CW00338309

THE CONSERVATIVE CHALLEN
GLOBALIZATION

THE CONSERVATIVE CHALLENGE TO GLOBALIZATION

Anglo-American Perspectives

RAY KIELY

agenda
publishing

To Will and Ella

© Ray Kiely 2020

This book is copyright under the Berne Convention.
No reproduction without permission.
All rights reserved.

First published in 2020 by Agenda Publishing

Agenda Publishing Limited
The Core
Bath Lane
Newcastle Helix
Newcastle upon Tyne
NE4 5TF
www.agendapub.com

ISBN 978-1-78821-096-6 (hardcover)
ISBN 978-1-78821-097-3 (paperback)

British Library Cataloguing-in-Publication Data
A catalogue record for this book is available from the British Library

Typeset by Newgen Publishing UK
Printed and bound in the UK by CPI Group (UK) Ltd, Croydon, CR0 4YY

CONTENTS

ACKNOWLEDGEMENTS

During the writing of this book, I have appreciated the music of (among others) Low, Spacemen 3 and early Spiritualized, This is the Kit, Julia Holter, Nadine Khouri, Funkadelic, Joy Division, Gene Clark, Laura Gibson, nineties Mercury Rev and The Beatles. This was a tricky book to write for a number of reasons, so many thanks to the following people: Tim Bale, Peter Brett, Denis Cattell, Jean Francois Drolet, James Dunkerley, Jane McAllister, Phil Mizen, Alfredo Saad-Filho, Rick Saull, David Williams. Many thanks to Peter, Rick, Alfredo and David in particular for detailed comments on the manuscript and for helping me to avoid some howlers. At Agenda, thanks to Alison Howson. Also thanks to family, some of whom deserve a special mention this time – Amy, Lee and Sophie, Louise, Sina, Maryam and Yasmin (but not those dogs!), Tristen, Grace and Eddie and, above all, Will and Ella, to whom this book is dedicated.

1

INTRODUCTION

In 1999, protests at a meeting of the World Trade Organization in Seattle put glo-balization under critical scrutiny. Advocates of globalization – above all British prime minister Tony Blair and US president Bill Clinton – had contended that it was a progressive development in world history, giving rise to open and free societies, poverty reduction, universal human rights, and so on. While many of globalization's advocates saw these developments as self-evident (Giddens 1998), the protestors at Seattle argued otherwise. For them globalization was associated with growing inequality, environmental destruction and the erosion of labour rights. Globalization's advocates argued that there was no turning back and that globalization was both inevitable and desirable (Desai 2000, 2002) and that "anti-globalization" was both backward-looking and parochial (Lloyd 2001). Most of this debate was against "anti-globalization" activists who were gener-ally associated with the political Left (Klein 2000), who in turn were at pains to point out that they were not anti-globalization *per se*. How could they be, when they drew on and utilized new technologies associated with globalization and organized across national boundaries? The argument used by these activists was that they were anti-neoliberal or corporate globalization, challenging North–South and wider inequality, the growing power of corporations, the erosion of the public sphere and the public sector, environmental destruction and then, after 2001, Western militarism and liberal intervention.

More recent years have seen the rise of another kind of anti-globalization. Some of this also questions liberal military intervention, and to some extent the growing power of corporate elites, and sometimes there is hostility to neo-liberalism. But this anti-globalization is essentially linked to the political Right and what we will call the populist Far Right (Mudde 2016). This takes the form of nativism and the valorization of certain ethnic groups within countries, a defence of national sovereignty against global forces, a defence of social con-servatism against liberal values including multiculturalism and a distrust but not outright rejection of liberal democracy. It involves a populist celebration of authentic peoples and marginalization of other groups within nation states, and thus a hostility to immigration, an impatience with democratic deliberation where liberal elites defend inauthentic groups and a preference for authoritarian executive power. Although there are significant differences between populist organizations and politicians, we can accurately include political leaders such as Vladimir Putin (Russia), Recep Erdogan (Turkey), Narendra Modi (India) and Viktor Orban (Hungary), and movements such as the Freedom Party (Austria), the National Front/National Rally (France), the Peoples Party (Switzerland), One Nation (Australia) and the AfD or Alternative for Germany. These organizations draw on much of the right-wing critique of globalization discussed in Chapters 2 and 3, though we will also see (particularly in Chapters 6 and 7) that the relationship between neoliberalism and right-wing populism is more ambiguous than one of outright rejection, and indeed often tends towards acceptance of the former (Betz 1994). This book therefore provides an analysis and critique of the broad ideas of conservative (anti-)globalization movements. But the book also considers two case studies, both of which might be considered "difficult" ones for understanding conservative anti-globalization, and more specifically conservative globalization. These two cases are those of British conservatism and Brexit, and American conservatism and Trump. In some respects, these can both be considered different from the conservative populist Far Right. Both emerged within mainstream political parties and, more specifically, there is some debate over whether Trump is a true conservative, and whether Brexit actually involves the extension and expansion of globalization. We will however argue that in some respects both cases overlap with the wider conservative populist turn, above all in challenging immigration, multiculturalism and cosmopolitan liberalism, and while both may draw on neoliberal ideas, so too in some respects do at least some conservative populist movements. These points are also important for challenging the idea that the main political divide today is between those supporting open polities and economies on the one hand, and thus advocating globalization, and those supporting more closed national polities, societies and economies, and thus advocating "anti-globalization" on the other (*The Economist* 2016; Goodhardt 2017; Global Future 2018). We will see in the following chapters that this characterization is too simplistic and assumes that those wanting free movement of capital also want free movement of people, when in fact the picture is more complex than this.

These issues are outlined and analyzed in the chapters that follow; for now, this introductory chapter does three things. First, it provides a brief and basic introduction to the concepts of globalization and anti-globalization, as a precursor to more detailed discussion in the rest of the book. Second, it provides a brief introduction to conservatism, which again is discussed in more depth in later chapters, both generally and with specific reference to globalization. Third, it provides an outline of the structure of the rest of the book, summarizing the chapters that follow and how these are used to develop a broad argument about contemporary conservative globalization and anti-globalization.

What are globalization and anti-globalization?

The concept of globalization has been used to describe a set of social relations that have been expanded beyond older territorial boundaries, so that "(t)here has been a shift in the nature and form of political life. The distinctive form this has taken in the contemporary period is the emergence of 'global politics' – the increasingly extensive form of political networks, interaction and rule-making activity" (Held & McGrew 2007: 20). This new global politics is said to challenge the previous Westphalian order of sovereign nation states, which presumably characterized the international order after 1648 (Held *et al.* 1999: 50). One impli-cation is that "(s)tate sovereignty depends on territorialism, where all events occur at fixed locations: either within territorial jurisdictions; or at designated points across tightly controlled borders. The end of territorialism has therefore brought the end of sovereignty" (Scholte 2000: 136).

This suggests that globalization involves the expansion of social interactions above, beyond and in part below the nation state, and therefore the undermining of state sovereignty. This provides the basis for a politics that rejects globaliza-tion in the name of sovereignty, and in some respects this conforms to the case studies discussed in Chapters 4 and 5. But at the same time, as we will see, a rigid dichotomy between state sovereignty and globalization is problematic and the state can be used to promote and enhance globalization. Historically, this is what the US state has done since at least 1945, and for this reason some argue – as does this book – that Trumpian conservatism is actually a threat to American hegemony. But also, as we will see, while there are a number of conservative Brexit visions, and all share a commitment to national sovereignty, some see this as the basis for an extension of, and not a retreat from, a global Britain.

Globalization and anti-globalization – and their relationship to state sover-eignty – thus comprise a far from straightforward issue, and, in some respects, this reflects certain confusion around the status of the concept. For as we will see in Chapters 2 and 3, much of the debate around globalization conflates social and spatial explanation (for a critique, see Rosenberg 2000; 2005: 10, 12, 54), and the latter is seen as the progressive alternative to national sovereignty. For example, Kaldor *et al.* (2003) celebrate the development of a global civil society beyond narrow, regressive national politics. The argument here is that global-ization promotes a space above the nation state and that this provides the basis for what is in effect a normative globalization, or cosmopolitanism. On the other hand, sovereignists argue that this is precisely what is problematic about global-ization, because it embodies a sphere above that of national politics, and one that in many respects is outside the bounds of politics (Bolton 2000; Fonte 2012). In each case the argument is couched in terms of a dichotomy between the national and the global, and the debate is over which one of these is more desir-able compared to the other. Conservative globalization and anti-globalization in some – though not all – respects repeat these arguments, as does the cosmo-politan, socially liberal neoliberalism that they partly challenge (see Chapter 3). Much of the current political debate is couched in terms of a conflict between the "somewheres" and the "everywheres", or those favouring openness against those supporting closure (Blond 2016; Gottfried 2016; Goodhardt 2017; Global Future 2018). This argument will be challenged in due course, but one should immedi-ately note here that it in fact betrays the kind of spatial fetishism that is challenged by Rosenberg (2000), and perhaps even more by Doreen Massey (2005: 101), who argued that "abstract spatial form in itself can guarantee nothing about the social, political or ethical content of the relations that construct that form". This is an argument considered further in later chapters, but we can reiterate here that such a dichotomy between the national and the global fails to account for very different national projects, some of which may promote globalization and some of which might not. Furthermore, we might also question which aspects of globalization are being promoted or restricted, and some forms of openness are different from others and might be challenged for very different reasons. As we will see in the next two chapters, then, there is a need for considerable nuance when talking about openness and globalization on the one hand, and closure and anti-globalization on the other.

What is conservatism?

Conservatism is also something that is not easy to define, not least because so many different viewpoints have been described as conservative, in part because of their historical and geographical context. In some respects, it is indeed this context that some self-styled conservatives consider to be most significant, and while conservatives might caution against change, they also to some extent accept that at least some change is inevitable and even desirable. Thus, in the past conservatives may have resisted votes for women or for ethnic minorities, but in most places conservatives have come to accept these things. This has led some – including some of those on the Right – to conclude that conservatives in fact have no principles (Hayek 2006: 343–56). One of the leading historians of conservatism thus suggests that it "is inherently resistant to precise definition" (Nash 2008: xiii). Huntington (1957) similarly suggested that conservatism was (in part) a positional doctrine based on support for and gradual change within a particular political and social order. For some conservatives this pragmatism and emphasis on contingency is precisely its strength. Michael Oakeshott (1962: 31), whose views overlapped in significant ways with Hayek, thus argued that:

> To be conservative, then, is to prefer the familiar to the unknown, to prefer the tried to the untried, fact to mystery, the actual to the possible, the limited to the unbounded, the near to the distant, the sufficient to the superabundant, the convenient to the perfect, present laughter to utopian bliss.

In 1933, Hearnshaw (cited in Gamble 1974: 1) traced conservatism back to the Garden of Eden, suggesting that "Adam was the person who represented the qualities of contentment and stability. Eve was the innovator, eager for novelty, ready for reckless experiment." In this account, then, conservatism focuses on the tried and tested, and recommends caution rather than radical change.

Oakeshott (1962: 31) thus famously argued that conservatism "is not a creed or a doctrine, but a disposition", and one that reveres the established, the traditional and the customary. This allows conservatives to focus on things higher than the dirty world of politics, such as the arts, culture, and so on (Hogg 1947: 46). But this begs the question of how certain practices become customary, and thus gain the acceptance of conservatives who only recently saw those same changes as potential threats to the order. One is left with the suspicion that the conservative emphasis on caution in the face of change gives no guidance in terms of what changes, if any, are desirable at a particular point in time (Hayek 2006: 343–56).

Related to this point, and more important for our purposes, is the question: what if society is threatened with change that is so radical it represents a call to arms to defend the existing order, or if society has changed so radically that the existing order should not be defended? Oakeshott (1962: 408) himself suggested that we most appreciate the familiar to the unknown when the former is threatened by the latter, and the American conservative Russell Kirk (cited in Robin 2018: 25) supported conservatism "with the vehemence of a radical". Fellow American conservative William Buckley described the new conservatives of the US in the 1950s as "the new radicals" (cited in Robin 2018: 25). Quentin Hogg (1947: 76) might have contended that conservatives focus on things higher than politics but he also wrote that if such things are threatened, then "once defeated, they will hold to this belief with the fanaticism of a Crusader and the doggedness of an Englishman". The American paleoconservative Mel Bradford (1999: 1) was perhaps most clear when he stated that, "merely to conserve is sometimes to per-petuate what is outrageous". In this account, to return to Hearnshaw, conserva-tism at times might endorse "reckless experiment". Karl Mannheim (1993: 263) was thus on to something when he suggested that conservatism "becomes conscious and reflective when other ways of life and thought appear on the scene, against which it is compelled to take up arms in the ideological struggle".

This is not insignificant as in many respects conservatives have continually argued that the familiar has been under threat since the French Revolution. This was the argument made by de Maistre (1994), who defended the absolute authority of the state and the monarch, who was answerable only to God, and thus rejected any idea of the sovereignty of the people. Burke (2003) also castigated the revolution on more pragmatic and empirical grounds, and argued that morally flawed human beings should not seek to overthrow the accumulated wisdom of generations and established institutions. Attempts to undermine hierarchy, deference and localism in the name of reason, universal abstractions, the nation and internationalism were bound to end in tears. He particularly feared the end of the old order and the attempt to create social levelling in a new order, where rule would be reduced to dictates by a numerical majority (Burke 2003: 44).

For conservatives since 1789, the nature of the threat has changed over time. It has included abstract calls to liberty, equality and fraternity, internationalism, capitalism, anti-capitalism, anti-racism, feminism, anti-colonialism and democracy. In keeping with their pragmatism, many conservatives have made their peace with at least some of these threats. That they have done so might again suggest that conservatism is an ideology without principle, based on pragmatic adaptation to the status quo in the ways suggested by Oakeshott (above). But these changes might tell us something else, about what conservativism might be in terms of *doctrine* as well as position (Huntington 1957). As we saw above, George Nash (2008: xiv) suggested that conservatism was hard to define but he went on to suggest that it is defined by "resistance to certain forces perceived to be leftist, revolutionary, and profoundly subversive of what conservatives at the time deemed worth cherishing, defending and perhaps dying for". That there was indeed "at the time" a context in no way means that conservatives simply adapt blindly to changing contexts; rather, they believe in certain principles, but – like (though perhaps more than) other ideologies – recognize that these will change over time. What unites conservatives across space and time, however, is the belief that the pursuit of excellence requires hierarchy, inequality and power (Robin 2018). Russell Kirk (2008: 8) thus argued that "civilized society requires orders and classes", while one of conservatism's leading critics suggests that its central position of principle is the belief "that some are fit, and thus ought, to rule others" (Robin 2018: 18).

This principle of course operates in different historical contexts, but we should not allow these differing contexts to substitute for an analysis of conservatism as a political position. But equally, we should not simply reduce this political position to a crude conspiracy theory, as though it were simply an ideology designed to defend particular privileged groups. Conservatism has been a successful ideology because it does talk to experiences of loss, not only for the most privileged in society, but for other groups. These groups might themselves enjoy some privileges over others, but in many cases they are far from being the most privileged in society – our cases will involve some discussion of white US southerners, the Tea Party and former manufacturing regions in the UK and US. Such groups may feel that they have lost something, and conservatism might in part speak to these concerns, and in this respect conservatism is not only an elitist, but a populist, doctrine (Robin 2018: 54–6).

If we take a more historical approach, we can see that conservatives were hostile to the initial impulses that led to the 1848 revolutions in Italy, France, Germany and the Austro-Hungarian Empire. Conservatives challenged liberal republicanism, anti-monarchism, liberal universalism and the recourse to abstract reason, all of which threatened the existing socio-political order. However, the defeat of these revolutions led the way to more doctrinal conservative positions (Huntington 1957) or a more "purposive" or "insurgent" rather than purely reactive conservatism (Goldman 2011; Taylor 2016). This included support for traditional social structures, which were under threat from liberalism and socialism. This did not just mean support for monarchs or authoritarian leaders at the apex of the social structure, but also for peasant and artisanal moral economies threatened by the processes of rationalization, urbanization and industrialization. From the 1870s, in the context of low agricultural prices and declining rural incomes, this gave rise to resentment against urban elites, especially bankers, much of which took an anti-Semitic form. After a brief period of acceptance of British-led free-trade policies in the 1860s, by the 1880s many European countries promoted protectionism at home and imperialism abroad. This was facilitated by social and political partnerships; in Germany, for instance, the Rye-Iron alliance promoted tariffs both for industries trying to develop in the face of established British competitors and agrarian groups suffering the consequences of declining agricultural prices.

Such alliances were conservative in nature. In contrast to the liberal republican nationalism of 1789 and 1848, a new conservative nationalism championed the centrality of the nation at the expense of individual liberty. Capitalist rationalization did emerge and in this sense the old regimes were changed, but at the same time they were not completely overthrown. These were in effect "revolutions from above" in which alliances based in the old order adopted and utilized technology, industrialization and science (Mayer 1981). This was done in part to promote what came to be called the national interest, and thus to avoid secondary status in a British-dominated international order (Polanyi 2001). This uneven development was in effect a kind of conservative modernization, which "could draw on the energies and emotions latent in the traditional society to create a powerful nationalism that was both ideologically opposed to the liberal ideology whilst embracing the fruits of industrialisation" (Gamble 1981: 143). In this way, "conservative defences of the old order helped in the creation of national cultures that promoted the growth of the nationalist and imperialist mass movements of the modern era" (Gamble 1981: 143).

At the same time this was also an era of new threats, which included democracy, socialism, cosmopolitan "others", "inferior races" and competitor nations. The late nineteenth century was an era of heightened geopolitical tensions, and included imperialist expansion and a new "scramble for Africa". In common with racist reactions to abolition and reconstruction in the US South, late nineteenth-century Europe saw the full development of the idea that the world was divided into separate races, in which biological differences were said to determine the behaviour of these different groups. Some were superior to others, and the so-called Aryan race was often deemed to be the one that was most fit to survive. This was a belief taken up by the Nazis but which had been common in nineteenth-century Europe and beyond, and conservatives saw this as one example of a natural hierarchy at the time. Conservatives in France such as Maurice Barres and Charles Maurras suggested that modernity had uprooted many people from their communities and led to moral decay, and that some groups in society were particularly rootless and a threat to French civilization, above all Jews (see Goldman 2011). This racism was also sometimes linked to the idea that both women and the lower classes were less rational than the higher orders. In late nineteenth-century France, Gustave Le Bon (1960) wrote about the mutual suggestibility, imitative behaviour and "feminine irrationality" of crowds (see Borch 2012: 49–63), and argued that crowd-like behaviour increasingly came to characterize so-called popular democracy and the threat of socialism.

While liberalism developed in the nineteenth century in ways that meant that the new liberals of the late nineteenth century accepted the extension of the franchise and the reality of mass democracy, there was some ambivalence about this process. In the 1830s, Tocqueville (2004: 428) warned that democracy could lead to enslavement because public opinion "does not persuade others to its beliefs, but it imposes on them and makes them permeate the thinking of everyone by a sort of enormous pressure of the mind of all upon the individual intelligence". In 1819, Benjamin Constant (1988: 215) argued for the representative principle, and specifically that in such "representative assemblies it is essential that those assemblies, whatever their further organization, should be formed by property holders". Even the far-from-conservative John Stuart Mill (2010: 133) expressed concern that the poor majority might impose its will on the rich minority, though he also argued that the market economy itself carried with it some dangerous threats to freedom. The concern here was the liberal one that the rise of "the masses" could lead to a stifling collectivism and conformity (Landa 2010; Mullholland 2011), as the movement for an extended franchise threatened not only absolutism, but also the sanctity of private property (Tocqueville 1997: 12–13).

In this way liberalism and conservatism shared some fears about the rise of the masses and the idea that democracy could lead to a tyranny of the majority in which the collective imposed its will on, and at the expense of the rights of, minorities. This begged the question of *which* minorities – an oppressed African American is somewhat different from a privileged property owner – and we will revisit these issues more concretely in later chapters. By the late nineteenth century, however, we begin to see a new development, which is also central to arguments to come: essentially, the development of a combination of conservative politics combined with liberal economics (see Kiely 2018: chapters 2 and 3). For example, Italian elite theorists of the late nineteenth and early twentieth centuries are often treated by political scientists as objective analysts of political processes who point to the reality of elite rule across political systems. In fact, Pareto (1966) and Mosca (2012: 158–63) both contrasted the rational economic actor with the irrational political actor and feared for the ways in which the latter might undermine the former (Bellamy 1988: chapter 2). Seen in this way, their work is normative, designed to uphold a liberal economic order through the promotion of a conservative political system. This meant support for authoritarian politics, and, in the case of Pareto at the end of his life, support for Mussolini (Bellamy 1988: 33). Robert Michels, the third of the classical elite theorists, also gave his support to Fascist Italy for the last 15 years of his life (Beetham 1977).

That conservatism is not simply a disposition that advocates gradual change is also clear if we briefly examine the relationship between conservative approaches and the international. Contemporary surveys of international relations theory tend to highlight two "mainstream" theories alongside more critical theories such as Marxism, postcolonialism and feminism. The former two are identified as conservative realism and liberal internationalism (see Burchill 2013), in which the former emphasizes anarchy and conflict, and the latter interdependence and the possibility of cooperation between states. Realism is seen as the main conservative theory in international relations (IR), where the emphasis is placed on states pursuing their national interest in a world of anarchy. It is then sub-divided into those that emphasize a more aggressive or offensive pursuit of this goal, and those that emphasize ("defensive") caution on the part of states in their interaction with other states. It is this latter approach that in some respects overlaps with the idea that conservatism emphasizes the tried and tested rather than radical change. These kinds of accounts are not necessarily incorrect so much as one-sided, as they tend to neglect both other conservative accounts of the international, and indeed the ways in which realism itself tended to marginalize these accounts (Drolet & Williams 2019a). Moreover, realism's emergence as the main

IR perspective in the US after 1945 occurred in the context of the promotion of a liberal international order, and so was less a critique of liberal internationalism and more an account of the international that promoted caution in the context of that particular order. Alternative conservative accounts thus promoted a more aggressive US foreign policy in contrast to the emphasis on containment of communism in the Cold War, and in this respect it mirrored precisely Nash's resistance to non-conservative forces and Kirk's call to do so with the vehemence of a radical (Diggins 1975). This is discussed further in Chapter 5.

This brief survey then shows how conservatism is indeed flexible and influenced by the changing social and political context. Equally, it shows how conservatism is not simply a passive, unprincipled reaction to such changes. Common principles and themes emerge, including the defence of elite rule, a sense that the forces of tradition must be defended, nostalgia and indeed – as we will see – populism. The concern of the book, then, is how some of these issues have manifested themselves in response to globalization, and to examine the ways in which tradition is defended, the search for a golden age and the ways in which the future is envisaged. This is done through two very prominent case studies – Brexit and Trumpian conservatism – and we highlight the similarities, but also the important differences, between these. We will also see that these two can be called awkward cases that reflect less the rise of Far-Right populist parties and more the mainstreaming of right-wing populist ideas within established parties (Mudde 2018: 76–7).

The structure of the book

The book has five basic themes. First, it provides an account of the "crisis of globalization" (inequality, financial crisis, deindustrialization, as outlined above), and the crisis of politics that became more visible in 2016 (Chapters 2, 3 and 6). Second, it considers projects for renewal in the face of neoliberal globalization and British decline in the face of Europeanization and the end of empire (Chapters 2, 3 and 4). Third, it examines conservatism in detail, with special attention paid to tensions in the (American) conservative tradition (Chapters 5, 6 and 7). Fourth, it examines the wider political economy and culture of globalization and suggests that conservative globalization and anti-globalization do not present a viable or desirable alternative (Chapters 2, 3 and 7). On the other hand, fifth, it accepts that in many respects actually existing globalization – or what I call cosmopolitan neoliberalism – has failed, and so there is a need for alternatives, but alternatives less flawed and indeed in some respects less dangerous than conservative ones (Chapters 2, 3, 6 and 8).

It should be clear, then, that these five themes are addressed in more than one chapter. Nonetheless, the book is structured in such a way that these arguments are gradually unpacked. Chapter 2 therefore considers or reconsiders what has been called the three waves of globalization, not simply by repeating old debates from the 1990s but also by exploring them again in the light of detailed consideration of both neoliberalism (something that – it will become clear – is central to the argument that follows) and conservative responses to globalization. In particular, the chapter suggests that conservative responses to globalization emerged as (partial) critiques of neoliberalism, and in particular what we will call the cosmopolitan neoliberalism of the third way. Chapter 3 examines in detail the ways in which globalization as a discourse – specifically the third way of the 1990s – conflated the logic of necessity and that of desirability, and in doing so became a normative project, and outlines the problems with this position, and where conservative positions challenge it. Chapter 4 then considers the first case of conservative globalization in more depth, that of British conservatism, which explores debates over free trade, the Anglosphere, the Empire and Brexit, and how these have interacted, both in the past and present. Chapter 5 then considers the second case, namely that of American conservatism and its current ostensibly "anti-globalization" form, associated with paleo rather than neoconservatism. Chapters 6 and 7 then examine conservative ideas around globalization and subject them to a detailed critique, in terms of both political economy and culture. Chapter 6 outlines and summarizes conservative critiques of actually existing globalization with particular reference to the liberal state and multiculturalism, and shows how these arguments overlap with the wider rise of conservative populism, examining why these responses are so problematic. Chapter 7 also provides a critique, this time with a focus on conservative responses to the liberal international order and the political economy of globalization. The argument is essentially that conservative responses provide no alternative and in many respects are complicit with the neoliberalism that is actually a central part of the problem. But this argument potentially leaves us facing a defence of a third-way cosmopolitan neoliberalism, which earlier chapters suggested was part of the problem. The concluding chapter therefore summarizes the main arguments of the book, but also tentatively explores possible "pro- and anti-globalization" alternatives, which problematize the nostalgia of much conservative globalization but which explore the question of a progressive moral economy in an age of globalization.

The argument of this book is that conservative approaches to globalization and anti-globalization – especially in their Anglo-American forms – are distinctive but also related to the wider rise of right-wing populism. Moreover, the two cases discussed in depth are themselves distinctive and not by any means identical. The British case has its own national trajectory, which is linked to Britain and especially England's historical development, and specific issues around the state of the union, empire and the perception that the nation should be the leader of a global Britain. While much of the Brexit vote could be linked to an argument that national identity and national sovereignty should be paramount, in its right-wing conservative form this argument is made not to retreat from but to extend globalization, albeit with Britain (alongside the US) as a global leader. The American case also has its own distinctive features, one linked to older notions of restricting immigration, "America first" and protectionism. In this regard current American conservatism around Trump can be regarded as far more anti-globalization than the British case. On the other hand, we will also see that there is a tension within the American case, which manifests itself within wider American conservative thought and the Trump administration itself. This is where isolationism and anti-globalization come up against the reality of the US's global commitments and a shift that is less one that challenges globalization *per se*, but rather endorses bilateralism rather than multilateralism. These specific cases, then, demonstrate an argument made throughout the book, and alluded to above – namely that it is too simplistic to reduce politics to a simplistic divide between those for and against globalization (*The Economist* 2016; Goodhardt 2017; Global Future 2018). This point applies also to the wider conservative populist turn, in both the Global North and South, which – in common with our two case studies, which have mainstreamed Far-Right thinking – challenges multiculturalism, cosmopolitanism and so-called liberal elites, but is far more ambiguous about the free movement of capital and neoliberalism.

While some of the literature on contemporary conservativism and the populist Right does a useful job in contextualizing its rise (Eatwell & Goodwin 2018), much of it is also far too limited in its approach. While the emphasis on context is useful in helping to take the rise of these forces and movements seriously, one can also argue that much of this work does not take this rise seriously and – above all – critically enough. Indeed, much of this work actually ends up, in effect, allowing the claims of right-wing forces to set the political agenda and to frame their own supposedly critical analysis of these same forces, and so at times easily falls into the trap of endorsing some of the ideas associated with the Right, both within and beyond Anglo-America. In contrast to these works (Goodhardt 2017; Eatwell & Goodwin 2018; Kaufmann 2018), this book considers the ideas of current conservativism and the wider Right seriously, but in doing so subjects these ideas to far more critical scrutiny and does not reduce them to "preferences" made within the "political market". These ideas must be subjected to critical scrutiny, not only in terms of context, but also content.

2

THE THREE WAVES OF GLOBALIZATION THEORY: REVISITING THE DEBATE IN THE LIGHT OF CONSERVATIVE ANALYSES

This chapter re-examines the so-called three waves of globalization theory: the hyper-globalization position, the sceptical position and the transformationalist position. In many respects, this is an old debate that has been covered many times, but the focus will be distinctive in that it will discuss how conservative populism links to these debates and, partly for this reason, we examine globalization and culture as well as political economy. The hyper-globalization position and the sceptical position are therefore examined in the first two sections, both generally and in relation to culture and to conservative populism. The third wave of globalization is slightly more complex because it can refer to two different approaches. First, the transformationalist or post-sceptical position contends that globalization should be seen less in terms of quantitative measures around trade or capital flows, and instead as a system of transformations. This includes increased capital flows, global value chains, financialization, multinational companies, systems of regulation that transcend nation states, the growing importance of international organizations, and so on (see Held *et al.* 1999; Holton 2005). Descriptively this is a perfectly acceptable contention (even if the empirical arguments do rest too much on the hyper-globalization thesis), but it has been subject to a powerful critique by Justin Rosenberg (2005), which questions globalization's status as both theory and history. While accepting his theoretical critique, the chapter is less convinced by his historical critique, and we argue that recent changes in global capitalism are central to understanding the reality of actually existing globalization and conservative responses to it, and, in particular, we need to understand the reality of *neoliberal globalization.*

It is at this point that we can usefully introduce a second way of understanding the third wave, namely Hay and Marsh's (2001) focus on how real changes have occurred in the international order, but specifically how these have been interpreted and constructed discursively. This is where the analytical account of globalization crosses over into a normative account, particularly in wider political discourse beyond the academy, for the discourse of globalization was increasingly adopted from the 1990s onwards by politicians associated with the third way (Clinton and Blair above all) to argue that globalization represents a new context in which politics operates, and that it creates certain imperatives to which governments must react because there is no alternative. While this was often presented as a *necessity*, the third way also put forward arguments to suggest that this was also *desirable* as well – and in this way the globalization debate increasingly became, even if implicitly, a normative one, and one that in some respects involves continuity with the neoliberalism that emerged in the 1980s. This argument is taken up further in the next chapter, where we suggest that a particular form of cosmopolitanism – a neoliberal one – is the normative "accompaniment" to globalization. The fourth section of this chapter, however, discusses in more detail the question of neoliberalism, in particular how this is related to globalization. Finally, this chapter briefly assesses the ways in which this globalization debate is relevant to the current rise of conservative globalization and anti-globalization. It does so first by periodically relating these three waves to contemporary conservatism throughout the chapter, and then returns to the issue in the conclusion.

The hyper-globalization thesis: political economy and culture

This approach is often set up as something of a "straw man", a position held by no one yet subject to all kinds of critiques. While there is some truth to this assertion, it is also something of an exaggeration because transformationalist positions often hold many assumptions – albeit with sceptical qualifications – derived from the hyper-globalization position. But more relevant for our purposes, conservative anti-globalization positions accept some of the analytical arguments made by hyper-globalizers, but then challenge the analytical and normative implications that follow. For this reason, it is worth considering the hyper-globalization position.

Essentially this position contends that the movement of things – capital, media flows and people – has grown so large as to have undermined and outgrown the nation state. The mobility of these things is so great that the relatively immobile nation state has been undermined. In terms of political economy, this position is often associated with the work of Kenichi Ohmae (1990, 2008). In his work, global markets are said to reflect the rational behavior of individual interests, and these therefore provide the basis for both the extension of individual freedom and economic efficiency. For this reason, he welcomes the development of global markets as they reflect individual interests and the social efficiency that emerges spontaneously from these interests. In economic terms, the rise of such mobile markets has in effect undermined the relatively immobile nation state, and this too is a welcome development because states are inefficient economic actors and indeed are threats to the freedom of the individual. It should be clear from this brief account, then, that Ohmae's case rests on a relatively straightforward – and perhaps simplistic – presentation of neoliberalism, something to which we will return throughout the book.

We should not, however, assume that hyper-globalist accounts automatically rest on neoliberal theories of the market. On the Left, there are a number of globalist accounts that suggest that globalization is the latest period of capitalist development, following earlier periods of mercantilism, laissez faire and imperialism (Robinson 2004, 2015). What is distinctive about this period is the rise of a transnational capitalist class, which has less interest in the national capitalism of previous eras of capitalist development (Sklair 2001). This is reflected in the intensification of capital flows, both in terms of financial flows moving across borders at rapid speed, but also the growing significance – central to this book – of global production networks or value chains, in which the production process is increasingly fragmented across national borders. This approach also argues that states are increasingly part of this globalization process, as they enter into international institutions of global governance (such as the EU, NAFTA or the WTO) and attempt to attract capital at the expense of the states (Cerny 1997) and discipline their labour forces in order to do so.

One possible effect of this development is a growing convergence between states, based less on a levelling-up whereby all states increasingly attract capital investment, and instead through a levelling-down or race to the bottom. In defending his transnational capitalism thesis, Robinson (2004: 99) contends that with the erosion of territorialized space, the "particular spatial form of the uneven development of capitalism is being overcome by the globalization of capital and markets and the *gradual equalization of accumulation conditions this entails*" (my emphasis). Although he has qualified this position at times (Robinson 2015), he has also contended that "(w)orldwide convergence, through the global restructuring of capitalism, means that the geographic breakdown of the world into north-south, core-periphery or First and Third worlds, while still significant, is diminishing in importance" (Burbach & Robinson 1999: 27–8). Becker and Sklar (1987: 14) similarly argue that "imperialism – the domination of one people by another – will be (is being) superseded by transnational class domination of the world as a whole". In this respect, the creation of a capitalist world market is leading to convergence between states and territories as all attempt to compete to attract capital investment, but also a growing divergence between a global capitalist class on the one hand, and a transnational proletariat on the other.

This argument in many respects repeats the earlier contentions of the German neo-Marxists, Frobel, Heinrichs and Kreye (1980). Writing in the 1970s, they suggested that the old colonial international division of labour, in which the "First World" produced manufactured goods and the "Third World" produced unfinished primary goods, was being displaced by a new international division of labour. In the 1960s and 1970s, First World capital faced a profit squeeze as labour won higher wages through strong unions and full employment, and so capital responded by increasingly internationalizing and investing in the so-called "Third World". In this way, new areas of manufacturing arose to take advantage of cheap labour in the "periphery". The rise of the newly industrializing East Asian countries – South Korea, Taiwan, Singapore and to some extent Hong Kong – was explained in this way. While Ohmae saw this phenomenon as a reflection of rationally self-interested individuals (at least mediated by corporations), and something that promoted a levelling-up in terms of development, Frobel and his colleagues suggested that in fact it was a negative development. This was because it led to unemployment and deindustrialization in the core countries of the First World, and super-exploitation of cheap labour in the peripheral countries of the Third (see also Frank 1981). This in effect was an earlier version of the race-to-the-bottom argument of Burbach and Robinson, and was one also employed at times in Naomi Klein's "anti-globalization" manifesto *No Logo*. Naomi Klein's tone is often similar, as when she writes that many multinationals base themselves on "a system of footloose factories employing footloose workers", with a "failure to live up to their traditional role as mass employers", as General Motors moves production to the low-wage maquiladoras, the manufacturing belt on the US–Mexico border (Klein 2000: 223). This gives the impression that there is a huge haemorrhage of jobs from the US to Mexico. But, like Robinson, Klein qualifies her case and elsewhere gives the total maquiladora workforce as 900,000 and recognizes that the GM workforce in Mexico is far less than it is in the US (Klein 2000: 205).

These debates around globalization are quite old, but in some respects they remain of great relevance for understanding the case for globalization, and anti-globalization, of both the Left and Right. In terms of supporting globalization, as we will see it is not only neoliberals like Ohmae who support the free movement of capital, but also the modified neoliberalism of the third way. In terms of anti-globalization, the argument that hyper-mobile capital leads to a race to the bottom and super-exploitation is associated with left-wing critics, most directly Naomi Klein (2000), but also in, say, anti-sweat-shop campaigns (Featherstone 2002). However, we will see in more detail in later chapters that both these positions share the assumption that capital has out-grown the nation state. Moreover, we will also see that right-wing anti-globalization can share similar assumptions to those associated with the race to the bottom. Frobel *et al*'s (1980) new international division of labour, namely that there is a zero-sum game between investment in the developed world on the one hand, and investment in the developing world on the other (de Benoist 1996; Mudde 2007: chapter 8). For instance, we might think here of the idea propagated by Donald Trump in his presidential campaign that American jobs were being stolen by Mexican or Chinese workers, and this was a major reason why the US had ongoing trade deficits with these countries (see further Chapters 5 and 7).

Although political economy is undoubtedly the main focus of the hyper-globalization position, we might also consider this perspective in terms of the relationship between globalization and culture. For while the hyper-globalization position is essentially arguing that the political economy of globalization has undermined the nation state, this parallels the argument that the globalization of culture has undermined national identity. Sometimes this analytical position takes the view that this development is a source of regret, while others see it as a reason for celebration. These positions do not necessarily easily fit into the three waves considered in this chapter, and indeed are not necessarily explicitly made in the academic globalization literature, but some consideration of globalization and culture within this framework is useful, not least as it is of crucial significance for understanding conservative responses to globalization.

Our starting point for understanding culture in terms of hyper-globalization is the contention that cultural flows have in some respects undermined different national identities. Like Ohmae's somewhat exaggerated thesis on political economy, this contention is something of a straw man, but nonetheless a number of writers do identify certain globalizing trends that are said to undermine national cultures. First, there are a number of pessimistic positions that suggest that cultural homogenization is occurring, an argument that in some respects mirrors those of Frobel *et al.* and Klein considered above. From the late 1960s, some leftists argued that cultural homogenization was occurring not only because of the spread of Western capital, technology, investment and aid, but also because of the spread of Western cultural products (Schiller 1969). For example, in 1971 Dorfman and Matellart (2019) argued that the Disney corporation did not simply produce innocent films to be consumed by audiences throughout the globe. Instead, products acted as propaganda tools, reinforcing not only a political and economic US hegemony, but a cultural one as well. The spread of Western consumer products, images, news channels, and so on thus constituted propaganda for the American dream and thus reinforced American hegemony (Klein 2000).

This cultural imperialism thesis was usually associated with the political Left, but fear of Americanization was also common on the Right as well, not least in the racist propaganda of the Nazi regimes, which attempted to ban "negro" jazz music, talked of Jewish conspiracies in the US (and elsewhere) and decried US multiculturalism (Evans 2006: 204–5). Not unrelatedly, in the inter-war period there was a great deal of conservative reaction to the weakness and decadence of liberal values, and conservative revolutionaries talked of the decline of the West and the need for strong leaders in Europe to restore the nation in the face of this challenge (Spengler 1991; Schmitt 1962). One German conservative radical, Moeller van den Bruck, even talked of the need for a Third Reich in Germany in the face of the decadence of the Weimar Republic, though he died eight years before Hitler won power, and so did not get to see the full gruesomeness of the Nazi regime (Lauryssens 1999). As we will see in later chapters, these kinds of arguments – about decline, the need for strong leaders, the restoration of the nation – are key components of versions of conservative anti-globalization, including the French and wider European New Right (O'Meara 2013), and the paleoconservatives in the United States (Francis 2016).

Perhaps the most sophisticated version of the cultural homogenization – or perhaps more accurately, the cultural *standardization* – thesis is that associated with George Ritzer's (1993) concept of McDonaldization. This thesis is not simply an argument about the power of one particular fast-food company to expand its global operations through marketing and so on, though this is part of the story. More important is how McDonalds is an exemplar of wider cultural trends, which reflect the way in which we – or at least many of us – live our lives. In particular, like many other companies, institutions, organizations, and so on, McDonalds is based on efficiency, calculability, pre-dictability and control (Ritzer 1993). This argument, essentially derived from Weber's rationalization thesis, suggests that the world is increasingly efficient but also dehumanized as we submit to the iron cage of rationality. In the pro-cess, the world is increasingly disenchanted as we submit to rules, which – though created by human invention – are deemed to be beyond our control. This system of rationalization is, however, only formally, rather than substan-tively, rational. We might eat fast food because we are in a hurry and it is cheap, but it is also part of an unhealthy lifestyle. Organizations – both private and public – might set goals that have all kinds of counter-productive effects, such as game-playing to ensure targets are met but at the cost of wider quality in terms of output and service provision. Ritzer's most famous example is the case of the car company that discovered a fault design before production, but calculated that the costs in lawsuits would be less than the cost of substantial re-design of the car (Ritzer 1993: 141). Seen in this way, rationalization is in many respects irrational, and indeed Ritzer (1993: 154) argues that "irration-ality means that rational systems are unreasonable systems. By that I mean that they deny the basic humanity, the human reason, of the people who work within or are served by them."

This kind of argument accords with those that suggest that cultural global-ization has been associated in part with a US-led cultural imperialism, but per-haps more importantly with "a culture of impetuous consumption necessary to selling puerile goods in a developed world that has few genuine needs" (Barber 2007: 173). The argument here, then, is that in the developed world at least, we live in a post-material society in which needs have been met but the economy is driven forward by the creation of new, disposable *wants* (Marcuse 2002; Inglehart 1977). As we will see this is an argument that links to explanations of the rise of conservative populisms based on a cultural backlash, where question of political economy and wealth and income inequality are less significant (Inglehart & Norris 2009, 2017). In this way, the speed of globalization, its hyper-mobility, has given rise to a "culture of immediacy" (Tomlinson 2007: 131), in which meaningless, throwaway and ultimately disposable consumerism dominates Western societies. Seen in this way, culture has become increasingly marketized (Bourdieu 2003).

Again, while this is an argument often associated with the (green) Left, it can take right-wing and conservative forms. For just as inter-war conservatives decried the decadence of, say, 1920s Berlin, so current conservatives might decry the carnage of the early twenty-first century and its encouragement of precisely this kind of individualist liberal nihilism (Gottfried 2001; de Benoist 2013; Dugin 2017). Similarly, the post-1945 period saw the development of a cultural Marxism that decried the disposable products of the US-led cultural industry (Adorno & Horkheimer 2002). In this way, capitalism integrated the organized working class and thus undermined the prospects for socialism. But this period also saw the development of a new conservatism in the US, which in contrast to the Frankfurt School's cultural Marxism welcomed the development of "free-market capitalism" and in some respects allied itself with what came to be the US New Right (see Chapter 5). However, in (partial) contrast to the neoliberals and "economic libertarians" in this New Right, the neoconservatives argued that capitalism might provide freedom and increased wealth, but while it satisfied individual preferences, without some conception of virtue there could be no social cohesion or any grounds for political obligation (Kristol 1970; see also Kiely 2018: chapter 4).

We will see in Chapter 5 that the current conservative populism in the US questions the neoconservative attempt to accommodate free-market capitalism, particularly in its globalized form, with social cohesion, and this brings us back to one final manifestation of the globalization of culture. This is the argument that global culture involves the rise of a cosmopolitan culture that is increasingly universalized. This is manifested not only in terms of the consumption of consumer goods, but also through the promotion of universal values, such as human rights, respect for others, and so on (Habermas 2001, 2006). This involves the dissemination of supposedly universal values such as human rights, market economies and liberal democracies, and recognition for excluded groups in society. This argument suggests that globalization has promoted these developments through, for example, the rise of institutions of global governance, which allows for the possibility of a system of multilateral governance. This system is not reducible to the national interests of nation states, and indeed involves the rise of non-government organizations operating in global civil society, as well as government actors, and which can act as a conscience for the world (Kaldor 2003; Willetts 1996). But it is also undoubtedly associated with a normative cosmopolitan project in which these same actors embrace and advance claims based on the argument that the rights of individuals across the world – global citizens – are more important than the sovereignty of nation states. Moreover, this cosmopolitanism can in turn lead to support for migration and the promotion of multiculturalism, in which migrants do not necessarily simply assimilate into the "host culture", but hold on to cultural ties derived from their countries of origin (Rattansi 2011). Equally, the argument of multiculturalism's advocates champions the contribution of migrants to the host culture, and in particular the argument is that migration can play a positive economic and cultural role. In some respects, the conservatives considered in the rest of this book accept that much of this process has occurred and is occurring, but take the normative position that this is cause for regret as it leads to the erosion of social cohesion and national identity. Indeed, seen in this way, for many anti-globalization conservatives, multiculturalism and cosmopolitanism are central parts of the liberal decadence and nihilism that needs to be reversed. This argument is considered further in the next section.

Global sceptics

The sceptical position on globalization essentially contends that the hyper-globalizers have exaggerated the degree to which the mobility of capital, culture and people has undermined the nation state (Hirst *et al.* 2009). Again, much of this debate is mainly focused on political economy but it is also worth considering questions of culture. In terms of political economy, the sceptical position broadly argues at least some of the following points.

- Capital mobility may not be any greater now than it was in the period up to 1914.
- While mobility may have increased in terms of finance, this is less the case for foreign investment in productive capital where sunk costs make an exit from a country much more costly and difficult.
- In fact, for much of the period of the so-called new international division of labour and/or the race to the bottom, capital flows have tended to concentrate more in the developed world and not shifted to the developing world.

• Insofar as there has been relocation to the developing world, this has been quite selective, both in terms of countries (East Asia in particular) and economic sectors (labour-intensive sectors in particular).

Above all, the sceptical position argues that the state still matters, and is not simply a prisoner or passive in the face of global capital. For instance, in terms of the new international division-of-labour approach of Frobel *et al.* (1980), this is at best limited as an explanation for the rise of the East Asian newly industrializing countries, not least because the state played such a central role in the development of Taiwan and South Korea (Amsden 1989; Wade 1990). This included the use of developmentalist policies whereby the state directed credit to certain industries, protected certain sectors from foreign competition, restricted the movement of capital overseas and restricted foreign capital investment in certain sectors. Indeed, for much of the period discussed by Frobel *et al.*, the proportion of foreign investment that went to the developing world actually fell, evidence that runs completely counter to their central contentions (Gordon 1988; Kiely 1994). More generally, if the state was passive, then we would see a convergence in terms of certain policies, such as taxation rates, welfare spending, labour and environmental standards and even wages, but there is little evidence of anything like absolute convergence on these issues, even within, say, the single market in the EU (Garrett 1998; Hay 2005; Hay & Wincott 2013). Indeed, at a most basic level the state remains of central importance and state spending as a proportion of GDP has hardly declined, as discussed below. Moreover, since the financial crisis of 2008, in which government stepped in and in effect bailed out failing private institutions, it is clear that the state still matters.

On one level, these are powerful arguments and the sceptical account undoubtedly has a point. However, this account does beg the question of what exactly follows from its critique of the hyper-globalization position. While it tells us something about the fact of the state's continued importance in recent years, it tells us rather less about what the state has done in those same years, and this is important both for questions of national sovereignty and national identity. In particular, while some of the arguments of the hyper-globalizers are exaggerated, they do at the same time point to important tendencies in the international order. This applies, for example, to financial flows and the rise of global production networks. Thus, while the sceptics use evidence such as trade/GDP ratios to question the extent to which globalization is unprecedented, they downplay the rise of global value chains in the world economy, the significance of which cannot be captured by the rise of these chains. Thus, if we examine merchandise trade as a percentage of merchandise value added, then there have been significant increases from 1913 to 2000 in France (23.3 to 68 per cent), Germany (29.2 to 78.5 per cent) and the United States (13.2 to 48.3 per cent). In the case of Britain, a much more globally integrated nation, there was a decline from 76.3 per cent in 1913, to 63.5 per cent in 2000, but this latter figure underestimates significant percentage increases from 1960 onwards, when the figure was 33.8 per cent (Perraton 2003: 43). In some respects these figures are misleading as there is considerable double-counting because of the fragmentation of the production process. Indeed, as much as 60 per cent of world trade is in intermediate goods and services linked to parts of this global production process (UNCTAD 2013: 123), but this in itself is why the sceptics' focus on trade/GDP ratios is out of date. Indeed, this global fragmentation is an important part of the analysis that will follow in later chapters. For now, though, we should emphasize that while the state is indeed still relevant, globalization sceptics tend to reify it, focusing more on what the state is and less on what it does. Thus while the hyper-globalization thesis tends to argue that states have to respond to globalizing forces outside of their control, the sceptics tend to downplay the significance of these forces. Instead, we might argue that states have in part actually helped to promote these globalizing forces, and this is a central argument of some conservative anti-globalization theorists (Francis 2016). What we might argue, then, is that many nation states have moved in a neoliberal direction since the 1980s, and away from neo-Keynesianism in the developed world and developmentalism in the developing world, and that states have been active agents in this process (Kiely 2005).

In terms of culture, like the hyper-globalization positions, a mapping of different accounts onto the sceptical position is far from straightforward. Nonetheless, some observations can be made and again we can make some preliminary observations about how these might be related to conservative anti-globalization. The first point to make is that sceptics would argue that the globalization of culture is at most far from complete, and at the very least a contested process. Most obviously, there are still different religions in the world, as well as different political systems, cultural values, and so on. Even in terms of consumer culture, much of the radical critique of cultural imperialism assumes that in fact globalization means Westernization and in effect the Americanization of the world (Tomlinson 1991). However, there are plenty of examples of cultural products that are not American, such as Bollywood, "national" foods, Latin American soap operas, and so on. Moreover, large corporations have found that in some respects they have had to localize their products, so that McDonalds products in India or MTV programmes in Asia are not the same as those in their American home base (Tomlinson 1999). For reasons such as these, some have suggested that, insofar as it exists, the globalization of culture has not given rise to homogenization so much as hybridization or creolization, in which the global and local interact in particular, localized ways (Pieterse 2004; Cohen 2007). Similarly, while patterns of migration might change national identity in various ways, multiculturalism does not necessarily mean the end of nationally specific cultural identities, not least because nations "are reconfigured by taking on the hybrid identity they have imported and created" (Martell 2017: 79).

This argument can be regarded as an optimistic sceptical position, which suggests that national identity and cultural diversity – within and between nations – is alive and well. One possible objection to this optimism is that claims for the existence of cultural hybridity downplay the role of power and how culture might be related to wider political, economic and social relations (Martell 2017: chapter 4). Moreover, while it might be true that the existence of cultural hybridization undermines simplistic accounts of cultural homogenization, this does not negate the fact that cultures across the world have become increasingly standardized in the sense that rationalization has become an increasingly prevalent tendency. For the Left, while this spread of neoliberal consumer capitalism might not be one that is reducible to the United States, it is still one in which American power is far greater than that of other countries (Scott 1997). For some American conservatives, and especially neoconservatives, this is less problematic because the US is a nation that is both exceptional and universal. Seen in this way, the US is indeed the leader of globalization, but it is something in which everyone can potentially benefit. In this approach, neoconservatives are sceptical about institutions of global governance, because this gives undemocratic nation states a potentially equal say in the international order, and gives too much tolerance to illiberal regimes and political movements. In particular, neoconservatives, like other conservatives, believe that the nation is central, but that there is something exceptional about the American nation, precisely because it is universal. But, unlike the conservative anti-globalists discussed in Chapters 5 and 6, neoconservatives believe that this is compatible with a liberal international order, provided it is one "with American power at the centre and with America as the indispensable nation" (Kagan 2002/3: 138–9). This involves some commitment to multilateral rules, the UN, and so on, but a conditional commitment in which the US is first among supposedly sovereign equals (Kagan 2004: 19). However, at the same time, the liberal international order and globalization are not only acceptable but desirable ends. In this way, the neoconservative strand of American conservatism is pro-globalization, though with some caveats, as we will see in Chapter 5. This support allows it to find common ground with liberal internationalists who see interdependence as desirable, and to an extent with those that suggest that the world order has – and should – become more cosmopolitan.

This leads us back to consideration of cosmopolitanism as the normative principle of globalization, as discussed in the previous section. As we saw there, cosmopolitanism supports the development of universal principles based on individual human rights, the spread of liberal democracies and (to some extent) market economies. It is here that we might identify a sceptical – and normative as well as analytical – critique of this cosmopolitanism, which contends that in fact this is not a genuinely universalist position at all, but actually an apology for imperialist power (Chandler 2000; Gowan 2001). This is an argument that unites critics derived from realist (Zolo 1997), postcolonial (Jabri 2012) and Marxist (Mieville 2005) accounts of international relations, which broadly argue that normative claims to universality are actually specific claims to power and the imperialist domination of some states over others. Thus, cosmopolitanism is in effect a form of cultural (and economic and political) imperialism. So-called ethical foreign policies and liberal humanitarian wars of intervention are not then about saving distant strangers from tyrannical regimes, but rather involve the implementation of power by some strong states over weaker ones. The disastrous post-Cold War interventions in Afghanistan, Iraq and Libya should be seen in this light (Davidson 2012), as should the wider postwar development project that involved the imposition of a culturally specific project on to developing countries (Escobar 1996), an argument central to the post-development critique of both globalization and development (Sachs 1992; Ziai 2007).

Much of this critique is associated with left-wing "anti-globalization" and the argument that in fact actually existing globalization is a new form of imperialism. But we should note that at least some of these contentions are also made by some conservatives, though obviously not the neoconservatives briefly discussed above. Samuel Huntington (1996) famously argued that global culture was not leading to one world but in fact to a clash of civilizations. This perspective contrasts sharply with Fukuyama's (1992) End of History thesis, the latter of which suggests that there is no viable alternative to liberal modernity, which was available to all cultures. These cultures might not have yet chosen liberalism but they will find that there is in fact no viable alternative to it in the long run. Fukuyama's thesis was written at a time when he was seen as a neoconservative thinker, a positon that he later rejected in the context of the Iraq war of 2003 (Fukuyama 2006). While in many respects his End of History thesis was considered to be triumphalist in the claims it made for Western liberalism, it did at times express some doubts that liberal individualism was sufficient for social cohesion to occur (Fukuyama 1992: part V). Huntington's conservatism, however, expressed far greater reservations, and indeed rejected any conception of the universality of Western ideas. Instead, he argued that the world was divided into nine major civilizations, Western, Confucian, Sinic, Japanese, Islamic, Buddhist, Slavic-Orthodox, Latin American and African, and it was cultural difference rather than the state system, nation, class or wealth that differentiated the world. In contrast to liberal internationalism and neoconservatism, Huntington argued that there was no international community or global society as such, but a variety of different cultures. Thus, while liberalism was accused of propagating a relativism *within* cultures and polities, Huntington – in contrast to liberal universalism – suggested a relativism *between* cultures. In the current era of globalization, "(p)eople and countries with similar cultures are coming together. People and countries with different cultures are coming apart" (Huntington 1996: 125). Huntington's thesis has been the subject of all kinds of criticisms. Among other things, it can be said that he conflates nation, ethnicity, polity and culture, tends to assume that cultures are static and fixed, believes that political differences can be read off from cultural difference, downplays conflict within cultures and assumes conflict between cultures (Halliday 1996; but for a nuanced close critical reading of Huntington, see Dunkerley 2017).

However, Huntington's (2004a) later work does not necessarily accept that nations and cultures overlap and he expresses a growing scepticism about multi-culturalism in the US. In particular, he suggests that American identity, or the American creed, has eroded since the 1960s due to globalization, the end of the Cold War, and migration and multiculturalism. He was particularly concerned with the rate of Mexican migration, particularly illegal immigration, and the failure of Mexicans to assimilate into the dominant American culture. Seen in this way, Huntington does not necessarily conflate culture and nation, but his criticisms of American multiculturalism still tend to essentialize cultures and do so in order to challenge the growing multiculturalism of the US. Huntington (2004b) argued that these developments in part reflected the "denationalization of the American elite", and a growing divide from "ordinary Americans" who supported the dominant American culture, and who feared for their jobs. On the other hand, for the liberal elite, which he called "Davos Men", "these concerns are secondary to participating in the global economy, supporting international trade and migration, strengthening international institutions, promoting American values abroad, and encouraging minority identities and cultures at home. The central distinction between the public and elites is ... nationalism versus cosmo-politanism" (Huntington 2004b: 5).

We will return to these arguments in relation to wider conservative arguments in later chapters. What we need to highlight here is a wider con-servative argument, not shared by neoconservatism, which questions the uni-versal aspirations of Western liberalism. Thus, the inter-war "conservative revolutionaries" argued that there was no universal human culture but rather a pluralism of cultures, each of which goes through cycles of growth and decline (Spengler 1991). Although at times these conservatives suggested a normative neutrality and a purely analytical account of the rise and fall of cultures, they also regretted the decline of the West, and placed the blame on liberalism. This was because liberalism was weak both domestically and internationally. The weak liberal democratic state allowed politics to be captured by strong vested interests operating in civil society and thus undermined the capacity of the sovereign to rule over the "masses" (Schmitt 1976). This was not just a question of weakness at the domestic level because the ability of the sovereign to decide definitively on questions of geopolitics was undermined by liberal individualism and subjectivism. This is most clear in the case of war between states, in which "the political entity must demand the sacrifice of life. Such a demand is in no way justifiable by the individualism of liberal thought. No consistent individualism can entrust to someone other than to the individual himself the right to dispose of the physical life of the individual" (Schmitt 1976: 71). Universalist ideas such as liberal internationalism – and, we might add, globalization – thus focus on global solidarity, which undermines sovereign state capacity and thus the ability to engage in an effective geopolitics (Schmitt 1962). We will see in Chapter 5 that the current form of conservative anti-globalization in the US – paleoconservatism – questions the supposed weakness of the liberal state as outlined by Schmitt, but at the same time it agrees with the inter-war conservatives that there is a close relationship between domestic and international liberalism. In particular the state has been captured by a new class that claims to promote equality but in fact is more interested in the extension of its own interests and power (Gottfried 2001: xi). This claim to universal equality is thus a claim to power, and it is one that operates both domestically and internationally so that the "drive toward extending equal citizenship at home and the opening of America's borders to larger and larger numbers of Third World immigrants became related tendencies" (Gottfried 2001: 96). Similarly, and in an argument in many respects similar to the postcolonial critique of development that suggests that the postwar development project is a form of cultural imperialism (Said 1978; Escobar 1996), paleoconservatives suggests that the postwar development project involved the imposition of supposedly universalist liberal internationalist ideas on alien cultures (Francis 2016: 471).

From global transformationalism to globalization as discursive neoliberalism

The transformationalist perspective attempts to provide both a middle ground and an alternative understanding of globalization. Like the hyper-globalizers, the transformationalists recognize the reality of globalization, but in contrast to them they suggest that it is a more complex process. In particular, they argue that contemporary globalization is part of a long-term historical process but recent events are unprecedented in terms of both intensity and scale. In particular, there are important changes such as an increase in the intensity of flows (of information, capital and to some extent people), institutions of global governance, and so on (see Held *et al.* 1999: 7–14; Martell 2017: 20–2).

In one sense, this position has an understandable appeal because it attempts to provide a more nuanced approach than the first two positions. In terms of a description of certain current events in the international order, the transformationalist position is an appealing one. But there are some issues with it. First, because it tends towards a half-way house between the first two positions, it at times can be accused of replicating one or the other of these. Thus, Martell (2017: 23–5) suggests that in many respects – the continued importance of the state, the unevenness of capital flows, the ways in which international institutions rest on nation states – the transformationalists are similar to the sceptics. At the same time, it could equally be argued that this approach also accepts key arguments of the hyper-globalization position, particularly around those related to the intensity of capital flows (Kiely 2014). This is not necessarily a problem, not least if we accept the importance of certain manifestations of globalization, and at the same time recognize that the state still matters. Nonetheless, the global transformationalists might be accused of being guilty of setting up too rigid a dichotomy between a "realist" past, when states were more or less all that mattered in the international order, and an unprecedented globalist present, where state power is seen as reduced in novel, but usually under-theorized, ways (see, for instance, Scholte 2005).

This point brings us closer to Rosenberg's powerful critique of globalization theory, to which we turn in a moment. Before doing so, there is one related issue that needs to be explored, and it relates back to the definitions of globalization briefly highlighted in the opening chapter of the book. For transformationalists, the global transformations that they refer to lead to an increase in what Holton (2005) has referred to as growing interconnectedness and interdependence. Again, descriptively, this is probably unobjectionable even if we need to qualify this with the recognition that sometimes historical novelty can be exaggerated for the reasons already suggested above. Indeed, this emphasis on interconnectedness is not so different from liberal internationalist theories of international relations (Keohane & Nye 1977), which combine an analysis of interconnections with a normative, liberal political project. But this begs the question of the nature of this interconnectedness, for is this one based on mutual interdependence, or does it involve unequal power relations based on what liberal internationalists called asymmetric interdependence (Keohane & Nye 1977)? Put more bluntly, what does this account have to say about the question of power, or, even more bluntly, what are the *politics* of globalization? This is an important point because sometimes this position appears to be so impressed by the novelty of globalization that the question of politics tends to fall away from the picture. For instance, some of the literature on globalization focuses on the ways in which changes in communications impact on the ways that people mobilize. This is an important question, but sometimes it is at the cost of examining why people mobilize at all.

For instance, there has been a lot of discussion of the ways in which social media were used to mobilize people in the Arab spring from 2011 onwards, but there has been far less focus on why people mobilized in the first place, which would bring us back to a consideration of politics and power (Gladwell 2010).

This point brings us on to a consideration of Rosenberg's (2000, 2005) critique of the global transformationalist position. As we have already seen, this position contends that globalization should be seen less in terms of quantitative measures around trade or capital flows; in fact, globalization should be seen as a system of transformations, which refer to increased capital flows, global value chains, financialization, multinational companies, systems of regulation that transcend national states, the growing importance of international organizations, and so on (see Held *et al.* 1999; Held & McGrew 2007). We might accept that these factors are in some respect novel and we might go further and – unlike Rosenberg – accept that these do indeed constitute a new period in the international (capitalist and state) order (Kiely 2014). But the transformationalist position goes further than this, and suggests that these changes, which in effect add up to something called globalization, can equally be explained by something we might call globalization. In other words, following Rosenberg, we might argue that globalization refers to a set of features (capital flows, global governance, and so on), and these are supposedly explained by the very same features that are used to otherwise describe globalization – in essence, globalization causes globalization. The result is that globalization – defined as the expansion of space – becomes the causal factor that explains the changes that occurred in the 1990s. As Rosenberg (2000: 2) argues, "globalisation as an outcome cannot be explained by invoking globalisation as a process tending towards that outcome". In this way, globalization became less something that needed to be explained and more something that did the explaining, and so "the causal properties of particular social relations that were undergoing spatio-temporal expansion or compression were instead attributed to the expansion or compression itself" (Rosenberg 2005: 13; see also Rosenberg 2000). Why, then, does globalization theory confuse globalization as process with globalization as explanation? The essential reason, as Rosenberg (2000; 2005: 10, 12, 54) argued, was that it substitutes a social for a spatial explanation.

For this reason, Rosenberg argues that globalization does not exist. This is the basis of his postmortem for globalization both as theory *and* as history or period of capitalist development. In many respects, Rosenberg is a globalization sceptic and he quite rightly argues that the state still matters. However, he tends towards the view that little has changed since, say, the era of imperialism in the period up to 1914 or 1945. This downplays both the important and significant changes that have taken place within the international capitalist order, and the changing role of states in that order, and above all the hegemonic capitalist state since 1945, the United States. What the US state has done is promote a global capitalism in which other states operate open-door policies in terms of investment, liberalize their trade and enter into agreements with other states based in part on promoting this globalized form of capitalism (Panitch & Gindin 2012). During the Cold War, the promotion of this liberal international order and global capitalism was in many respects compromised by the existence of the Soviet Union and its allies, and the promotion of a statist, developmentalist capitalism in what used to be called the Third World. But since the end of the Cold War, and alongside the rise of neoliberalism from the 1980s, this liberal order and globalized capitalism has in many respects intensified (Kiely 2010). While Rosenberg's (2007: 420) theoretical postmortem is very convincing, his historical postmortem is not (Kiely 2014).

So far, then, we have suggested that the hyper-globalization position is exaggerated, above all in terms of its arguments concerning the mobility of capital. At the same time it captures some important changes in terms of the restructuring of capitalism, including an increase in cross-border flows, state openness to investment and the growing significance of global production networks (Dicken 2015). Nonetheless, this does not mean that the state has declined in importance and it is a central institution both in its own right and in terms of its interaction with these capital flows. In this regard the sceptics are correct. However, these analytical considerations beg the question of what political – and normative – questions follow from these changes. As we will see, conservative globalization and anti-globalization draw certain conclusions from some of these changes, while at the same time downplaying the significance of some of these as well. But this is to get ahead of ourselves; first we need to introduce an alternative approach to understanding globalization, which accepts elements of both the hyper-globalization and sceptical positions, but then adds a new twist. This is the argument that globalization is best understood as a discourse (Hay & Marsh 2001), or a particular way of understanding, interpreting and acting on the world.

This argument links academic analysis more closely to the way that globalization was deployed in the world of formal politics, perhaps above all in the United States under Bill Clinton and the United Kingdom under Tony Blair. In particular, from the 1990s onwards, and especially the long boom of 1992 to 2007 (Schwartz 2009), it was argued that globalization represents a new context in which politics operates, one that creates certain imperatives to which governments must react because there is no alternative. While this was often presented as a necessity, the third way also put forward arguments to suggest that this was also desirable – and in this way the globalization debate increasingly became, even if implicitly, a normative one. What interests those working with this discursive approach is the ways in which globalization comes to be perceived as an established fact by thinkers, agents, and so on, and how these perceptions become self-fulfilling prophecies. In particular, the inevitability of globalization leads to policymakers carrying out decisions (that is, making choices) that the discourse itself deems to be both inevitable and necessary. In this way, globalization should be regarded less as a reality, and more as a political project (Hay & Watson 2003). These are the grounds on which Hay and Watson (1999) suggest that the work of Anthony Giddens, and the third way more generally, easily accommodates itself to neoliberalism. If we accept Giddens' claim that globalization is irreversible, then "(l)ike it or not, to accept the radical stance on globalization as unquestioningly as Giddens does is to appeal to a set of ideas which have long been taken hostage by a distinctively neo-liberal articulation of systemic economic 'imperatives'. Moreover, so long as this continues to be understood as just 'how things are', the political space for democratising globalising tendencies and once more laying neo-liberal 'common-sense' open to question would appear to be strictly limited" (Hay & Watson 1999: 422). States must therefore adopt the correct policies in order to draw on the opportunities that globalization presents. In other words, globalization theory too easily accepts the political parameters established by the victory of neoliberalism in the 1980s. This point leads us to ask the question of what exactly neoliberalism is, something discussed in the next section.

Neoliberalism and globalization

Neoliberalism is itself a contested concept and has recently been the subject of widespread criticism (*Progress* 2015; Venugopal 2015; Talbot 2016; Dunn 2017). Much of this critique rests on a particular definition of neoliberalism, which suggests that it can be defined as the promotion of the so-called free market and thus the roll-back of the state, followed by the argument that the state in fact has never gone out of business (Weiss 2012). This is reflected in, among other factors, continued high state expenditure/GDP ratios, continued high rates of social spending and new forms of protectionism for high-tech industries in the developed world (Weiss 2012: 30–1). Talbot (2016) provides extensive data to show that by around 1980 the state "was more than four times the size it had been in 1870". Since then, there has barely been any roll-back of the state, so that among OECD countries, public spending averaged 40.5 per cent in 1986, and 40.1 by cent by 2005. Therefore "(w)e are no nearer the 'neoliberal state' now than we were in 1980". Although less critical of the term, Wren-Lewis (2016) similarly argues that "(o)ne of the defining characteristics of neoliberalism as far as I am concerned is a dislike of 'big government'. In the period from 1998 to 2010, government consumption as a share of GDP rose from 17 per cent to 22 per cent, in contrast to the Conservatives from 1979 to 1997", and thus, "(w)hen it comes to the rather important issue of the size of the state, New Labour was not neoliberal" (Wren-Lewis 2016).

The problem with these kinds of arguments is that they want to reduce ideas and practices to easily identifiable "things" that either exist or do not exist. One therefore only needs to point to easily identifiable measures – such as state spending – to show whether neoliberalism is indeed "a thing". There is a certain irony in the case of *Progress* (2015) magazine's rejection of the concept as an example of an "absence of clearly defined terms" that permits "sloppiness, laziness and downright sophistry". This is not only because *Progress* is associated with the third way and thus – as we will argue in the next chapter – is in many respects a neoliberal journal. It is also because other concepts, which are not clearly defined – modernization, social capital – are central features of the third way project, and indeed this is a project that is forever changing in response to the demands of globalization, itself a concept that, as should now be clear, is far from easy to define. Furthermore, as we will see in the next chapter, the third way itself tends to reduce the concept of the market to a thing, something beyond human capacity and agency to change, and this is a central reason why the third way is complicit with neoliberalism (Watson 2018).

None of this tells us what neoliberalism actually means, however. In some respects, neoliberalism does refer to the promotion of the market, and indeed does include privatization, trade, investment and financial liberalization as central features of its project (though, as we will see in later chapters, it is far more ambiguous about the free movement of labour). We might also accept that neoliberal thought contains within it a libertarian promise that the market can displace the state. But it is mistaken to conclude from this that neoliberalism is simply about extending the market on the one hand, and minimizing the state on the other (Kiely 2018), as though there were a zero-sum game between the two. Perhaps the most famous neoliberal theorist, Hayek, argued in *The Road to Serfdom* that "(t)he question whether the state should or should not 'act' or 'interfere' is a highly ambiguous and misleading description of the principles on which a liberal policy is based" (Hayek 2001: 84). He later argued in *The Constitution of Liberty* that "it is the character rather than the volume of government activity that is important" (Hayek 2006: 194). What is important, then, is not the amount or extent of state intervention, but the particular forms and character of that intervention. This can be illustrated through a brief examination of neoliberal ideas that emerged – like the conservative revolutionaries discussed above – in the inter-war period and developed further after 1945. In particular, the brief discussion here will focus on German ordoliberalism in the 1930s, the Chicago School after 1945 and Hayek's distinction between spontaneous and constructed orders.

Ordoliberalism emerged in the context of the crisis of the Weimar Republic in Germany in the early 1930s. As we saw above, one of the conservative revolutionaries, Carl Schmitt (1976: 216), argued that Germany needed a strong state because Weimar had in effect been captured by vested interests operating in civil society, which put pressure on the weak Republic. Schmitt was briefly a member of the Nazi Party in the period from 1933 to 1936, before he fell out of favour, but the reason he was sympathetic to the Nazi takeover was that it could provide a strong leader that could rule over the competing interests that existed in civil society. Ordoliberals were also concerned with the rise of competing interests in the weak pluralist state, and the ways in which this undermined the market order. Instead of German Fascism, they supported an authoritarian liberalism (Heller 2015) in which a strong state stood above civil society, and made sure that no particular interest could undermine the rule of the market order. What was needed was a strong state that, in the words of Rustow (who first used the term neoliberalism in the 1930s), could "look outside the market for that integration which is lacking within it" (cited in Bonefeld 2013: 111). The ordoliberals were particularly concerned by the rise of large corporate monopolies on the one hand (Röpke 2009: 10), and proletarianization and the welfare state on the other. The result was the development of a mass society dominated by large corporations and the millions of propertyless workers who worked for an "industrial mammoth" (Röpke 2009: 140). There is thus a need to de-proletarianize these workers through the extension of property ownership and independent production. What was needed was a *vitalpolitik*, a politics of life, which contained the proletarianization of society through the fostering of a combination of entrepreneurship and civic engagement through family and community. The welfare state simply exacerbates the proletarian condition, exposing the masses to commercialism and cheap materialism. The masses benefit from the creation of wealth that arises from the market society but they do not fully understand it, and so social policy is needed to reconcile the market and individual responsibility, and which maintains "society as an enterprise society" (Bonefeld 2013: 107). In contrast to the welfare state, this involves the extension of private property through "restoring small property ownership" (Campbell 2009: xvi). In one respect these ideas sound hopelessly romantic, though we will see that in fact they have had some influence over anti-globalization ideas (Chapter 5), including those associated with the Left (Chapter 8). But an important legacy of Röpke's work is its focus on individual empowerment through property ownership, and thus his vision of the individual as, in the words of Foucault (2008: 241), "an enterprise". Ordoliberals therefore argued for a strong state, but one that was strong enough only to provide the order necessary for a market economy to flourish. Rustow thus used the term "free economy-strong state" to describe the ordoliberal postion (Turner 2008: 84).

The second strand of neoliberalism that is important for our purposes is the Chicago School, and its offshoot the Virginia School, particularly as it developed in the postwar period. Initially, there was widespread agreement among neoliberals that the state was necessary to promote the market order and that large corporations were as much of a problem as trade unions and the collective demands for (social) democracy. In 1944, Hayek (2001: 200) argued that "the impetus of the movement toward totalitarianism comes mainly from the two great vested interests: organized capital and organized labour". From the Chicago School, Milton Friedman argued in 1951 that neoliberalism would "accept the nineteenth century liberal emphasis in the fundamental importance of the individual, but it would substitute for the nineteenth century goal of laissez faire as a means to this end, the goal of a competitive order" (Friedman 1951: 5). This position placed him close to that of the ordoliberals, who had similarly argued for a strong state to promote and foster competition, in contrast to nineteenth-century laissez faire, which "underestimated the danger that private individuals could through agreement and combination usurp power and effectively limit the freedom of other individuals" (Friedman 1951: 4).

This unity was eventually undermined, not least through debates at the main neoliberal think tank, the Mont Pelerin Society, which was founded after the war. From the late 1950s to the early 1960s, the German ordoliberals gradually left the Society (see Burgin 2012: chapter 4; Hartwell 1995: chapter 5). By this time the Chicago School and Hayek had made their peace with large corporations and therefore had broken with the earlier arguments of ordoliberalism. In particular, both the Chicago School and the Virginia School of public choice theory (Buchanan & Tullock 1962) argued that government regulation carried costs that might be greater than those associated with private monopoly (Coase 1960). Insofar as monopoly was the product of competition, this reflected the efficiency of the company that emerged as a monopoly and its capacity to respond to the needs of consumer welfare (Bork 1978; Posner 2001). Ronald Coase (1960) argued that neoclassical economists had previously assumed costless transactions and then placed their focus on externalities, and on that basis made a case for regulation to deal with this market failure. But Coase argued that transaction costs also apply in cases of regulation, and that therefore economists should focus on examining which legal arrangements are the least costly in the aggregate, *relative to other courses of action* (see Davies 2013: 50). He argued, for example, that the clarification of property rights between two individuals might be more efficient than a system of general (government) regulation, and they could settle damages among themselves. This argument implied that these costs and benefits can be quantified and measured on the basis of their capacity to enhance efficiency. This was taken up and developed further by the Law and Economics approach at Chicago, which essentially argued that law's "basic function ... is to alter incentives" (Posner 1981: 75).

This argument was important not only because it gave intellectual support to private monopoly and thus large corporations, which are an important part of the globalization and anti-globalization story. It was also important because it laid the ground for the extension of market principles into an ever-expanding range of public institutions, for the Chicago School increasingly argued that, as Davies (2014: 85) describes, "faced with a range of options (be they market or not), individuals will select the one which delivers the greatest welfare to them-selves, however understood ... any situation can therefore be analyzed *as if* it were a market, even when it *appears* that choice making behaviour is neither free nor calculated."

Classical liberalism essentially attempted to deal with the question of the appropriate boundaries between state and market. As we saw above, critics of the concept of neoliberalism use this demarcation as the basis for an argument that neoliberalism does not exist. But this definition is problematic because neo-liberalism is a project designed to *eradicate and not separate* such boundaries, so that the state could be conquered on the grounds that it should be analyzed and assessed *as if* it was a market. This meant extending market principles into ever-expanding fields, such as culture, education, government and, indeed – in this regard consistent with ordoliberalism – the enterprising individual (see Brown 2003; Davies 2014; Foucault 2008: 163). Gary Becker (1976) argued that economics is not simply the study of the production, distribution and con-sumption of goods but is actually a science of human behaviour. All areas of life can be analyzed through cost-benefit analyses that can thus tell us which par-ticular choice enhances our welfare or utility (Becker 1976: 3–4; see also Lazear 2000). This kind of cost-benefit analysis can be applied to all walks of life. This is important because neoliberalism emerged in part as a critique of the top-down planning associated with socialist experts (Lavoie 1985), but neoliberalism in effect enhanced the role of a particular kind of expert, because people are not "necessarily conscious of efforts to maximize their utility" (Becker 1976: 5). In other words, the principles and methods of Chicago economists can be deployed to analyze utility maximization at an aggregate level. In this way monopoly is theorized as a reflection of aggregate consumer preferences. But as important, the principle can be applied not just in the sphere of markets, but in all areas of social life, as a kind of imperialism of the discipline of economics (Lazear 2000; Fine and Milonakis 2009). Febrero and Schwartz (1995: xx–xxi) thus contend that many non-economic activities "are actually economic problems. Economic theory can thus help explain phenomena traditionally located outside the scope of economics, in the areas of law, sociology, biology, political science and anthro-pology." Indeed, they approvingly refer to Becker's methodology as "economic imperialism". Davies (2016c) is thus on to something when he suggests that "(t)he reason 'neoliberalism' appears to defy easy definition (especially to those with an orthodox training in economics or policy science) is that it refers to a necessarily interdisciplinary, colonising process. It is not about the use of markets or competition to solve narrowly economic problems, but about extending them to address fundamental problems of modernity – a sociological concept if ever there was one. For the same reasons, it remains endlessly incomplete, pushing the boundaries of economic rationality into more and more new territories."

The implications here should be clear, for what neoliberalism essentially means is not a rigid demarcation of the state on the one hand, and the market on the other, but rather the increased domination of the latter by the former, namely the "*marketization of the public institution*" (Dardot & Laval 2014: 218). Neoliberalism is then "a general philosophy of market society, and not some narrow set of doctrines related to economics" and "(f)ar from trying to preserve society against the unintended consequences of the operations of markets, as democratic liberalism sought to do, neoliberal doctrine instead set out actively to dismantle those aspects of society which might resist the purported inexorable logic of the catallaxy, and to shape it in the market's image" (Mirowski 2014: 8, 12). In fact, neoliberalism is less about the separation of the state and the market, and should instead be regarded as a project designed to extend the market to all spheres of society (Mirowski 2013; Davies 2014; Kiely 2018).

Polanyi (2001) argued against the idea that laissez faire was based on the development of a market economy independently of the state, suggesting that the former was closely linked to the development of money, central banking, war, the corporation and limited liability and contracts (see also Chang 2002; Knafo 2013). The expansion of the market thus went hand-in-hand with the expansion of bureaucracy, and so the free market "required a thousand times more paperwork than a Louis XIV-style absolutist monarchy" (Graeber 2015: 9; see also Harcourt 2011). In other words, the so-called free market requires all kinds of regulation, an important factor in understanding both populism and conservative anti-globalization. Similarly, in the case of recent reform of the public sector, Pollitt (1990) sees the state not as external to the market order, but instead it becomes "an entity completely integrated into the space of exchange, into the interdependent system of economic agents" (Dardot & Laval 2014: 238). What has taken place in effect is that, in the name of consumerism for the customer and entrepreneurialism for the public servant, bureaucratization (or, if one prefers, rationalization or McDonaldization) has increased in order to both measure and administer reforms such as meeting key performance indicators, targets, and so on. This is a process where the "enterprise must replace bureaucracy whenever possible and, when this is not possible, bureaucrats must as far as possible conduct themselves *like entrepreneurs*" (Dardot & Laval 2014: 238).

But, in contrast to the new spirit of capitalism's self-image, this takes place not through the end of Weberian bureaucratic rationalization, but its *extension*. In this new spirit of capitalism, everyone is expected to construct their own iron cage, and will be audited to check if they do so, and therefore instrumental rationality further erodes professional vocation. Thus, "(i)n reality, an act of judgement, involving ethical and political criteria, is replaced by a measure of efficiency that is alleged to be ideologically neutral. The purpose of each institution thus tends to be obscured in favour of an identical accounting norm, as if each institution did not possess constitutive values that are peculiar to it" (Dardot & Laval 2014: 249).

But this then begs the question of "(w)ho in effect evaluates the evaluation? One verifies only what one has constructed; one measures only what can be reduced to being measurable" (Dardot & Laval 2014: 251). We can therefore see where rationalization has actually intensified, for "(t)he three Es of management – 'economy, effectiveness and efficiency' have erased the categories of professional duty and conscience from the logic of power" (Dardot & Laval 2014: 254). Where this does differ from Weber is that neoliberal rationalization rests on the increased role of experts that have authority because of the methods that they use, which are essentially efficiency measures based on metrics and auditing, and which are then applied across the field. In contrast, for Weber bureaucrats derive their authority from their specialized knowledge in their field of expertise. Moreover, the rise of new public management has not led to cost savings. Hood and Dixon (2015) suggest that in Britain from the late 1980s to mid-2010s, while the civil service was cut by one third, public spending doubled and administration costs rose by as much as 40 per cent.

Nonetheless, irrespective of this state encroachment, neoliberalism does promise a free market, a free individual and spontaneous development. Hayek (1967: 63) sets up a rigid demarcation of the spontaneous order of the market, or *cosmos*, which is the outcome of individual interactions but not consciously designed by any one individual, against designed or rationally constructed orders, or *taxis*. Thus, spontaneous order is "a state of affairs in which a multiplicity of elements of various kinds are so related to each other that we may learn from our acquaintance with some spatial or temporal part of the whole to form correct expectations concerning the rest, or at least expectations which have a good chance of proving correct" (Hayek 2013: 35). He suggests that tradition is supposed to provide at least some basis for his defence of the market order and the rule of law, so that good rules will evolve over time and bad ones will gradually disappear. But, at the same time, he also provides a "negative" test of whether or not change is compatible with the adaptation of universalizable rules (Hayek 2013: 194–5). This sounds suspiciously like an argument rooted in the constructivist rationalism that he otherwise wants to reject, for, as Gamble (1996: 30) points out, "paradoxically, it seems that in this modern era we can no longer rely on cultural selection alone to do the job for us. Hayek implies that we now need understanding of the nature of the Great Society, so that we can safeguard it against the dangers that threaten it. What was a spontaneous process can now be preserved only through the conscious appli-cation, if not of planning, then at least of anti-planning." Seen in this way, "his whole project is an exercise in constructivist rationalism" (Gamble 1996: 36). Hayek was especially concerned to find ways to resist mass democracy and support what he considered to be individual freedom. He therefore proposed ways in which democracy (which he reduced to majority rule) could be resisted by rulers insulated from (presumably constructivist) mass demands, and who had superior wisdom. This is an argument hardly compatible with the idea of a spontaneous evolutionary logic (Hayek 2013: 443–7; see also Gamble 1996: 40), and indeed one rather close to Schmitt (see Kiely 2018: chapter 3). Hayek's promise that markets could eliminate politics and bureaucracy should be seen in this light, for the reality is that the world has seen an extension of bureau-cracy *in the name of the market* (Harcourt 2011; Graeber 2015). This point applies not only to the expense of auditing public-sector reform, but also to the costs of regulations, which are often not restrictive of, but actually the basis for, free markets (Vogel 1998). This is important for understanding how con-temporary conservative populism and anti-globalization, which emerged partly to challenge the technocracy of and expertize associated with neoliberalism, including regulations in the US and within the European Union. But, as we have also implied, neoliberalism is a project that in many respects is anti-state, even as it relies on the state to carry out its project, and this is the heart of the neoliberal paradox (Kiely 2018). Thus, the fact that neoliberalism requires intervention is one that may undermine its intellectual coherence, but equally it is one that is a source of constant renewal for the interventionist neoliberal project. For as Mirowski (2009: 449–50) argues:

> The constant bewailing of the size of government is a win-win situation for neoliberals: they complain about recent growth of government, which they themselves fostered, use the outrage they fan to "privatize" more functions, which only leads to more spending and a more intru-sive infrastructure of government operations.

Neoliberals thus attempt to have it both ways, as they try

> to stridently warn of the perils of expanding purview of state activity *while simultaneously* imagining the strong state of their liking rendered harmless through some instrumentality of "natural" regulation; to posit

their "free market" as an effortless generator and conveyor belt of information *while simultaneously* strenuously and ruthlessly prosecuting a
"war of ideas" on the ground; asserting that their program would lead to
unfettered economic growth and enhanced human welfare *while simultaneously* suggesting that no human mind could ever really know such
thing, and therefore that it was illegitimate to justify their program by
its consequences; to portray the market as something natural, *yet simultaneously* in need of solicitous attention to continually reconstruct it;
to portray their version of the market as the *ne plus ultra* of all human
institutions, *while simultaneously* suggesting that the market is in itself
insufficient to attain and nourish trans-economic values of a political,
social, religious and cultural character.   (Mirowski 2013: 69)

While this extended discussion tells us something important about
definitions of neoliberalism, it does not tell us how neoliberal practice and globalization emerged. This was linked to the crisis of the 1970s, when inflation
increased and for some "was taken as vindicating the monetarist critique of
Keynesianism" (Gamble 1988: 79). It was certainly true that the reflation after
1972 was made easier by the end of the fixed exchange rate system established
at Bretton Woods. Friedman supported the shift to floating exchange rates but
also argued that governments should meet monetary targets and not attempt to
reflate in a futile effort to maintain full employment. This ignored the US policy
of deficit financing, much of which paid for the war in Vietnam, and the massive
oil price rises of 1973 and 1974 (Brett 1983). Nonetheless, the monetarist critique of Keynesianism had an instinctive appeal in the context of growing or high
rates of inflation in much of the 1970s. It was above all the economic crisis, and
specifically inflation, and the perceived power of the trade unions that were central to the increasing influence of the New Right in the 1970s (Hayek 1972: 119).
In this way, monetarism acted as a "battering ram" as government policy shifted
to controlling inflation (Gamble 1986: 32). In the US, Paul Volcker was appointed
Chair of the Federal Reserve in 1979; from October of that year interest rates
were increased and a number of further hikes followed, and targets were set for
monetary growth.
    This laid the ground for a shift from neo-Keynesian full-employment policies
in the developed world, facilitated by controls on the movement of capital, to a
shift to neoliberalism. While the money supply was never seriously controlled,
and nor could it be, neoliberal government emerged that liberalized trade and
investment policies, and removed controls on the movement of capital as part
of a much wider process of financial liberalization. In the US and Britain these
policies were started by Democrat and Labour governments of the "Left", as they
were also in Australia and New Zealand, but it was the New Right governments

of Reagan and Thatcher that really promoted a wider shift to economically liberal policies (Kiely 2018: chapter 6). What was perhaps more important than the monetarist attempt to control the money supply was the wider political rationale for this shift. For despite the very significant differences, the inflationary crisis of the 1970s was related closely by neoliberals to the crisis of the Weimar Republic in the 1930s. The question thus faced by neoliberals in the 1960s and 1970s was similar to that asked in the 1930s, namely: in the context of the rise of collectivism, how can mass democracy be limited, at least in the developed world (the transition to neoliberalism in the developing world is considered in the next chapter)? Put slightly differently, how do governments deal with the problem of what Schmitt had earlier called the politicization of the economy and what in the 1970s was called government overload (Crozier *et al.* 1975; Buchanan *et al.* 1978)? Samuel Brittan (1975: 129) argued that the crisis of the 1970s was generated by excessive expectations placed on government and the closely related "disruptive effects of the pursuit of group self-interest in the market place". This resulted in an *"excessive burden ... placed on the 'sharing out' function of government"* (Brittan 1975: 130). For public choice theorists, this led to an economic and cultural crisis, for inflation and welfare had undermined family responsibility, and the commitment of both government and households to balanced budgets had given way to instant gratification, increased debt and a cultural crisis of capitalism (Buchanan *et al.* 1978; Bell 1976). In this way the economic critique of Keynesianism combined with the conservative critique of the decline in family values and responsibility (Krippner 2012; Cooper 2017).

We can therefore argue that neoliberalism emerged in the 1930s as an intellectual project designed to deal with collectivist demands generated by liberal mass democracy, and it emerged as a governing force from the late 1970s for similar reasons, namely a perceived crisis of politics and democracy. Seen in this way, neoliberalism is a *de-politicizing political project*. This brings globalization right back into the discussion because it too can be a de-politicizing political project, one that accepts the parameters set by the neoliberal governance that emerged in the 1970s. These parameters can easily be accepted because globalization theory relies on spatial explanations that effectively sever the link between social actors and historical and political processes. In this way, globalization serves to de-politicize deeply political questions (Burnham 1999), as reinforced by claims that globalization is inevitable, an "explanation" that ignores the ways in which agents have promoted globalization in the first place. This discussion suggests, then, that in contrast to both Rosenberg and to some extent the transformationalists, a focus on the contingent – and contested – nature of globalization is useful, but above all globalization is itself (in part) a political project, and in many ways a neoliberal one. We might also add that conservative populism and conservative globalization have emerged in part to put politics back on to the agenda, and in effect "re-enchant" the world (Schmitt 1976).

Finally, central to neoliberalism is the focus on competition. As we briefly saw above, this includes the promotion of the enterprising individual, if necessary through appropriate state policy, an issue we return to in the next chapter. This includes individuals working in the public sector, so that the marketization of the state involves the promotion of competition within the state. But equally, in the context of the liberalization of capital flows, it involves competition between states (Cerny 1997), not least in terms of attracting this capital. This competition does not necessarily mean convergence in terms of state spending, welfare policies, fiscal policy, and so on, though it might – and does – involves some converging tendencies through some degree of standardization. This applies not just in terms of reduced tariffs, but also in terms of standards related to the environment, intellectual property, labour and food safety. As well as competition, this might involve high degrees of cooperation, for instance, in regional trade agreements and indeed the extension of the EU. This leads to questions over whether poorer countries might not be able to afford such standards, and thus face continued protectionism through non-tariff barriers. But it has also involved accusations that such standards undermine state sovereignty, including in the rich world, and indeed that poorer countries might somehow be evading such standards. These issues are also central features of current conservative critiques of globalization, as we will see.

Conclusion

This chapter has discussed a wide range of issues, focusing mainly on old debates on globalization, but also suggesting ways in which these debates might help us to understand both neoliberal globalization and the rise of conservative globalization and anti-globalization (see Table 2.1). Given the wide range covered, and not least the focus on culture as well as political economy, the following table provides an overview of various positions on globalization. It uses the three perspectives on globalization but then looks at normative positions from both Right and Left that follow from particular analyses, and incorporates neoliberalism into the analysis. The table unavoidably oversimplifies and should just be taken as a snapshot of certain positions in the globalization debate. There are areas of overlap and the table cannot capture important points of difference, not least among cosmopolitans, who might be social democratic or neoliberal, or who even might try to combine the two. What is perhaps most important, and is illustrated both in the table and the wider discussion in the chapter, is that though in many respects the debate on globalization is in part an analytical one,

Table 2.1 Positions on globalization

Positions	Analytical political economy	Normative political economy	Analytical cultural	Normative cultural
Hyper-globalization of Right	Capital and markets have, in some respects, undermined states through their mobility.	The undermining of the state is welcome insofar as the market mechanism is efficient.	Cultural flows have also intensified and have sharply changed national and "traditional" cultural identities.	Some disagreement here. Third way perspectives welcome cosmopolitanism and multiculturalism. Many conservatives are more sceptical and ambivalent.
Hyper-globalization of Left	Capital and markets have, in some respects, undermined states through their mobility.	The undermining of the state is part of the story – the undermining of labour is central and led to a global race to the bottom.	Cultural flows are not outside of wider power relations, and can be a form of cultural imperialism, state domination and the extension of consumer culture.	Cultural flows beyond states are not intrinsically bad, but their current forms should largely be resisted, including liberal interventions, which represent the imperialism of human rights.
Global sceptics of Right	Capital flows are in some respects restricted by states and not as mobile as is often suggested.	No united position – conservatives might suggest that capital flows undermine good jobs in the developed world (e.g., Trump) while others suggest capital flows should be liberated from state regulations (e.g., Brexit).	Cultural flows have increased and national identity has changed.	States should exercise their sovereignty to protect national identity, which entails suspicion of or outright hostility to immigration.
Global sceptics of Left	The state is still a central actor and the mobility of capital is exaggerated.	This allows space for social democracy and development.	Cultural flows have increased but this has not ended cultural diversity or undermined national identity.	Cultural flows may be welcome but also can be problematic as they promote the marketization of culture (and some leftists are suspicious of migration).

(continued)

Table 2.1 (*Cont.*)

Positions	Analytical political economy	Normative political economy	Analytical cultural	Normative cultural
Transformationalist	Globalization involves a number of transformations such as intensified capital flows, new technology, media flows and migration.	Increased capital flows are generally welcome but need to be harnessed by the state (the question of how is a matter of some difference – see above positions).	Among the flows are increased culture and media flows, migration, and so on, and these are not one-way (so not just Americanization).	Global culture, even if there are specific localized, hybrid manifestations, is a good thing, and part of an unfolding cosmopolitanism.
Neoliberal	Global flows increase competitiveness but may still be restricted by state regulations, though some neoliberals recognize that states play a role in enhancing markets (see the third way, for example).	Increased global flows are welcome – see right-wing hyper-globalization – even if still sometimes undermined by states and regionalism (see right-wing sceptics).	Increased cultural flows are happening as a result of the expansion of the market and the freedom of the individual and the choices that arise from such flows.	Divided – some welcome increased cultural flows, but some neoliberals suggest that markets are culturally or socially embedded. Some cultures might undermine the foundations of the market. Also some neoliberals are associated with a cultural conservatism (see the Anglo-American New Right), while third way neoliberals combine cultural liberals and economic liberalism – and thus promote a neoliberal cosmopolitanism.

we can still identify normative positions within the broad debate. Conservative globalization and anti-globalization (also far from a united project, as we will see) can in some respects be seen as a normative project designed to uphold the nation state, either to challenge or indeed facilitate the hyper-mobility of capital, and in this way we can see how it overlaps with the first two positions in the debate. It also arises as a critique of the discursive neoliberal cosmopolitanism that has been discussed briefly in this chapter, to be considered in more detail in the next one.

3

A FOURTH WAVE OF GLOBALIZATION: FROM THE THIRD WAY TO CONSERVATIVE (ANTI-)GLOBALIZATION

This chapter examines in detail the ways in which globalization as a discourse conflated the logic of necessity and that of desirability, and in doing so became a normative project. This was associated with revised social democracy and the third way, above all in the US and UK but also in other parts of the world, both developed and developing, such as Germany, Brazil and France. In particular it was argued that globalization amounts to a "logic" to which nation states must respond (Giddens 1998; Blair & Schroeder 1999), which in many respects represents a continuation and extension of neoliberal principles – in terms of trade and investment liberalization, financial liberalization and public-sector reform, which made public bodies act in ways more consistent with (imagined) market principles. But unlike the neoliberalism of the 1980s, led by the New Right and conservative social policy, in some respects this was associated with a new social liberalism that (selectively) championed progressive social policy including women's rights, gay rights and anti-racist policies so that these groups could properly participate in the "free market". This was sometimes associated with a new, progressive capitalism in which these policies are socially just and economically efficient (Florida 2002).

This era of globalization can be linked closely to the long "1990s boom" of 1992 to 2007 (Schwartz 2009). This enhanced a number of wider claims made about the benefits of globalization, related to the rise of a post-industrial information economy in the developed world, and manufacturing and poverty reduction in the developing world. Central to these claims was the wider one that we are increasingly living in a globally interdependent world and that many of these interconnections are to be welcomed. These include the development of new skills, entrepreneurship and positive sum interactions between individuals, regions and countries, and the development of a cosmopolitan human rights culture enforced by liberal global governance. As part of this post-Cold War world, liberal multiculturalism was enhanced by migration, and humanitarian intervention promoted the integration of the developing world into the liberal zone of peace.

The rest of the chapter examines these issues in four sections. First it examines third way claims made about the "new economy" in the developed world, and second the issue of poverty reduction and liberal intervention in the developing world. The third section then assesses the claims of the third way, for example, through an assessment of the limits of multiculturalism (including incarceration in the US and UK), the focus on entrepreneurialism and the impact of the financial crisis of 2007–8 and its aftermath. The overall argument that globalization is inclusive provided individuals and states behave in appropriate (market-conforming) ways, and with it globalization's normative position of liberal cosmopolitanism, is outlined. The chapter then moves on to examine the problems with many of these claims, suggesting that the outcomes of these global interconnections were more problematic than third way cosmopolitans suggested. The third section of the chapter then asks the question of what was wrong with actually existing globalization. It particularly identifies a number of problems, such as the 2007–8 financial crisis, and how this was so damaging to some of the optimistic claims made by third way neoliberals, and some of the fall-out from liberal wars of intervention. More broadly, this third section also examines wider concerns around inequality, debt, social exclusion and how these were perceived by some on the Right to be associated with the rise of the South, and indeed "the South in the North" in the form of immigration and multiculturalism. This section attempts to provide some kind of sociological context for the cases that follow in the next two chapters, namely the rise of a distinctive isolationist conservatism in the US, and of an anti-EU Brexit in Britain. It will be suggested – but not argued in any detail in this chapter – that this rise of conservative (anti-)globalization does *sometimes* address real issues of concern, though later chapters will argue that the explanations – as opposed to descriptions – of these problems are often hugely problematic, and rest on a misplaced nostalgia for the past (Bauman 2017).

Globalization and the developed world

As we saw in the last chapter, in some respects we can argue that much of the debate on globalization focuses on analytical questions and the extent to which globalization has occurred. This does not mean that normative questions were irrelevant and in many cases these analytical issues combined with an understanding of whether or not these developments were welcome or causes for concern. This is most certainly the case with the varieties of conservative globalization and anti-globalization considered in the next two chapters. But it is also the case with what we briefly identified as the third way in the last chapter. As we saw there, neoliberalism emerged in a variety of forms from the 1980s, and in the case of Britain and the US, it was first associated with the New Right, which combined a free-market approach to economics with more conservative approaches to social and cultural questions. The third way, however, combined liberal economics with liberal social and cultural policy (with some significant exceptions, as we will see). Seen in this way, in terms of both the political economy and culture of globalization, the third way was in many respects cosmopolitan. What this in effect meant was that globalization was not only associated with openness in terms of trade and capital flows, but also in terms of a growing universalization of lifestyles, culture and human rights. This also meant support for migration and multiculturalism as this led to both economic and cultural development for liberal countries (see previous chapter). Indeed, one theorist of the new economy associated with third way thinking argued that entrepreneurial regions have developed on the basis of a high creativity index, part of which includes the existence of cultural diversity, as entrepreneurs sell to all irrespective of gender, race or sexuality (Florida 2002).

The third way focus on entrepreneurship is important and we will return to it in the final section below. For now, though, we need to emphasize the way in which the third way understood the political economy of globalization, and in particular deployed a particular understanding of the international division of labour. Briefly, the best route to development for the developing world is to promote open policies towards foreign investment, alongside trade (and perhaps financial) liberalization, and this will allow those countries to absorb underemployed labour by producing labour-intensive goods. At the same time, the developed world can specialize in higher-value, skilled, high-technology goods and services (Grossman & Helpman 1991; Krugman 1986), a view also endorsed by Ulrich Beck (2000: 92–4; 2006: 108–9). He advocated an international division of labour in which low-skilled jobs are concentrated in poor countries, and skilled jobs concentrate in the developed world. In the developing world the third way also supports a modified neoliberalism, the post-Washington Consensus (see below), and the promotion of the post-industrial new economy in the developed world. Crucially, the third way assumed that this move from manufacturing to services meant that class solidarity had ended, and everybody could potentially be an entrepreneur.

The idea of the third way was developed in the 1990s by the Democrats in the United States and, under their influence, "New Labour" in Britain. It was supposed to be an alternative to the statist socialism of both the former Soviet Union and social democracy in the postwar period on the one hand, and of the market fundamentalism of neoliberalism on the other. In particular, the third way developed in the context of debates around globalization, post-industrial society and the new economy in the West (Castells 1996). The crucial argument of the third way was that these developments changed the context in which politics took place, in some respects changing the very meaning of politics. In particular, modernizing forces had placed demands on states, which needed appropriate policies to respond to these changes. This meant both continuity with and a break from Thatcherism and Reaganism. The third way essentially tried to reconcile the market economy and its tendency to uproot and dis-embed all social relations, with the development of a cultural, social and institutional infrastructure, which would allow the market economy to operate in the first place.

Much of the focus of the third way was thus on how globalization had laid the ground for a new era of politics. What was required in this new era of globalization was the modernization of the state, against those "forces of conservatism" that "kept people down" and "stunted people's potential" (Blair 1998). In particular, social change has swept away the postwar social democratic consensus and the market fundamentalism of neoliberalism, and this includes the rise of global markets, global culture, the information revolution and the changing role of women (Blair 1998). In contrast to Thatcherism and the New Right, a state and politics were needed that reacted appropriately to these changes.

The rise of the information economy has increased the importance of knowledge, and thus everyone has the chance to fulfil their potential. Human capital was central to the third way project and "(p)eople are the contemporary resources that matters [sic]" (Blair 1998). The role of government is to promote a "dynamic knowledge-based economy founded on individual empowerment and opportunity, where governments enable, not command, and the power of the market is harnessed to the public interest" (Blair 1998). Government must create "a positive climate for entrepreneurial independence and initiative" (Blair & Schroeder 1999: 5). Thus, Tony Blair (2000) asserted that: "Because 90% of new jobs will need skills with computers, there will be 6000 centres round Britain, giving access to the internet and help with technology. Everyone will get an 80% discount on computer courses, the unemployed will get it for free."

In this account, social justice was reformulated from a social democratic argument concerning the need to alleviate inequality through redistribution of wealth and social protection in the workplace, to one where the new era of globalization presented a challenge for everyone, rich and poor. The most successful "enterprises", from firms to individuals, would respond to the competitive challenge by harnessing their skills, knowledge and creativity. The state therefore had a crucial role in the enhancement of human capital, and so employees became targets of investment whose skills needed to be harnessed to the changing demands of globalization (see Finlayson 2009: 404).

In contrast to New Right neoliberalism, the third way did not assume that this harnessing and adaptation would occur relatively spontaneously, albeit with a strong state to protect the market order. Instead, the third way promoted a strong state that changed individual behaviour so that it became more market-conforming. In this regard, the concept of social capital was very important, and this "refers to trust networks that individuals can draw upon for social support just as financial capital can be drawn upon to be used for investment. Like financial capital, social capital can be expanded – invested and reinvested" (Giddens 2000: 78). Social capital is therefore central in providing a social underpinning to the market. Important here is the work of James Coleman (1988), who argued that the rational utility-maximizing individual does not exist in isolation but in specific social relations. Seen in this way, social relations function to secure individual interests, based on "the notion of different actions (or in some cases, different goods) having a particular utility for the actor and is accompanied by a principle of action which can be exercised by saying that the actor chooses the action which will maximise utility" (Coleman 1990: 13–14). On the face of it, this sounds like a challenge to the methodological individualism of Hayekian neoliberalism. But what is significant about this usage of the concept of social capital is that it "facilitates the interpretation of social phenomena and problems in the language of economics" (Finlayson 2003: 159). Social relations are thus always economic activities. The economy (through globalization and the information revolution) is something to which we must all respond, and this lays the ground for a new kind of state intervention. In the foreword to the 1998 White Paper on competitiveness, Blair (cited in Finlayson 2003: 177–8) argued that "(t)he Government must promote competition, stimulating enterprise, flexibility and innovation by opening markets … In Government, in business, in our universities and throughout society we must do much more to foster a new entrepreneurial spirit."

In particular, this meant the elimination of social exclusion. In contrast to the New Right, the third way embraced a social liberalism that challenged discrimination on the basis of race, gender or sexuality, partly as a progressive end in itself, but partly also to eliminate distortions in the labour market, so that all could contribute to the production of wealth for society. Indeed, central to the elimination of social exclusion was the participation of everybody in the new economy, and therefore the equipping of all individuals with the necessary human and social capital that would enable them to enter the labour market. The third way saw an important role for the "social investment state", particularly investment in skills and education (Giddens 1998: 99), and Blair was keen to emphasize social justice, equal opportunity and the importance of society and community in third way thinking (Blair 1995). Government is therefore both an "enabler" (World Bank 1997), allowing market forces to do their job effectively, and also regulates the conduct of individuals in order to make them behave in more market-conforming ways.

Government intervention was necessary but of a kind designed to construct individual responsibility. For New Labour, this meant a rejection of old Labour in government and its close ties to unions, commitment to redistribution and social protection. Welfare policies were acceptable provided they played the role of promoting individual responsibility by equipping individuals with the capital needed to participate in the labour market (Mandelson & Liddle 1996). Thus in the US, Bill Clinton's "end of welfare as we know it" was introduced through the 1996 Personal Responsibility and Work Opportunity Reconciliation Act, which abolished automatic aid to families with dependent children, and replaced it with Temporary Assistance to Needy Families (TANF). Together these Acts devolved welfare provision to individual states, and cut grant levels to those states that failed to meet targets to get people off welfare and into work (Levitas 2005: 18).

Under the third way, in many respects the public sector expanded. This, however, is compatible with neoliberalism as was argued in the last chapter, as this expansion promoted reforms that were part of a wider process of marketization. Indeed, "(a)n assumption of the Thatcher, Major and Blair governments has been that public services will flourish through adopting the entrepreneurialism, efficiency and customer focus of the market" (Needham 2007: 67–8). Anthony Giddens (1998: 74–5) was quite clear that "(m)ost governments still have a great deal to learn from business best practice – for instance target controls, effective auditing, flexible decision structures and increased employee participation". In practice this meant policies such as outsourcing and competitive bidding to private companies, public–private partnerships in which private investments were underwritten by the state and competitive audit, league tables and performance targets within public institutions (Burton 2013). These reforms were designed to foster a spirit of entrepreneurialism within the public sector (Triantafillou 2017), including a new customer orientation to consumers of public services.

More broadly, the imperatives of globalization were used to justify the argument that Keynesian economic policies must be rejected. Macro-economic policy had to prioritize low inflation above full employment and high welfare bills (Balls 1992). New Labour gave operational independence to the Bank of England to set interest rates, in order to meet a target of annual retail price inflation of 2.5 per cent, while at the same time being far more relaxed about asset price inflation. In this respect both the Democrats and New Labour gradually shifted their focus away from so much emphasis on the new economy after 2001 (when the dotcom bubble burst), though this remains important, as we will see in the final section of this chapter. In practice, though, New Labour in Britain and, from 2001, the George W. Bush presidency to some extent moved their focus away from individuals and the labour market and focused on promoting the expansion of the housing market.

This Anglo-American liberal growth "model" rested on a booming property market, easy access to credit and low interest rates (Hay 2013: 22–32). It also rested on highly securitized mortgage markets, so that mortgages were repackaged and sold on as new debts. It was also fully compatible with the third way emphasis on individual responsibility, which was reflected not only in greater conditions attached to welfare, but also in the promotion of an entrepreneurial spirit that envisaged all individuals saving and investing in assets, above all housing, for their future welfare (Langley 2008; Watson 2013: 14). This also had the macro-economic "benefit" that it demonstrated to financial markets that government was serious about controlling public spending. At the same time, the increase in paper wealth that came from the housing boom led to a wider boom in which demand was sustained in part by growing debt, but it was envisaged that this was acceptable because of the increase in asset prices, above all in housing (see Kiely 2018: chapter 8). This in turn increased tax receipts as the economy continued to boom, but this in effect hit a wall due to the financial crisis that started in 2007. Both the boom and the bust are explored further in the next section.

Globalization and the developing world

For the developing world, the 1990s saw a shift in dominant development policy. The 1980s were in many respects the start of neoliberal globalization in the developing world in the context of the 1982 debt crisis. A number of large Latin American countries could not meet their increasing interest payment obligations on their debts, as interest rates rose sharply in the period from 1979 to 1982. Faced with the threat of default, creditors (largely Western banks) faced the prospect of not receiving regular payments on their loans and so were no longer willing – or indeed able – to make further loans. This led to the risk of global financial panic in the international payments system as no individual bank was willing to put up new loans, but such loans were necessary for the system (and therefore each individual bank) to continue lending. Indeed, in some cases, banks had committed such large amounts of capital to Latin America that they faced the prospect of bankruptcy.

There was thus a need for an agency to resolve this collective action problem. The International Monetary Fund was a creation of the Bretton Woods conference in 1944 and it was envisaged that it could play a crucial role in lending at favourable rates of interest to countries that faced short-term payments crises. This institution thus had the potential to be a Keynesian one that recycled money from surplus to deficit countries at favourable rates of interest. Indeed, this was the role that Keynes envisaged for the IMF in 1944, but in fact the IMF never received anything like enough funding to work in this way. Therefore, not surprisingly, in the postwar era neoliberals were relatively hostile to the existence of that particular institution, as well as the main organization that dispensed international aid, the World Bank, which also emerged from Bretton Woods (Bauer 1971). However, by the early 1980s, both institutions had in effect internalized the neoliberal critique of development (see Toye 1987), and challenged the dominant postwar development strategy in what was called the Third World, namely import substitution industrialization (ISI). ISI essentially envisaged all developing countries promoting the development of the manufacturing industry and this substitution for the import of relatively high-cost manufacturing goods, at least in some sectors. This would be done through the selective protection of targeted industries, through policies like high tariffs, import quotes and subsidies. This was necessary because in a situation of free trade, new industries would be out-competed by imports from overseas competitors.

By 1982, the IMF – and indeed the World Bank (1981) – argued that the reason why Latin American countries and developing countries in general could not meet their interest payment obligations was not because of high interest rates that were in effect set by the United States, but because of their bad domestic policies, and specifically because of ISI. It was therefore counterproductive to throw new money at these countries because it would be wasted on further poor development policies, which in effect protected high-cost and inefficient industries. If developing countries were to receive further money, either from private sources or from the IMF (or indeed aid from the World Bank), then they needed some kind of seal of approval by which these loans would be subject to certain conditions. While these conditions were subject to negotiations and were unevenly implemented across different countries, there was a certain similarity between them, as they involved the roll-back of ISI and promotion of neoliberal policies of privatization, and trade and investment liberalization. In effect then, these countries were to "globalize" in terms of their economic policies.

The rationale for such policies was that they would encourage individuals and countries to focus on those sectors where they were most competitive, rather than protect inefficient sectors. This in turn would lead to increased output and exports, the latter of which would generate foreign exchange so that countries could meet their interest payments. In the short term, in many cases countries met their interest payment obligations, but did so less by increasing exports and more by rapidly cutting government spending, output and imports. This led to a lost decade of development, where living standards in much of the developing world declined, something that was repeated in the early 1990s in the context of shock therapy in Eastern Europe. Even the IMF (1989) admitted that the results of its policies were disappointing.

However, this pessimism gave rise to optimism in the 1990s. The IMF argued that its policies in themselves were not the problem but rather they had not been properly implemented. Thus, just as the third way envisaged a focus on state policy and institutional change to supplement and better promote the market in the developed world, neoliberal development shifted from a sole focus on the economic conditionality associated with structural adjustment in the 1980s, known as the Washington Consensus. The post-Washington Consensus 1990s still supported neoliberal economic policies, but supplemented these with institutional reform (World Bank 1992), which emphasized good governance. This did not, however, mean the abandonment of pro-market policies of the Washington Consensus, so much as their reformulation through a post-Washington Consensus, as the World Bank (1989, 1992) encouraged institutional reforms that in some respects paralleled public-sector reforms carried out in the developed world. Good governance was defined as transparent, open and accountable government, and a commitment to the rule of law (World Bank 1994), something that on paper was uncontentious but that in practice meant a commitment to reforms that would help to facilitate more effective market-friendly intervention (World Bank 1993, 1994).

In terms of the market, the language changed from that of neoliberalism to that of globalization. In particular, and consistent with 1980s neoliberalism, the argument was made that the problem for poor countries must be internal to those countries. Giddens (2000: 129) suggests that the problems of underdevelopment "don't come from the global economy itself, or from the self-seeking behaviour on the part of the richer nations. They lie mainly in the societies themselves – in authoritarian government, corruption, conflict, over-regulation and the low level of emancipation of women." The 1990s saw significant rates of economic growth in the developing world, and it was argued that this was caused by policies of trade and investment liberalization – in other words, by the decision of countries of the South to embrace the opportunities afforded by globalization. Poverty still existed but was a residual problem, a result of insufficient globalization, reflecting poor policy choices by some states in the South. Good policies are those that encourage competition and specialization, rather than protection, which means tariff and subsidy reduction, the removal of import controls and an openness to foreign investment. It may also mean financial liberalization, the freer movement of money into (and out of) countries, but there is some disagreement over the extent to which this should occur (a point that also applies to the free movement of labour).

The basic argument was that trade liberalization encouraged specialization in those sectors in which countries have a comparative advantage, and that investment liberalization encouraged investment by transnational companies, thus leading to a shift of investment from capital-rich to capital-poor areas – an argument not unlike the hyper-globalization thesis. Following earlier neoliberal work that attacked state-guided development in the third world (Krueger

1974; Lal 1984), a number of writers have suggested that export promotion of manufacturing has been a resounding success, and this was often linked to the argument that global poverty has been reduced in recent years (Krueger 1998; Ben-David & Loewy 1998). This is an argument consistently made, albeit with some qualifications, by the World Bank since at least 1987, namely that trade and investment (and perhaps capital account) liberalization allow developing countries to exercise their comparative advantage and attract foreign investment and savings (World Bank 1987, 1993, 1994, 2002). In contrast, those countries that have failed to develop are said to be insufficiently globalized, as they have failed to capture the opportunities presented by globalization, and instead continued with poor, globalization-unfriendly policies (World Bank 2002).

Since the early 1990s, there has been a large increase in direct foreign investment, from $59 billion in 1982 to $1.45 trillion in 2013 (UNCTAD 2014: 2). It is true that in this period much of this investment tended to concentrate in the developed world, with about two-thirds in the developed countries and one-third to developing (and transition) economies for much of this period. However, if we compare 1980 and 2010, the share of the Global South increased from 25 per cent to 47 per cent (UNCTAD 2013: 3), and by 2015 developing and transition economies accounted for 55 per cent of global FDI inflows. Although post-financial crisis the growth of foreign direct investment has slowed down, and in 2016 the South's share fell to 41 per cent (UNCTAD 2016: 222, 2, 10), we have still seen the rise of the so-called BRIC (Brazil, Russia, India and China) countries or emerging powers. In 2013 China was the second-largest recipient (and Hong Kong fourth), Russia third, Brazil fifth and India fourteenth (UNCTAD 2014). Furthermore, the BRICS (including South Africa) countries have also emerged as major foreign investors themselves, and in 2013 outward FDI flows from developing countries stood at 32.2 per cent of the total outflows (of $1.41 trillion), in contrast to 1998 when the proportion (of a much lower figure) was just 7 per cent (UNCTAD 2014). On the face of it, then, this would appear to conform to the optimistic hyper-globalization thesis discussed in the last chapter, at least up to a point, which suggested that the movement of capital throughout the globe was promoting a levelling-up process across the world. Indeed, it could be argued that the rise of China, and to some extent other BRIC countries, has meant that "the world's economic centre of gravity has moved towards the east and south, from OECD members to emerging economies ... This realignment of the world economy ... represents a structural change of historical significance" (OECD 2010: 15). Although the OECD itself saw this as reason for optimism for the world economy as a whole (see also O'Neill 2013), one could also make a hyper-globalization pessimistic case that in fact these countries in the South have developed at the expense of the West, and the US in particular. This argument may focus on China as a geopolitical threat to the liberal West, as it presents a state capitalist alternative, in which the so-called Beijing Consensus threatens to usurp the post-Washington Consensus. In this account, China's authoritarianism combined with rapid capitalist development threatens to undermine the liberal West, as it represents a new model of development and involves active support for authoritarian regimes in the developing world (Halper 2010). This has led some conservative writers, from a variety of theoretical perspectives, to conclude that China's rise is bound to lead to geopolitical conflict and even possibly war (Navarro & Autry 2011; Mearsheimer 2006). This is an argument that has been made by the Trump administration, of which Peter Navarro is a member, above all by the once influential Steve Bannon, who was eventually forced out of the administration.

These are issues discussed further in the next section and later in the book. For now, though, we need to return to one final issue about the third way and development: wars of liberal intervention. In terms of arguments for military intervention, two cases can be considered here, first that of neoconservatism and second that of third way liberal cosmopolitanism. In the case of the former, we saw briefly in the last chapter that neoconservatives in many respects welcome the so-called free market, but are simultaneously suspicious about the cultural consequences of modernity (Bell 1976). This is because liberal individualism can lead to social anomie and thus undermine both social cohesion and political obligation (Kristol 1970). The so-called free market therefore has to be embedded in a particular socio-cultural framework that goes beyond the liberal individual and the free market. Whether or not neoliberalism believed in a disembedded free market in the ways that Kristol suggests is questionable, and something to which we will return in later chapters (see Cooper 2017; Kiely 2018: chapters 4 and 6), not least as it is important for understanding the relationship between global markets and state regulation, and indeed current nostalgic responses to actually existing globalization. For now though we should emphasize that Kristol argued that neoliberalism alone is insufficient because the state needs something beyond the market, and specifically the state should play the role of a moral tutor, enforcing individual responsibility, hard work and family values. The state is thus an institution designed to promote particular values, and ones that in many respects combine private vice and social virtue (Himmelfarb 2008). These arguments led the neoconservatives to play a leading role in the culture wars from the 1960s in US domestic politics, and what they saw as the increased liberal nihilism not just of neoliberals, but also of the New Left and its celebration of what was deemed to be moral relativism. What is important here though is that for neoconservatives the view that the state should act as a moral leader carried over directly into their view of the international sphere. Thus, just as there may be a crisis in domestic politics that must be overcome by cultural reconstruction, so too is there a need for a more virtuous foreign policy. This involves the promotion of a "future oriented conservatism" (Williams 2004: 314), whereby neoconservatives attempt to recover a specifically American, republican virtue that attempts to combine liberal individualism with public responsibility. In domestic politics, the state plays the role of reconnecting the individual to the community through the promotion of republican virtue, but the state should also lead in foreign affairs. This is part of a historical narrative of American empire, based on the exceptional but universal nature of American nationalism, which is differentiated from the particular nationalisms of Europe. In the words of two prominent neoconservatives:

> American nationalism – the nationalism of Alexander Hamilton and Teddy Roosevelt – has never been European blood and soil nationalism … Our nationalism is that of an exceptional nation founded on a universal principle, on what Lincoln called "an abstract truth, applicable to all men at all times." Our pride in settling the frontier, welcoming immigrants and advancing the cause of freedom around the world is related to our dedication to our principles.   (Kristol & Kagan 1996: 31)

In this way, both foreign and domestic policy is central to US national identity, and the national interest. This is an argument that is distinctive from both conservative realism and liberal internationalism, but has more common ground with the latter than the former. Realist theories of international relations suggest that there are potential enemies in an anarchical world order made up of self-interested nation states. This is true but insufficient for the neoconservatives because it does not clearly identify actual, as opposed to potential, enemies. Indeed, a realist analysis too easily accepts that the national interest is best preserved by a policy of isolationism, something strongly rejected by neoconservatives, who explicitly promote the need to identify enemies, both at home and abroad. As Kristol suggested in early 2001, "(i)n politics, being deprived of an enemy is a very serious matter. You tend to get relaxed and dispirited. Turn inward" (cited in Drolet 2007: 274). Furthermore, realists suffer from the same problems as those associated with the neoliberal state, which is that they both sever values from interests, and specifically the national interest. But just as self-interested material calculation is never enough for the neoliberal state at home, nor is it sufficient for the state in the international arena. Michael Williams (2004: 321) suggests that:

> In this vision, the national interest cannot be reduced to an analytical concept of foreign policy or a narrowly defined material interest. It is a political principle – a symbol and requirement of the political virtue needed for a healthy modern polity. A clear, commonly shared understanding and commitment to the national interest is the sign of a

healthy social order domestically and a basis for a strong and consistent action internationally.

Neoconservatives argue that there is something almost decadent about realism and modern liberalism, in that both fail to provide the basis for social stability. This crisis lies at the heart of liberal modernity, and has led to social break-down at home, and US decline and international disorder abroad. Despite this bleak scenario, neoconservatives argue there are also grounds for optimism, and that these have increased since September 2001. This is because (so it is asserted) the views of neoconservatives resonate with those of the "average American", who similarly regards republican virtues as central to American values (Brooks 2004). This focus on the centrality of values allows neoconservatives to reach out to wider constituencies, not least those of the religious Right, in their attempt to promote a backlash against what they consider to be a liberal, intellectual elite. Neoconservatives therefore suggest that "(j)ust as 'average' Americans are victimized by a culture that systematically misunderstands them and attacks their lifestyle and values, so too America is victimized by a world that is irration-ally, decadently, or perfidiously hostile towards it" (Williams 2007: 117).

The second approach is that of contemporary liberal cosmopolitanism, which from a more universalist perspective argues that the rights of individuals are more important than the sovereignty of states – an argument that is compat-ible with the hyper-globalization cultural optimists and the transformationalists discussed in the last chapter. Current advocates suggest that a cosmopolitan order is more likely in a post-Cold War world, where nation states can be influenced more by ethical considerations than old-fashioned power politics (Cooper 2003; Beck 2006; Kaldor 2006). This argument is often backed up by liberal democratic peace theory, which broadly suggests that war is less likely to take place between liberal democracies, due to a combination of commercial interdependence and/ or liberal democratic accountability (Doyle 1984; Starr 1997). This theory can be traced back to Kantian notions of perpetual peace, based on the idea of a world republic of peaceful nation states, which champion a spirit of commerce and a "universal community" (Habermas 2001: 1). The case for liberal peace was unsuccessfully re-made in the inter-war period, particularly by Woodrow Wilson, and has been revived in the context of the post-Cold War world of glo-balization, due in part to the partial erosion of geopolitical conflict and to the rise of global governance (Held & McGrew 2007). The question then arises as to the relationship between liberal and non-liberal states in the international order. Some cosmopolitans argue for considerable caution in cases of military intervention, above all because of the question of who has the right to inter-vene (Habermas 2006). On the other hand, in the context of post-Cold War and especially post-2001 interventions, some have argued that liberal democracy represents a more progressive form of government than, say, Ba'athist dicta-torship, and so there is a strong case for liberal democracies to intervene in the affairs of non-liberal states. Indeed, in some accounts the domestic structure of liberal democracies, and the implications this has for (peaceful) international relations, is itself sufficient for such states to have established the moral high ground (Cushman 2005).

These arguments are not identical to neoconservative claims, but equally they are not entirely incompatible with them. In his famous Chicago speech of 1999, Tony Blair (1999b) set out a number of principles that must be met for a war to be considered just. These included: certainty that war is the only means; that dip-lomatic options have been exhausted; that there has been a practical assessment of military operations; that intervention is prepared for a long-term haul; that national interests had changed in the context of globalization; and that the United Nations will be the central pillar of promoting international norms. It is debat-able that the interventions in Afghanistan, Iraq and Libya met these criteria, but for some liberal cosmopolitans – and of course American neoconservatives – there was clearly some continuity. It should be noted, too, that these wars of liberal intervention were supported by American conservatives, but also most liberal internationalists in the Democrat Party, and of course third way advocates in the British Labour Party.

Seen in this way, while neoconservatism saw such interventions as necessary ones made by the rightful global moral tutor, the third way supported them on the grounds of active social engineering. As we have seen above, the third way essentially saw an active role for the state in constructing appropriate market-conforming behaviour. This point applied not only to public-sector reform and the construction of the liberal individual, but also in the more extreme form of constructing market-conforming states. Post-Cold War military intervention attempted to construct neoliberal states and eliminate rogue and failed states (Barnett 2005), and in doing so forge a path to development through the pro-motion of open market policies. These would then incorporate countries into the liberal zone of peace, and so promote both the development of these coun-tries and the security of the whole world. Thomas Barnett (2003, 2005) thus wrote of a "functioning core" and a "non-integrating gap", and argued that the latter should be integrated into the former, in part by expanding the sphere of "globalization". This is in many ways the military version of the "globalization-friendly" policies advocated by the World Bank (2002). Some influential foreign policy advisers and academics suggested that for the US in the post-Cold War world, the nineteenth-century British Empire was the model to follow (Haass 2000; Ferguson 2003, 2004), and that the core, functioning states had an obli-gation to intervene into non-functioning states that had limited rights of sover-eignty, a duty that increased after the attacks on 11 September 2001 (see Mazarr

(2003: 508). In this way, security and development were closely linked, so that "dark" globalization could be displaced by liberal military interventionist policies alongside wider neoliberal policies (Roberts *et al.* 2003).

The problem with "actually existing globalization"

So far this chapter has outlined what in effect became the case for globalization from the 1990s and into the 2000s. While this was not necessarily a smooth process, and there were considerable setbacks such as financial crisis, problems with particular military interventions, recessions, and so on, this was still an era where globalization's advocates in effect were confident about their contentions. While there was some disagreement between, say, liberal internationalists, third way cosmopolitans and neoconservatives, above all on the agents necessary to realize their goals, there was also considerable common ground. This involved arguments that economic globalization was both necessary and desirable, and indeed that the era of boom and bust might be over. It also involved arguments that the liberal international order was progressive compared to previous geopolitical orders, and that threats to that order were based on cultural and political reaction, by rogue states or terrorists linked to failed states. And the belief was that the "globalization-friendly" parts of the South were integrating into this order, and that interdependence between Global North and South were based on positive sum transactions.

The rest of this section outlines why at least some of these claims are problematic. Its focus is more or less solely on the developed countries, two of which are the focus of the following chapters, though we will examine some claims made about the South by conservatives in the North. We return to questions about development and the South in Chapters 6 and 7, however, not only to problematize some of the conservative claims made about the South's rise, but also to question some of the optimistic claims made about its rise in this chapter (and the rise of populism in parts of the South). For now, in focusing on the developed world, this section identifies the following factors: (i) the 2007–8 financial crisis and its aftermath; (ii) the question of debt, inequality and social exclusion; (iii) the question of the South, including the rise of emerging powers, the fall-out from liberal wars of intervention, the question of immigration and of multiculturalism. This section will largely focus on certain manifestations of these issues, though it will also briefly show how some conservatives – discussed in Chapters 4 to 6 – have interpreted them. At this stage, a sustained critique of these conservative interpretations will not be made (though there will be points at which I hint at what these might be). As will become clear, especially in Chapter 6, the absence of a critique here does not mean endorsement of these conservative views.

First there was the financial crisis of 2007–8, and its aftermath. In terms of the crisis itself, we can be relatively brief (see Gamble 2009; FCIC 2011; Kiely 2015: chapter 5; 2018: chapter 8). The world economy entered difficulties in 2007 and September and October 2008 saw the possibility of financial meltdown. On 15 September, the leading investment bank Lehman Brothers collapsed (FCIC 2011: 324–42). The following day, the US government agreed a major bail-out and an 80 per cent share in the main insurance group in the US, American Insurance Group (AIG). AIG was increasingly exposed to the drying-up of short-term lending by money markets, and the declining value of its collateral, much of which was in mortgage-backed securities (MBSs). Finally, AIG increasingly had to pay out to counterparties that had insured against falling securities, leaving it exposed to massive pay-outs but with little access to short-term credit (FCIC 2011: 344). Panic ensued and lending between banks, crucial to the circulation of credit, effectively dried up, as the interest rate at which banks were prepared to lend to one another increased substantially. This rate is usually quite close to the rate at which it costs governments – and the US government in particular – to borrow, with an average discrepancy of around 0.3 points, but on 18 September, it reached 3.02 percentage points. At the same time, the cost of borrowing for non-financial firms increased from around 2 to 8 per cent (Mason 2009: 17).

The collapse of Lehman Brothers led to stock market volatility, with significant losses on Wall Street, London and elsewhere, which were then counteracted at rumours of impending government bail-outs. The Troubled Assets Relief Programme (TARP) planned a US government bail-out of $700 billion to buy up Wall Street's toxic debts. This led to considerable opposition from both the anti-corporate Left and the libertarian Right, and an initial defeat of the bail-out plan in Congress on 29 September. This again led to substantial stock market falls. Meanwhile in Europe, banks were desperate to purchase dollars in a market where there was limited availability, and simultaneously were exposed to the bad debts of Lehman Brothers and AIG. In the UK, Bradford and Bingley was nationalized and sold on to Santander, and there was pressure on HBOS, Lloyds TSB and RBS. Hypo Real Estate was bailed out by the German government and the joint Dutch–Belgian operation Fortis was semi-nationalized, while Iceland and Ireland saw the removal of money from their banks, which in the case of the latter was only reversed when the government stepped in to guarantee all deposits in its major banks.

While nationalizations and bail-outs spread across Iceland, Russia and Spain, Britain and the US dithered until it became clear once again that there was a need for bail-outs and nationalizations. Eventually, after considerable opposition from Congress, the $700-billion Troubled Asset Relief Programme (TARP) was passed in early October 2008 (Doran 2008). This in essence meant that the US state bought up the bad debts of banks at prices that were advantageous to the banks (that is, above the market rate at that point in time). In Britain, a £500-billion bail-out was implemented on 8 October 2008. These were only the first stages of a number of bail-outs and nationalizations of loss-making financial companies (see Gamble 2009: chapter 1). Much of these bad debts originated in the US mortgage market. However, in keeping with wider debates around globalization, these markets were not isolated from the rest of the financial sector and indeed the wider economy, as US mortgages had been securitized. What this meant was that mortgages were packaged together with other debts into MBSs or into a more general package that included mortgages and other forms of debt called collateralized debt obligations (CDOs). These were then sold on to new parties, not just in the US but elsewhere. For this reasons, the aforementioned government bail-outs and nationalizations was widespread. For some, this constituted the potential end of neoliberalism, as the state stepped in, seemingly at the expense of the free market. But – in keeping with our discussion of neoliberalism in the last chapter – this was not a straightforward "return of the state", but rather the state bailing out private companies to save the market, and then carrying out austerity policies on the grounds that these were necessary to tackle ongoing fiscal deficits and rising government debt. But these deficits and increased debt were caused by the slowdown in growth that led to fiscal crisis, and the government policies that were designed to save the market (Fine 2012: 54). With the bail-outs and the slowdown in growth, the crisis increasingly came to be seen as a sovereign debt crisis, particularly in Europe.

This in turn led to a new assumption that the crisis was not one caused by instability generated by financial markets, but rather was caused by the state. For some economic libertarians, then, the crisis was caused by politics, and specifically state actors distorting markets (see Wallison 2009; Friedman 2009; for critiques see Min 2011; Payne 2012; Kiely 2018). Briefly, US libertarians argued that the state set home ownership targets for minorities in the US, and these distorted the housing market (Wallison 2009). However, while such targets were periodically set, they were never met, and one libertarian, Peter Wallison, was critical of *limited* home ownership among minorities as late as 2006, placing the blame on the state (Payne 2012: 160). Most of the high-risk, sub-prime mortgages were issued by private companies *independently of* government directives or of the involvement of the Government Sponsored Enterprises[1] (GSEs), Fannie Mae

---

1. Attempts to blame the GSEs (see Pinto 2009) have relied on definitions of sub-prime that are so wide as to be meaningless. Edward Pinto identified 27 million sub-prime mortgages and argued that 19–25 million of these were attributable to government steering of the housing market. He then highlighted a serious default rate of 25 per cent, but this (accepted figure) of 25 per cent does not refer to his figure of 27 million. Pinto's figures include loans completely outside the remit of the Community Reinvestment Act, and indeed 65 per cent of Pinto's high-risk loans were outside of government targets (Min 2011: 3).

and Freddie Mac. By 2005–6, at the height of the bubble, Wall Street invest-ment banks securitized one-third more loans than the GSEs, and sub-prime mortgages rose from 8 per cent of mortgage originations in 2003 to 20 per cent in 2005 (FCIC 2010: 102, 104). GSEs did attempt to become more involved in sub-prime securitization, but this was in response to falling market share. Wallison implies (but cannot prove) a causal link from the Community Reinvestment Act to targets to private lending, suggesting that such lending was a victim of government distortion, but the private sector was not forced to do anything. Indeed, what *was* central was the emergence of a shadow banking system that the government allowed and encouraged – insofar as regulation existed, it was designed to expand and not distort the market. In fact, private securitization mortgages defaulted at over six times the rate of those originated by Fannie Mae and Freddie Mac (Min 2011: 2). Furthermore, the financial crisis was not just caused by a housing market bubble, but included real estate (Palley 2012: 83–5), where there were no "distorting" GSEs, and the crisis was not just confined to the US, but to countries like the UK, Ireland and Spain, where there were no GSEs (Mirowski 2013: 316). In Britain, while David Cameron's Conservative-led coalition was on the whole socially liberal, its economic policy was one that increasingly placed the blame for the crisis on over-spending by the Labour gov-ernment. In fact, the Conservatives said nothing about Labour "over-spending" prior to the crisis, and indeed had committed themselves to Labour's spending plans (Conservative Home 2007). The public debt/GDP ratio was 37 per cent on the eve of the financial crisis, while in 1997, when Labour entered office, the figure was 42 per cent. In 1997 the budget deficit stood at 3.9 per cent of GDP while in 2008 it was 2.1 per cent (Weeks 2012). In the Euro crisis, there were problems with specific areas of government spending and revenue collection in Greece, where the latter was particularly poorly coordinated and debt/GDP ratios were much higher, but Ireland's debt/GDP ratio was just 12 per cent in 2007, and Spain's was 26 per cent, while Germany's stood at 50 per cent (Blyth 2013: 65).

Meanwhile, financial institutions were seriously exposed to risk. The assets of the top six US banks in the third quarter of 2008 amounted to 61 per cent of US GDP and so they were unsurprisingly considered too big to fail. In Europe the situation was even worse; in France in 2008 the assets of the top three banks amounted to 316 per cent of French GDP, and in Germany the figure was 114 per cent of German GDP. Deutsche Bank alone had assets equivalent to 80 per cent of GDP. Outside the Eurozone, the top four banks in Britain had assets that amounted to 394 per cent of British GDP (Blyth 2013: 83). Banks acquired much of this money through short-term borrowing and by June 2011, $755 billion of the $1.66 trillion in US money market funds was held in the form of short-term European bank debt. European banks were also heavily exposed to US mortgage markets, and when this combined with the sovereign debt crisis from 2010, banks found that they were unable to fund themselves through further short-term borrowing. This was exacerbated by the fact that asset prices were falling and so banks had to put up more funds as collateral for further loans. By 2010, Eurozone banks had a collective exposure to Spain of $727 billion, $402 billion to Ireland, $206 billion to Greece and it has been estimated that French and German exposure to the "PIIGS" countries (Portugal, Ireland, Italy, Greece and Spain) was close to $1 trillion (Blyth 2013: 86).

Nonetheless, the crisis was increasingly reimagined as one caused by inappropriate intervention by government rather than instability caused by the behaviour of financial institutions. This laid the grounds for a renewal of neoliberalism, which essentially took the form of austerity, itself premised on the assumption that the state was to blame for the financial crisis. Austerity is "a form of voluntary deflation in which the economy adjusts through the reduction of wages, prices, and public spending to restore competitiveness, which is (supposedly) best achieved by cutting the state's budget, debts and deficits" (Blyth 2013: 2). The case made for austerity rests on a number of contentions, but in essence it asserts that the private sector must lead the recovery and so should not be crowded out by the public sector, and so governments should not run budget deficits. Keynesian stimulus policies can in this respect be regarded as harmful as they take money away from the private sector (Cochrane 2009; Alesina & Ardagna 1998) and try to solve crises through the creation of more debt. The problem with this argument is that "we cannot all cut our way to growth at the same time" (Blyth 2013: 7, 8). In other words, the paradox of thrift suggests that while it makes sense for any individual debtor to pay back its debts, it makes no sense for all to do so as this would lead to stagnation. It was for this reason that Keynes made the case for fiscal stimulus, because in the context of everyone cutting back, recovery would be delayed, something that would carry both social and economic costs. The state – or the macro-economy – is not like an individual household, precisely because of the interconnections and interdependencies between individuals, corporations and government (Gamble 2013). Fiscal expansion is thus necessary to deal with shortfalls in demand and is not "crowding out" private investment. Indeed, it is a supplement to, and a stimulus for, such investment (Keynes 1973: 217–18).

The debate on austerity after 2008 took a number of forms. In the US, President Obama's fiscal stimulus was criticized as insufficient by Keynesians and unnecessary and counter-productive by those favouring austerity, and this led to confrontations in Congress in 2011 and 2013. In Britain government expenditure (at constant prices) showed a slight increase in 2010–11 and a small decrease in 2012–13, but for the year 2013–14, government spending still amounted to 41.2 per cent of GDP (Wren-Lewis 2015). There were important cuts from 2010 in local authority grants, school building, capital expenditure and flood prevention (Pearce 2013). There was also increased pressure to cut welfare benefits for individuals but, as we have seen, this was hardly new and had taken place since the 1970s. The Office for Budget Responsibility has estimated that austerity in 2010–11 and 2011–12, even in this mild form, led to reduction in GDP of around 1 per cent each year, and this seriously undermined the recovery that had begun to take place in early 2010 (Wren-Lewis 2015: 9–11). In the 2010 plans for austerity, it was envisaged that the budget deficit would be reduced from 7.5 per cent of GDP in 2010–11 to 5.75 per cent in 2011–12, 4 per cent in 2012–13, around 2.3 per cent for 2013–14 and less than 1 per cent by 2014–15, and zero by 2015–16. In fact, while the 2010–11 target was more than achieved, by 2011–12 the target was not met, in 2012–13 the actual figure was 5 per cent and in 2013–14 it was 4.24 per cent, around 2 percentage points higher than the original plan (Wren-Lewis 2015: 10). Insofar as there was recovery after the great recession, it was slow and uneven, and was not caused by austerity policies. Moreover, in Europe, where such policies were more severe, there was a much sharper recession, which was a factor in the rise of populist movements (see Chapter 6). In May 2010, Greece received a €110-billion loan in exchange for a 20 per cent cut in public-sector pay, a 10 per cent pension cut, and tax increases. The troika forecast a return to growth by 2012, but instead Greece received a further bail-out in July 2011, which was extended in October 2011. Ireland and Portugal also received substantial bail-outs, which were subject to similar conditions. For most countries in the Eurozone, the threat of widespread default declined somewhat once the European Central Bank started to act as a lender of last resort, purchasing bonds from issuing countries like Spain (Gamble 2014: 180).

Long-term unemployment in the OECD countries increased by 85 per cent in the period from 2008 to 2016 (Le Baron 2016). According to the *New York Times*, in 2014 corporate profits were at their highest level for at least 85 years, while employee compensation was at its lowest for 65 years (Le Baron 2016). From 2007 to 2015, Britain experienced the second-biggest fall in real wages in a developed country (after Greece) (Allen & Elliott 2016). Government policy after 2010 – and specifically cuts to benefits and tax credits – led to a decline in real incomes for the bottom fifth of the population of around 10 per cent on average, with some groups (such as the disabled) suffering far more. This had the effect of increasing the number of children in poverty by an estimated 1.5 million. Meanwhile the top fifth of the population saw little or no change to their income (Portes 2018). In the US, much hope rested on the "new Roosevelt", Barack Obama, who it was hoped would reverse years of decline and growing inequality. However, the promised stimulus was severely watered down by Republican intransigence, and in the period from September 2008 to the end of 2015, 6 million Americans lost their homes. An estimated 70 per cent of people in the developed world experienced income stagnation in the period from 2005 to 2014, a figure that rises to as much as 97 per cent for Italy in that period (Davies 2018a: 78). In terms of wealth, in the US the wealth Gini coefficient increased substantially between 2007 and 2016, from 0.82 to 0.86 (Kuhn *et al.* 2018).

The post-2008 years also saw the exacerbation of trends that stretched back to the 1980s. In the US, the top-1-per-cent income group increased its share of national income from 8 per cent in 1979 to 18 per cent in 2007, and if capital gains are included, then the figures are 8.5 per cent (1979) and 23.5 per cent (UNCTAD 2012: 49–50). The overall income Gini rose from a postwar low of 0.43 in 1971 to 0.58 in 2016 (Kuhn *et al.* 2018). From 1993 to 2000, the top 1 per cent of income earners captured 45 per cent of total pre-tax income in the US, and in the 2002–6 period the figure was as much as 73 per cent (Palma 2009: 842). In 2010 alone, 93 per cent of the additional income created in the US went to just 1 per cent of taxpayers, and 37 per cent went to the top 0.1 per cent (Streeck 2014: 53). Thomas Kochan (in Streeck 2014: 52–3) has estimated that while productivity, household income and average hourly wage rates increased more or less at the same rate from 1945 to 1975 in the US, since then, while productivity increased from 200 in 1975 to 400 in 2010, wages remained at their 1975 level of 200. From 1973 to 2006, the average annual income of the bottom 90 per cent fell in real terms – from $31,300 to $30,700 at 2006 prices (Palma 2009: 841). The ratio of CEO pay to average wages in the US increased from 20:1 in 1965 to 270:1 in 2017 (Coates 2018: 118). Clinton's 1996 welfare reform, the Temporary Assistance for Needy Families Act, had the effect of protecting about 1 million households with children from extreme poverty, but by 2011 this figure had fallen to 300,000. In the US in 2016, around 1.5 million households (involving 3 million children) lived below the extreme poverty line, double the number in 1996, and an estimated 6.7 million households used a foodbank or other food charity in 2014 (Edin & Schaefer 2015).

In Britain, from 1979 to 2012, the bottom 20 per cent saw a decline in income of 12.1 per cent. The next quintile (20–40 per cent) also saw a small decline, of 0.1 per cent, while the 80-to-100 per-cent quintile saw an increase of 48.8 per cent. Most tellingly, however, the top 0.01 per cent saw an increase in income of 685 per cent (Hindmoor 2018). Even under New Labour the much-trumpeted and very real successes in terms of poverty reduction (Hindmoor 2018: 142) – due to the minimum wage and tax credits – were still limited. While there was increased welfare spending and significant falls in pensioner and child poverty in Britain, there was also an increase in poverty among those of working age without children (IFS 2016) and poverty reduction targets were not met. Child poverty rates declined from about 26 per cent in 1997 to 18 per cent in 2010, but this was still higher than the 14 per cent when Thatcher entered office. Overall poverty rates fell from 19 to 16 per cent in the same period, compared to 13 per cent in 1979 (Hills 2013). Moreover, in the 2010 election campaign, Labour committed itself to austerity measures that might have increased poverty rates had Labour entered office (although falling incomes for so many might have had the perverse effect of lowering the poverty line). In terms of income inequality after tax and benefits, Britain was the fifth-most unequal society among industrialized countries in 2010–11 (Hills 2015: 28–9). Since 1980, the share of wages in GDP fell by 5 percentage points or more in Australia, Belgium, Finland, France, the Netherlands, Norway, Sweden, the UK and the US, and by 10 points or more in Austria, Germany, Ireland, New Zealand and Portugal (UNCTAD 2012: 52).

In the 1980s, Britain was promised a property-owning democracy based on home ownership. But in fact wealth inequality increased massively. Home ownership fell from 69 per cent in 2001 to 64 per cent of homeowners in 2011 (Savage 2015: 77). With the financial crisis, house prices fell but quickly recovered in the context of central bank action, support for homeowners, foreign purchases of luxury homes and acute housing shortages. The amount of personal wealth in Britain tripled from £2 trillion in 1980 to £6 trillion by 2005 (at constant prices), and the proportion of wealth as a percentage of GDP doubled from less than 300 per cent to over 500 per cent (Savage 2015: 73). At constant 2005 prices, the average marketable wealth of the top 1 per cent more than tripled from £700,000 in 1976 to £2,230,000 by 2005. The average wealth of the bottom 50 per cent increased from £5,000 to £13,000 in the same period (Savage 2015: 74). In Britain in the period from 1961 to 1981, the richest and poorest households spent a broadly similar share of their final income on housing. By 2015–16, the richest 5 per cent of households spent 9 per cent of their income on housing, while the bottom 5 per cent spent 44 per cent of their income on housing (Hindmoor 2018: 149). At the same time, this period also saw a sharp rise in debt. G7 household liabilities as a percentage of household income rose from 53 per cent in 1985 to 74 per cent in 1996, and US household debt as a percentage of GDP rose from 11–12 per cent in the 1960s to 51 per cent by 1980, and 69 per cent by 1997 (Langley 2008: 140). In the United States, student loan debt increased from $90 billion in 1999 to $550 billion in 2011, a 511 per cent increase (Birch 2015: 131). By June 2008, aggregate (household, corporate and government) debt had reached a total of $51 trillion, compared to a GDP of $14 trillion (Lazzarato 2012: 112). This is a problem that in some respects has not receded since 2008, and in the first quarter of 2017, total household debt stood at $12.7 trillion, a figure higher than it was at the height of the crisis (Coates 2018: 2).

Alongside debt, there is a common – if sometimes exaggerated – trend towards greater precarity in the workplace. This refers less to the limited growth of the so-called gig economy, and rather more to the loss of important benefits as well as stagnant wages. Thus, in the US, rates of job tenure appear not to have changed too much, with average job tenures for those in various age categories (25–34, 35–44 and 45–54) declining in the period from 1979 to 2006, but not in ways that accord with the idea that almost all work is precarious in the US (Moody 2017: 25). More significant is the fact that most workers have lost important gains that were made for many workers in the period up to 1973. Female entry into the official labour force is due in part to stagnant wage growth and the need for both partners to earn a wage, and even then, this has not halted a sharp increase in household debt. By 2011, around 28 per cent of all workers earned less than the official poverty-level wage of $11.06, and around 30 per cent of the workforce rely on public assistance (Moody 2017: 30). The period since 1973 has also seen a significant decline in employer-sponsored benefits such as health care and pension schemes, despite significant state subsidy. In 1979, 69 per cent of employees had some form of employer-provided health care benefit, but by 2010 this had fallen to 53 per cent (Moody 2017: 30). By 2010, only 43 per cent of employees had employer-provided pensions, and secure defined benefit plans had fallen sharply so that they accounted for 29 per cent of all pensions in 1980 to 18 per cent in 2004 (Moody 2017: 30). In the period from 1984 to 2010, US workers that lost their job found work with a wage on average 15–20 per cent lower than their previous post. The impact of the turn to defined contribution plans, the value of which depend on financial investments, was felt in the period after 2008, when an average work-based savings account pension fell by an estimated 27 per cent. This meant that 56–61-year-olds who would have retired in 2013 saw median family savings fall from $35,929 in 2007 to around $17,000 in 2013 (Moody 2017: 31). Seen in this way, precarity is felt most acutely at or near retirement, alongside those who enter the labour market among the 18–24 age group.

In the US, while official unemployment has fallen substantially, including under Trump, labour market participation rates for working-age men fell, with 11.5 million men aged 24–55 neither employed nor looking for a job (Coates 2018: 2–3). Indeed, in April 2017 the labour market participation rate reached a ten-year low of 62.9 per cent (Coates 2018: 54). At 24.8 per cent, the US has the highest proportion of its labour force earning less than two-thirds of the median wage (Coates 2018: 59). Before 2008, the average annual hours worked in the US exceeded those of German workers by as much as 350 hours a year, which is in effect nine extra 40-hour weeks. There was also a very high rate of work-related illness and injury with fatal consequences, and around 40 million American workers lack access to any sick pay (Coates 2018: 61, 139). Meanwhile in Britain, according to the TUC, and drawing on OECD data, average real wages in Britain fell by almost 10 per cent in the period from 2008 to 2016. There is also a major productivity crisis, with British output per hour 36 percentage points lower than Germany, 31 per cent lower than France and 30 per cent lower than the US (Coates 2018: 5).

This has occurred in the context of relatively lower rates of growth and higher rates of debt than in the period of the postwar boom. In the United States, private investment as a share of GDP fell from 18.5 per cent in 1979 to 15.5 per cent in 2007 (Palma 2009: 851). In the same period, US corporate tax as a percentage of public expenditure fell from 15 per cent in 1978 to 6 per cent in 1982, while the government deficit rose from 6 to 16 per cent of total public spending (Palma 2009: 858). Similarly, consumer spending has been sustained not by real wage increases but rising debt and the hope of rising asset prices, and so the bottom 90 per cent of consumers also saw a big increase in debt levels. This period saw a partial shift from developed world economies based on increased production and rising consumption financed by increases in wages to ones based increasingly on asset creation and increasing consumption based on increases in asset values and debt. In practice consumption and rising asset values are often linked, and indeed wage earners themselves have an interest in rising asset prices, as this can help to fuel further consumption through the selling of assets or the purchase of debt that is guaranteed by rising asset prices. This applies most obviously to rising house prices (see above), and the pre-2008 housing boom at least went some way towards compensating for stagnant wages and precarious work. At the same time, in the US, personal savings for the bottom 90 per cent of the population fell from around 16 per cent of disposable personal income in 1981 to about 0.5 per cent in 2006 (Palma 2009: 850). If we compared the growth of aggregate income of the bottom 90 per cent between 1950 and 1980, and then 1980 and 2006, we see a sharp fall in the rate of growth, with a figure of 3.5 per cent for the first period and 1.8 per cent for the second. However, in both periods the rate of growth of personal consumption was 3.5 per cent (Palma 2009: 858). The shortfall was made up of increased debt, which itself was financed by asset price increases and expectations of continued increases, which came to an abrupt end in 2007 and 2008. Consumer credit as a percentage of wages and salaries increased from around 25 per cent in the early 1980s to over 40 per cent by 2007 (Palma 2009: 859). Similar processes took place in Britain and elsewhere.

What we have seen, then, is a growing pattern of relatively slow or stagnant wage growth with less benefits, some increase in precarious work or more benefit reductions for those in work and rising debt for significant sections of the population in many OECD countries. We have focused mainly on the US and Britain, our two main case studies, but there are some similar (if less pronounced) trends in other parts of the developed world. Chetty *et al.* (2017) estimate that in the US, the rate of absolute mobility, defined as the ideal that children will have a higher standard of living than their parents, has declined from around 90 per cent for children born in 1940 to around 50 per cent for children born in the 1980s. Moreover, in parts of the US, from 1999 to 2013, in some locations there has been a rise in morbidity and mortality rates among white non-Hispanic middle-aged men, linked to alcohol and narcotic abuse, and high rates of suicide (Case & Deaton 2015). From 1999 to 2017, over 200,000 Americans died of opiate overdoses, more than three times the number of American deaths in Vietnam, and by 2017 opioid overdoses were the leading cause of deaths among Americans under the age of 50 (Davies 2018a: 116). What we have seen then is the "hollowing of the middle class" (Pew Research Center 2015: 1), characterized by increasing returns for upper-middle-income groups, and above all for the super-rich. In 2015, 160,000 families (0.1 per cent of US households) "owned nearly as much as everyone from the very poor to the upper middle class combined – 90 per cent of the country, some 145 million in total" (Ehrenfreund 2015).

In this context, much has been made of the decline of relatively secure jobs in manufacturing and the resentment of the so-called "white working class", an issue discussed further in the next two chapters. We should, however, briefly address how these issues relate more specifically to the question of globalization. For the third way, like other varieties of neoliberalism, growing inequality *per se* is not necessarily a problem. The key question is that equal opportunity exists and so unequal outcomes reflect a meritocratic society (Bell 1972; Wooldridge 1995). There are numerous problems with this argument, however. Much faith has been placed in the university, and the expansion of higher education, as a means to promote social mobility and promote meritocratic outcomes in both the US and the UK from the 1990s in the context of the post-industrial new economy. In the US, there has been the growth of a significant wage gap between those who were educated up to university level and those with only high school qualifications, and this increased sharply in the 1980s and 1990s (Autor 2019), and is one reason why the university is a source of populist resentment (see further, Chapter 6). At the same time, as we saw above, the expansion of higher education has not led to a massive proliferation of high-paid, skilled jobs – in Britain almost half of all graduates are in jobs that do not require degrees, and as we have seen in both countries there is the issue of growing student debt (Chakraborty 2018). In terms of the wider question of meritocracy, equal opportunity will lead to unequal outcomes but this in effect then undermines equal opportunity for the next generation. Moreover, this offers little to those "left behind" by globalization beyond exhorting them to further develop their human capital. In this way, the idea that some were neglected by globalization gradually morphed into the argument that being left behind was the responsibility of these individuals (Kenny 2017: 264; Harris 2018; Frank 2016). Neoliberal meritocracy in effect gives a green light to globalization's winners, for they are the rightful winners of the competitive game, thus allowing them to shed any wider notion of social responsibility (Littler 2018).

It is of course true that the third way is also associated with ideas like philanthropy and corporate social responsibility. But charitable donations by corporations have actually fallen in the last 30 years or so, from a high of 2.1 per cent of pre-tax profits in the mid-1980s to 0.8 per cent of profits in 2012 (McGoey 2015). At the same time, corporations have successfully avoided taxation, in parts through states lowering rates for wealthy individuals and companies and in part through the growth of tax havens. Estimates vary, but possibly as much as $21 trillion was held offshore in 2010, the equivalent of the combined GDPs of the US and Japan (Urry 2014: 47). Since 2008, many companies have combined high levels of corporate savings (cash hoarding) with the use of tax havens, a practice particularly common among IT companies, where both Apple and Microsoft hold over 90 per cent of their vast reserves in offshore accounts (Srnicek 2017: 31). In the period from 2008 to 2014, offshore wealth grew by as much as 25 per cent (Srnicek 2017: 32). This accords with some of the claims made by the pessimistic hyper-globalization thesis, but at the same time it needs to be understood how states themselves actively facilitate such practices.

At the same time as this green light provided to the wealthy, there is a red light for the left-behinds, who are said to have simply failed to keep pace with globalization. The third way's meritocratic belief that these can catch up through developing their human capital ignores the reality of the jobs created in the last 30 years (see above), alongside stagnant wages and rising debt. While the long boom from 1992 to 2007 at least hid the worst manifestations of these processes, the financial crisis and its aftermath exacerbated them and brought them to the foreground. In essence it exposed the third way's fallacious assumption that everyone could be an entrepreneur, for "if everyone really did, none of them would be. Individually, everyone could be, but not everyone together. This fact of a general possibility that can only be realized in a select few, forces the individual to self-optimize on the economic terms dictated by the entrepreneurial self, at the same time accusing those lagging behind of being personally responsible for their failure" (Brockling 2016: 77).

Finlayson makes a similar point explicitly related to the financial crisis:

> New Labour, in its redefinition of social justice and reinvention of government, has instituted policies intended to spread the skills and attitudes required to become wealthy. In this respect, rather than

challenge oligarchy it has attempted to increase the number of persons competing to be oligarchs. Instead of seeking to cultivate an egalitarian ethos it has encouraged and sought to facilitate the growth of
the financialised individual. Asset-based welfare is fundamental to this.
The sub-prime mortgage crisis, therefore, does not undermine one or
two policies of the UK government but deals a blow to the ethos it has
sought to instil in the nation.   (Finlayson 2009: 415–16)

It is here that we can introduce again the idea of conservative anti-
globalization because in many respects we can accept that it recognizes at least
some of these problems. Thus, Prime Minister Theresa May talked of the "just-
about-managing" after the Brexit vote in 2016, and President Trump talked
of the "forgotten Americans" before and after his election. In the period from
1999 to 2013, the global number of industrial workers rose from 533 million
to 724 million, but in the same period, the number in the developed world fell
from 122 million to 107 million (Moody 2017: 1). In the United Kingdom, over
the course of the twentieth century the proportion of manual workers in the
labour force fell from 75 to 38 per cent and the proportion of managers and
professionals increased from 8 to 34 per cent (Gest 2016: 2). In the US, in 1940,
74 per cent of US workers were white non-professionals, but by 2006 this figure
had fallen to 43 per cent (Gest 2016: 2). In the same period the proportion of
adults that were white with no college degree fell from 86 per cent to 48 per
cent (Gest 2016: 2). In the US from 1979 to 2010, the net loss in manufacturing
non-supervisory jobs fell by 5.7 million and it was particularly acute in certain sectors, such as primary metals, textiles, apparel and electronics, which
together accounted for 25 per cent of the decline in industrial employment over
this period (Moody 2017: 8).

What is distinctive about conservative responses is their explanation for
why these problems have occurred, and this is where these political-economic
developments overlap with cultural ones. One version of conservative anti-
globalization, associated with our American case study in Chapter 5, suggests
that the deindustrialization of the West (and specifically the US) is closely linked,
and indeed caused by, the rise of emerging powers in the South. This suggests
a zero-sum game between trading nations in which some exploit their position
at the expense of others, or at least there have been bad trade deals between the
US and other countries, such as the North American Free Trade Agreement
(NAFTA). Although many countries from the South (and some from the Global
North) are accused of cheating, China is seen as the biggest cheat. Its rise is said
to be due to its alleged policies of currency manipulation, illegal export subsidies
and wider abusive trade practices (Navarro and Autry 2011), further encouraged
in 2001 by its entry into the World Trade Organization (WTO). These problems

are exacerbated by stifling regulations, and so there is a need to deregulate the economy. This is a position shared by both Trump and Conservative Brexiteers, the former blaming regulations on the federal state, the latter on the European Union and Brussels. But in the case of the latter, at least one global Britain vision of Brexit suggests that these regulations can be overcome and form the basis for the construction of a renewed global Britain based on free trade, albeit – as we will see in the next chapter – with an appropriate institutional regulatory framework. While in both cases, then, there is a (neoliberal) promise of spontaneity, there is also some recognition of a (neoliberal) reality of constructivism and how markets are embedded in institutional frameworks. We will see in the chapters that follow that such frameworks often draw on arguments around culture and globalization, and particularly the idea – discussed in relation to Huntington in Chapter 2 – that some civilizations are not compatible with perceived Western cultural traditions.

This has led to suspicion of liberal cosmopolitanism and multiculturalism both domestically and in the international sphere. In terms of the former, this has led to hostility to migration, particularly against certain ethnic minorities. In Britain since 2004, the proportion of ethnic minority groups has almost doubled and minorities account for around 80 per cent of population growth (Gest 2016: 6). In the US, the non-white population stood at 37 per cent of the population in 2015, but the figure for under-5-year-olds was over 50 per cent (Gest 2016: 6). Some, though not all, conservatives are generally hostile to immigration on economic and cultural grounds. In terms of the former, the argument is essentially that immigration constitutes a drain on government resources, especially in the context of austerity following the financial crisis, and may serve to lower wages as it increases the supply of labour. These arguments are hugely problematic and are criticized in Chapter 6, but the second conservative argument is one that is harder to pin down empirically. This is the idea that immigration leads to the promotion of multiculturalism, which undermines national identity and is thus a threat to the dominant culture, an argument discussed in relation to Huntington in the last chapter. This is also discussed in later chapters, but for now we should just stress that some conservatives are essentially contending that liberal multiculturalism is having some pernicious effects within certain societies, and at the very least immigration should be restricted. Related to this argument, but often less noted, is that some conservatives question liberal wars of intervention on similar grounds, arguing that this is in effect an example of multicultural intervention, albeit at the level of foreign rather than domestic policy. This is an argument made by much of the populist radical Right (see Chapter 6) and American paleoconservatives (Chapter 5). Parts of the argument have also been made by Trump and his administration, though this has not stopped continued military involvement, but it is less prominent in the case of Brexiteers committed to the leading role of the Anglosphere in world affairs (Chapter 4). Like many on the Left, the conservative critique contends that these liberal wars have involved all kinds of justifications based on half-truths and what we now call "fake news". Above all the threat posed by the Saddam Hussein regime in Iraq prior to 2003 was exaggerated, as were justifications both before and after the war from cosmopolitan liberals like Blair and neoconservatives associated with the Bush II presidency in the US. As important were the promises of rapid victories and peace, and the postwar realities in places like Afghanistan, Iraq and Libya, and, indeed, in the US the high casualty rates in regions already neglected by the liberal cosmopolitan elite that promoted such wars (Weiss 2017).

Seen in this way, the commitment of the Blairite third way to cosmopolitanism and neoconservative claims to promoting liberal humanitarianism were severely compromised. A similar point applied to domestic politics and multiculturalism as well, not least in the Clinton administration of the 1990s. This has included the promotion of welfare reforms and extended incarceration, which disproportionately affected black men. This included cuts in benefits at an individual level, more conditions and the introduction of workfare policies that tied welfare provision to particular conditions. It has also involved the expansion of what Wacquant (2009) has called "prisonfare", involving the vigorous deployment of police, courts and prisons in marginalized and resistant spaces. In the 1980s, the state of California passed almost 1,000 laws to expand the use of prison sentences, alongside reduced public assistance, and the Clinton administration complemented its welfare reform policies in 1996 with the Violent Control and Law Enforcement Act 1993 and No Frills Prison Act 1996 (Wacquant 2010: 202). Seen in this way, the "misery of American welfare and the grandeur of American prisonfare at century's turn are the two sides of the same political coin" (Wacquant 2010: 203). In the US the number of incarcerated adults has quadrupled since 1980, and around 2 million adults are in prison. This means that in recent years around 1 in every 100 adults, and 1 in every 9 African American men in the US, is incarcerated. This took place at a time when there was no significant increase in crime in the preceding years, and indeed there was some reduction in crime rates.[2] Moreover, outside of homicide and assault, US crime rates were not noticeably higher than in Western Europe, but incarceration rates were much higher in the US. Within Europe they were significantly higher in Britain and much of this took place under the third way premiership of Tony Blair, just as rates substantially increased in the US under Clinton (Wacquant 2010: 215).

2. Incarceration rates, and the gap in incarceration between whites and African Americans, both also declined in the 2010s, but only after a massive spike from the 1980s and 1990s onwards.

Conclusion: the failure of globalization as context, but not explanation, for the rise of conservative (anti-)globalization

This chapter has examined globalization as a political project, and particularly linked this to a particular version of neoliberal cosmopolitanism, and specifically the third way in both Britain and the US. As Table 3.1 shows, this involved, in some respects, the expansion of the public sector, and in contrast to New Right neoliberalism the (uneven and unequal) promotion of cosmopolitan ideals and multiculturalism. But it relied heavily on the idea that people needed to develop their human capital in ways that enabled them to participate in markets. This idea was undermined in part by the end of the dotcom boom in 2001, and with it some of the claims made for a new economy were challenged (though far from defeated). But it was also undermined by the financial crisis of 2007–8, which was a problem for both the third way in Britain and the neoconservative-influenced Bush II administration in the US. This was further exacerbated by the disastrous liberal wars of intervention in the 2000s, particularly in Iraq. But even the boom from 1992 to 2007 hid longer-term issues, such as deindustrialization, rising debt, in some respects rising inequality and rising rates of incarceration (which certainly compromised celebrations of multiculturalism).

Table 3.1 Neoliberal cosmopolitanism

Issue	Neoliberal cosmopolitan	Neoliberal Anglo-American New Right and neoconservatives	Current conservative (anti-)globalization
Trade and investment	Open policies.	Open policies but some exceptions.	Divided.
The state	Pro-state spending but often to promote marketization of state.	In theory critical of state spending but practice was different in economy and law and order.	State protection for "real" citizens, strong law and order. Divided over protectionism versus free trade.
Multiculturalism	Supportive in some respects and pro-migration but also strong racialized incarceration policies.	Hostile in many respects.	Outright hostility.
Liberal intervention	Supportive in name of cosmopolitanism.	Supportive in name of Western power plus human rights.	Generally sceptical with exceptions such as British conservativism.
Inequality	Acceptable so long as equal opportunities exist and thus support meritocracy.	Acceptable.	Natural order of things.

These socio-economic issues are important for understanding the rise of right-wing populism and conservative ideas on globalization that challenge third way neoliberal cosmopolitanism. But at the same time we need to be careful here, for three reasons. First, while we might identify certain global trends, these have their own specific national manifestations, with different levels of right-wing populism and differing fates for left-wing parties. We might, however, observe that social democratic parties that have adapted to neoliberalism have generally faced political crisis. Second, and related to this point, there is no single conservative position on globalization. The next two chapters examine cases that – in some respects – are actually contrasting responses to actually existing globalization. To over-simplify, Brexit can in some respects be seen as an attempt to extend neoliberal globalization, while Trump (and certainly paleoconservatism) is to an extent attempting to roll it back. This is an over-simplification, as we will see, but this contrast is not without merit, even if we will substantially qualify it. Third, while we have stressed the socio-economic context for the rise of populism, outlined in the final section to examine our two cases, we cannot map on to these anything like a straightforward, causal explanation, for the Brexit and Trump votes in 2016. It is one thing to point to the failures of actually existing globalization, but quite another to then assume that this itself constitutes an explanation for the success of conservative populism, as if the latter was simply a functional effect of the former. Indeed, much of the literature on globalization and the so-called left-behinds is guilty of precisely this fallacy, which ignores the complexity of the vote for conservatives, including our cases, but even more fails to consider seriously the *content* of these conservative ideas and the support for them among different social groups. Indeed, conservative intellectuals, popular journalists and political movements have all decried growing inequality, social dislocation, deindustrial-ization and (in some cases) liberal wars of intervention (Mount 2012; Gottfried 2016; Francis 2016; Letts 2017; Carlson 2018; Sasse 2018). Glowing in the immediate aftermath of the EU referendum and looking forward to the US presidential election, former UKIP leader Nigel Farage (2016) argued that:

> The similarities between the different sides in this election are very like our own recent battle. As the rich get richer and big companies dominate the global economy, voters all across the West are being left behind. The blue-collar workers in the valleys of South Wales angry with Chinese steel dumping voted Brexit in their droves. In the American rust belt, traditional manufacturing industries have declined, and it is to these people that Trump speaks very effectively.

This speaks to some of the failures of actually existing globalization, though as we will see the causes are far more complex than competition from cheap imports. But what is distinctive about conservative populism is the explanation for why these things have occurred. Here the focus is on the ways in which liberal elites and the promotion of multiculturalism and open borders have created these problems, and why more controlled immigration and a focus on nativism rather than neoliberalism *per se* offers the solution, an argument not limited to conservative populists (Salam 2018). In short, the problem is not one of neoliberal economic policy but rather liberal social and cultural policy, an argument also made by some otherwise critical of conservative populism (Goodhardt 2017; Eatwell & Goodwin 2018; Kaufmann 2018). But in contrast to much of the Left that focuses on the structural imperatives of neoliberal, financialized capitalism, conservative critics seek to blame specific groups or even individuals, and this usually takes a racialized form. This in effect is less a systemic critique and more a personalized attack on those who have supposedly betrayed society, whether they be liberal elites, Washington, Wall Street, Silicon Valley, ethnic minorities, the European Union, Muslims or Jewish "globalists". We therefore need to take a much more detailed look at conservative populist ideas, and this is considered through the two "difficult" cases of Brexit and American conservatism, in Chapters 4 and 5, and through a wider critical analysis of conservative populism in Chapter 6.

4

BRITISH CONSERVATISM AND THE INTERNATIONAL: FREE TRADE, THE ANGLOSPHERE AND BREXIT

The opening chapter examined – and challenged – the idea that conservatism was simply a "positional" doctrine, adapting to change in a pragmatic, gradualist and peaceful manner. This depended on circumstances and conservatives were prepared to fight with "the fanaticism of a Crusader" (Hogg 1947: 76) to defend their values if they were threatened. These values were above all the promotion of virtue and excellence but crucially these could only exist in a hierarchical elitist order. This preparedness to fight was something like what Huntington had in mind when he talked of a doctrinal conservatism. But in Britain – and more specifically England – there would appear to be some strong grounds for suggesting that conservatism is simply a positional doctrine, or what Oakeshott (1962) called conservatism as a disposition (Freedland 2019; Saunders 2019). This is in part because the circumstances have been so different from those in continental Europe. In short, Britain had no 1789 or 1848, and in the 30-year crisis from 1914 to 1945, the political order was much more stable than in much of Europe (and indeed a case can be made that the greatest potential threat was external, namely the fear of German invasion in 1940). A further reason is that the Conservative Party itself has pragmatically adapted to wider social change in ways that appear to conform to positional, rather than doctrinal, conservatism. This chapter addresses – and questions – this characterization of British conservatism (and Conservatism). It particularly suggests that conservatives have been particularly animated by the question of *decline*, and that this has always been intimately related to Britain's role in the international order – and that Brexit is the latest manifestation of this doctrinal conservatism. This chapter therefore focuses mainly on how the question of decline links to questions of the international. Its particular focus is on free trade and the Anglosphere, the latter idea having changed over time, but which refers to the assumed "values, peoples or histories of the core five countries of the UK, Canada, Australia, New Zealand and the USA" (Kenny & Pearce 2018: 5). It should be stressed, however, that these values and histories are highly selective, and indeed the countries that form part of the Anglosphere have changed over time.

The chapter investigates these issues in five sections. First, conservatism is examined from the early to the late nineteenth century, with a particular focus on the repeal of the Corn Laws in 1846, and Disraeli's reconstruction of the Conservative Party in the 1860s, in part as the party of empire. Second, the period from the 1880s to 1945 is addressed, with a particular emphasis on Joseph Chamberlain's call for tariff reform at the turn of the century, the eventual shift to imperial preference in the 1930s and war. The third section examines the postwar period with a focus on the end of empire, postwar Commonwealth migration and the turn to Europe. The fourth section examines the Thatcherite revolution and, despite Thatcher's initial commitment to the European Community, the rise of Euroscepticism. Finally, the fifth section examines Brexit in some depth, detailing how this has some continuity with earlier disputes in the Conservative Party (particularly in 1846 and 1903), future scenarios for Brexit Britain and the question – already alluded to in Chapter 3 – of the extent to which the referendum vote was a protest against Europe and globalization.

Conservatism in the nineteenth century: landed interest, free trade, one nation and empire

As we saw in the first chapter, though a Whig, Burke was in many respects one of the first conservative thinkers. Unlike de Maistre in France, he was pro-reform and did not call for unquestioned obedience to the state or to God. He argued against equality and "social levelling", and was pro-hierarchy, deference and cultural difference. He emphasized the limits to reason, statism and inter-nationalism, and promoted localism, community and grounded citizenship. As humans were morally flawed, they should not seek to radically overthrow tradition, accumulated wisdom or established institutions (though there was little reflection on the possible relationship between being morally flawed and accumulated wisdom). In a precursor to conservative suspicion of globaliza-tion, Burke was particularly critical of abstract theorizing and liberal claims to universalism, both of which posed threats to the established social and political order. This sounded very much like a reactive, positional conservatism, but it was still one rooted in the doctrine that hierarchy is the basis for social and cul-tural excellence. Burke (2003: 44) also feared government by arithmetic, which was in effect his version of fear of the tyranny of the majority that, as we saw in Chapter 1, was also something of concern to many liberals in the nineteenth and twentieth centuries.

Conservative thought in the nineteenth century focused on concerns about democracy, but also liberalism, and more specifically economic liberalism. The likes of Thomas Carlyle, John Ruskin and Matthew Arnold all rejected laissez faire and liberal individualism. In his 1843 book *Past and Present*, Carlyle (2009) condemned the dehumanization of the mechanical age and hated the cash nexus, whereby everything was valued according to its price. Ruskin also disliked Victorian materialism, while in *Culture and Anarchy* (1869) Arnold (2009) feared that high culture was threatened by a vulgar, materialist culture and focused on the ways in which democracy could be civilized for the new mechanical age. In each of these cases there was some sympathy for the human condition and the "common man" (somewhat less was said about women), and indeed "the conservative and the socialist could find common ground in their shared protest at the consequences of economic and social liberalism" (Goldman 2011: 706). Indeed, these writers influenced later British socialist thought, though on what conservatives and socialists "proposed to do about it they differed widely" (Goldman 2011: 706). Carlyle proposed a benevolent authoritarianism in which great men ruled for the common good, and he therefore rejected democracy. Both Ruskin and Arnold tended to see high culture as the preserve of the privileged few, out of reach to the untutored "masses". This suspicion of democracy applied to empire as well as "mother country". Following the Morant Bay rebellion in Jamaica in 1865, the Jamaica Committee was set up to prosecute Edward Eyre, the Governor of Jamaica, following his authoritarian response to the protests in which over 400 people were killed and many more were flogged. Among its members were John Stuart Mill and British free-trader John Bright. Carlyle set up a committee to defend Eyre, which included Ruskin among its supporters.

Much of this conservative thought was in many respects based on a romantic critique of industrial society, and in the early nineteenth century the Tory Party was essentially a party of agrarian landed interests. Following the 1832 Great Reform Act, the Tory Party became the Conservative Party in 1834, and with an extended (though still very small) electorate attempted to expand its social base. Industry now had political representation and industrialists called for the promotion of free trade in order to expand potential overseas markets for their products. This policy would also mean the repeal of measures designed to protect British agriculture, and specifically it meant the repeal of the Corn Laws. This was precisely the policy of laissez faire that the likes of Carlyle rejected, but it was a Conservative prime minister, Robert Peel, who successfully led the repeal in 1846, albeit with support from the Whig Party. This cost Peel the support of two-thirds of his own party and condemned a divided and outdated Conservative Party to years of opposition (Baker *et al.* 1993) or minority governments, broken only by the 1874 Disraeli government. Meanwhile, the Peelites merged with the

Whigs and Radicals to form the Liberal Party, which had a far stronger foothold in government until the 1880s, when it faced its own divisions over Irish Home Rule.

It was in this context, and under the leadership of the former protectionist who was influenced by Carlyle, that Benjamin Disraeli led the attempt to expand the conservative social base. In practical terms, this was quite limited, but Disraeli's emphasis on One Nation conservatism was significant, particularly in influencing the post-Disraeli years from the late nineteenth century onwards. In 1870 at Crystal Palace, Disraeli emphasized institutional continuity, empire and the elevation of the conditions of the British people as the chief characteristics of the Conservative Party. In this new account of conservatism, emphasis was placed on strong leadership, the national interest and national consensus rather than class interest. This approach paved the way for the Conservatives becoming the party of empire and of social reform. This included a defence of property, but this was more one of property in general rather than of landed interests. The Conservative Party was in some respects hostile to empire before and after 1846. While the Whigs supported colonization and expansion, Tories often were critical of costly imperial ventures. As late as 1852, Disraeli described the colonies as a "millstone round our necks" (cited in Gamble 2003: 75). However, in this period and beyond the Conservative Party gradually shifted its identity. This took place in the context of further industrialization and urbanization, the extension of the franchise, agitation for Home Rule in Ireland and the undermining of the power of the House of Lords. On the face of it, these developments were hardly conducive to a party dominated by rural landowners and hostile to the extension of the franchise, but the Conservatives identified as the party of individualism at home and empire abroad. This was facilitated in turn by divisions in the Liberal Party (over Home Rule) and the rise of the Labour Party from 1900, which the Conservatives saw as a threat to the individual and to private property.

Conservatism, 1880 to 1945: decline, empire and war

Empire, then, became crucial to changes in the Conservative Party from the late nineteenth century onwards. But the British Empire in some respects represented more than one kind of empire, for while it was in part an empire of territorial control, it was also one that mainly focused on cosmopolitanism, free trade and internationalism (Bell 2007). These two types of empire are not mutually exclusive and the latter was facilitated in part by the former; recent apologists for the British Empire and its legacy often emphasize the latter and its continuity with the open-door policy of US hegemony after 1945 (Ferguson 2003). The late nineteenth century also saw a resurgence of empires that focused more on territorial control and, insofar as this involved commercial transactions, these were often exclusive in terms of trade and investment between colonizer and colonized (Kiely 2010), in contrast to the free-trade imperialism of Britain (Gallagher & Robinson 1953). While apologists often argue that this showed the moral superiority of the British Empire over the Japanese and other European empires (Ferguson 2003), the late nineteenth-century colonialism of the latter was in part a reaction to British hegemony, and a challenge that involved protectionism at home and colonialism abroad (Polanyi 2001; Kiely 2010; Palen 2016). Moreover, this did not preclude repression, indifference and massive suffering in the British Empire and many new liberals distinguished between imperialism and empire on this basis (Bell 2016).

Moreover, in the late nineteenth century in Britain, some Conservatives began to advocate a new social imperialism, which included reform at home and some forms of protectionism abroad, in part because the competitive challenge from the new protectionist-imperialists was undermining British hegemony and competitiveness. As we saw in the opening chapter, this social imperialism existed in Europe and above all in Bismarck's Germany, and it referred to a new imperialism where "entrepreneurs and other elements woo the workers by means of social welfare concessions which appear to depend on the success of export monopolism" (Schumpeter 1951: 114). While the specific linkage of social welfare to the export of capital was in many respects questionable (see Kiely 2010), what was envisaged was the use of colonial tribute to help finance social reforms in the context of the threat of democracy and the rise of the working class. In the words of Cecil Rhodes:

> My cherished idea is a solution for the social problem, i.e. in order to save the 40,000,000 inhabitants of the United Kingdom from a bloody civil war, we colonial statesmen must acquire news lands to settle the surplus population, to provide new markets for the goods produced by them in the factories and mines. The Empire, as I have always said, is a bread and butter question. If you want to avoid civil war you must become imperialists. (Cited in Lenin 1977: 225)

In conservative Britain, this social imperialist position was most associated with Joseph Chamberlain. He was an industrialist who, as mayor, transformed Birmingham in the late nineteenth century, and who actually developed a decent public infrastructure in the city, which included publicly owned water and gas, new housing, decent sanitation, new civic building and a prominent university. In this respect, Chamberlain promoted social reform in part through the public sector, and in this regard his views accord with so-called Red Tories, discussed further below. What is more relevant here, however, is that Chamberlain was originally a Liberal, but one who broke with that party over Home Rule for Ireland, and became the colonial secretary under the arch-imperialist Lord Salisbury in 1895. In other words, like Bismarck, Chamberlain combined social reform at home with support for imperialism abroad.

In 1903, Chamberlain resigned from government as he gave support for imperial preference over global free trade. After the repeal of the Corn Laws in 1846, Britain had in effect exercised its hegemony through the promotion of a low-tariff, free-trade policy between countries, an argument pursued above all by Richard Cobden and John Bright. The 1860s was in many ways the high-point of this liberal internationalism, and the idea was promoted that commercial inter-dependence between nations would enhance wealth, freedom, prosperity and peace. In that decade, a number of free-trade agreements were signed, such as the Cobden Chevalier Treaty of 1860. Many free-trade advocates suggested that it represented the interests of all nations, as each participant would make abso-lute gains from trade, and interdependence would promote peaceful relations between states (see Sylvest 2009). It seemed, then, that for a while Europe would be committed to free trade along the lines propagated by Britain. This commitment to so-called laissez faire and free trade came across two problems, namely poor working and social conditions at home, and increased opposition abroad (Polanyi 2001). We saw above how cultural conservatives like Carlyle and Ruskin deplored the consequences of the Industrial Revolution, the rise of the cash nexus and the urban squalor that accompanied industrialization. By the mid- to late nineteenth century there was in effect no turning back to a romantic vision of pre-industrial Britain, and with the extension of the franchise (particu-larly in 1884) and the rise of working-class organizations, conservatism needed to respond to this new social context. In some respects, Carlyle and Ruskin acted as a kind of link to earlier and later conservatism, in their support for Governor Eyre in his response to the Morant Bay rebellion in Jamaica in 1865, discussed above. For in contrast to Cobden, Bright and Mill, all of whom called for the prosecution of Eyre, they in effect gave an uncritical apology to imperialism, an argument developed further from the 1880s onwards. For in this period there was a new vigour given to the promotion of empire, in part to deal with the threat of democracy and socialism at home, and in part to promote a Greater Britain abroad (Seeley 2001). In the context of urban poverty and potential social unrest, the British colonial empire needed to be taken more seriously by the British public, because it provided a solution to these problems (Bell 2016: 167–71). This was reinforced by the urgency of the question of Home Rule in Ireland, and the 1880s and 1890s saw the formation of a series of pro-empire organizations such as the Imperial Federation League, the United Empire League and the British Empire League. Some of this was inspired by the apparent success of the United States, which suggested that large-scale federations could work (Seeley 2001).

At the same time, Europe and the United States gradually turned against a commitment to free trade, and instead developed protectionist policies designed to foster domestic industry, and in Britain thus replace British industrial imports with their own domestically produced goods. The rationale for this switch was that free trade favoured the already established and competitive economy – Britain's – at the expense of other economies, and thus in effect forced other countries to specialize in lower-value, non-industrial production, rather than potentially higher-productivity manufacturing, which also fostered important links with the rest of the economy (List 1966). As one Whig participant in the debate on the repeal of the Corn Laws argued in 1846, free trade was the means by which "foreign nations would become valuable colonies to us, without imposing on us the responsibility of governing them" (cited in Gamble 1994: 51). If this was the case then it was not surprising that countries resisted this informal colonial status, and began a process of protectionism at home and imperialism abroad. This national protectionism was also combined with social reform, such as sickness and old-age insurance in Germany. It also saw a new wave of imperial expansion abroad, as European countries and the US searched for raw materials to fuel their industrial revolutions, and guaranteed markets for their surplus goods. In this way, "(s)ocial imperialism was designed to draw all classes together in defence of the nation and empire and aimed to prove to the least well to do class that its interests were inseparable from those of the nation" (Semmel 1960: 12).

These kinds of arguments were influenced by the development of a social Darwinism that talked of the survival of the fittest. This term is usually associated with Herbert Spencer, a laissez-faire liberal who was also involved in the attempt to prosecute Governor Eyre after the Morant Bay rebellion. However, Spencer mainly used this concept to refer to the competition between individuals in the competitive market place. By the late nineteenth century the idea was increasingly used to refer to competition between nations and indeed races, and was therefore often associated with the increased formalization of biologically based theories of "scientific racism". Thus, rather than advocating individual responsibility to deal with domestic social problems, as did Spencer, Benjamin Kidd (2009) argued that the condition of the working class needed to be improved through social reforms at home. This was necessary not only to protect the nation from domestic threats, but also from international ones, for survival of the fittest also meant the need for nations to survive in a competitive international order. Kidd particularly promoted the need for the survival of the "virile" Anglo-Saxon race, and the need for close ties between Britain and its (past and present) settler colonies in Australia, New Zealand, parts of South Africa and North America.

It was in this context that Chamberlain called for Britain to respond with its own imperial exclusivity, and in particular promote a Greater Britain, led by the white settler colonies. He argued that Britain should respond to competitive pressures by increasing tariffs, but at the same time maintain a system of low-tariff preferences within the empire. The revenue that accrued from such tariffs could be used to finance social reform at home, thereby leading to social improvement and expanding the social base of support for the Conservative Party. In 1903, he called for tariffs of two shillings a quarter on flour and all imported grain except maize, a duty of 5 per cent on meat and dairy products and an average tariff of 10 per cent on all manufactured imports, but none of these duties would be applied to imports from the colonies (Semmel 1960: 83). In effect, this meant an exclusive, preferential trading area within the Empire of Greater Britain. Leadership of this trading area should lie in the hands of an Anglosphere, composed not of rootless cosmopolitans, but of a global culture rooted in Anglo-Saxon cultural ties, religion, trade and migration (see Kenny & Pearce 2018). Home Rule was abhorrent because it meant domination by "another race and religion" (quoted in Kenny & Pearce 2018). As colonial secretary, Chamberlain did not support overt discrimination but instead supported education qualifications to limit immigration, which laid the foundation for white supremacy in the white settler colonies. Chamberlain was unsuccessful in his demand for imperial preferences, and was incapacitated by a stroke in 1906. However, in the context of the rise of the Labour Party, social unrest, fear of immigration and the revived Liberal government from 1906, by 1910 Conservative leader Arthur Balfour was advocating tariff reform, a position rejected by some Conservatives like Winston Churchill, who defected to the Liberal Party. The Liberals themselves were not anti-imperialist, and they also defended empire, but in contrast to Chamberlain argued that free trade was the best way of maintaining British hegemony overseas (see Gallagher & Robinson 1953; Kiely 2010). In effect, then, the tariff reformers called for imperial protection and tariffs and argued that tariff revenue could be used to finance social reform. Domestic taxation, particularly direct tax, should be kept as low as possible. In contrast, Liberals were divided but they included pro-empire free-traders who believed in continued free trade to maintain British interests abroad, and increased direct taxation at home to finance social reform. This divide was most stark in debates over the 1909 budget, where Chancellor Lloyd George consolidated and extended direct taxation, for instance, in the form of a super-tax for the rich, land taxes and death duties. By then, the promotion of imperial tariff reform was largely abandoned, though not without continued debate and division into the 1920s.

The post-First World War period saw growing concern about the rise of the Labour Party, the extension of the franchise in 1918 and 1928, wage cuts and industrial confrontation in the context of the return to the Gold Standard in 1925 and the continued promotion of free trade. However, it was in the period of the Great Depression that something closer to Chamberlain's reforms were introduced, after the Imperial Economic Conference in Ottawa in 1932. Following the Ottawa conference, Britain's proportion of trade with the Empire increased, from 33 per cent of imports (1932) to 37 per cent in 1936, and from 41 per cent of exports in 1932 to 47 per cent in 1936 (Dilley 2016). However, this increase was in the context of decline or slow growth in world trade and growing protectionism on the part of the established powers, and did not accord with Chamberlain's vision of a strong Anglosphere dominating the international order, as he had envisaged in 1903.

Finally, the Conservative Party again came close to splitting in 1940 over whether or not to forge peace with Hitler. The 1930s saw various attempts to appease an expansionist Germany. Some on the Right (both within and outside of the Conservative Party) were relaxed about the Nazis, partly because they were considered an important counterweight to Communism, and partly because of some sympathy with their authoritarianism and racism (Griffiths 2013). The main reasons for appeasement, however, were fear of another destructive war, but the Conservative Party in particular also combined this with the belief that any new war would threaten the existence of the British Empire and the City of London (Dalton 1986). This was the prime reason that some recommended that Britain sign a peace treaty with Hitler once Britain stood alone after the fall of much of Western Europe in the early summer of 1940. It was, however, another Conservative, Winston Churchill, who won the day, and Britain continued the war. In 1941, it was joined by allies decisive to the victory in the Second World War, as Germany invaded the Soviet Union, Japan bombed Pearl Harbour and Germany declared war on the US.

Britain after 1945: the end of empire, Atlanticism, Europe and multiculturalism

In one sense the appeasers were correct, and the aftermath of war did lead to the end of empire. Britain was weakened by the war and the US and the Soviet Union both supported the end of European empires, including Britain's. Moreover, anti-colonial movements strengthened in the immediate aftermath of war, not least as many countries of the Empire had fought in the war (and sustained greater losses than Britain), and the war had been fought for freedom against tyranny, which undermined the case for empire. Britain was reluctant to give up its empire and it took a period of often bloody conflict for it to end. Furthermore, the US's failure to support Britain's attempt to re-capture the western part of the Suez Canal from Egypt in 1956 in effect gave the country a reality check in the postwar world. Over the next 40 years or so, Britain gave up almost all of its empire.

This did not mean that the Empire, or Commonwealth, as it came to be known in the late 1940s, was no longer relevant. The postwar Labour government passed the British Nationality Act in 1948, which granted British citizenship to all citizens of the Commonwealth or Empire. In some respects this was an attempt to hold the Empire together in the context of postwar constraints, and reflected close ties with the dominions. But it also meant that migration from the non-white Commonwealth countries increased, alongside white immigration and emigration out of Britain. From the outset, there was some panic about the extent of migration into Britain even as it was encouraged to deal with postwar labour shortages. It was, however, in the context of heightened racism and race riots from 1958 that the Conservatives passed the Commonwealth Immigrants Act in 1962, and, together with a further Act passed by Labour in 1968, restricted the right of entry to those Commonwealth citizens born in Britain or who had at least one parent or grandparent naturalized in Britain. These postwar developments – the end of empire, postwar migration and domestic resentment of migrants – were to have important consequences through later debates on multiculturalism, as we will see later in this chapter. What was clear, though, was that if the Conservatives were to continue a policy of one-nation conservatism, they increasingly had to do so without an empire abroad.

Churchill had expressed growing concerns over non-white migration to Britain in the 1950s (Kenny & Pearce 2018: 58–9), but it was above all Enoch Powell who took up the mantle of anti-immigration, particularly in the 1960s. His focus on national culture, anti-immigration and state sovereignty on the face of it look like a turn away from the idea of the Anglosphere and Greater Britain, but as Kenny and Pearce (2018: 85–6) have convincingly shown, in many respects "Powell reworked some of the constituent themes of Anglosphere thinking rather than rejecting them altogether". Consistent with pro-empire British conservatism, Powell believed that Britain had a glorious past that included its empire, and indeed he even forged a plan early in his career for Britain to reconquer India (see Heffer 2008: 111; Schofield 2013: 70). But the process of decolonization and the removal of troops from Suez in June 1956 led Powell to alter his views on empire. In particular, while upholding the view that Britain had a proud imperial history, he argued that at the same time the Empire had created and released forces that undermined the nation. Internationally, he was particularly critical of the idea of a Commonwealth based on a partnership between independent nations, and abstractions like supposedly universal human rights (Schofield 2013: 90). Domestically, he argued that with the end of empire there was a need to forge a new patriotism based on commitment to Britain based on an entrepreneurial spirit operating in a natural, hierarchical market order, and against a state that, increasingly and misguidedly, claimed to have moral purpose. Like many other conservatives forces in the twentieth century, he argued that socio-political developments that had once promoted hierarchy and virtue now undermined it. We came across this argument in the context of American neoconservative views of capitalism in Chapter 2, and much of this argument drew heavily on Weber (1994) and Schumpeter (1976), and in some respects Hayek (2001) and the destructive force of market rationalization. Powell's vision of decline, however, was focused more on the nation and empire and he argued that British (or English) greatness paved the way for empire, but then gave rise to forces that undermined the nation. In particular, Britain saw itself as a nation beyond its borders, and the 1948 British Nationality Act was a case in point. This gave rise to the undermining of national loyalty, custom and tradition by other traditions (Gamble 1974) – what we referred to in Chapter 3 as liberal multiculturalism. This has led, Powell infamously claimed in his 1968 "Rivers of Blood" speech, to "the sense of being a persecuted minority which is growing among ordinary English people" (quoted in Kenny & Pearce 2018: 93; see also Schwartz 2011: 34–52). Powell was dismissed from the Conservative front bench after this speech and he was increasingly regarded as a populist outsider among the political class. Many of the letters of support sent to Powell after his speech likened postwar migration to the threatened invasion by Germany in 1940, and asserted that ordinary people had fought in the war to prevent such invasions (see O'Toole 2018: 91). Powell encouraged such views in his rejection of the idea that the period up to 1945 represented a people's war, which culminated in the social democracy of 1945 onwards, one that even subsequent Conservative governments in many respects accepted. Instead, Powell characterized the legacy of 1945 as one in which an over-stretched government became the enemy of a people constantly under siege, a self-reliant people undermined by the liberal state, committed to partnerships and human rights overseas and migration at home (see Schofield 2013: chapter 4). His arguments about "ordinary people" have close parallels with the debate over Brexit (see below), and indeed American paleoconservatism, as we will see in the next chapter.

Powell's outsider status was further secured by his Euroscepticism and opposition to Britain's entry into the European Community, and he even advised people to vote for the more Eurosceptic Labour Party in the February 1974 election. He was sceptical of formal political unions beyond the nation state, and suspicious of Britain's closer ties with the US. Powell (1965, 1971) therefore emphasized sovereignty and national identity but did so in a way that reworked rather than rejected the idea of the Anglosphere,[1] suggesting that it in effect needed to "come home" and recognize the reality of the end of empire. Seen in this way, for Powell, Churchill's English-speaking peoples were no longer

---

1. Powell (1977) wrote a nuanced biography of Joseph Chamberlain, which can also be read in a similar way.

part of a Greater Britain but "an overlooked and increasingly resentful nation whose cultural traditions and interests were being dangerously neglected by their own state" (Kenny & Pearce 2018: 102). This did not, however, mean an isolationist stance because Powell also emphasized that Britain's greatness was reflected in its role as a nation committed to free trade, and sovereignty could be used to restore this commitment – a central part of the Brexit project. Along with his Euroscepticism and suspicion of the cultural consequences of postwar migration, one can see that Powell in fact is an important formative link to the Thatcherite Euroscepticism that emerged from the 1990s onwards.

Much to Powell's disappointment, the postwar period also saw Britain forge closer ties with the US. While many conservatives saw the US as vulgar, particularly in terms of its culture, and in effect revived the arguments of Matthew Arnold to criticize the import of cheap cultural goods,[2] most accepted that Britain had a special relationship with America. This was partly because of the Cold War and the formation of NATO, and initially Britain being outside of the newly formed European Community (founded in 1957). But for many conservatives, Churchill among them, the special relationship reflected shared language, culture and the promotion of a cosmopolitan ideal based on consensus. This was an example of an "imagined community" (Anderson 1983) that went beyond national borders and joined the English-speaking peoples of the world (Churchill 2001). It thus resonated with earlier Conservative defences of empire and of the Anglosphere found in Disraeli and Chamberlain. This did not mean that Churchill was a Eurosceptic in the way that some have contended (see Johnson 2015), and he did at times refer to a United States of Europe, so that some have regarded him as a pioneer of the European ideal (Klos 2017). In fact, Churchill tended to see Britain as an integral part of three international political alliances, taking in the "special relationship" with the US, the Empire and the Commonwealth, and Europe, which suggests that he was neither a Eurosceptic nor a Europhile (Kenny & Pearce 2018: 56–7).

While the Anglo-US special relationship was clear under Churchill and Roosevelt, it did experience some tensions, particularly in the period of Suez and Britain's failure to give effective support to US intervention in Vietnam. But the 1980s saw a close relationship between President Reagan and Prime Minister Thatcher, partly because of increased tensions in the second Cold War (Halliday 1983), but also because of a shared commitment to a particular brand of Anglo-American capitalism. This combined a neoliberal commitment to the

2. This was not exclusive to the conservative Right, however, and the Left feared that authentic folk culture was being displaced by inauthentic mass culture. See, for example, Hoggart (1957). This kind of argument was also present as late as the 1990s in the "Britpop" phenomenon, much of which drew on old anti-American ideas.

so-called free market, with more traditional conservative social and cultural policies, which is discussed further in the next section.

The final postwar issue for the Conservative Party was its relationship to Europe. The US strongly supported the construction of the European Economic Community (EEC), which came into being in 1957 with the signing of the Treaty of Rome. Britain was initially outside of this community, but from 1961 to 1973 it negotiated entry into the EEC, after two rejections by the EEC and Charles De Gaulle in particular, in 1961 and 1967. It did, however, join in 1973, membership of which was further reconfirmed by a referendum in 1975. Much of the opposition to EEC entry was based on the notion that it undermined national sovereignty, an argument that cut across Left and Right divisions. The Conservatives, however, often combined their defence of national sovereignty with support for the continuation of empire, a recurring theme in the history of British conservatism. Under Macmillan, however, they came to accept the gradual decline of empire and disappointment with the Commonwealth, and – reinforced by some degree of business pressure – they came to accept the need for closer ties with Europe. Some objections continued, particularly over the extent to which the European Community was based on a perceived supranational customs union, and thus a threat to national sovereignty. There was in the late 1950s and early 1960s more support for a looser and less rigid European Free Trade Association, but the Party gradually came to support joining the European Community. While most Conservatives voted for entry in 1973 in the parliamentary vote of 1971, 39 Conservatives voted against (while the majority of Labour MPs voted against, 69 voted for entry).

This issue of the relationship between empire and Europe also reflected Britain's changing economic partnerships. Following imperial preference, trade with what came to be the Commonwealth did increase in the 1940s, and reached a peak of 49 per cent of British trade (both exports and imports) by 1953, but again this was in part because of historically specific factors such as the devastation of Europe due to war and exchange controls in the sterling area. More important, following postwar recovery and the growing internationalization of capital, Britain became more dependent on trade with Europe even before it joined the European Economic Community in 1973. Thus, in 1957, the original six members of the EEC accounted for 12 per cent of UK imports and 14 per cent of exports, but by 1973 the figures had risen to 25 and 23 per cent, respectively (Dilley 2016). For the Commonwealth, there had been a sharp decline, with British imports from the Commonwealth accounting for around 15 per cent and British exports to the Commonwealth around 18 per cent of Britain's total by 1973 (Dilley 2016). This decline continued after 1973, albeit with a slight revival after 1998, so that by 2010, the Commonwealth accounted for about 11 per cent of Britain's imports and 10 per cent of its exports (Dilley 2016).

Thatcherism and Euroscepticism

This section examines Thatcherism, and how it laid the grounds for a new Euroscepticism, which culminated in the Brexit referendum. Thatcherism emerged in the context of stagflation in the 1970s, and essentially argued for a break from the perceived postwar consensus. For Conservatives, this meant acceptance of the welfare state and social reform, and in this respect it was consistent with Disraeli's one-nation conservatism. It was also in some respects compatible with Chamberlain's emphasis on social reform, but this coincided with what was the loss of empire, which is an important component part of the Brexit story.

Thatcher argued for a break from this consensus and the promotion of market-friendly policies such as trade, investment and financial liberalization, and privatization. But these policies existed alongside traditionalist policies on social and cultural issues, and in some respects the state expanded. While this was partly because of unexpected consequences (such as welfare spending expanding as more people became dependent on welfare even as the value of individual welfare benefits declined), it was also deliberate in some sectors, such as security, and reflected continued demands made by the electorate (Kiely 2018: chapters 4 and 6).

All of this took place when Britain was said to be ungovernable, as the state was a prisoner of vested interests, which undermined individual freedom and economic efficiency. As a result governments attempted to buy the votes of the electorate, leading to inflation (Brittan 1975; Buchanan *et al.* 1978). At the same time, one of the worst vested interests, the trade union movement, used its monopoly and hence coercive power in the marketplace (Hayek 1972), leading to unemployment because it was not possible to "in the long-run increase real wages for all wishing to work, above the level that would establish itself in a free market" (Hayek 2006: 267). This, then, was an economic crisis, but it was also a crisis of politics and indeed morality, caused by threats to the social and political order, above all, youth rebellion, black immigration and trade union militancy (Hall *et al.* 1978). For Thatcher, "(w)e are reaping what was sown in the sixties … The fashionable theories and permissive claptrap set the scene for a society in which the old virtues of discipline and self-restraint were disregarded" (quoted in Edgar 1986: 55). The rise of multiculturalism was linked to the rise of a liberal elite, and Alfred Sherman argued in the *Daily Telegraph* in September 1976 that "the imposition of mass immigration from backward alien cultures" was an attack on "all that is English and wholesome" (quoted in Edgar 1986: 71). Feminism was equally problematic and the importance of the family with the male as head of the household was central to the alliance between neoliberalism and neoconservatism (Cooper 2017). Thus, just as Irving Kristol (1970) argued that instant gratification was encouraged and facilitated by Keynesianism, Buchanan *et al.* (1978) argued that inflation was a moral as well as economic threat as welfare undermined individual and family responsibility.

Seen in this way, Thatcherism was a purposive, doctrinal conservative project. For Ian Gilmour (1977), one of Thatcher's strongest critics from inside the Conservative Party, this was precisely why Thatcher was not a true conservative. He drew on the legacy of Oakeshott, who rejected the idea that the state should be organized as an enterprise, dedicated to the pursuit of a common purpose. Instead, much like Powell argued, the state should be a civil association, which allowed individuals to make their own choices and set their own goals. In terms of the Conservative Party in the 1980s, Gilmour (1977) claimed the mantle of Oakeshott, and suggest that the Thatcherite project was too rationalist and dedicated to a blueprint for the future, based on the promotion of the so-called free market. In this way Thatcherism was a project based on the state as an enterprise and not a civil association. However, in keeping with the discussion of conservatism in the opening chapter, the Thatcher government was committed to certain common principles, but these were necessary for the state to operate as a civil association in the first place, as without them the market order could not exist and so individuals would not be able to pursue their choices and goals. Thatcher, like American neoconservatives, but unlike Powell and (theoretically) American paleoconservatives (Fleming 2005), did indeed want to use the state for particular moral ends, albeit ones very different from the postwar state (Schofield 2013: 319–46). Second, its advocates argued that the grand project of Thatcherism was necessary to reverse the growth of the enterprise rather than the civil state (see Gamble 1988: 160). Indeed, some Conservatives argue that the period from 1945 to 1975 was actually the anomaly in Conservative history, and not 1979 onwards (Blake 1976). Certainly, Thatcherism had some echoes of Peel's support for free trade, deflationary politics in the inter-war period and fear of politicized interests in the public sphere, and the two traditions of collectivism and libertarianism in British politics have always cut across party lines (Greenleaf 1983).

How, then, does this relate to the question of Europe? The referendum in 1975 saw divisions in the two main parties, but most Labour MPs were against and most Conservatives, including Thatcher, were for continued membership of the European Community. The result itself saw an easy win – by 67 to 33 per cent – for those who wanted to remain in the European Community. By the 1990s, although both parties were still divided, Labour was more pro-European and the Conservatives more Eurosceptic. While Thatcher was pro-Europe, her position gradually shifted over this period. She supported the development of the single market, and thus supported the Single European Act 1986, which committed the European Community to a single market area by 1992; the European Union was officially founded in 1993, following the 1991 Maastricht Treaty. Thatcher was in favour of a free-trade area, but there was a growing divide between Thatcherite pro- and anti-Europeans, as "they increasingly differed as to how the single market was to be achieved and maintained, and the extent to which it was desirable to create common economic institutions to underpin the single market" (Gamble 2003: 121).

Conservative opposition to the European Union was increasingly based on a combination of nationalism and defence of national sovereignty combined with a commitment to a global free market. Seen in this way, the EU undermined both British sovereignty and global free trade, and in this respect was deemed to be protectionist. The latter emphasis on free trade tended towards a view that markets could be accessed through spontaneous free trade, or through the construction of closer ties with the US (an intensified Atlanticism) and the old empire. The former emphasis was based on concerns that the move to a single currency would transfer monetary responsibilities to the European Central Bank, and fiscal responsibility to the European Commission, and wider objections to what was considered to be a corporatist, excessively regulatory Europe. This was a particular concern among Conservative Eurosceptics because they believed that the European Union was in many respects social democratic in nature. EU fiscal rules were actually very conservative, but there was some attempt to promote a social Europe, which was a cause for concern among Conservatives – and one reason why the Labour Party increasingly moved in a pro-European direction. The Conservative government opted out of the social clause in the Maastricht Treaty, and committed to engage in monetary union plans, but no more than that. The Black Wednesday run on sterling in 1992, whose value was fixed as part of the Exchange Rate Mechanism, further fuelled Euroscepticism and in 1996, 74 backbenchers supported Bill Cash's motion calling for a referendum before any further European integration. Euroscepticism was further reinforced by the extension of European power without any referenda within Britain, particularly over the Lisbon Treaty of 2007, which switched voting on many issues to the majority principle rather than countries having the right to exercise a veto.

These developments reflected the basic dilemma faced by Conservative Eurosceptics and the wider Thatcherite and neoliberal shift in the Conservative Party. As Gamble (2003: 122–3) states:

> The Thatcherite programme in Britain had targeted the political obstacles to the working of the free market and had endeavoured to sweep many of them away. It followed that if there was to be a real single market at the European level there had to be supranational administrative and legal institutions to ensure that local political obstacles to various nation states were exposed and overcome. The problem

for many Thatcherites however, including Thatcher herself, was that although they agreed with the goal they were not prepared to will the means if this meant transferring what they regarded as core aspects of British national sovereignty to Brussels.

Thatcher (1988) herself argued in her famous Bruges speech that "(w)e have not successfully rolled back the frontiers of the state in Britain only to see them re-imposed at a European level with a European super-state exercising dominance in Brussels". This speech paved the way for a number of Eurosceptic think tanks, including the Bruges Group (founded in 1989), the European Constitutional Group (1992) and the Centre for the New Europe (1993), all of which were hostile to what they saw, particularly after Maastricht, as a growing federal super-state. There was particular hostility to what Eurosceptic neoliberals considered redistribution policies through expanded structural and regional funds, and the Delors emphasis on a social union. In addition, as well as entrenched opposition to the European Common Agricultural Policy, many neoliberals opposed the single currency. Many argued for the continuation of a number of currencies, while some also argued for the introduction of a European-wide currency to compete with national currencies, an argument that drew heavily on Hayek's work on the denationalization of money in the 1970s (Hayek 1976; Friedman 1997; see Slobodian & Plehwe 2019). This was ironic, given that the euro was used to discipline indebted countries, once the Eurozone crisis broke following the 2008 financial crisis (Blyth 2013; Kiely 2018: chapter 8). But what is important for our purposes is to recognize that while there are strong arguments for characterizing the European Union as in many respects neoliberal, there were just as many, if not more, neoliberal ideas associated with Euroscepticism. Indeed, while many Eurosceptics hoped for reform, by 1996 the Bruges Group had effectively abandoned hope of reform and published what was in effect a manifesto, which asked the question *Better Off Out?* (Hindley 1996). This brings us to the question of Brexit.

Conservative Euroscepticism and the question of Brexit

The idea of the Anglosphere was essentially revived in the post-Thatcher Conservative Party in the context of the rise of globalization. In some respects British Eurosceptic Conservatives essentially envisage a vision of globalization that parallels the claims made by the hyper-globalizers discussed in Chapter 2, though with some exceptions such as more ambiguous positions on the free movement of labour. This Euroscepticism is derived from the view that the European Union and the single market is a regionalist constraint on globalization

THE CONSERVATIVE CHALLENGE TO GLOBALIZATION

and not an extension of it. This argument is supposedly reinforced by the rise of Asia and new growth centres in the South such as the so-called BRICS countries (Brazil, Russia, China, India and South Africa), which provide both an economic opportunity and a geopolitical challenge. In this way, we might argue that conservative globalization in Britain is forward-looking and not based on nostalgia, as it is based on a global future "at odds with the idea that unelected bureaucrats in Brussels and judges in Luxembourg have aggregated so much power over our lives" (D'Ancona 2016). In particular, it is argued that while Britain entered the European Community from a position of weakness, post-Thatcherite Britain can re-enter the world from a position of strength. Seen in this way, the problem with the European Union is that it is "not modern enough", particularly in the context of a modern, new economy where there is a need for greater decentralization, accountability and transparency (D'Ancona 2016). Thus, just as Blair argued that the New Right was not sufficiently modernizing, the argument here is that the third way's Europeanism means that it suffers from the same problem because European bureaucratization is not as modernizing as real globalization. On the other hand, as we saw above, support for an Anglosphere might be seen as an institutional foundation for global free trade to happen, but the current case for global free trade often relies in part on the idea that this can be generated spontaneously. This tension notwithstanding, much of the Conservative case for Brexit has tried to square these circles based on the belief that Britain should return to its role as, in the words of Theresa May, "a great, global trading nation", which is part of its "unique and proud global relationships" (cited in El-Elnany 2017). As we will see in a moment this argument can imply a nostalgia for global free trade, the return of the Anglosphere and the revival of Britain's (or more accurately England's) supposedly glorious past (see O'Toole 2018).

In terms of spontaneous free trade, the most clear argument for a Brexit followed by no trade deal was made by the groups Economists for Brexit (2016) and Economists for Free Trade (2018). According to the main author of these reports (Minford 2016), if Britain left the EU without a trade deal and unilaterally removed all tariff barriers, GDP could be boosted by as much as 4 per cent. According to former chancellor of the exchequer Nigel Lawson, Britain needs "nothing more, nothing less" than trade with the EU under WTO rules. The basis for this argument is that the European Union is not based on free trade, but rather is a protectionist bloc. More specifically, Minford suggests that with the end of EU protectionism, prices paid to EU consumers for manufacturing and agricultural goods would fall by 10 per cent, which in turn will facilitate an increase in GDP of 4 per cent. This 10 per cent figure is not derived from actual tariff levels (which are around 3 per cent), but from the differences in producer price levels between the UK and some other countries, with the implication that these differentials are the product of EU trade barriers. Britain's post-Brexit future thus rests on a truly global free trade in contrast to the restrictive trade policies of the European Union, in which trade can be enhanced in a global context, as opposed to the diverted trade that has taken place through the EU. This might involve some degree of creative destruction, and Minford accepts that unilateral trade liberalization might lead to the complete elimination of manufacturing in Britain and growing wage inequality, but it will also promote much greater opportunity through the global rather than European market. The most libertarian position suggests that new trade deals are not necessary, while less extreme positions suggest that new trade deals will be forthcoming once (or even before) Britain leaves the EU.

Related to this argument is the contention that the European Union is inward-looking, and that Brexit instead provides the chance to revive the idea of a Greater or global Britain, as opposed to a presumably European one (Nelson 2016). This argument has embraced a range of alternatives, including the construction of a Commonwealth trading area, or one that embraces the supposedly similar "Anglo-Saxon" cultures of Canada, Australia, New Zealand and Britain, as well as possibly the United States (Bennett 2004, 2016). The idea is that the British "pick up where we left off in 1973" and establish closer commercial relations with those countries with which we have historic links (Roberts 2016). Important here is the idea of close cultural ties between the English-speaking peoples (Roberts 2006), as we have seen an idea supported in part by, among others, Winston Churchill (2001), in his four-volume history originally published between 1956 and 1958. There are a number of variants on the idea, sometime referred to as the Anglosphere or CANZUK, but essentially the argument is that these countries have a common heritage rooted in a common head of state, a common language, a legal system based on Magna Carta and the rule of law, a Westminster system of politics and a history of cooperation (Bennett 2016).

This turn to what in effect is a revived Anglosphere can be traced back to two conferences in 1999 and 2000, in Washington, DC and Berkshire (Lloyd 2000), attended by, among others, the politicians Margaret Thatcher (and former adviser John O'Sullivan) and David Davis, intellectuals such as Francis Fukuyama, Kenneth Minogue and Robert Conquest, and public figures such as tycoon Conrad Black and James Bennett, as well as writers of numerous books on the Anglosphere (Bennett 2004, 2007). Black (1998) had linked this idea to Euroscepticism, suggesting that the EU artificially tied global Britain to Europe. Conquest (2001: chapters 14 and 15) argued in 2001 that in the context of new geopolitical and security challenges, the EU was not fit for purpose and suggested that the Anglosphere was a viable alternative, united by historic and cultural ties and similar political institutions. But it was James Bennett (2004, 2007) who most explicitly suggested a forward-looking Anglosphere whereby historic ties based on language, culture and institutions could unite with the realities of contemporary globalization, based on intensified information and capital flows, which actually enhanced the importance of English as a global language. This turn to the Anglosphere or (parts of) the Commonwealth has been supported by a number of prominent pro-Leave campaigners, including Nigel Farage, Liam Fox and Daniel Hannan (2015), the latter of whom has explicitly called for a "union with other English speaking democracies". This renewal of an "Anglosphere Association" or "English Speaking Union" (Conquest 1999) is based on "a common law tradition, respect for private property, continuous representative government, and a culture that nurtures civil society and entrepreneurial enterprise" (Bennett 2004: 64). Though there are differences between advocates, what in essence they argue for is a "Peelite" global commitment to free trade, which is different from Chamberlain's preferential treatment within the empire scenario, but at the same time, like Chamberlain, they argue that this needs to be embedded in a specific cultural-political context, in which the Anglosphere plays a leading role. Some stretch the concept of the Anglosphere to include Ireland and India (Hannan 2013; Nalapat 2011), Hong Kong, Singapore and the Philippines (Congdon 1992), which again reflects the changing world economy and the supposed economic opportunities that have emerged with the rise of these countries. Indeed, in some respects the dominant conservative Brexit position is one that calls for a revival of global Britain based on an intensification of the Anglo-liberal model of capitalism. "Britannia unchained" will compete in the world economy through the further intensification of low taxes, public spending cuts, further labour market flexibility and limited social and environmental protections (Kwarteng *et al.* 2012). In this scenario, Britain can leave the EU without a deal and instead adopt WTO rules or even simply just impose unilateral free trade (Economists for Brexit 2016). In addition, a trade deal with the US would further aid the shift to a lower-tax, "deregulated" Britain where there would for instance be fewer rights for workers, or tax and environmental regulation designed to limit capital (Lawson 2016; Farand & Hope 2018).

At the same time, this combination of Cobdenite free trade and appropriate institutional support (such as the Anglosphere) has led to some ambiguities, not least over the relationship between globalization on the one hand, and national sovereignty on the other. Much of the Brexit campaign focused far less on global Britain and much more on sovereignty and the rhetoric of taking back control. Under Prime Minister May this initially appeared to include a commitment to state policies that challenged important components of neoliberal public policy, including possible controls on capital and its movement, a focus on social and political obligations and much tighter curbs on immigration policy. This drew on Chamberlain but less through the Anglosphere and the international, and more in terms of domestic policy, and it was one that owed something to the idea of Red Toryism (Blond 2010). This tradition proposes a communitarian vision of traditionalist conservatism, challenging both the welfare state and large corporations and emphasizes the importance of local communities, small enterprises embedded in community and the importance of voluntary associations in promoting community and relieving poverty. The importance of the local or "somewhere" is contrasted with rootless cosmopolitans whose focus is on "anywhere", and in this respect it can be seen as in some respects anti-globalization. Blond (2016; see also Timothy 2016) thus argues that "Britain is a very strong civic nation and it was the fear that we were letting in those who would break this civic compact that I think tipped the balance to taking back control ... For example, for the new British PM Theresa May, immigration is indeed the issue, she developed a deep distrust of mass migrant flows, firstly on the security issue, as Home Secretary she was on the front line defending the UK against terrorist threats. And the mass importation of cultures hostile to Western values and the structural dangers of this I suspect made her think migration was perhaps the key security threat to Britain. Given mass EU sponsored multiculturalism and the denial of a values affinity approach to immigration, Europe itself draws in those hostile to its foundations."

The prospects for a new era of "Mayism" were, however, seriously undermined by the general election result of 2017 when the Conservatives lost their majority and May and her advisers took much of the blame, and thus came to rely on the support of the Democratic Unionist Party from Northern Ireland. This alliance begged a number of questions about the future of the union, particularly in the context of the Irish mainland border, and implementing Brexit proved to be a task beyond May in the context of a divided House of Commons and the reality of what leaving the EU would likely mean both socially and economically. But there was also a clear ambiguity between advocates of a global Britain and the question of taking back control, not least over the question of immigration, with May and much of the Brexit vote focusing primarily on sovereignty and immigration, while many global Britain advocates were far less hostile to immigration and its importance to the Anglo-liberal growth model. This position was certainly more ambiguous than advocacy of open borders, and indeed sometimes involved cultural opposition to certain kinds of immigration, based especially on arguments that certain migrants are cultural threats to the Anglosphere. But at the same time it did not involve the same commitment to immigration reduction as Theresa May had envisaged.

Conversely, May herself did advocate a "global Britain" as part of the post-referendum Plan for Britain, and emphasized Britain's tradition as a "great, global trading nation" (May 2016, 2017). Indeed, after the Brexit vote, the question of global Britain returned with a vengeance as the government quickly cast its eye

on post-EU trade deals. David Davis (2016) had contended before the referendum that leaving the EU "is an opportunity to renew our strong relationships
with Commonwealth and Anglophone countries. These parts of the world are
growing faster than Europe. We share history, culture and language. We have
family ties. We even share similar legal systems. The usual barriers to trade
are largely absent." In 2013, Boris Johnson (2013) argued that in 1973 "we
betrayed our relationship with Commonwealth countries such as Australia and
New Zealand". The argument here was that national sovereignty could be the
basis for the return of an open-sea, "world island" Britain in a truly global age
(Pocock 1992), and that Brexit provided the basis for a renewed Anglosphere or
what Bennett (2016) called CANZUK. Some conservative historians had long
argued the case made by Seeley that Britain was an exceptional nation (Roberts
2006), and the British Empire "undeniably pioneered free trade, free capital
movements and, with the abolition of slavery, free labour" (Ferguson 2004: 366).
It is for reasons such as these that some referred – in part, satirically – to the
post-Brexit project as Empire 2.0 (Olusoga 2017). This does not of course mean
that the Brexit project simply meant advocacy of a return to empire, which is
indeed history (Johnson 2018a). But what the conservative Brexit project does
include is the notion that global Britain can be reinvigorated, and this was a
project intimately linked to empire, which many Brexiteers not only accept, but
actually endorse (Thackeray & Toye 2019), an argument we consider further in
Chapters 6 and 7.

Much of this, then, is clearly not a case of conservative anti-globalization,
but rather an attempt to expand and extend globalization, in opposition to the
regionalist and supposedly protectionist European Union. Seen in this way,
Brexit is not part of the conservative populist anti-globalization trends that
exist in much of Europe, in parts of the developing world and in some respects
with Trump and the current condition of American conservatism. Indeed,
some pro-Brexit advocates of the Left have argued that a complete break with
the European Union is necessary precisely to avoid Britain seeing a right-wing
populist backlash (The Full Brexit 2018). The argument here is that the vote
restored national sovereignty, and undermined any right-wing populist turn, as
the United Kingdom Independence Party (UKIP) was undermined after the referendum, and the rise of the Brexit Party in 2019 simply reflected the failure to
leave the European Union by 29 March 2019.

On the other hand, there are significant areas of overlap between Brexit
and the wider conservative populist turn. First, as we will see in Chapter 6, the
anti-globalization of much of the populist Right is often ambiguous, and while
there is universal hostility to the free movement of labour, there are far more
ambivalent views on the free movement of capital and free trade. Second, immigration (together with sovereignty and "control over borders") was the major

Table 4.1 British conservatism and the international

Issue and year	Brief details	Outcomes/consequences
Free trade, 1846	Peel supports free trade against Conservative protectionist interests.	Conservative Party splits and years of opposition. Conservative Party shifts to one nation, empire and union.
Imperial preference, 1903	Joseph Chamberlain resigns from the Conservative Party, supporting the protectionist imperial preference within the Empire and the promotion of an Anglosphere abroad and social reform at home.	Some shift towards tariff reform with some defections to the Liberal Party, but the fear of Labour dominated. 1932 saw imperial preference introduced in the context of the Great Depression.
Isolation and peace with Hitler, 1940	Conservative pressure to make peace with Germany in the context of German expansion and British isolation, motivated by the fear of war, but also anti-Communism, and the belief that the Empire could be preserved through peace and some sympathies with Fascism.	Rejected by Churchill and Labour. War continues with empire and decisive intervention of the US and especially the USSR, as was empire (which in turn led to a new wave of anti-colonial resistance after 1945).
Europe and Brexit, around 2016	Ongoing Conservative divisions from the late 1980s over Europe, leading to the referendum in 2016. The Conservative Eurosceptic Right supports a combination of the Anglosphere and global Britain as a free-trade nation.	Continued divisions in the Conservative (and Labour) Parties, including the resignations of four Conservative prime ministers (Thatcher, Major, Cameron, May) over Europe.

issue in the vote (Ashcroft 2016: table 59; Ipsos Mori 2016). While leading Leave campaigners generally kept their distance from UKIP and Nigel Farage, they were also happy to draw on scare stories about the issue, with claims that Turkey's supposed imminent entry into the EU would encourage further immigration, and that Britain's borders would soon extend to Iraq and Syria (Kenny & Pearce 2018: 154–5). Indeed, the reason why a referendum was called in the first place had more to do with internal Conservative Party politics and fear of UKIP than any wider demand for a referendum on the issue. Seen in this way, using the later marginalization of UKIP as evidence for the lack of conservative populism in Britain is misleading, first because it ignores the fact that UKIP's central focus had effectively gone, and second because in any case UKIP's ideas had so strongly influenced the Conservative Party, and indeed the Conservatives had influenced UKIP (Bale 2018).

Given that immigration was such a major issue, this suggests that there is some significant degree of conflict between Conservative plans for Global

Britain and the reasons why the referendum was won in the first place. For what happened in essence was that the EU became "a lightning rod through which UKIP and other promoters of Brexit were able to channel or funnel a broader set of social frustrations" (Flinders 2018: 183). This of course brings us back to the question considered in the last chapter, namely the ways in which "actually existing globalization" has failed and encouraged resentment and a "cultural backlash" in the context of stagnant or even declining living standards, and more specifically how this linked to the Brexit vote. As is well known, Scotland and Northern Ireland voted Remain, while Wales voted to Leave. But the Leave vote was essentially won in England, where every region outside of London voted for Brexit: 58 per cent in the Northeast, 54 per cent in the Northwest, 58 per cent in Yorkshire and Humberside, 59 per cent in the East Midlands, 56 per cent in the East, 52 per cent in the Southeast and 53 per cent in the Southwest (Hazeldine 2017: 52). Indeed, while there is an undoubted tension between the Conservative Brexit project, which projects the return of a global Britain, and the Brexit vote in post-industrial areas that wanted more protectionism, there is some overlap in that both projects were centred on England. Those more likely to identify as English were far more likely to vote Brexit than those who identified as British (O'Toole 2018: 186–7, 190–1), and indeed English Euroscepticism has emerged in response to devolution and the rise of a more inclusive national identity in Scotland (Henderson *et al.* 2016).

Survey evidence suggests that the vote for Leave was around 30 per cent higher among those who left school at 16 than among those who have a university degree. It was 20 per cent higher among those aged 65 than those aged 25, and 10 per cent higher among those who earned less than £20,000 a year than those who earned over £60,000 (Flinders 2018: 187). This has led to widespread consideration of the vote of the so-called white working class, not only in terms of Brexit but also the presidential vote for Trump a few months later (see Chapter 5). As in the case of Trump, we need to exercise considerable caution here, and not only for the most obvious victories for remain in Scotland and Northern Ireland. According to the Ashcroft Brexit polls (Ashcroft 2016), economically well-off upper- and upper-middle-class voters account for less than 25 per cent of the adult population but made up around one-third of the Leave vote. Antonucci *et al.* (2017) suggest that two groups with intermediate levels of education (those with good GCSEs and A-Levels but no more than that) were more pro-Leave than those with low GCSE grades or no formal education. Dorling (2016) thus suggests that the middle-class vote was central to the Leave vote, particularly in the south of England, and the proportion of Leave voters in the lowest social classes is less than one-third, largely because turnout among these groups was lower than for middle-class groups. Indeed, while lower-social class categories DE and C2 were proportionately more likely to vote Leave than social class categories C1 and AB, when abstentions[3] are factored in, the differences among social groups is marginal. Indeed, if we then also compare percentages among these groups with the size of each group among the national population, then AB (9.49 per cent) and C1 (11.2 per cent) "become the largest purveyors of vote for Leave, above both C2 (9.02 per cent) and DE (9.14 per cent)" (Mondon 2017: 361).

Nonetheless, there are some contextual features that in part help to explain some of the Brexit vote, above all those 6 million Leave voters in England's historic industrial regions (Hazeldine 2017: 53), and areas that were or remain heavily dependent on manufacturing were more likely to vote Leave (Becker *et al.* 2017). We have explored broader trends such as deindustrialization, stagnant wages, rising debt and increasing inequality in the last chapter, and these can be more explicitly linked to Brexit through a more regional focus. In particular, New Labour attempted to compensate for longer-term deindustrialization through investment led by the public sector. Indeed, deindustrialization trends continued under New Labour, with financial services growing at twice the overall growth rate, while the manufacturing contribution to GDP fell from 19 to 10 per cent. In the North, manufacturing's contribution to regional output fell from 24 to 15 per cent, while in the West Midlands the equivalent figures were 27 to 13 per cent (Hazeldine 2017: 57–8). From 1999 to 2006, public spending increased by around 6 per cent a year, and this was central to attempts to revitalize the deindustrialized North. Public-sector jobs and state-funded jobs in the private sector (through outsourcing) accounted for 73 per cent of employment growth in the Northeast, 67 per cent in Yorkshire and Humberside, and 62 per cent in the Northwest. While some of this involved higher-paid supervisory and auditing jobs in the marketized public sector (Hood & Dixon 2015), most of it involved low-paid service work. Not surprisingly, Labour's vote in the three Northern England regions declined from 4.1 to 2.6 million from 1997 to 2010 (Hazeldine 2017: 61). Austerity actually exacerbated these problems for while financial services received bail-outs following the 2008 crisis, the public sector was cut and this disproportionately affected Northern England, where (along with Scotland and Wales) one in four employees worked in the public sector compared to one in six in London and the Southeast (Hazeldine 2017: 63). While there was a great deal promised in terms of overcoming regional imbalance and the promotion of a Northern powerhouse, job creation was far more rapid in the Southeast, and under the 2010–15 coalition government median household

---

3. The figures for abstentions are far from perfect as there are no commonly known data on abstentions among different social classes for the 2016 referendum. Mondon (2017) uses estimates extrapolated from abstentions across social classes in the 2015 general election, a far from scientific exercise, but one that at least serves the useful purpose of further undermining the myth of Brexit as a (white) working-class revolt.

wealth increased by 14 per cent in London but fell by 8 per cent in Yorkshire and Humberside (Hazeldine 2017: 68).

Regional differences are thus important not only in explaining the uneven development associated with both national economic strategies and globalization. However, there is again a need for considerable caution in drawing relevant conclusions. For example, as the Farage quote in the previous chapter makes clear, an influential argument associated with the rise of the populist Right, and specifically UKIP in Britain, is that the older, traditional working class has been marginalized by globalization, and in this context cultural concerns have become increasingly important. These involve distrust of government, economic pessimism, concern about immigration and resentment aimed at university-educated, cosmopolitan elites (Ford & Goodwin 2014). This is an argument we first came across in terms of debates around globalization and culture in Chapter 2, and the attack on the socially liberal (and economically neoliberal) "Davos Man" (Huntington 2004a). This kind of argument has also been used to explain the rise of Trump (Inglehart & Norris 2019) and indeed closely parallels the paleoconservative worldview, as we will see in the next chapter. Furthermore, the Conservative strategy in the 2017 general election in many respects rested on this view, as Prime Minister May referred to families that were just about managing, and attempted to focus on immigration controls, national sovereignty and leaving the European Union, as well as reviving 1950s policies such as the planned national renewal of grammar schools. In some respects, this strategy echoed that of Chamberlain and his success in winning the votes of at least a section of the organized working class in the early 1900s for the Conservatives. But as Jennings and Stoker (2017) suggest, this strategy in part met with only limited success because it relies on an overly simplistic social analysis. In particular, while a place like London does have a proportionately larger economic elite compared to the rest of the country, it also has significant numbers of low-paid and insecure workers, who indeed might still have university degrees and significant amounts of social and cultural capital. These younger workers face considerable insecurity, especially limited or no access to the housing market and student debt, but they also have considerable cosmopolitan sympathies. To reduce these people to a cosmopolitan elite because of their location is far too one-sided. Moreover, while it is true that the Conservatives made some inroads in terms of winning traditional working-class votes, this was true throughout the twentieth century, and in the 2017 election Labour did well in areas of traditional routine manual occupations. Indeed, Labour saw no decrease in support among traditional working-class voters, and indeed saw slight increase in votes in areas where there has been a fall in real wages (Jennings & Stoker 2017: 363). Labour's strategy in the run-up to the 2019 European Parliament elections appeared to be based on trying not to alienate either its Leave or Remain supporters, but its fence-sitting alienated both sides. Crucially, though, polling evidence suggests that Remain voters were far more likely to be alienated than Leave voters, and indeed there was little to no "punishment" of Remain-supporting Labour MPs in the 2017 election. Moreover, based on a survey of 25,000 voters, the largest block of Leave voters were, first, middle-class Conservatives and, second, working-class Conservatives. In fact, working-class Leave voters accounted for just 12.5 per cent of the total (Kellner 2019).

The pro-Brexit Labour response to these figures is to point to the fact that Labour lost significant numbers of working-class supporters from 2001 onwards, which is indeed true, and reflects the fact that third way rhetoric around globalization and the new economy never matched reality. But what is less clear is how this *necessarily* translates into a case for supporting Brexit, either in narrow electoral or wider socio-political terms. The implication of the argument is that globalization's losers have moved to support the populist Right, but the evidence for this, as we have seen, is limited at best (though it did occur to some extent in the December 2019 election). Above all, a majority for Leave in the EU referendum in Labour constituencies does not mean that the majority of Labour voters supported Leave, and indeed the evidence here suggests that Labour voters tended to vote Remain (at least until the December 2019 election). Moreover, given that the dominant project for Brexit is a right-wing conservative one, it is difficult to see how the pro-Brexit Labour position makes any sense, at least beyond immediate narrow electoral strategy. As we will see in Chapter 8, the EU is a highly problematic institution, but to suggest that it is responsible for Labour losing working-class votes after 2001 is unconvincing. Furthermore, a 2019 survey of attitudes to Leave and Remain showed that Remain supporters tended to have stronger commitments to their position than Leavers and, if anything, support for a no-deal Brexit was slightly stronger among more financially secure voters (Stager *et al.* 2019). This suggests again that while the rise of the conservative Right is a real phenomenon, there is a need for considerable care in examining its social base. Similarly, while it is simplistic to reduce the Leave vote in 2016 to a revolt by the so-called traditional or white working class, particularly as so many higher-income voters also voted Leave, it is also true that deindustrialization and relative decline was a significant factor for some, particularly older voters (especially in December 2019). Indeed, age was in many respects the most significant factor in the vote and "a majority of 18–34 year olds in every social class voted to remain, while a majority of those aged 55+ in every class voted to leave"[4] (Ipsos Mori 2016). But this is still a long way from a simple vote by the left-behinds and the traditional working class.

4. There was however one notable exception to this trend as those over 90 voted Remain. The numbers of course were small but the symbolic significance is great, for as this chapter has shown, much of the Leave case drew on "memories" – albeit highly selective ones – from the Second World War. Those who actually lived through the war did not share Nigel Farage's vision.

Indeed, probably the best way of understanding the "material basis" for the coalition that eventually supported a no-deal Brexit in 2019 is to relate it to the question of assets that was discussed in the last chapter (Davies 2019; Lucas 2019). This is a coalition in which "grassroots" Leavers are committed to the ideology of English exceptionalism, but also tends to be composed of older people who have paid off the mortgages on their homes and are living off assets paid for by their pension funds. At the same time, leaders and funders of Leave campaigns tend to be composed of precisely the footloose capital associated with the hyper-globalization thesis – the kind of capital that can move rapidly and with ease of exit not associated with productive capital (which fears a massive interruption in supply chains through Brexit). In this way, an asset-rich middle class has united with footloose capital that favours de-regulation, particularly labour and environmental deregulation, and which in some respects is based on a transatlantic alliance that supports closer trade ties between the US and Britain, and where there are considerable financial links between the Trump and Brexit projects (Farand & Hope 2018), to be considered further in Chapter 7.

Conclusion: Brexit, the "peculiarities of the English" and neoliberalism

This chapter has examined British conservatism through a consideration of the international, and demonstrated how current debates about national sovereignty, global Britain and Brexit have long roots in the Conservative Party and among conservative intellectuals. Some of the current debates draw in selective ways on older controversies around Robert Peel, Joseph Chamberlain, Winston Churchill, Enoch Powell and Margaret Thatcher. It should be clear from the discussion above that this represents a conservatism that is not simply about stability, and while it is certainly the case that much of the current debate over Brexit draws on a nostalgia for nineteenth-century Britain, we should also note that is not *simply* a backward-looking idea. The revival of the Anglosphere has been "reworked for a global, rather than, imperial era" (Wellings & Baxendale 2015: 123). In particular, much of the current Conservative Euroscepticism rests on the idea that the hyper-globalization thesis, as outlined in Chapter 2, is not yet a current reality but an aspirational political project. But in contrast to the claim made by the hyper-globalization thesis that the nation state is dead, the Conservative argument is that hyper-globalization can only be achieved through what Margaret Thatcher called "good Anglo-Saxon traditions" of commerce and culture (cited in Lloyd 2000), because a "borderless economy" requires cultural cohesion and civic strength (Bennett 2016). This is an argument that is not necessarily against immigration controls, which can be rationalized on ethno-cultural grounds (see Chapter 6), but this focus on global Britain is somewhat different from the protectionist impulses that drove much of the Brexit vote. Any critique of conservative views of the Anglosphere certainly need to focus on the ways that problematic accounts of the past and of empire are presented in these accounts, but also the problems associated with how the present is conceptualized. In this way we can consider whether or not, to cite Hearnshaw once again (Chapter 1), Brexit is a "reckless experiment". This task is undertaken, as part of wider critique of conservativism and globalization, in Chapters 6 and 7.

Finally, as was suggested in earlier chapters, to understand the emergence of right-wing populism in recent years we need to pay attention to both general and specific features. As is clear by now, the former include growing inequality, declining trust and the rise of post-politics, and the impact of the financial crisis. This chapter has addressed more specific features and the ways in which British conservatism has been periodically divided by international questions (see Table 4.1). This in turn links to specifics of English and British history and the ways in which British capitalism linked to the union, empire, decline, an archaic class structure and a "pre-modern" state. For some this reflects the incomplete-ness of English and British capitalist development and the compromise with landed interests, the centrality of financial capitalism and high levels of over-seas investment (Anderson 1964; Nairn 1977, 1988). Much of this argument was developed during the postwar boom years when Britain grew in absolute terms but fell behind relative to other countries, a process that began in the late nineteenth century, as Joseph Chamberlain recognized. By the 1970s, wider economic problems suggested that British decline was not necessarily unique. Moreover, the idea that British archaic capitalism could be contrasted to mod-ernizing European or American capitalism ignored the ways in which catch-up countries used existing institutions to modernize. The European "ancien regimes" and European conservatism in this way modernized in the context of growing rivalries between advanced powers (Thompson 1965; Mayer 1981; Teschke 2003), an argument partially accepted by Anderson (1992: chapter 4) in later work.

Nonetheless, we can still accept some specific features of English and British capitalism, which in part reflect not the incompleteness but rather the success of early capitalist development, and the ways in which Britain was then unable to effectively deal with the question of competitive rivalries once it was no longer the workshop of the world (Wood 1991). In terms of ideology, one might argue that England in particular did not develop a civic nationalism in response to this, but instead drew on nostalgia and English exceptionalism, primacy and its role as a trading nation (Barnett 2017; Nairn 1977). This does not explain the diverse reasons for the Brexit vote, but it does link closely to the Conservative Brexit project and what Barnett (2017) has called imperial fantasy and the ideology of "Churchillism". This involves a focus on empire (such as the Anglosphere, albeit combined with free trade), English exceptionalism in terms of its institutions and subordination to the US (though this is not specific to Conservatism, as the Blair era demonstrated). This in turn can be linked to changes in the British state, which has seen a partial shift away from some of its archaic features and the partial undermining of "the Establishment" (Sampson 1962). This was associated with one-nation Toryism and rested on an overwhelmingly white, public school-educated state elite that had a paternalist commitment to "public service". But in contrast to the hopes of Thatcherite (and Blairite) modernizers, this was only partially displaced, and was succeeded by an even more short-termist ethos, greater domination by the City, a high turnover of generalist rather than specialist staff, an ever greater focus on marketing and public relations and subordination to the economic rule of metrics.

In some respects, this undermined the old Establishment (Davis 2018), but at the cost of anything resembling a coherent political class or political project, and instead saw the rise of a "political media caste" (Barnett 2017) that effectively attempts to cover up this absence of anything like rationality. This is not necessarily specific to the British state, and indeed much of these developments took place in the Blair era, but what is exceptional is how these developments have combined with older conservative ideas of Englishness. This was combined with a mis-diagnosis of the crisis of 2016, which essentially argued that just as 1979 saw a revolt against the British state, which was responsible for the 1970s downturn, so Britain can revive by taking on the EU super-state, which supposedly was the cause of Britain's problems over the last 30 years. As we saw in Chapter 2, the 1970s crisis was said to have been caused by monetary irresponsibility, and specifically state over-spending to buy votes and families living beyond their means. In fact the crisis had its roots in the breakdown of the Bretton Woods system, the role of the dollar as both a national and international reserve currency, falling profits and the oil price, which, combined with trade union attempts to maintain living standards, all contributed to the inflationary crisis. In terms of the British economy, the period from 1980 to 2011 saw Britain's share of manufacturing exports fall from 5.41 per cent to 2.59 per cent (Head 2016).

This period saw the significant decline of British manufacturing (Comfort 2012), in which companies like GEC bought up US IT companies just as the dotcom bubble was about to burst (in 2001), and Rover was in effect asset-stripped by the so-called Phoenix Four, leaving the company bankrupt in 2005. Even in financial services, there were widespread takeovers by foreign capital after the Big Bang in 1986 (Kynaston 2001). It is for reasons such as these that some historians otherwise critical of the decline thesis do accept that in recent years at least Britain has indeed experienced something that we can accurately call "decline" (Edgerton 2019). On the other hand, as we saw in Chapter 2, some theorists of globalization would suggest that none of this matters so long as a country is successful in attracting capital investment, and so Britain's success in attracting foreign capital compensated for the loss of "national capital". On the other hand, foreign investment has located in Britain partly because of low costs, including wages, but also because of Britain's access to the single market. In this way, the EU has not so much caused British decline but actually *helped to compensate for it*. This of course makes Brexit very problematic because there is no longer guaranteed access to the single market. In terms of trade and global value chains, we consider this in more depth in Chapter 7. However, we might immediately note that even the hyper-globalization theorist Kenichi Ohmae (see Chapter 2), who had previously advised companies to invest in Britain, was now advising against this in the context of Brexit and the disruption of supply lines within this market (Head 2016). This is also a problem in financial services where both EU governments and the European Commission have increasingly called for transactions in euro-dominated bonds and securities to only take place in countries where the euro is the actual currency. Britain resisted this development but this would be much more difficult outside of the EU, which shows how vulnerable the British economy would be to European regulatory change.

Thus, while it certainly was not a straightforward vote of the so-called left-behinds, the crisis that culminated in the Brexit vote did have its roots in decline, reflected in deindustrialization and growing inequality, the former of which is considered further in Chapter 7. But it was also rooted in a further manifestation of neoliberal reform, namely the fragmentation and marketization of the state, the latter of which included both high-cost and low-quality service delivery at great expense to the taxpayer, and exacerbated by lower rates of taxation and tax avoidance. The result was an increasing audit culture, which attempted to counter the problems that arose from previous rounds of marketization, and which further undermined the capacity of the state to govern in an effective way. In other words, state failure was not an intrinsic feature of governance but a product of the reforms designed to promote the market. Seen in this way, Brexit was a stark manifestation of these processes. In terms of the conservative project, old imperial fantasies were seen as sufficient and enough to compensate for the fact that Conservative Eurosceptics wanted exit without having any concrete idea of what should happen next – beyond the never-ending fantasy of a pristine market that lay at the heart of the problems of governance in the last 30 years. The fiascos of 2018–19, when fantasy continued with the rise of the Brexit Party, the Conservative Party leadership campaign and the election of Boris Johnson, could not escape this underlying reality. Indeed, given the demands made by hard Brexiteers and protest entrepreneurs like Farage, it is difficult to see what exactly would be a satisfactory Brexit (Bush 2019). One of the great ironies of the Brexit project was that, in many respects, it was part of the culture wars against the cultural Left that emerged in the 1960s, but by 2019 it increasingly relied on the feel-good-factor, can-do optimism generated by Boris Johnson, and the fanciful idea that a successful Brexit could be delivered through positive psychology. This legacy of self-help and happiness as an enterprise can of course be traced back to the otherwise derided 1960s (Binkley 2014).

But this hides a darker reality, namely

> that Johnson/Farage is a symptom of prolonged financialisation, in which capital pulls increasingly towards unproductive investments, relying on balance sheet manipulation, negative interest rates and liquidity for its returns (aided substantially by quantitative easing over the past decade). To put that more starkly, these are seriously morbid symptoms, in which all productive opportunities have already been seized, no new ideas or technologies are likely, and no new spheres of social or environmental life are left to exploit and commodify. These are socially nihilistic interests whose only concern with the future involves their children and grandchildren, but otherwise believe that everything good is in the past. The term "late capitalism" was over-used in the past, but this certainly feels like *very* late capitalism.   (Davies 2019)

We explore both the legacy of the 1960s and the fantasies and realities of Brexit further in Chapters 6 and 7.

5

US CONSERVATIVISM: TRUMPING GLOBALIZATION?

This chapter examines right-wing anti-globalization through a consideration of the conservatism in the US, with attention paid to the period from around the 1950s, through to the conservatism that has at least in part influenced the Trump administration. It traces the shift from a position that in effect supported neo-liberal globalization, particularly in the Reagan era, and which continued under Bush II. The Trump presidential campaign of 2016 was much more critical of globalization, promoting an America-first isolationism, a more sceptical account of international commitments and institutions, including liberal interventionist wars, a hostility to migration and a questioning of the liberal cosmopolitanism associated with the Democrats and many Republicans, including, to some extent, neoconservatives. The chapter therefore highlights differences within the conservative movement, particularly between the more "pro-globalization" neoconservatism (initially associated with Irving Kristol in the 1960s and now William Kristol) on the one hand, and Patrick Buchanan and Paul Gottfried's paleoconservatism on the other, which promotes a more isolationist stance that is in some respects more sceptical of global "free markets". The chapter is largely an exposition and not a critique, but some criticisms are implied and sometimes made more explicit. A fuller critique is developed in Chapters 6 and 7.

The chapter starts by discussing how conservatism developed in the US in the period before 1945. It particularly outlines conservatism's seemingly ambiguous relationship with capitalism, and especially its antagonism to liber-alism, socialism and "mass society". The second section then examines the devel-opment of conservatism after 1945, particularly the development of a postwar American conservatism that essentially made its peace with capitalism, and in its neoconservative form essentially allied itself with neoliberalism from the 1960s onwards. The third section examines alternative conservative thought in the US and specifically the paleoconservative tradition, which is hostile to neoconser-vatism and indeed to globalization. Finally, the fourth section examines the links between different strands of conservative thought and the rise of the Trump phenomenon. This will look in particular at the question of what Trump stood for during his presidential campaign, and in developing some of the themes discussed in the last section of the previous chapter will look at the social basis of support for Trump and the rise of anti-globalization resentment. I will also make some preliminary observations about the relationship of paleoconservatism to other American conservative traditions, and in particular to neoliberalism and how this is linked to the question of resentment.

Conservatism in America (and elsewhere) before 1945

Louis Hartz (1991) famously argued that in the absence of a monarchy, a feudal order and an established Church, there is no conservative tradition in the US. This argument is further reinforced by the fact that industrialization and (limited) democracy evolved together, and there has been no lasting socialist tradition to threaten the liberal order. On the other hand, the constitution was designed, in part, not only to provide checks and balances between different branches of government, but also to ensure state rights for minorities and an electoral college that would supposedly ensure that no tyrant could emerge to manipulate the democratic masses. But it was also clear that the electoral college quickly developed in such a way that local state rights amounted to a defence of the practice of slavery in the South. Moreover, the agrarian South established a conservative tradition in the context of slavery and, after abolition, through the promotion of an authentic Southern order, which contrasted to the commercialism of the North. In the nineteenth century, the case for slavery was made, above all by George Fitzhugh and John Calhoun. The former, in his 1854 work *Sociology for the South: or the Failure of Free Society*, argued that slavery was based on a paternalist social order where slave-owners felt a moral obligation towards their slaves. In contrast, liberal economies left people atomized and isolated, and wage slavery left no social obligation on the part of employers to their employees. Indeed, slavery was "a beautiful example of communism, where each one receives not according to his labour, but according to his wants" (Fitzhugh 2013: 29). John Calhoun, who from 1825 to 1832 was vice president of the US, made the case for local state rights in the face of majority votes at the federal level, an argument that laid the ground for Southern secession in 1860–1 and thus the Civil War. The case for states' rights has since regularly been made, including in the period after the Civil War and the failure of reconstruction in the Southern states, and the institutionalization of racism in the South from the 1880s and 1890s onwards. This Southern tradition was one of the first examples of American conservatism. This conservatism around slavery and the post-1865 order was based on the idea that this was a natural order and any attempt to undermine it would lead to the end of social cohesion and the promotion of more radical ideas, such as those taking place in Europe in 1848 (Kolozi 2017: chapter 1). The case for slavery was of course full of hypocrisy and slaves were subject to brutal treatment if they demanded equality with whites. Moreover, for all the suggestiveness of the criticisms made of capitalism in the North, slavery was itself integrated into a capitalist world order through, for instance, the selling of cotton to British manufacturers. After 1865, slave-owners themselves became capitalists, though the failure of reconstruction did mean that the Southern order remained different from that in the North.

But a new form of conservatism also emerged in the North in the late nineteenth century, one that had some parallels with the conservatism that developed in Western Europe at around the same time. This period saw rapid westward expansion and indeed formal colonization in the Pacific in particular, and the growth of increasingly large manufacturing companies. This was the Gilded Age, which saw the concentration and centralization of capital and the emergence of robber-baron industrialists who enriched themselves in the context of corruption. This was also a period of agrarian crises, recession and high unemployment. Although it was a period of migration, it was also one in which the Republican Party developed a commitment to protectionism for manufacturers, and the argument was made that free trade was a conspiracy propagated by the British to promote their own interests as the most competitive industrial power at the time (see Palen 2016). This was a tradition that pre-dated the party and stretched back to the independence era. In 1791, Hamilton (2017) argued that manufacturing should be fostered through protectionist policies, so that a more advanced division of labour, more specialist machinery and technical spin-offs and export dependence on agriculture could be avoided. Hamilton's arguments were later made in Germany by Friedrich List (1966: 79), who argued that, "A country like England which is far in advance of all its competitors cannot better maintain and extend its manufacturing and commercial industry that by trade as free as possible from all restrictions. For such a country, the cosmopolitan and the national principle are one and the same thing. This explains the fervour with which the most enlightened economists of England regard free trade, and the reluctance of the wise and prudent of other countries to adopt this principle in the actual state of the world." On becoming US President in1869, Ulysses Grant similarly argued that:

> For centuries England has relied on protection, has carried it to extremes and has obtained satisfactory results from it. There is no doubt that it is to this system that it owes its present strength. After two centuries, England has found it convenient to adopt free trade because it thinks that protection can no longer offer it anything. Very well then, Gentleman,

> my knowledge of our country leads me to believe that within two hun-
> dred years, when America has gotten out of protection all that it can
> offer, it to will adopt free trade.   (cited in Chang 2006: 287)

In the 1872 presidential election, a small group of free-trade Republicans unsuccessfully challenged President Grant to be the Republican presidential candidate, and in 1884 liberal Republicans gave their support to the Democrat candidate Grover Cleveland, who went on to become president. From this period the liberal Republicans, known as Mugwumps, left their party, leaving the Republicans as the party of protectionism and the Democrats as the party of free trade, a situation that changed only as late as the 1930s. What was conservative about this protectionism was that it combined with elitism, anti-egalitarianism and imperialism, as well as social reform designed to ward off the threat of Left-populism and socialism. The intellectual Brooks Adams (1848–1927) and the politician Theodore Roosevelt (1858–1918) were particularly important in developing this new conservatism. Both held a social Darwinist account of society, not at the level of the individual but through an understanding of competition between nations. The competitive liberal individual could not form the basis for an orderly society and in this regard was a threat to social disorder. In this way, capitalism lacked the kind of virtuous elite necessary to generate stability, an argument previously made by apologists for slavery in the South 50 years earlier. Capitalism was therefore in need of an invigorating spirit, a "martial man" (Kolozi 2017: 54–5). In Europe, Weber had argued that early capitalism rested on a Protestant spirit in which the individual found his calling on Earth to do God's will, but regretted that the further development of capitalist rationalization had undermined this spirit. Roosevelt and Adams in effect were searching for a new spirit, not to challenge but to supplement capitalism. Commercial society privileged accumulation and consumption over masculine martial values, and what was needed was a love of glory as well as a love of material comfort. This was in effect a "warrior critique" of capitalism (see Kolozi 2017: chapter 2). Adams argued in *The Law of Civilization and Decay*, published in 1896, that societies oscillate between barbarism and civilization, and suggested that US decline was inevitable, an argument that had some overlap with conservative revolutionaries in Europe between the wars (see below). Roosevelt (and Adams) argued that decline was not inevitable, so long as a new responsible sovereign emerged. A public-spirited aristocracy would promote virility, self-sacrifice and masculinity, or the martial spirit, in contrast to bankers and Jews. Roosevelt saw white Anglo-Saxons as the leaders, who would promote the martial spirit through the expansion of the frontier, both westwards in North America and overseas through empire. For Roosevelt, this "spread of English-speaking peoples over the world's waste spaces has been not only the most striking feature in the world's history but also the event of all others most far reaching in its effects and its importance" (quoted in Kolozi 2017: 67). For Roosevelt this involved the centralization of federal power, something that contrasted sharply with the Southern apologists for slavery. Although in many respects different from later American conservatisms, particularly over protectionism, the search for an elite to promote virtue alongside capitalism was something that interested later conservatives. Like much of Europe, this was a period if imperialism and social reform, growing state power, the concentration and centralization of capital and a fear of socialism and mass democracy.

Indeed, the inter-war period saw a great deal of reflection among conservatives about the emergence of mass society. This in part followed on from conservative and some liberal theory from the eighteenth century that expressed fear of "the mob", "the crowd" and "the masses", and in particular feared the ways in which egalitarian and democratic impulses might lead to cultural decline, and how there was a need for strong nationalist leaders to control the passive, "feminine" masses. As we saw in the opening chapter, in various ways this was present in the work of, among others, de Maistre and Burke, and liberals like Tocqueville and Mill. The fears of cultural decline through a tyranny of the majority became more compelling through the shift away from a relatively small-scale capitalist modernity to one where social organization became increasingly "massified", as embodied through urbanization, the rise of labour movements, the large corporation and wider-scale rationalization. This was clear in the work of, among others, Pareto, Mosca, Michels and Ortega y Gasset, and in more sophisticated and different ways in Weber and Nietzsche, and was briefly discussed in the opening chapter of this book.

Although Nietzsche was critical of modern conservatism, his focus on cultural decline was attractive to conservative nationalists who rejected bourgeois liberal decadence, particularly in the period from 1918 to 1939. Oswald Spengler famously argued that the West was just one of a number of civilizations that was no better than any other, and, as with other cultures, it had passed through a process of growth and was now entering a period of civilizational decline. This decline-of-the-West thesis is well known, but less well known is that in his *Man and Technics* he argued (Spengler 2015: 76) that this decline was in part due to industrial "off-shoring", and the import of foreign workers through immigration policies that have undermined white supremacy – what today might be called globalization. Alongside globalization was the problem of liberal subjectivity and the process whereby individual calculation and individual preference rendered politics a meaningless spectacle in which the state became subordinate to self-interested individuals and groups representing such individuals. Liberalism thus weakened the state, reducing it to an empty shell devoid of purpose or meaning, a theme considered in Chapter 2 in the case of Weimar and Carl Schmitt. This weakness was most clear in the international sphere, where the sovereign is most undermined. This is first because of the inability of the state to call on the need for national sacrifice as individual self-interest dominates. Second, on the other hand, war is made not for clearly defined goals but according to abstract principles that are unlikely to be met, and thus lay the ground for endless war in the name of, say, human rights. In both cases the sovereignty of the state is severely compromised.

While inter-war conservatives were pessimistic about liberal modernity, they also held the hope that renewed nationalist communities could emerged in the context of mass society, above all in Germany. This was especially true given the industrial carnage of the First World War, the consequences of which might lay the grounds for cultural re-evaluation, which revived stable, authoritarian rule against weak liberal decadence and its offshoots, including Wilsonian liberal and Leninist socialist internationalism. Thus, Schmitt was initially optimistic about the Nazis and supported the end of the weak Weimar Republic, and even joined the Nazi Party before falling out of favour with it in 1936. The problem for this conservative nationalism of course was that the Nazis replayed the carnage of 1914–18, in unprecedentedly brutal ways.[1]

In the US in this period, conservative responses to these threats varied in the North and the South. This occurred in the context of the roaring twenties and the Great Depression of the 1930s. By this time, the US had become a major economic power, had advanced westward and penetrated foreign markets, but had not quite matched the hopes of Teddy Roosevelt and Brooks Adams in developing a major empire led by warrior-like statesmen. Instead there was Wilsonian liberal internationalism, which threatened to embroil the US in the chaos of Europe, as had happened after 1917, and a shift towards mass consumption alongside mass production, which threatened to undermine excellence by promoting individual interest and utility maximization as the dominant values in society.

Conservative resistance in the South to these developments occurred in the context of the further decline of the agrarian South and growing labour unrest. This occurred in the booming 1920s as well as the depressed 1930s, as agricultural prices and wages for labourers fell, and foreclosures and rural-urban migration increased. The so-called Southern Agrarians, a group of Southern intellectuals and artists, developed their manifesto in response to these developments in

1. I leave aside the debate here over the extent to which Nazi policies were a simple continuation of European colonial policy, or indeed American treatment of Native Americans. Certainly there are similarities, but Arendt's (1966) boomerang effect in which colonial policies "over there" came back to haunt Nazi expansionist policies, especially in the East, also usefully reminds us of the unique determination to wipe out a perceived race of people, rather than mass murder being the collateral damage of earlier colonial policies associated with colonial labour regimes.

1930, entitled *I'll Take my Stand: The South and the Agrarian Question* (Ransom *et al.* 1977). This work was hostile to laissez faire and corporate capitalism, but also to Communism and Fascism, and argued for the preservation of the Southern tradition through the promotion of small farmers and the partial redistribution of private property. It was argued that private ownership on a small scale promoted and reinforced authentic values, whereas corporate capitalism undermined tradition and local roots (Lanier 1977). One of the main intellectuals of the movement, Lyle Lanier (in Kolozi 2017: 51), argued that large corporations are the "instruments of economic fascism threatening American democracy". Frank Owsley (2001: 206) argued against what he called "twentieth century robber barons" who were buying up indebted small farms in the South, and promoting the government purchase of land from absentee landlords and the redistribution of land. While initially hopeful that the Franklin D. Roosevelt presidency would protect small farms, there was growing disillusionment that the main beneficiaries of his agricultural policies were large farmers, who benefited most from higher prices and restricted production.

In many respects, the Southern Agrarians revisited many of the themes and arguments of the intellectuals and politicians of the slave-owning South. Indeed, this new defence of the South was also racist and the proposed redistribution of land did not apply to African Americans, or indeed the poorest whites (Owsley 2001: 204; Kolozi 2017: chapter 3). While their views differed on specifics, some defended lynching, supported the Ku Klux Klan and those who lived into the 1960s condemned the Civil Rights movement (Hawley 2016: chapter 3; Kolozi 2017: chapter 3). While the aims of the movement reflected the specific history of the US South, the Southern Agrarians had a number of things in common with wider conservative ideas. These included the defence of private property against corporate capitalism, which was not dissimilar to the German ordoliberal tradition, the linking of small-scale production with tradition and community, the quest for a golden age that had been destroyed and the fear of Communism and Fascism. Perhaps above all, it championed what postwar conservative Richard Weaver called "social bond individualism" (quoted in Kolozi 2017: 91), which influenced later conservatives, including twenty-first-century anti-globalization conservatives, as we will see.

Alongside the Southern tradition, there also emerged a conservativism led by the very same corporate capitalists that the South considered their enemies. In the 1930s, this was tentative and it developed much further in the postwar period, but it emerged initially in response to Franklin D. Roosevelt's New Deal policies of the 1930s. This included the Liberty League in the North, founded in 1934 and committed to a rejection of the New Deal in the name of economic liberalism (Phillips-Fein 2009: chapter 1). In the West, and particularly California, agribusiness organized against struggles for labour rights. The Associated Farmers was an organization ostensibly committed to small-scale yeoman farmers and traditional American values, much like the Southern Agrarian tradition, but in contrast to those it was committed to the increasing dominance of agricultural plantations and the dominance of agribusiness (Kolozi 2017: chapter 3). These ideas – a combination of economic liberalism, corporate capitalism, antagonism to the New Deal and support for traditional values – became increasingly significant in the postwar era and in the context of the Cold War.

American conservatism after 1945

In the postwar period, and particularly under President Eisenhower, the Republican Party increasingly made its peace with the New Deal. This was a position shared by some conservative intellectuals such as Peter Viereck (2005), who argued for state intervention to defend cultural standards and virtue in the face of liberal individualism, and as a necessary bulwark against more radical ideas like socialism. In this way he argued that the New Deal represented an organic development in American society, as opposed to the more radical social engineering proposed by those on the liberal Left. At the same time, in terms of foreign policy, while there was hostility to Communism, this was accompanied by a "realist" policy of containment rather than outright confrontation, at least in Europe.

However, this acceptance of the New Deal and pragmatic anti-Communism was increasingly undermined by the emergence of new conservatives in the postwar period. Viereck himself was ostracized by these new conservatives in the 1950s and was accused of in effect being a New Deal liberal (Kolozi 2017: chapter 4). In this period, new conservative intellectuals were increasingly suspicious of the state and the New Deal and often conflated the two. Some of the most sophisticated conservative intellectuals drew on the influence of Burke, Tocqueville and others and argued for the need for community groups and civil society association as a necessary mediator between the state and the market. Russell Kirk (2008) was critical of large corporations and the state, and argued, like ordoliberals and the Southern Agrarians, that a capitalism of small-scale owners and proprietors was the way forward in the face of large-scale capitalism and the big state (Kolozi 2017: 128–9). Robert Nisbet (2010) echoed the concerns of Weber and Schumpeter and argued that capitalism had undermined its own institutional foundations, and corporate capitalism existed alongside both the big state and the dominant ideology of individual interest. Nisbet (2010), however, placed much of the blame for these developments on the state, rather than the competitive market, which might itself give rise to a growing concentration and centralization of capital. In this way, Kirk laid the grounds for a conservative promise of tradition, small-scale production and community while Nisbet blamed much of the negative developments of the period on the state. Both of these were central features of the fusionism, which emerged in this period.

Some of the postwar conservative Right embraced some of the positions of the inter-war Right, particularly the aversion to liberal decadence, the relativism of the West and the hostility to globalization. Schmitt (1962) argued that the Cold War was a division between two camps that shared the same sociotechnical organization, even suggesting that it was a conflict between private and state capitalism. But in terms of American conservatism, this was very much a minority position after 1945. As we saw in the previous section, Schmitt's hope for an anti-liberal re-enchantment through the rise of an elite politics and strong nationalist leaders gave rise to the even greater horrors of Nazi totalitarianism (Hayek 2001). The rejection of the total state of Nazism was applied after 1945 to the Soviet Union in the Cold War, and in the process conservatism in many respects made its peace with capitalism in the face of the threat of the totalitarianism of the Soviet Union (Friedrich & Brzezinksi 1965). In the United States it gave rise to "fusionism" (Buckley 1951; Meyer 1969), which combined suspicion of the domestic state and the New Deal and communism, support for the state in a robust foreign policy against (perceived and real) Communism, and support for traditional values such as family and religion. The conservative–libertarian fusion energized the Goldwater presidential campaign in 1964 and the victorious Reagan presidencies in the 1980s.

The challenge to both Communism and to the New Deal was central to the rise of this fusionism. US conservatives saw individual, "negative" freedom as the most important liberty and argued that property ownership was necessary for this to operate as it gave individuals independence from the state. In contrast, the New Deal's interventionism was considered a threat to individual freedom, and in this way postwar conservatism broke with both the warrior aristocrat and Southern Agrarian traditions, as well as Republican protectionism, all of which saw the state as necessary to restrict capitalism. By the early 1960s, a new conservatism emerged around the Arizona senator Barry Goldwater, whose economic advisers included the neoliberal economist Milton Friedman, and foreign policy advisers such as Stefan Possony and Gerhart Niemeyer, who rejected containment of Communism in favour of sharper confrontation (Drolet & Williams 2019a). Goldwater (2007: 81) was a critic of the New Deal at home, and the Republican Party's acceptance of, and compromise with, communism abroad. While he was defeated as the Republican presidential candidate in 1964, this was still a significant moment in the rise of a New Right that challenged both the New Deal and the containment of Communism, and which eventually paved the way for the electoral victory of Ronald Reagan in 1980. As we saw in Chapter 2, neoliberalism, particularly in its Chicago form, supported the so-called free market against discretionary state interventions such as those associated with the New Deal, and did so in the name of both freedom and economic efficiency.

This New Right was, however, about far more than the promotion of economic liberalism. As Horwitz (2013: 9) states, since 1980 "anti-establishment conservatism has manifested in an effective, if somewhat discordant alliance of re-energized anti-New Deal business, the Christian or evangelical right (embodying social conservatism), neoconservatism ... and the libertarian conservative tradition now embodied in the Tea Party movement." In the 1930s, though Roosevelt enjoyed widespread support, there were also significant pockets of opposition from some industrialists, leading Republicans and some Democrats. Some leading Republicans such as Robert Taft were critical of the New Deal, as were some industrialists and a growing number of conservative think tanks, such as the American Enterprise Institute and the Foundation for Economic Education (Phillips-Fein 2009). Nonetheless, by the 1950s both political parties were committed to New Deal policies. At the same time, the 1950s was a period of rabid anti-Communism, culminating in the McCarthy era, which purged different sectors of the economy of alleged Communist influences. This period saw the beginning of the conservative–libertarian fusion that characterized the New Right, led initially by William F. Buckley, who became the first president of the Intercollegiate Society of Individualists in 1953, and set up the influential organ the *National Review* in 1955. Founded in 1958 by Robert Welch, the John Birch Society claimed that between 40 to 60 per cent of the US government was controlled by Communists, and was hostile to what it claimed to be the "Communist" Civil Rights movement (McGirr 2001). Anti-Communism *per se* was not the exclusive preserve of the conservative Right, and many New Deal Democrats called for a more aggressive anti-Communist foreign policy.

The New Right, however, emerged around Goldwater, and the publication of his 1960 book *The Conscience of a Conservative*. Goldwater attacked welfare policies, and Civil Rights, not in the name of an overt racism, but rather in support of the right of local government freedom against encroaching federal government. This was very significant in terms of the breakdown of the coalition that gave rise to the New Deal (Katznelson 2014), and the rise of a New Right. The New Deal won the support of Southern Democrats in the 1930s, in part through playing down Civil Rights. The price of support for neo-Keynesian public and social policies was therefore a failure to fully confront the question of racism and segregation, particularly (though not exclusively) in the South (although we qualify this argument in Chapter 8). This uneasy tension was sometimes exposed, such as with the move to promote full racial integration of the armed forces in 1948, and especially with the decision in the *Brown v. Board of Education* case in 1954, which outlawed the segregation of public schools. Goldwater (2007: 31) argued that he supported the objectives of the *Brown* case, but he was not prepared "to impose that judgment of mine on the people of Mississippi or South Carolina". The conservative critique of such cases echoed those of disillusioned Southern Democrats that, in the words of Charles Wallace Collins (founder of the States' Rights Democratic Party, or Dixiecrats) rejected both "Negro equality" and "state capitalism" (cited in Horwitz 2013: 57). In the 1944 election, around 80 per cent of Southern whites voted for Roosevelt, but by 1948 only 50 per cent voted for Truman. In that latter election, the Dixiecrats won Louisiana, Mississippi, Alabama and South Carolina. By 1964, the Goldwater election, all of these states plus Georgia were won by the Republicans. Although these states (except South Carolina) were lost in 1968, this was to George Wallace's American Independent Party and not to the Democrats. This reflected a gradual breakdown in support among Southern whites for the Democrats, and by the time of Ronald Reagan's second presidential election victory in 1984, the majority of these had shifted to supporting the Republican Party (Horwitz 2013: 56–7).

Although the New Deal remained in place, the 1960s saw growing anxiety around what some considered the growing encroachment of the federal state on the lives of individuals, alongside growing polarization around the question of race. Conservatives exploited these concerns. Employing a growing populist rhetoric, conservatives appealed to the "forgotten American", to Middle America, to those (largely white) men said to be increasingly left out of American society at the expense of a new liberal elite, welfare recipients, anti-war protestors, rioters, students and so on. This was central to the Goldwater campaign in 1964 and Nixon's Southern strategy employed from 1968 onwards (Phillips 1969). Religion – and specifically the rise of a new Christian, predominantly Protestant Right – was a central part of this populism. Though previously relatively apolitical, by the early 1980s Christian evangelicals were the most politically engaged religious group among Christians (Horwitz 2013: 78–9). Like the question of race, this was partly a response to federal state encroachment, including the legalization of abortion.

It was in this context that the neoconservative movement emerged in the 1960s. As was outlined in Chapter 2, much of the concerns of this group of intellectuals in the post-Cold War period concerns America's engagement in the international order, and how the re-moralization of the republic internationally is linked to this ideal domestically. Neoconservatism thus emerged in the 1960s and was critical of US containment rather than roll-back of Communism, but it also challenged Lynden Johnson's Great Society programme, and the rise of a new class that promoted relativism and nihilism, and culminated in the rise of student radicalism, the counter-culture, Black Power and welfare dependency (see Chapter 2). Moynihan's (1965) report *The Negro Family: The Case for National*

Action was indicative of the New Right argument that African American poverty was a cultural problem caused by high rates of illegitimacy, welfare participation and self-destruction. Social welfare was not about enhancing the life chances of under-privileged groups, but rather reflected the growth of an increasingly self-sustaining liberal, metropolitan elite. At its heart was a critique of collectivism, which was regarded as being part of an overt (the Soviet Union) and covert (the New Deal) expansion of the Communist ideal.

But as we saw in Chapter 2, even neoconservatives – the conservative faction most supportive of capitalism and indeed neoliberalism – had their concerns about capitalism. In particular they worried that while capitalism promoted both the (supposed) freedom of the individual and efficiency through wealth creation, it was far less successful at promoting virtue, a principle needed to allow society to cohere around shared values, rather than individual market calculation (Kristol 1970). In other words, conservatives constantly feared that the republican tradition was under threat because of capitalism's excessive individualism, relativism and expansion, which undermined tradition, established orders and the nation. The challenge to the welfare state was important here and specifically the argument that it was not only providing social safety nets to the deserving poor, but was showing compassion for the undeserving poor, and thus encouraging welfare dependency (Moynihan 1965). Neoconservatives hoped that welfare reform and the promotion of supply-side economics would restore the virtue of the individual entrepreneur, though there remained an ongoing tension between market individualism and social cohesion. Nonetheless, like neoliberals, neoconservatives believed that the spirit of competition was essential for the resurgence of the entrepreneur, and this included the promotion of free trade and the end of protectionism, as well as financial liberalization, as occurred in the Reagan era and beyond.

In effect, then, neoconservatives promoted a cultural revolution, in which the liberal elite is challenged and the welfare state restructured. The New Deal state has produced a culture of dependency, and not unrelated to this a white liberal romanticization of "blackness", part of which involves seeing crime as somehow more normal than employment (Himmelfarb 1995). The neoliberal focus is on individual responsibility, and thus welfare retrenchment is not enough, for there needs to be a cultural shift, part of which is the establishment of a conservative welfare state. This would involve provision for those unable to work, such as the old and the ill, but also the recovery of American values such as hard work and family values. In this way, the welfare state is regarded less as an institution to promote social solidarity by providing social safety nets for the poor, and more one in which it acts as a moral tutor. It thus "substitutes the 'rehabilitative' and 'solidarist' rationale that underpinned the post-war approach to social security for a retributive one by which welfare and social security benefits are made conditional upon certain moral behaviours" (Drolet 2011: 113–14; see also Cooper 2017).

Neoconservatism thus sees a central role for the state in acting as a moral tutor, while also being prepared to deal with enemies both at home and abroad. It draws on Carl Schmitt's critique of liberalism, in which politics is based on a distinction between "us" and "them", "friend" and "enemy". As Drolet argues:

> Neoconservatism negotiates the tension between its commitment to market capitalism and liberal democracy on the one hand, and its commitment to conservative socio-cultural values on the other, by means of a symbolic politics of security that places the myth of the undesirable other and the enemy of society at the centre of public policy debates. By doing so, neoconservative practices of statecraft translate into an executive-centred conception of politics in which the elite must produce social order through the sovereign allocation of right and wrong. Whether it is the demoralised street criminal, the welfare cheat, the illegal immigrant, the godless communist or the religious fanatic, the moment of antagonism and unease prompted by the identification of the enemy forces the liberal state to abandon its claim to value neutrality and give normative substance to the relationship between protection and obedience. It forces a transcendent element of irrationalism not admitting of compromise into the public sphere that negates liberal and pluralist conceptions of politics altogether.   (Drolet 2011: 119)

At around the same time as the emergence of neoconservatism, neoliberalism emerged to challenge the premise of the New Deal. This made the theoretical case for "smaller" government at home, through a challenge to the expansion of welfare policies, an argument that overlapped with neoconservative concerns about the future of the nuclear family led by a male breadwinner (see Cooper 2017). Alongside the anti-inflationary policies introduced towards the end of the Carter administration, above all the interest rate hikes under Federal Reserve Chair Paul Volcker from 1979, the Reagan presidency was the start of the triumph of the conservative fusionist movement, with its commitment to neoliberal economic policy, anti-Communism and conservative cultural policies. This included tax cuts for the rich, enhanced military spending and attempts to cut relief for and change the behaviour of the poor (Murray 1984).

Although often now seen as a golden age for American conservatism, the Reagan years were also a source of some discontent for American conservatives, from neoconservative frustration with Reagan's "appeasement" of Gorbachev (now largely "forgotten"), through to the running of annual deficits of an unprecedented size, in both government budgets and international trade. These deficits were financed by capital inflows to the US, initially attracted by higher interest rates and the continued dominant role of the dollar in the international economic order. Suspicion of Reagan quickly gave rise to triumphalism as Communism collapsed in the Bush, Sr. years and American hegemony was uncontested in the 1990s. But these seeming triumphs still hid some continued tensions. The end of the Cold War led to conservative disagreements over the US's international role, with older paleoconservatives, now organized around Pat Buchanan in the 1992 and 1996 Republican primary campaign, arguing the case for a less interventionist and indeed isolationist international role in the name of "America first". Neoconservatives on the other hand argued that the principle of America first should operate in the international as well as domestic sphere, and this meant that America should use its exceptional status to lead the post-Cold War order. In particular, the decadence of the 1990s was replaced by the post-2001 renewal of what amounted to empire through a "neo-Reaganite" foreign policy, so that republican virtue could exist alongside the so-called free market (Kristol & Kagan 1996).[2]

For the paleoconservatives, this was just a new version of Wilsonian liberal internationalism (Francis 2005). This division also expressed itself domestically as well, not least as the Clinton administration effectively accepted neoliberal economic policies but merged these with socially liberal policies, albeit with racialized policies of incarceration (Wacquant 2009). What this in effect meant, then, was that the liberal managerial class associated with the New Deal and Great Society programmes had not gone away and in fact had expanded, certainly in the Clinton years and to some extent even under Reagan. In effect, Reagan had failed to win cultural power and the Right had lost the cultural wars (Buchanan 1992). Even worse, power still lay in the hands of a liberal elite, as was shown by the Clinton administration and his promotion of globalization, including the signing of the North American Free Trade Agreement in 1994 (agreed under the Bush I administration) and involvement in wars in the former Yugoslavia. Neoconservatives regarded the Clinton era as years of half-hearted involvement in international affairs (PNAC 1997), but reinvigoration came in the form of American responses to the terrorist attacks of September 2001 and the wars in Afghanistan and Iraq (Kagan 2004, 2008). The Obama administration was a return in some respects to American weakness, though the intervention in Libya saw agreement between Democrat liberal internationalists and Republican hawks, including neoconservatives (see Walt 2011). Paleoconservatives on the

2. It should be noted in passing that this call for a neo-Reaganite foreign policy is based on selective memory on the part of neoconservatives, some of whom accused Reagan of appeasement of the Soviet Union in the early 1980s. See, for instance, Podhoretz (1983).

other hand saw this alliance as indicative of a wider Wilsonian consensus in which Democrats and Republicans were committed to liberal internationalism and the ideology of globalism (see below). We now turn our attention to the conservative anti-globalization ideas of the paleoconservatives.

Paleoconservatism and anti-globalization

Paleoconservatism was a term coined by Thomas Fleming and Paul Gottfried in 1986, in order to distinguish it from other factions within American conservatism and above all neoconservatism (Scotchie 1999). Much of the dispute between these branches of conservative thought developed after the Reagan presidency but the initial selection of Mel Bradford as Chair of the National Endowment for the Humanities in 1981 was a sign of things to come. Bradford is regarded as one of the first paleoconservatives and his selection caused some consternation in conservative circles because he was a supporter of the old Confederacy and had even compared Abraham Lincoln to Hitler (Will 1981). In this regard, the paleoconservatives were the heirs of Richard Weaver, an American conservative who had drawn on the decline thesis of European inter-war conservatives briefly discussed in the first section. In the case of Weaver, he Americanized this thesis and argued that the American South represented the kind of ordered society that had largely been displaced in Europe (Weaver 1948). Indeed, he argued that anti-segregationist policies would lead to the kind of mass society that meant the decline of the US. Bradford had supported the segregationist governor and presidential candidate George Wallace in the 1960s. Criticizing the appointment of Bradford, the leading neoconservative Irving Kristol favoured William Bennett, and Bradford withdrew. This was the start of a bitter dispute between paleo- and neoconservatives, culminating in divisions over liberal wars of intervention in the post-Cold War world (see Frum 2003).

In some respects, the paleoconservatives looked for a return to the right-wing isolationism that had existed in the 1930s, associated with John Flynn and the America First Committee, which opposed US entry into the Second World War. Flynn argued that Roosevelt represented the extension of Fascism in the United States, and that this ironically occurred in the name of anti-Fascism, an argument sometimes deployed by conservatives against so-called Left liberal fascists today (Goldberg 2008). In the post-Cold War world, the principle of isolationism was taken up by Pat Buchanan, who unsuccessfully attempted to secure the Republican ticket for the 1992 and 1996 presidential elections.[3] In this

3. In addition there was the independent populist candidate Ross Perot, who advocated protectionism, and whose vice presidential candidate, James Stockdale, was a paleoconservative.

period, he outlined the main themes of the paleoconservative worldview, identifying various symptoms of US decline, which for him meant the decline of US manufacturing, too much immigration, the erosion of solid cultural foundations, US military over-reach and nihilism (Buchanan 1999). His isolationism also rested on arguments about the international sphere, such as that the Second World War was unnecessary and that Britain should take a great deal of the blame for it, and that the US was the true aggressor in Eastern Europe as NATO expanded further. He also attacked the NAFTA agreement and, invoking the spirit of Alexander Hamilton, argued that free trade was not a good thing and that "no nation has ever risen to pre-eminence through free trade" (Buchanan 1994). Like Huntington, Buchanan argued that mass immigration was a product of a porous southern border, and a combination of low "native" birth rates and high immigration was a deliberate attempt to "dissolve the people", which would lead to the death of the West (Buchanan 2004). By 2011, in the context of an African American president, Buchanan despaired that the US was in effect committing suicide and would not last until 2025, unless there was a conservative counter-attack, which would include the end of mass immigration, the closure of overseas military bases, protectionism and conservative policies in the culture wars (Buchanan 2011). He also expressed fear for what he called "the end of white America" (Buchanan 2011: chapter 4). Although the targets have changed over time, this echoes a long history of anti-immigrant rhetoric in the US. This stretches back to the (oddly named) Native American Party, or Know Nothing Movement, in the 1850s, through to the periodic upsurge in support for the Ku Klux Klan (post-1865, 1915 and in the 1950s/1960s).[4]

While Buchanan is identified as the main public figure associated with paleoconservatism, there are also a number of intellectuals allied to it, above all Paul Gottfried and the late Samuel Francis. These intellectuals link US decline to what they call the liberal managerial state, and show how this has given rise to a global, or transnational, post-American elite (see Drolet & Williams 2019b). Like other conservative traditions, paleoconservatives are concerned to reconcile capitalism with tradition. While paleoconservativism had little problem with anti-Communism in the Cold War, it was far more suspicious of interventionism and internationalist commitments in the post-Cold War world. While private enterprise and capitalism should be supported, free trade and internationalism have undermined the American republic. Samuel Francis (2016) argued that American identity had been undermined by an alliance of a managerial elite and

---

4. This includes notorious racist tracts such as that produced by Lothrop Stoddard (2019) in 1920. Stoddard was a Northern member of the Ku Klux Klan who was later a Nazi sympathizer who spent time in Germany. He advocated segregated societies based on supposed biological racial distinctions, an argument considered in the context of race science in Chapter 6.

multinational companies, neither of whom put America first. As we saw above, inter-war European conservatives decried the ways in which the mass state was weakened by competing interests in civil society, and thus led to weak states like the Weimar Republic. The American paleoconservative tradition instead argues that the postwar managerial state is strong and has led to new sources of social power. This argument owes something to the theory of a new class. Neoliberals were critical of self-interested state elites that represented no one but themselves (Buchanan & Tullock 1962), while neoconservatives around Irving Kristol (1995) followed Schumpeter (1976) and talked of a new class that had emerged within the state. The paleoconservatives argued something similar but distinctive, namely that liberal elites dominate and exercise power through control of cultural, educational and legal institutions. In this way liberal relativism is problematic not only because it undermines social order, but also because it is a new form of power and domination within that order. Managerial liberalism takes place both domestically and internationally, and globalization is the product of liberal rule and power and not – as in many Left accounts – simply the economic rule of capital. In particular, globalization combines rootless cosmopolitanism, bureaucratic and legal power, transnational capital and borderless cultural flows. This does not lead to a weakened nation state so much as a new era of global governance, energised only by abstract principles and not by any concrete content. Thus, international human rights undermines appeals to particularist or nativist values, and in this way global liberalism is an extension of domestic liberalism. Paleoconservatives in the US (alongside various European conservatives) are hostile to international institutions and commitments and, above all, liberal wars of intervention (Gottfried 2001; Dugin 2017). This is a particular interpretation of the theory of the new class, one that draws on and develops James Burnham's contention that a managerial revolution had taken place that undermined the virtue of the entrepreneur. Unlike Schumpeter (1976), however, Burnham argued that this development was reversible, and indeed had to be reversed in order to prevent the self-destructive suicide of the Western world (Burnham 2014). While this argument is still in many respects compatible with neoconservative and neoliberal critiques of self-interested state elites in the context of the New Deal and Great Society, paleoconservatives argue that that this liberal managerial state persisted *after* Reagan and the end of the Cold War. Neoliberals and neoconservatives argued that the American republic had been undermined by the Left liberalism associated with Roosevelt and Johnson, and it needed to be revived through the promotion of an American bourgeois populism committed to legal but not economic or cultural egalitarianism (Kristol 1970). For paleoconservatives, the Reagan takeover failed because of changing sociocultural conditions; in the nineteenth century classical liberalism co-existed with traditional aristocracy "in a still partly aristocratic world" (Gottfried 2001: 136).

In contrast, the culture of the current state is based on a purely instrumental managerialism in which individualism and meritocracy are paramount, and so traditional values no longer take precedence (Francis 2016). Neoconservative hopes that the bourgeois ethos could be revived through a conservative welfare state simply exacerbated the problem because it enhanced the managerial state rather than dismantled it. Neoconservatives thus fall for the trap of separating the new class from wider political-economic structures of power, and specifically attempt to separate the new class from government administration and multinational companies.

For paleoconservatives, then, the new class identified by neoconservatives did not lose power with the rise of the New Right. This new class is part of the cosmopolitan elite that has betrayed the American republic. In particular, this elite promotes globalization, allies itself with rootless multinational companies who invest overseas and outsource production, and promotes immigration and multiculturalism – and, we will see in the next chapter, also promotes rule by experts. The end result is a political economy and culture that cannot be separated from each other. What has occurred is deindustrialization and the undermining of traditional American culture, and in particular a white middle America that is squeezed between a cosmopolitan corporate elite and poor ethnic minorities (Francis 1994). State elites themselves claim to be the prisoners of various interest groups but in fact these liberal social planners "hide rather than flaunt the power they exercise. This however does not render their power any less real, though it is not individuals but a class of experts who speak out against inequality and monopolize this rule" (Gottfried 2001: xi).

Buchanan thus argued that that the economic liberalism of the 1980s also saw the rise of social liberalism that was epitomized by the loathed Clinton administrations of the 1990s, and talked of the need to win the culture wars (Buchanan 1992). He emphasized the need to save America from foreign do-gooders, bureaucrats, career victims and corporate elites, so that the market can re-embed itself within virtuous conservative traditions. This meant that the US should not become embroiled in liberal wars of intervention and should leave burdensome international agreements. Samuel Francis (2016) expanded on these arguments and suggested that the postwar liberal managerial state had become embroiled in the "development" and "modernization" of the Third World, with the result that new regimes had been created that had no ties to local and/or national communities. Seen in this way, "Islamic fundamentalism" was a perfectly understandable reaction to the homogenization associated with the global development project, and thus in some respects mirrored the particularism of the American paleoconservative project.

Both globalization and development are based on abstract universalist principles derived from Kant, and not the real general will of the people. The notion that universal principles can be derived from the idea that no rational person would reject such principles (Habermas 2003: 110) is a myth, and in effect leads to the imposition of particular liberal universalist values on diverse cultural communities. Given Buchanan's more favourable view of this historical figure (see further below), Francis (1992) interestingly places much of the blame for this on a tradition derived from Alexander Hamilton, who is linked to the American Northeast, and promoted industrialization and a national currency at the expense of the traditional agrarian South. For Francis, this gave way in the post-Civil War period to the ideas of Manifest Destiny, territorial expansion, the imperialism of Teddy Roosevelt and ultimately to the liberal internationalism of Woodrow Wilson (Francis 1992: 21). This paleoconservative critique of Wilsonian liberal internationalism is central to its critique of contemporary globalization. Gottfried argues that involvement in the First World War from 1917 led to an unjust peace, and was in part caused by the influence of a white English Protestant tradition in the Northeastern US, as against the influence of German Protestants in the rest of the US (Gottfried 2007b, 2011: 36). Thus, the claim to liberal universalism was actually the imposition of an ethnic nativism on others. This was apparent in the support for segregation and immigration controls at home by these same internationalists, which particularly targeted Eastern European Jews and Southern European Catholics, and the shift to isolationism between the wars, which saw disproportionate representation among white Anglo-Saxon Protestants. Liberal internationalism was not universalist at all, but in effect the particularist imposition of one culture onto others – an argument we came across in the context of contemporary globalization in Chapter 2.

Moreover, there is a link between liberal universalism abroad and the expansion of the managerial state at home, as wars for human rights overseas also lead to demands for the extension of citizenship at home. Seen in this way, there is a close connection between warfare abroad and welfare at home. But there is a further reason, which is that attempts to export human rights overseas also lead to attempts to "import" human rights through liberal immigration policies. The European migrations to the US of the nineteenth century were perfectly acceptable because the US "derives from and is an integral part of European civilization" and the US "should remain European" (Council of Conservative Citizens 2005). In the twentieth century, in contrast, the liberal managerial state has expanded non-European migration, and this has led to a fear of "cultural extinction" (Buchanan 2002; Francis 2001). The result is precisely the mass society that conservatives feared in the early twentieth century, where the rise of (political) liberalism and democracy (and socialism) lead to a mass society, and the dissolution of all class and race differences into a massified population with no common identity or meaningful political will. What is needed, then, is a populism that speaks for the abandoned Middle America, and that champions limited federal government, local and state government, a true free market promoting entrepreneurship and a return of the true individualism associated with classical (economic) liberalism (Francis 1994). In contrast, the liberal managerial state's promotion of globalization has meant that largely white and middle-class Americans "find that their jobs are insecure, their savings stripped of value, neighbourhoods and schools and homes unsafe, their elected leaders indifferent and often crooked, their moral beliefs and religious professions and social codes under perpetual attack even from their own government, their children taught to despise what they believe, their very identity and heritage as a people threatened, and their future ... uncertain" (Francis 1992: 19).

The American republic has been lost since the New Deal and even the Reagan counter-revolution has not undermined the liberal managerial state. The task of American conservatives is not to accommodate themselves with this state, but rather to destroy it. This is not dissimilar to the worldview of sometime Trump confidante, ally and former administration team member Steve Bannon. Influenced by Strauss and Howe's (1997) account of history, in which the US has gone through four periods of crisis, namely independence in 1776, Civil War in the 1860s, the Second World War in the 1940s and the period from 2008 onwards. Each period of around 80 years is characterized by a high, or period of strong institutionalism and weak individualism, followed by an awakening and then unravelling, in which institutions are increasingly challenged by individuals, culminating in crisis (Howe 2017). A crisis period is one where there is a creative destruction of public institutions. Like a number of other conservative traditions that can be traced back to Weber and Schumpeter, Bannon argues that capitalism needs to be moored in particular cultural traditions, and in particular the Judeo-Christian tradition. While critical of the state capitalist tradition in Russia and China, Bannon also rejects the libertarian capitalism associated with "neoliberal capitalism", which in effect reduces people to commodities and leads to secularization. Like Gottfried, he argues that neoliberalism has given rise to a global managerial elite where "people in New York ... feel closer to people in London and in Berlin" (cited in Feder 2017). Bannon argues that this liberal managerial state must be destroyed.

Furthermore, this state has been at the forefront of the promotion of globalization, and indeed has led to a convergence between Left and Right on economic issues, and economic and cultural decline as a consequence (Gottfried 2001). What is instead needed is a reaffirmation of American cultural identity against the liberal individualism, multiculturalism and relativism fostered by the managerial state (Francis 1994: 203). For Francis (1992) "(t)his is the true meaning of 'America First'. America must be first not only among other nations but first among the other (individual or class or sectional) interests of its people." Thus "anti-globalization" abroad is intrinsically linked to "anti-globalization" at home, and America should be seen not as an abstraction that represents the equality of all of humanity, but rather a specific, historical community. Pat Buchanan thus suggests that immigration has changed the cultural cohesion of the US and by 2011 argued that it was committing cultural suicide with the possibility of the end of white America. In order to reverse this trend he proposed that immigration should be ended and all illegal immigrants removed, the closure of American military bases overseas, massive government spending cuts, economic protectionism and a renewed conservative counter-attack in the culture wars (Buchanan 2002, 2011).

Like Francis, Buchanan linked the dangers of multiculturalism, which was a threat to the US cultural heritage, to the dangers of free trade, which threatened its economic strength. The US's cultural heritage needed to be restored through the promotion of a white, European, Christian nationalism. But while Francis argued that this reflected an American tradition that stretched back to Hamilton, Buchanan is far more willing to invoke the spirit in a more favourable way, linking Hamilton's case for protectionism to develop American manufacturing (Buchanan 2003), arguing that "no nation has risen to pre-eminence through free trade" (Buchanan 1994). We will see in Chapter 7 that this difference is not a minor one and goes to the heart of the limits of the conservative anti-globalization associated with American paleoconservatism.

But first we need to expand a little more on the paleoconservative view regarding globalization. In terms of postwar foreign policy, American realism was essentially one committed to the American liberal tradition, but combined this at times with a pragmatic – if often highly racialized – *Realpolitik*, even as this led to all kinds of aggressive and belligerent policies during the Cold War. It was precisely this pragmatism that concerned neoconservatives, and so even Henry Kissinger was criticized for his 1970s policy of detente with the Soviet Union, because it underestimated Soviet ambition and in effect compromised on the American principle of universalism. As we have seen, this is precisely the case made for a neo-Reaganite foreign policy by neoconservatives, which involves a re-moralization of America and American universalism both at home and abroad. In contrast, the paleoconservative position combines nationalism and political realism in a different way, one based not on supposed universal categories but instead on the reality of a plurality of cultures in the international order (Gottfried 2007a). In this way, realism is based not on pragmatic strategy at a particular point in time, but rather on the integrity of the American nation in the context of unavoidable cultural difference. In this regard at least, the paleoconservative worldview has some overlap with Huntington's (1996) "clash of civilizations" thesis, discussed in Chapter 2. For Steve Bannon, the West faces a war against multiculturalism, including against "jihadist Islamic fascism" (cited in

Feder 2017). The argument here is that the problem of terrorism is not one based on politics and various movements that have different grievances and mobilize in the name of Islam (*Islamism*), but rather that in some respects these groups' image of themselves is in fact correct, and they do indeed represent the authentic face of *Islam*. This is an argument made by Trump associates and former administration members Michael Flynn and Sebastien Gorka (Shariatmadari 2017), both of whom suggest that various Islamist groups, despite their radically different agendas, have the capacity to unite against "the far enemy", namely the West.

This does beg question about how cultures can peacefully co-exist, but for now we need only emphasize that this worldview is sharply different from the neoconservative one. It is one that rejects the idea that the US is committed to a perpetual crusade in the world order based on a mythical notion of democratic globalism (Gottfried 2001). It therefore follows that – like Schmitt argued – the US should disengage from international commitments and thus terminate all foreign aid, leave the North American Free Trade Agreement (NAFTA), leave the North Atlantic Treaty Organization (NATO) and instead uphold a conservative vision of statehood, as should every other country. For this reason, Buchanan (2013) even suggests that Vladimir Putin might be "one of us", namely a paleoconservative. Although he does not directly answer his own question, he does state that:

> He is seeking to redefine the "Us vs. Them" world conflict of the future as one in which conservatives, traditionalists and nationalists of all continents and countries stand up against the cultural and ideological imperialism of what he sees as a decadent west.
>
> "We do not infringe on anyone's interests," said Putin, "or try to teach anyone how to live." The adversary he has identified is not the America we grew up in, but the America we live in, which Putin sees as pagan and wildly progressive.

Paleoconservatism and Trump

It is probably fair to say that paleoconservatism as an organized political movement does not exist, at least in the same way that neoconservatism does, and indeed Paul Gottfried (2017) has stressed that while he prefers Trump to the neoconservatives, he is still no enthusiastic supporter of Trump. While there are various journals that essentially hold a paleoconservative worldview, above all *Chronicles* and *The American Conservative*, and there are others such as *Taki's* and *American Renaissance* that are more overtly white supremacist, none of these appear to have directly influenced Trump and those around him.

On the other hand, there is also the direct link between Samuel Francis and Paul Gottfried to Patrick Buchanan, and Steven Bannon and Stephen Miller appear to have some knowledge of, and are influenced by, paleoconservative ideas. During the 2016 presidential election campaign, the paleoconservative William Lind met Donald Trump and gave him a copy of his co-written book *The Next Conservative* (Weyrich & Lind 2009). In this book, the authors rejected liberal wars of intervention, regretted growing trade and budget deficits under Bush II, decried deindustrialization, and called for the restoration of the primacy of Western, Judeo-Christian culture in the US (Weyrich & Lind 2007, 2009). They also called for a new conservative onslaught on the supposed Marxist influence in the culture wars, control over US borders and a revival of the Southern agrarian tradition[5] (Weyrich & Lind 2007). However, the influence of this book on the Trump administration is unlikely to have been that great.

But more important is the fact that we can identify, paraphrasing Oakeshott, a paleoconservative disposition, which talks to the current Republican mood, and this is why we need to pay so much attention to paleoconservative ideas. Above all, paleoconservative hostility to free trade and immigration, suspicion of international commitments and liberal wars of intervention, the promotion of economic nationalism and protectionism and the return of American manufacturing jobs sounds remarkably like Donald Trump's programme during his presidential campaign. Although there is a history of conflict between Buchanan and Trump, specifically over the Reform Party presidential candidacy in 2000 when Trump was far more socially liberal (Kornacki 2018), Buchanan (2016) himself argued in 2016 that Trump is "Middle America's Messenger". Trump (2017) argued at his inaugural speech that "We must protect our borders from the ravages of other countries making our products, stealing our companies and destroying our jobs. Protection will lead to great prosperity and strength." In the summer of 2017, he promised that "I will bring jobs back and get wages up" (cited in Greenhouse 2017).

Before his election victory, the conservative *National Review* (2016) contended that "Trump is a philosophically unmoored political opportunist who would trash the broad ideological consensus within the GOP in favor of a free-floating populism with strongman overtones." This is based on a narrow understanding of conservativism, which reduces it to a pragmatic acceptance of, and cautious adaptation to, the status quo. As Chapters 1 and 2 showed, this leaves aside those cases in history where conservatives have argued that tradition and hierarchy

---

5. Indeed, under the pseudonym Thomas Hobbes (2014), Lind wrote a novel about the break-up of the republic and the restoration of slavery, and has frequently suggested that the problem of race in the US was caused by the fall-out from the reconstruction era, rather than slavery or white supremacism.

have become so distorted that there is a need for reconstruction, rather than cautious acceptance, an argument that overlaps with Huntington's (1957) characterization of *doctrinal* conservatism in times of perceived reversal and decline. Seen in this way, Trump and the paleoconservatives are doctrinal conservatives that attempt to reconstruct the US in the context of the loss of the true republican tradition.

But this still begs the question of who exactly are the Middle American Radicals and, more specifically, who voted for Trump in the 2016 presidential election? Put slightly differently, what is the relationship between the socioeconomic changes that we considered in Chapter 3 (deindustrialization, peripheralization, growing inequality, stagnant real wages, growing household debt, uneven regional development) and the election result of 2016? If we look at some aggregate figures, the election appears to represent something close to business as usual. Trump won 306 and Clinton 232 of the electoral college seats, though Clinton with almost 66 million votes won the popular vote – 48.5 per cent compared to Trump's almost 63 million or 46.4 per cent. Turnout has been estimated at 55.7 per cent, which is quite low but in line with general recent trends other than 2008 (CNN 2016). Around 91 per cent voted for the political party that they normally vote for (McQuarrie 2017: 124). This fact has led some political scientists to conclude that "Trump won because the overwhelming majority of Republicans voted for the Republican candidate" and that therefore 2016 was a more or less ordinary election (Bartels 2016). In other words, for all the talk of this election representing a realignment in American electoral politics, the result was actually consistent with previous ones. The implication is that talk of a 2016 revolt against globalization is not borne out by the election result. Further fuel could be added to this argument by focusing on the question of timing, for the socio-economic changes outlined in Chapter 3, such as deindustrialization and growing inequality, have been occurring since the 1970s and 1980s, and though the post-2008 period might have exacerbated these, the actual election outcome was consistent with previous elections.

However, this focus on the aggregate numbers and the election result leaves out some important issues. Above all, while the Republican vote held up, Trump was a far from ordinary Republican candidate, at least judged by the pro-free trade, pro-military intervention candidates of recent years. Similarly, on the Democrat side, Bernie Sanders ran a campaign – unsuccessful in that he failed to become the candidate but still one that exceeded all expectations – that was far to the left of any Democrat candidate in recent years. In both cases this did impact on the election campaign, above all in the massive increase in small donations for both the Trump and Sanders campaigns. This reflected the fact that much of the electorate did not consider either party as representing their interests, and so gave small contributions (less than $200) to outside candidates on a large scale

(Ferguson *et al.* 2018). The mid-term 2014 Congressional elections were much more business-as-usual elections, and though these do often see low turnouts, in 2014 these were unprecedented, with massive drops compared to 2012, and rates of voting in some areas not seen since the early nineteenth century when the ballot was restricted (see Burnham & Ferguson 2014). That the turnout stood up fairly well in 2016 was more a reflection that at least one of the candidates was different – in this sense, the timing of the revolt was significant.

Indeed, if we focus on small donations, the usual historical pattern is that Democrats are far more reliant on these than the Republicans, who tend to get more money from big business. Once Sanders was out of the equation, Trump in effect reversed this practice and it was Clinton who was the favoured candidate for most of big business, and Trump the recipient of small donations. Trump of course also relied on money from his own personal fortune, and as the campaign entered its final stage, business poured money into Senate Republican campaigns, the results of which correlated closely with the presidential results (Ferguson *et al.* 2018: 20). Trump also received increasing amounts of money late in his campaign from the Mercer family, followed by a whole range of donations from various sectors of big business, both before and after his victory, the latter of which was used to finance inaugural celebrations (Ferguson *et al.* 2018: 43–7). This pattern may reflect in part the fact that Trump (in some respects like previous Republican candidates) was in many ways a populist candidate but also a plutocrat president, a question we will consider further in Chapter 6. But the fact remains that Trump the candidate did represent something different from the recent Republican norm, and this was reflected in campaign donations. Moreover, the 2000-plus counties won by Trump represent a much lower share of GDP than the areas that voted for Clinton, and so in this regard we can says that "Trump won the economic periphery while Clinton won the economic core" (McQuarrie 2017: 123).

But also in terms of the details of the results, there were significant changes. Exit poll data suggest that while Clinton won places of higher wealth, the vote was still differentiated so that Clinton won lower-income voters as a whole, albeit by much smaller margins than Obama. Thus Clinton won 53 to 40 per cent among those earning under $30,000, and 52 to 41 per cent among those earning $30,000 to $49,999 a year, while those on $50,000 to $99,999 dollars went 49 to 46 per cent for Trump (CNN 2016). Trump and Clinton won broadly similar levels of support among higher-income groups. Unionized workers who actually voted tended to opt for Hillary Clinton, albeit by small margins, and were less pro-Democrat than in the past (CNN 2016). What was significant, however, was continued relatively low turnout in the election, and a (small) continuation of a trend in which the Democrats lost some of their former working-class base, particularly in Rustbelt states. Indeed, in the period 2008 to 2016, there were significant declines in union membership in Wisconsin, Michigan and Pennsylvania (Ferguson *et al.* 2018: 19). Trump was more successful in winning votes among those who had an unfavourable view of both candidates, around half of whom had a favourable view of Obama (Anderson 2017; Mound 2017), and insofar as sections of workers supported Trump and had an impact on the election, it was significant above all in Michigan, Wisconsin and Pennsylvania, where a swing at the margins helped Trump to victory in all those states (McQuarrie 2016). Although there was a 16 per cent national shift among poorer voters to Trump, in the Rustbelt Five (Iowa, Michigan, Pennsylvania, Ohio and Wisconsin) a 10.6 per cent point swing to Trump was significantly less than the 21.7 per cent swing away from the Democrats in the same states (Kilibarda & Roithmayr 2016). These were all solid Democrat states that voted Obama in 2008, and again though less enthusiastically in 2012, and defeat in three of them was enough to clinch the Whitehouse for Trump. Clinton's support fell among all ethnic groups, and not just white voters – indeed the 13 per cent decline for Clinton among Rustbelt white voters was almost matched by the black, indigenous and people-of-colour vote in the same territories, which saw an 11.5 per cent decline. In the Rustbelt Five, Clinton lost 1.35 million votes and only 590,000 shifted to Trump, while the rest either voted for a third candidate or stayed at home (Kilibarda & Roithmayr 2016). In many respects, there was limited expectation that President Trump in office would lead to social improvement, and given that these people had very little to lose in the first place, they often expressed a kind of negative solidarity whereby if they have to suffer, then so should everyone else (Davies 2016a).

The complexity of these arguments has led to some debate over the extent to which the Trump vote was about materialist, economic issues or ideational, cultural issues. For example, Inglehart and Norris (2019) find that support for Trump is best explained not by rising economic insecurity but rather by a cultural backlash to progressive social change. In this way the result reflected longer-term trends in which some of the electorate voted for a backlash against cultural globalization, and specifically cosmopolitan and multiculturalism. Thomas Frank (2004) has long argued that the culture wars have provided an ideological cover whereby workers vote against their own (self/class) interests. As Frank himself suggests, the Democrats have offered little more than the Republicans in government in this regard. But, despite their very real differences, both these arguments are based on an artificial separation of culture and economy, and indeed much is couched in a methodologically individualist account of voting behaviour, with the culturalist explanation reducing culture to the revealed preferences of authoritarian tendencies of voters and the economic explanation regretting that voters do not vote for their economic self-interest. This is ironic given that this methodology mirrors precisely the technocratic neoliberalism, based on rational-choice models and revealed preferences in the (political) market, which is at the source of resentment and protest. The idea of "uneducated whites" is often used as a proxy for the white working class, but this downplays the large numbers of small business owners in this category. Furthermore, some definitions lead to very odd conclusions. Thus, Joan Williams' (2017) book on the white working class defines it as those on an annual median income of $75,144, which gives room for those on an income of between $41,005 and $131,962 a year. This excludes the poor, but perhaps even more problematically much of the educated cosmopolitan elite could fit into this income bracket, but it is precisely this group that is supposed to be the source of resentment among the white working class (Roediger 2017). This might suggest that the source of resentment is not economic but cultural, but this begs a number of questions about the timing of any cultural backlash and the rise of "authoritarian values", why this is confined to certain places and why these places are often areas of relatively low migration.

Rather than explanations based purely on economic or cultural variables, it is more fruitful to explore how these two factors overlap and reinforce each other. Thus, the decline of communities does exist as a social reality but also as a "social resource" in which a narrative of decline is constructed, and in which even better-off members of these communities blame urban elites more interested in Wall Street or liberal wars of intervention, and regulation hits small business far more than the corporate elite. We thus have the growth of a politics of resentment, such as a "rural consciousness" that believes that rural areas are being ignored, marginalized and misunderstood by urban elites (Cramer 2016; Davies 2018a: 61). Hochschild (2016: 145) shows how in Louisiana, where people directly experience the destruction of the environment, there is rage less against environmental polluters such as large corporations, and more against the hypocrisy of federal government, which is seen as rewarding and facilitating joblessness and delinquency. These are indicative of a worldview in which life is seen as harsh, but the American dream would exist if people were prepared to "wait in line" to reap their rewards. This has been undermined by the growth of those who are thought to jump the queue, such as welfare recipients, immigrants and "privileged" identity groups, all encouraged by a Washington elite that instruct outsiders to show empathy and endorse political correctness. That these are myths is in many respects less significant than the fact that these are *powerful* myths, and indeed ones that accord closely with the paleoconservative worldview. These are powerful precisely because there are significant levels of despair in the US, as we saw in Chapter 3. Indeed, economic *anxiety* rather than income *per se* appears to have been a significant factor in the election, with Trump's support stronger than Romney's in 2012 among those with low credit ratings, in counties where men had stopped working, where people had sub-prime loans before 2008 or where more residents received high disability payments. This, then, is a story less about income *per se*, and more about identifying areas where economic prospects have declined most steeply, and Trump's support in these areas was significant (Hohmann 2016; Casselman 2017). Trump won 2,584 counties to Clinton's 472, but the latter accounted for 64 per cent of US GDP in 2016 (Muro & Liu 2016). Indeed, Trump won two-thirds of the vote of those who felt that life for the next generation would be worse than it is for the current one, and a similar figure among those who said that their financial situation had become worse since 2012 (CNN 2016). This is, then, in some sense a question about the politics of place and the sense that, whatever one's own personal situation, a community's future holds out little prospect of hope, except insofar as it can become one in which a mythical past is recaptured, and thereby security and freedom are reconciled in "retrotopia" (Bauman 2017). In this vision, "the future is transformed from the national habitat of hopes and rightful expectations into the sight of nightmares: horrors of losing your job together with its attached social standing, of having your home together with the rest of life's goals and chattels 'repossessed', of helplessly watching your children sliding down the well-being-cum-prestige slope and your own laboriously learned and memorized skills stripped of whatever has been left of their market value" (Bauman 2017: 6). This is the reality of the "end" of the American Dream, not only for those groups always excluded, such as African Americans and Native Americans, but increasingly (if still unequally) for all sections of the population. Put bluntly, spaces of hope have turned to spaces of despair. This, then, is not so much a revolt of the white working class, but rather a revolt – both cultural and economic – that cuts across classes. Indeed, much of its ideological appeal is middle-class, as it rests on precisely the image of rugged individualism and the republican ideal that the liberal managerial state and globalization has supposedly eroded.

The rise of the Tea Party is of some relevance in this regard. Although often seen as a libertarian critique of continued government involvement in the economy, the movement was in fact more ambiguous that that. Indeed, the movement emerged "in part, by the threat its supporters perceive to their share in the economic legacy of the New Deal" (Disch 2010). While Tea Party rhetoric often talked of rolling back government, repealing Obamacare and reducing government deficits, supporters also talked of support for social security and Medicare (Skocpol & Williamson 2012). These were legacies of the New Deal, but were largely available only to the white population (Katznelson 2014). Although this was contested before Civil Rights in the 1960s (see Chapter 8), the New Deal was still highly racialized, and social security was introduced less in terms of universal rights and more in terms of "race based privileges" (Disch 2010). Seen in this way, the Tea Party is a product of a racialized liberal America, and in this regard the paleoconservatives' characterization of Middle American Radicals as intrinsically anti-liberal is problematic. But at the same time, in terms of the emergence of a new version of the discourse of the forgotten American, and the notion that welfare has been extended from the deserving to undeserving poor, this feeds directly into the arguments made by Gottfried, Francis, Buchanan and indeed Trump. For the Tea Party are "moved to act by a rhetoric that taps not a black-white binary but a powerful cultural scenario that configures a relation among the poor, an elite of intellectual do-good social engineers, and the hard working 'forgotten man' who'll foot the bill" (Disch 2010). This is precisely the discourse of resentment discussed above. Thus for all their supposed libertarian principles, many of the Tea Party that emerged in 2009 switched their support to Trump in 2016,[6] not least because of hostility to the liberal managerial state.

Conclusion: contemporary American conservatism, neoliberalism and globalization

This chapter has surveyed various conservative moments in American politics and concluded that in some respects we might call the Trump era a paleoconservative one. We need to be quite precise though about what we mean by a paleoconservative moment. In contrast to, say, protectionist republicanism in the 1870s onwards, the new conservatism around Goldwater in 1964 and Reagan in 1980, and the neoconservatives around Bush II in the US (and neoliberals from 1964 onwards), paleoconservative intellectuals, think tanks and individuals have little influence. Steve Bannon was the most obvious exception, and there are the Alt-Right and Alt-Lite movements, which are to some extent influenced by paleoconservatism. Bannon was, however, quickly removed from the administration and these other movements are, despite a significant online presence and widespread individual acts of racist violence, pretty disparate and relatively small-scale and disorganized. There is thus little in the way of an organized paleoconservative movement today.

But we might still talk of a paleoconservative moment for reasons suggested in the last two sections of this chapter, namely that their ideas resonate with a significant social base in the Republican Party. These ideas include hostility to Wall Street, Washington and to some extent big capital (like Southern Agrarians), an obsession with American greatness (like Teddy Roosevelt and the neoconservatives), an appeal to local state rights, tradition and authenticity

---

6. A CNN poll in February 2016 suggested that 16 per cent of Tea Party affiliates supported Ted Cruz, while as much as 56 per cent supported Trump. See Aronoff (2016). The 1990s also saw something of a paleoconservative–libertarian alliance and support for Buchanan in 1992, around Thomas Fleming and Murray Rothbard. Both sides were hostile to immigration, the libertarian side because immigrants support more statist policies (Hawley 2016).

Table 5.1 American conservatism

Issue and year	Brief details	Key features
Pre-1945 American conservatism	Slavery in the South (up to 1865), protectionism in the North (1870s onwards), expansion and militarism (Theodore Roosevelt), Southern Agrarians in the 1930s.	Initial suspicion of capitalism in favour of racialized paternalism, revived in the 1930s by Southern Agrarians. Gradual acceptance and co-existence with capitalism through the search for other forms of hierarchy, such as masculine war-like virility.
Post-1945 American conservatism	Growing rejection of the New Deal and Republican realism. The Goldwater campaign 1964.	Acceptance of capitalism. Fusionism – tradition, capitalist enterprise and religion. Anti-Communism.
Neoconservatism	More theoretically developed fusion of neoliberalism and conservative ideas, part of the Anglo-American New Right.	Rejection of the statist new class and commitment to the neoliberal "roll-back" of the state but a crucial role for the state as moral tutor, both domestically (personal responsibility, rejection of welfare for the undeserving poor) and internationally (American moral exceptionalism justifies wars of intervention, including in the post-Cold War world). Support free-market economics but still with a need for virtue.
Paleoconservatism	Partial return of the Old Right, rejection of American universalism. Split with neoconservatism in the 1980s.	Rejection of the statist new class, which neoconservatism and liberalism have both sustained. Pragmatic ethno-nationalism with racialized overtones, but not as extreme as the Alt-Right. Generally hostile to migration and multiculturalism, and to globalization. Support protectionism though also nostalgia for small-scale production and independent producers.

(like new conservatives, neoliberals and Southern Agrarians) and a hostility to immigrants and Muslims, a common feature of American conservatives, including neoconservatives. Much of this adds up to a suspicion of globalization, including multiculturalism, the movement of capital overseas (and deindustrialization) and the rise of a liberal managerial elite that promotes these things and supposedly puts immigrants "at the front of the queue" in the context of American decline. Gottfried (2017: 140) thus challenges both the neoconservative Right and the Democrat liberal internationalist "Left" who both support "a liberal internationalist American foreign policy, governmentally negotiated free trade agreements, and a globalist understanding of nationhood" and talks of "a populist insurgency from a transformed, energized Right. Unlike the American conservative movement, this populist Right does not genuflect before the gods of capitalism. In fact, it is not this Right but the social left that is warming to a globalist economy run by a multinational capitalist class. It is the multicultural left in the new political constellation that can make its peace with the immigration politics and 'human rights' internationalism of, say, the *Wall Street Journal* or *Commentary*" (Gottfried 2017: 140).

In some respects, then, the paleoconservative tradition argues that the Republic has been betrayed by a liberal elite. Here, though, we can begin to see some of the *theoretical* tensions within this tradition, as a precursor to how these are played out through the reality of actually existing globalization in Chapters 6 and 7. First, there is a clear tension between Patrick Buchanan's support for a conservatism based on "the patriotism of Theodore Roosevelt" on the one hand and the decentralized "humane economic vision of Wilhelm Röpke on the other" (Buchanan 1998: 289). Roosevelt was a strong advocate of empire and in that regard at least is closer to the neoconservative vision of America. But more interesting is Buchanan's favourable reference to the ordoliberal Wilhelm Röpke and his hope for a society based on free and independent producers, which would appear to conform to the republican ideal (and the neoliberal – undeliverable – promise of pristine free markets). But at the same time, Buchanan (1998: 93–4) also talked of his admiration for the capitalists of the Gilded Age, rejecting the notion that they were robber-barons and instead suggesting that they were patriotic Americans. This argument flies in the face of both the growing managerialism of these large corporations and indeed their proto-globalization strategies, which involved the expansion of American capital overseas. Moreover, Buchanan's case for protectionism for manufacturing rests less on a defence of the Old Right conservatism and its links with the South, and rather more on the Union's case for protection for manufacturing in the North before and after the Civil War, right through to 1945. Indeed, Buchanan's favourable view of Hamilton contrasts sharply with that of paleoconservative thinkers like Francis (1992: 18), who argues that Hamiltonian nationalism undermined tradition in the nineteenth century. Weyrich and Lind (2007) also decry the rise of large corporations who have "no concern for the homeland", while Gottfried (2005, 2017) claims allegiance to Hayekian Austrian economics even while giving support to protectionism. This inconsistency is reflective of a conservative tradition, which, like Kirk, claims support for small businesses – those Middle American Radicals – that are so important to Trump, but which often in effect support large corporations. Moreover, as we saw in Chapter 2, this gap between rhetoric and reality is a central feature of neoliberalism, and the ordoliberal support for small business, echoed in places by Chicago and Hayek after 1945, but which, via Coase and Becker, ended up rejecting anti-trust laws and developing a theoretical case for private monopoly. We clearly have, then, a tension between a conservative (and neoliberal) version of "small is beautiful" on the one hand, and support for "large" private monopoly on the other. This in turn leads us to consider the most significant difference between paleoconservatism on the one hand, and neoliberalism on the other, and this is over the question of protectionism against free trade, the latter of which was of course an important part of the Reagan administration that both sides claim allegiance to, albeit with some qualifications.[7] In contemporary political discourse, this is a tension between ("small") paleo anti-globalization and ("large") neoliberal globalization. This is discussed in depth in Chapter 7. But it is precisely here where we can see some of the tensions between (and within) the paleoconservative and neoliberal ideals, and the reality of the US (and indeed global) political economy.

In one respect Trump represents a re-politicization of the world in the face of the technocratic de-politicization of actually existing neoliberalism since the 1980s and the third way in the 1990s. This also feeds into the populist discourse in which technocratic economism has existed alongside competition, so that the losers in this competitive game – individuals, localities, even countries – are somehow less worthy precisely because they have lost in this competitive game (Davies 2014). There are some parallels (and differences, as we will see) with the radical conservatives of 1930s Germany, as Trump can be seen as an attempt to re-enchant a world of bureaucratic rationalization, albeit this time one where the rationalization has occurred through the market (Graeber 2015). As Brown (2017: 32) suggests: "If not a man of the people in his billions, he is in his impulsive, opinionated, misinformed and insulting style, and his indifference to facts, evidence, even consistency. These qualities constitute his lack of qualifications for the presidency, but are what make him Everyman, and were not irrelevant but crucial to his appeal."

This, however, is not simply a populist response to neoliberal reason, though it is partly this. Trump sees himself as the CEO of the US, supposedly running the country as he runs his company, and his promise to drain the swamp should be seen in this way, for it "was not a promise to get Wall Street or wealth out of politics – it was a promise to get politics and politicians out of politics" (Brown 2017: 34). For it was the case that "neoliberalism generated the hostility to

---

7. For the paleoconservatives there was the failure to undertake a cultural revolution that would challenge the liberal managerial state, and for the neoliberals there was the failure to tackle state spending and, above all, the reality of massive increases in budget deficits.

politics, to social justice and even to democracy in favour of market justice and rationalities, combined with heavy statism" (Brown 2017: 35). The result is a nihilism "abetted by neoliberal reason. A nihlilism that makes truth and reason a plaything, that makes values fungible, that vitiates conscience and felt responsibility for the present and future by the powerful and the powerless alike" (Brown 2017: 35–6). Moreover, while Trump's protectionism did not find support among companies that utilized global value chains (see Chapter 7), sections of American capital supported tax cuts for corporations and the wealthy, the roll-back of environmental regulations and resistance to any attempt to curtail finance following 2007–8 (Mason 2019: 22–8). That Trump represents a conservatism that only partially breaks with neoliberalism is considered further in the next two chapters.

6

CONSERVATISM, POPULISM AND
THE LIBERAL STATE: A CRITIQUE

This chapter is the first of two that provide a detailed critique of conservative responses to globalization, examining both the socio-cultural and political economy responses made by conservatives. This chapter focuses on the former and provides a critique of contemporary conservative globalization and anti-globalization with a particular focus on the liberal state, cosmopolitanism and multiculturalism. This is carried out in three sections. The first section provides a summary of British and American conservative (anti-)globalization, and examines the differences and similarities between them. The second section then compares this to other forms of right-wing anti-globalization, and discusses right-wing populism and populist movements in different parts of the world. The third section then provides a detailed critique, with particular though not exclusive reference to Britain and the US, with a focus on conservative views of the liberal state, of liberal cosmopolitanism and multiculturalism.

British and American conservativism and globalization: summary, differences and similarities

It should be clear from the two cases discussed in Chapters 4 and 5 that there is no single conservative position on contemporary globalization. Indeed, in some respects, we might argue that the two cases are very different, with the British case essentially arguing for more globalization through the promotion of a Greater or global Britain, and the American case arguing, albeit with considerable qualification and ambiguity, for "America first" through isolationist policies such as protectionist tariffs, border walls and more restricted immigration policies. On the other hand, there are also important similarities, as both are critical of actually existing globalization, and particularly argue that globalization is too liberal and cosmopolitan, and this has undermined national sovereignty and led to national decline.

Briefly, then, the British case is based on a critique of the European Union. The case against the EU is that it has promoted both too much and too little globalization. It has promoted too much because it has subject the British state to rules made in Brussels and thus undermined national sovereignty. Part of this claim is the (problematic – see below) argument that Britain no longer has control of its borders as the EU has promoted the free movement of labour. Brussels and the European Court of Justice have also subjected Britain to rules that restrict the nation's freedom to make its own laws. Much of this sounds like a defence of national sovereignty and indeed in many respects it is. At the same time, much of the conservative case for Brexit has not been made in order to suggest that Britain simply retreat from the international order, although it might do in the case of migration, and other areas, as we will see below. What is envisaged by leading conservative Brexiteers is a globalization more conducive to Britain's national sovereignty and national interest, one that reflects Britain's leading role in the international order. For some Brexiteers, this involves the promotion of trade deals with the rest of the world. Some are happy for Britain to trade under WTO rules (Economists for Brexit 2016) or indeed believe that international trade can be organized without formal trade agreements, presumably through spontaneous interaction and competition, sometimes known as a "world trade deal" (Economists for Free Trade 2018). Others, however, argue that there is a need for an institutional underpinning to trade and so-called global free markets, and this might lead to closer ties with Britain's former empire and the Commonwealth (Bennett 2016), or at least with those countries in the Commonwealth that share the closest ties with Greater Britain, namely the Anglosphere (Roberts 2016). Seen in this way, then, conservative positions regard the EU as a regionalist hindrance to a much broader globalization, one whose rules actually undermine the movement towards truly global free markets (Hindley 1996).

The American case is in many respects different from this. Chapter 5 suggested that an organized conservative movement around Trump is limited (compared to, say, neoconservative influences on Reagan and Bush II) but at the same time Trump represents a social base whose views in many respects accord with those of paleoconservatism. This worldview essentially argues that the US has declined and this is because of a globalist, transnational, post-American elite, both within the liberal managerial states, and among the corporate class. The loyalty of this privileged group is to globalization rather than to America, and this manifests itself through the promotion of "uncontrolled" immigration, a welfare state without limits that protects immigrants and minorities, deindustrialization, weak trade deals and the erosion of the American republican ideal. The way forward is for the US to protect itself, both in terms of supposedly uncontrolled migration, and in terms of tariffs to protect industry deemed necessary for the national interest (or to forge better trade deals). The US can be made great again them through selective "de-globalization", not in the sense of a complete shift away from all aspects of globalization, but through global integration based on selectivity, bilateral rather than multilateral deals and the possibility of complete withdrawal in certain cases (Stokes 2018). This is because the international order is based on zero-sum transactions in which one side wins at the expense of another, and so the US should engage only when it is a winner – or at least it should use this rhetoric to ensure "better deals" within the existing liberal order. To some extent, this is how Trump has treated trade deals, international organizations like the UN and NATO and international agreements such as the Paris climate agreement.

On the face of it, then, our two cases point to two sharply different approaches to globalization, one broadly promoting its extension and one a retreat. On the other hand, we can also point to some areas of overlap and similarity. Both argue that "actually existing globalization" in some forms has not worked for the national interest, be it the restrictive Brussels bureaucracy, unfair trade agreements or unrestricted migration. Both are committed to the defence of state sovereignty and the national interest, which have been undermined by the dominant forms of globalization. In both cases, there is a sense of regret and national decline, and (despite claims to the contrary) a nostalgia for a lost golden age, and an attempt to construct a retrotopia that will "make America great again" or restore Britain's "rightful place as a world leader" through the restoration of the idea of a Greater Britain. As we have seen in some respects the British case argues for a more global Britain while the US involves in part a less global America, but both cases draw on a free-market vision, both of the past and the future. In particular, both argue that actually existing globalization can be challenged and its shackles overcome, in some respects by the promotion of a "true free market" unencumbered by Washington or Brussels regulations. This might mean protection from unfair foreign competition in the case of the US, but both focus on the need to promote a purer free market of sorts.

In terms of solutions to globalization, conservative responses to these questions vary but essentially contend that there is a need for a proper market economy either within the US or globally, supported by an appropriate institutional infrastructure (though there is great disagreement over what this might be). The problem of deindustrialization can be overcome either through the (supposed) return of manufacturing jobs "stolen" by the South (Trump), or through the creation of new jobs appropriate to the demands of the new global economy, facilitated by lower taxation and (predominantly financial) services (Brexit). This feeds into the idea of the free market because these developments will secure more employment, through an enhanced entrepreneurial vision based on the rugged individual of the republic or Britain's role as a commercial leader. This will involve cultural change that challenges liberal multiculturalism, feminism and "gender ideology" and political correctness, and thus restricts the free movement of labour and promotes traditional family values, hyper-masculinity and a maternal femininity (see Graff *et al.* 2019). On the Far Right, this has involved a racialized masculinity that blames immigrants for stealing both jobs and native women, and that suggests that authentic masculinity can be reclaimed through fighting the "Other" (Kimmel 2018), in the process protecting women and children through reclaiming the "true nation" (Belew 2018). Although usually expressed in less violent ways, much of this rhetoric is central to the broader conservative movement in the US, where the reclaiming of the true America is closely linked to the restoration of authentic masculinity (Kimmel 2013). As we will see in the next chapter, Trump pays far more attention to job losses in certain sectors of manufacturing where men were mainly employed, and far less in those sectors where women are employed (and which in fact are more likely to suffer from import competition than those sectors where men have been more widely employed).

In terms of the Global South, there are sharply contrasting visions. Some Brexiteers see the South as representing an opportunity for the renewal of the Commonwealth and imperial relations. Trump and many paleoconservatives, on the other hand, suggest that many parts of the South have cheated on trade deals and undermined job security and so protectionism is justified. Chapter 4 showed how Red Toryism has some suspicion of the free movement of capital as well as labour. Capital should recognize some social and national obligations, and the question then is one of partially challenging the *mobility* of capital, as opposed to left-wing anti-globalization, which often involves a challenge to *capital itself*, something we will consider in Chapter 8. But the main conservative Brexit vision is in fact to take advantage of capital mobility and free trade and this is very different to the Trump paleoconservative view.

Finally, and perhaps most obviously, though both have longer-term causes, as we saw in Chapter 3, these were intensified by the fall-out from the financial crisis of 2007–8 and its aftermath. A focus on the causes of this crisis is not particularly prominent among British and American conservatives. However, there are common positions that argue that this crisis was a product of poor regulations and government overspending, aided by the absence of conservative virtue and social obligation, particularly on the part of a complacent Wall Street swamp, itself said to be a product of the nihilist 1960s (Bannon 2010; Anderson 2005). While it would be mistaken to say that there is a direct line of causality from 2008 to the Brexit and Trump votes of 2016, it is likely that neither would have happened without the crisis. Seen in this respect, we might consider these two cases in relation to broader populist trends since 2008, and this is considered in the next section.

Populism and conservative globalization

The populist radical Right is not a new phenomenon. This book has also argued that there is a need for considerable caution in exaggerating the rise of conservative populism and that to some degree the rise reflects a wider fragmentation of mainstream electoral politics, particularly in the developed world. Nonetheless, it has enjoyed some degree of success both before and in the wake of the fall-out from the financial crisis. In the 2009 European elections, there were 25 radical Right populist parties, the most successful of which was the Party for Freedom in the Netherlands. By 2017, across 22 European countries support for populist radical Right parties was higher than at any time over the past 30 years, with populist parties winning 16 per cent of the overall vote on average in the most recent parliamentary election in each country, up from 11 per cent a decade earlier and 5 per cent in 1997 (Bloomberg 2017). Populist parties in Europe more than tripled their vote from 1998 to 2018, and populist leaders have found government posts in 11 countries in the continent (Lewis *et al.* 2018), including in Poland, Hungary, Norway, Finland and, in 2018, Italy. In addition, we can identify some resurgence of right-wing populism in the developing world, including in Turkey, India, the Philippines and Brazil, which in 2018 saw the election of Jair Bolsonaro, an authoritarian nativist committed to the extension of neoliberal policies.

Mudde (2007) argues that there are three key features of the contemporary radical Right, namely nativism, authoritarianism and populism. Nativism manifests itself above all through anti-immigration and anti-minority rhetoric, while authoritarianism expresses itself through a strong emphasis on law and order, so that terrorism, for example, is seen simply as purely a security issue and one that is strongly linked to open borders. Populism is in part the idea that there is a corrupt elite working against the general will of the people. In the words of Jean Marie Le Pen in 2007, "I will give voice to the people. Because in democracy only the people can be right" (cited in Baker 2019). In this account populism is a thin ideology in which the authentic people and the corrupt elite can vary over time (Mudde 2004).

The word populism is ordinarily used in a pejorative sense, but if this is so then it begs a number of questions about how we think about the people. First and most obviously, all politicians claim to speak for the people but not all of them are populist. Populists therefore suggest that political institutions and mainstream political parties have lost touch with the people. But if populism is problematic, then this implies that the people have in effect fallen prey to irrational ideas and demagogues, an argument that ironically replicates older conservative ideas, discussed in Chapter 1, that talked of fear of the mob and the problem of democratic demands in mass society (d'Eramo 2013). What has changed is that whereas conservatives (and some liberals, especially neoliberals) called for authoritarian solutions to the problem of mass society, today's centrists call for economic technocracy as an alternative to populism. For some on the Left, then, and in different ways, the rise of populism is not so much a cause for regret as something that should be celebrated, because it challenges the rule of neoliberal technocracy through the revival of politics, something that is always based on conflict (Mouffe 2006; d'Eramo 2013; Streeck 2019).

However, one can certainly recognize the rise of populism, specifically in its conservative form, and the very real reasons for its (re-)emergence, without then accepting that it is intrinsically a welcome development. Moreover, Left critiques of actually existing globalization focus on systemic critique rather than recourse to often racist conspiracy theories, but at the same time systemic critique is based on the notion that there are elites and power at the expense of certain groups in society. Not unrelated to this point, one should not conflate populism and democracy, and we need to be more careful in recognizing that the former is actually a challenge to the latter. Crucially, conservative populism is combined with nativism so that the construction of the people is not simply based on including all people outside of the corrupt elite, but only the true people (Mudde 2004). Populism is thus not only an idea that claims to speak for the people, it is one that *excludes* many – scapegoats – because they are not an authentic part of the people (Muller 2016). Mudde (2016: 8) suggests that right-wing populism is an "illiberal democratic response to an undemocratic response to an undemocratic liberalism" that "asks the right questions but provides the wrong answers." The second of these statements is correct but the first, I would suggest, needs some amending. It in effect suggests that populism represents a kind of general will, or will of the people, unmediated by dominant institutions of representation in liberal democracy. But this rests on a purely majoritarian account of democracy, in which the rights of minorities can be excluded, and a conflation of the sum of individual wills and a general will. In this way populism lays the ground for what is in effect a tyranny of the majority through the emergence of a totalitarian democracy (Talmon 1970) in which democratic collectivism undermines individual rights. Rousseau (1968) is often regarded as one of the main culprits in this regard, but for him the general will reflected something more than aggregate individual interests, and rather a will in which individuals committed to something beyond their own individual interests, or at least selected those interests that were congruent with the wider political community. We might go further and argue that while democracy involves majority rule, it does not advocate this at the expense of the rights or interests of *excluded* minorities (though it might challenge the rights of *privileged* minorities). Seen in this way, given that populism speaks for a people but dehumanizes "non-peoples", it cannot be considered democratic, even if it does involve re-politicization in the context of neoliberal technocracy. This is the point at which right-wing populism challenges globalization.

In particular, populists argue that liberal democracy has been usurped by a liberal cultural elite. For example, in Brazil Bolsonaro places much of the blame for the country's ills on supposedly (cultural) Marxist universities, feminism and communism as well as an exaggerated sense that corruption is a problem exclusive to the political Left (Garcia 2019). While populism has emerged in part as a response to neoliberal de-politicization, in many respects it is a symptom rather than a solution to this phenomenon. Populism in part reflects a growing distrust of experts and in this respect challenges the growing technocracy associated with the neoliberal period. But at the same time, in dismissing the idea that there is any possibility of a genuinely public knowledge developed in part by disinterested and objective experts, populism exacerbates the post-political condition, and indeed extends neoliberal ideas about the limits of public knowledge. Hayek (1972) in particular argued that experts tended to encourage ideas that were not conducive to freedom as they used their expertise to promote social engineering that involved the exercise of power by intellectuals over others. Tacit knowledge, based on practical know how, was far more important in a changing, uncertain world, and as a result it was entrepreneurs rather than intellectuals that were "more open to new ideas" (Friedman 1978: xi). The search for laws and regularities failed to represent this world, but instead led to the imposition of expert systems over the wider population, and was in effect simply another type of Soviet central planning (Hayek 1941, 2010 [1945]; Mises 1944; Lavoie 1985). Much more important were those people with practical know how who used their knowledge to change the world, and who in effect "know how", rather than "know what". These are the entrepreneurs who act on and change the world, in contrast to self-serving experts (Davies 2018a: 162), an argument that in effect leads to considerable overlap between neoliberal theories of self-interested rent seekers and conservative theories of the new class (Buchanan & Tullock 1962; Schumpeter 1976; Burnham 1972; Kristol 1995). While on the face of it this would appear to challenge rule by technocracy, and possibly the technocracy that has emerged from actually existing neoliberalism, where neoliberals and populists overlap is in their rejection of the possibility of a public sphere or, in other words, a sphere where political deliberation and debate is possible. This in many respects reflects the legacy of neoliberal hegemony and the ways in which populism does not challenge it so much as extend it. In focusing on knowledge and neoliberal rule, Davies suggests that:

> The more transformative and disconcerting claim was that it could reduce the need for public, centralised experts as such. One might go further still and say that they reduced the need for truth. Dating back to Mises' 1920 pamphlet on economic calculation, an ideal had

developed that, so long as markets were relatively unimpaired by government intervention, they could become the organising principle of an otherwise disorganised, unplanned, even ignorant society. As long as there was a way of coordinating people peacefully, in real time, why the need for experts or facts at all ... If experts *really* want to be neutral, they should give up trying to understand what is happening, and simply focus on creating the conditions for competition to take place ... The market is therefore a type of "post-truth" institution, that saves us from having to know what is going on overall. It actually works *better* if we ignore the facts of the system at large, and focus only on the part of it that concerns us ... Understood as real time monitoring devices, markets are not so much tools for producing facts but for gauging our feelings. This is where faith in the market maps onto populism and nationalism, for all these creeds see politics as little other than mass public coordination via shared feeling.   (Davies 2018a: 166, 167)

It therefore follows that experts are not disinterested observers trying to understand the world, but rather self-serving elites attempting to impose their worldview on everyone else, and not subject to the competition of the marketplace, unlike entrepreneurs. Michael Gove's contention while campaigning for Brexit that "people in this country have had enough of experts" (Mance 2016) is but one example of this kind of thinking, and one where marketization and social media combine to effectively marketize and fragment the production of knowledge, including of the news[1] (Mirowski 2017). Furthermore, as Davies (2018b) suggests:

One way to understand the rise of reactionary populism today is as the revenge of sovereignty on government. This is not simply a backlash after decades of globalization, but against the form of political power that facilitated it, which is technocratic, multilateral and increasingly divorced from local identities ... A common thread linking "hard" Brexiteers to nationalists across the globe is that they resent the very idea of governing as a complex, modern, fact-based set of activities that requires technical expertise and permanent officials.

This distrust of government also brings us back to the overlap between neoliberal public choice theory on the one hand, and conservative theories of the

---

1. The journalist Jeffrey Lord, who had worked in the Reagan administration, argued in 2016, that "this fact checking business ... [is] one more sort of out of touch, eitist, media type thing" (cited in Mirowski 2017: 23).

new class on the other. In the words of Australian populist Pauline Hanson (1996), a new class controls industries "servicing Aboriginals, multiculturalists and a host of other minorities" at the expense of "ordinary Australians". This populist argument is thus a celebration of the feelings of supposedly "ordinary national citizens" and a rejection of reason and wider notions of truth, and one that feeds into wider rejections of cosmopolitan liberalism and multiculturalism. The Belgian Right populist Filip Dewinter has argued that the old Left–Right conflict has ended and the post-Cold War world has led to a new divide between identity on the one hand, and multiculturalism on the other, and indeed he cites Huntington's clash of civilisations thesis (Betz & Johnson 2017: 72). This leads to a celebration of the authentic people, but also a rejection of minorities who will not assimilate into the desired culture. Democracy has been betrayed by a cosmopolitan elite who do not listen to ordinary people. Moreover, the argument of the populist Right is that they are the ones who genuinely celebrate difference. In the words of the Italian Northern League, or Lega Nord, "(t)hose who fight for the survival of their nations represent the camp of the diversity of cultures, true tolerance, and freedom, whereas the America like multiculturalism ... represents the camp of uniformity, deracination and enslavement" (cited in Betz & Johnson 2017: 72).

The argument is not anti-immigration *per se*, but it is anti-migration from what is perceived to be alien cultures that will not assimilate into the dominant culture. This has included the targeting of Asian migrants in Australia and New Zealand but there is above all particular hostility to Islam. Lega Nord thus refer to Islam's "incompatibility with regard to European culture" and so conclude that there is no chance of integration. Multiculturalism, according to the Swiss People's Party (SVP), is a "resigned reaction" to the failure of migrants to assimilate (quoted in Betz & Johnson 2017: 75). In particular, the radical Right argue that the cosmopolitan elite have promoted globalization at the expense of the ethno-nation, and have allegedly bestowed welfare privileges on outsiders at the expense of the home population – an argument that also resonates with the Tea Party in the US (Disch 2010; Skocpol & Williamson 2012). These problems are caused not only by migration and multiculturalism at home, but also a global project of liberal interventionism and indeed a totalitarian democracy that undermines the nation, culture and diversity. Regional agreements and organizations such as the European Union are thus integral to this globalization project and should be rejected.

The parallels between these arguments and the two case studies should be clear. Many of the arguments made by the European populist Right are shared by the paleoconservatives in the US. As we have seen, there is hostility to a liberal elite, to migration and multiculturalism, to multilateral organizations and, albeit ambiguously, to so-called free trade. Brexit is more complicated, as we have seen, for while there is a sovereignist and anti-immigrant wing associated with former prime minister May, and indeed the Brexit vote, much of the conservative case for Brexit is actually about the creation of a more global Britain. This has included populist arguments against the EU, some suspicion of migration and some nostalgia for a golden age, but this call for sovereignty is made in part not at the expense of, but to actually intensify, important aspects of globalization. We might also note more generally the radical Right claim that there is a Western tradition that should be defended against the liberal elite and outsiders. This claim to support the democracy of "ordinary people" does feed into some of the rhetoric around Brexit as well as Trump, but "the apparent arguments for genuine democracy are actually arguments for excluding some groups from democratic representation" (Betz and Johnson 2017: 72).

As we have seen throughout the book, a common argument is that this populist Right represents a rejection of globalization in favour of relatively closed national political and economic systems, reflecting the fact that the old Left–Right divide has been displaced. A parallel argument is that the age of neoliberalism has been undermined by the rise of populism, which represents a more or less straightforward neo-nationalist break from neoliberal globalization (Blyth 2016). In contrast to these contentions, we have suggested that while this characterization might be applied to immigration, it is less convincing when generalized across other forms of openness such as the free movement of capital. This is most clear in our case study of Brexit, where many advocates in the Conservative Party actually support a "global" rather than "European" Britain, and in essence see the EU as insufficiently neoliberal, even if at the same time they advocate tighter immigration controls. Again, though, we could usefully recall that Hayek was no straightforward supporter of the free movement of labour and advocated tighter immigration controls in Britain in the 1970s (see Edgar 1986: 71). Furthermore, while neoliberalism has historically been hostile to protectionist European empires, it has been far more sympathetic to empires that promote free trade and the free movement of capital, including the British and Habsburg Empires (Lal 2004; Slobodian 2018a). As decolonization advanced in the postwar period, this was increasingly associated with neo-Keynesian and neo-developmentalism, both part of the much-derided global New Deal that neoliberals rejected. In this context, neoliberals began to support empire and reject decolonization and democracy in the developing world as this led to the extension of protectionist policies (Slobodian 2018a: 94). Empire – particularly Anglo-American empire – thus provided a potential institutional framework for the market order to operate (Lal 2004; Ferguson 2004). This argument often took explicitly racialized forms. Wilhelm Röpke, for instance, denounced the brutality and barbarism of imperialism in the 1930s (see Slobodian 2018a: 180), but by the 1960s was arguing that the appropriate "moral infrastructure" for the market order did not exist in some cultures. He advocated apartheid and segregation in southern Africa, on the spurious grounds that "the South African Negro ... stems from a completely different type and level of civilisation", and went on to contend that full equality between the black and white "races" would amount to "national suicide" (cited in Slobodian 2018a: 162, 153). A similar argument was made by William Buckley in *National Review* in 1957, where, in the context of the rise of Civil Rights movements in the US and decolonization overseas, he referred to whites as "the advanced race" (Buckley 1957). Another prominent neoliberal intellectual, William Hutt, wrote what is often considered to be a case against apartheid in 1964, in his book *The Economics of the Colour Bar*, based on the argument that the market did not discriminate and was colour-blind. But he argued against the tyranny of the majority and thus equal voting rights for blacks and whites on the Hayekian grounds that excessive democracy would undermine the freedom of the marketplace (Hutt 1964). He therefore called for a system of weighted franchise whereby the vote of richer people would count more than those of the poor, which in effect meant advocating a continued colour bar within the political system. In the 1970s, in letters to both US President Jimmy Carter and California Governor Ronald Reagan, Hutt even suggested that Rhodesia was "the only genuine anti-racist democracy in Africa" (cited in Slobodian 2018a: 176). While most neoliberals avoided the vulgarity of Röpke's views, and American conservatives tended to prefer more covert forms of racism than Buckley's views in 1957, both were committed to allowing non-democratic institutional structures to exist in defence of what they saw as market freedom. Thus even a market populist like Milton Friedman (1976) argued in 1976 that the isolation of Rhodesia was a mistake and indeed cited paleoconservative hero James Burnham to suggest that it was indicative of the "suicide of the west" (Burnham 2014). He developed this theme further in 1991, invoking the spirit of Oswald Spengler when talking of American decline (Friedman 1991). This decline could only be reversed through conservative victory on the part of "Tocquevillians", in the culture wars against socially liberal "Gramscians", which in part meant ensuring that the market was embedded in an appropriately conservative cultural framework (Fonte 2000/2001).

Crucially for our purposes, in some respects these observations apply to at least some of the populist movements that are often characterized as being anti-globalization and against neoliberalism. Although movements vary, and there has been some shift in response to the 2008 financial crisis, much of the populist Right combines nativism and authoritarianism with a commitment to economic liberalism (Betz 1994; Mudde 2016; Otjes *et al.* 2018). In parts of the developing world, there has been a marked turn towards "authoritarian neoliberalism" (Bruff 2014) in which the non-market institutional foundations for marketization policies take an increasingly authoritarian turn. Privatization, economic liberalization and the marketization of the state exist side by side with an increased "propensity to employ coercion and legal/extra-legal intimidation" (Tansel 2017: 3), including intensified efforts by the state to control civil society through attacks on minorities, the press, universities, and so on. While each case has its nationally specific features, we can identify some common trends along these lines in, among other places, the Philippines (De Jong 2016), Turkey (Ozden *et al.* 2017), Brazil (Boffo *et al.* 2018) and Egypt (De Smet & Bogaert 2017). In many respects, though, the most telling example from the developing world is Modi's India, in which the ruling Bharatiya Janata Party (BJP) has drawn heavily on repressive measures to curtail dissent, some of which date back to the State of Emergency in the 1970s and even the colonial era (Chacko 2018). It has also drawn on a narrowly majoritarian approach to democracy, which has meant that minority rights have been downplayed or ignored. The focus has instead been on security, law and order and the rights of the silent Hindu majority in the face of hostile minorities, and their defenders, which are essentially identified as India's liberal elite (Chacko 2018: 541–2, 555–7). While much of the support for this populism has come from those that have not benefited from neoliberal policies, Modi and the BJP have – to some extent at least – successfully blamed these outcomes on the corruption of these policies by liberal elites and minorities, and in the process deployed this populism to enhance neoliberal reform. Seen in this way, the populist turn is not necessarily a challenge to neoliberalism and in many respects it has coincided with its expansion. In Brazil, the conservative turn under Bolsonaro has been accompanied by an intensification of economic liberalism under the influence of the Chicago-trained economist Paulo Guedes. Within the state a new super-ministry of the economy has been created under Guedes, alongside new secretariats, for de-bureaucratization, and for de-nationalization and de-investment. The main priorities for the economy have been pension reform, privatization, trade liberalization and more access to indigenous land for corporations (Garcia 2019).

In Europe, even the Austrian Freedom Party and the AfD (or Alternative for Germany) have prominent advisers and leading figures with links to neoliberal think tanks including the Hayek Institute and the Mont Pelerin Society. While both parties are critical of the European Union, this is based on the argument that it has not sufficiently promoted so-called free markets and instead has created new bureaucratic structures that hinder such markets. In other words, the neoliberal promise of pristine markets has come up against the reality of the need for institutional structures to promote such markets, something we saw in the cases of Brexit and American conservatism. This in turn brings us back to the fact that neoliberalism often emerged in the 1970s and 1980s in the context of the rise of the Anglo-American New Right, which combined social conservatism with neoliberalism. Much like the ethno-nationalism of the populist Far Right, for neoliberal thinkers like Hans-Hermann Hoppe, Erich Weede and Gerard Radnitzky (see Slobodian 2018b), the argument is made that some cultures or even races are more conducive to the promotion of a market economy than others. The social liberalism of the third way has undermined the virtuous circle between private vice and public virtue, and this can only be restored through appropriate interventions designed to promote social conservativism and free-market economics (Anderson 2005). Historically, neoliberalism has promoted spontaneous free markets but has also centrally understood that these rely on state construction, but also that there may be other appropriate institutional foundations related to cultural evolution (Hayek 1988: chapter 1; 2013: chapter 1), or indeed race science (Murray and Herrnstein 1994) or social Darwinism (see Slobodian 2018b). This is not something new about neoliberalism but was in effect present at the start of its development. In 1944, Hayek argued that:

> We have progressively abandoned that freedom in economic affairs without which personal and political freedom has never existed in the past ... We are rapidly abandoning not the views merely of Cobden and Bright, of Adam Smith and Hume, or even of Locke and Milton, but of the salient characteristics of Western Civilisation as it has grown from the foundations laid by Christianity and the Greeks and Romans.
>
> (Hayek 2001: 13)

What *is* new is the way in which neoliberals and right-wing populists have both revived race science and debates around IQ, and how they have argued that egalitarianism is a "revolt against nature" (Rothbard 1974), an argument that eventually led Rothbard to support race science and some of the other concerns associated with the contemporary Far Right (Raimondo 2000: 166). This can be seen as a "de-politicizing" response to the politicization associated with the new social movements of the 1960s onwards, and feminism, anti-racism, sexual liberation and anti-colonialism. For conservative neoliberals as well as conservative populists, the socially liberal neoliberalism of the third way is part of this movement and this is why the culture wars – or recourse to biological racism – are so important to them. This focus on the superiority of Judeo-Christian culture is a common assertion made by right-wing populists. Furthermore, even though his work mainly focused on cultural evolution, Hayek (2006: 79) flirted with eugenics when he argued that "there are some socially valuable qualities which will be rarely acquired in a single generation but which will generally be formed, only by the continuous efforts of two or three." The prominent neoliberal intellectual Peter Boettke (2017) has argued that neoliberalism's focus has increasingly shifted from "getting the prices right" in the 1980s, to "getting the institutions right" in the 1990s, to a focus now on "getting the culture right"

(World Bank 2015). Boetkke is critical of the populist Right (see also Horn 2015) but, as Slobodian points out, it is precisely this kind of argument that has been taken up by what he calls "neoliberalism's populist bastards". This has included suggestions for immigration to be allowed to the highest bidder, an argument formerly made by prominent Chicago economist Gary Becker (1976), to the suggestion made by another prominent American neoliberal, Richard Posner, that IQ tests should be used to determine the right of migration (see Slobodian 2018c). In both cases this is justified with reference to the entrepreneurial individual and the maximization of human capital (see Sandel 2012). This leads to the argument that in some respects, closed borders are necessary to preserve globalization, because some cultures and/or races are more anti-globalization that others, and immigrants are more likely to depend on welfare (an argument challenged below) and behave in market-non-conforming ways. It was precisely on these grounds that paleoconservatives made an alliance with libertarians in the US in the 1990s, sometimes known as the "redneck strategy", and which included support for "race realism", the right of states to ignore the federal state and strong immigration controls (Hawley 2016; Ganz 2018). This strategy also had some influence on the Centre for the New Europe, a neoliberal Eurosceptic think tank that promoted state sovereignty, neoliberal economic policies and social and cultural conservatism, above all around immigration and anti-Islamic rhetoric (Slobodian & Plehwe 2019). Rothbard's protégé, Hans-Hermann Hoppe (2017), has argued that a libertarian order can only exist within specific cultures, and it is only in the West (and Central Europe) that liberty-loving cultures exist.

In Europe, both the AFP and AfD remain critical of the EU but support global competitiveness, further trade liberalization through the WTO, fiscal conservatism, an end to inheritance tax and free school choice. The AfD also explicitly links its economic policies to the ordoliberal account of the social market economy that was developed in the 1930s (see Chapter 2), citing prominent ordoliberals like Röpke, Rustow and Muller-Armack in its 2016 programme (see Havertz 2018: 7). While critical of the European Central Bank policy of quantitative easing (QE), the AfD highlights natural inequalities between individuals, cultures and communities within the EU, and suggests that QE policies simply bailed out inferior, lazy cultures, rather than making both individuals and countries responsible for their own actions. In what amounts to a competitive populism, the authentic, disciplined German people is contrasted with undeserving individuals and communities, especially those poorer countries of Southern Europe (Havertz 2018: 13). Although in 2018 the AfD moved away from some of its neoliberal origins, and particularly focused on attacking corporate tax evasion, and talked of social justice, the latter was very much based on the distinction between deserving and undeserving poor that was central to the neoliberal–neoconservative alliances in the 1980s (Cooper 2017). In these ways, populist conservatism combines with neoliberalism, and indeed the prominent AfD member Marc Jongen (see Havertz 2018) has contended that German ordoliberalism was a central part of the conservative revolution that occurred in the inter-war period, above all in Germany, which was discussed in Chapter 2.

This section has suggested, then, that while the conservative populist turn in recent years can in part be seen as a response to neoliberalism, it is not necessarily the case that it represents an unambiguous break from it. Nonetheless, the populist Right is in part a reaction to one specific form of neoliberalism, namely the third way and its support for cosmopolitanism and multiculturalism, and we consider these issues in the next section.

Conservativism and the liberal multicultural state: a critique

Dehistoricizing the liberal state

As we saw in Chapters 2 and 3, while neoliberalism carries the promise of spontaneity, freedom and the market, it continually relies on constructivism and the state to carry out this project. Even the project of marketization always relies on something outside of the market, namely the sovereign state. While technocratic neoliberalism dominated in the years of third way neoliberalism, there is another form of neoliberalism, which involves de-politicization through authoritarian rule. German ordoliberalism emerged in the 1930s as an authoritarian liberal response to Weimar and an alternative to the Nazis. A number of ordoliberals shared views close to Schmitt's case for the sovereign to exercise exceptional power in response to the politicization of the economy, and though Hayek was dismissive of "Adolf Hitler's crown jurist" (Hayek 1967: 169), his case for market freedom was similar to Schmitt's view. Schmitt's argument rested on a distinction between general legal norms and specific commands, and he claimed that only the former could satisfy the condition of upholding the rule of law. His problem with the Weimar Republic was that as a pluralist-party state it led to rule through specific discretionary demands. The state was the prisoner of powerful interest groups that therefore undermined the rule of law, and was thus entangled in far too many activities and this undermined the constitutional order. For Schmitt (1976: 226–7), "only a strong state can depoliticize, only a strong state can openly and effectively decree that certain activities ... remain its privilege and as such ought to be administered by it, that other activities belong to the ... sphere of self-management, and that all the rest be given to the domain of a free economy."

Neoliberalism promises, but does not and cannot realize, a truly free market based on free producers working and exchanging independently of the state. But neoliberalism requires the state to realize that goal, and so can never escape the reality of regulation. However, cases of market failure can then be perpetually explained by the existence of regulation and so the neoliberal promise is, potentially at least, continually renewed. Thus, for instance, technocratic neoliberalism relies on the state, and this is as much the sovereign as well as the marketized state, as the response to the 2008 financial crisis makes clear. But – and here the overlap with Schmitt is significant – this applies also to neoliberalism and the authoritarian liberalism that is also associated with the neoliberal project of de-politicization. Furthermore, the search for re-enchantment is not simply about a strong leader exercising executive power, because there is also a neoliberal discourse of heroic entrepreneurs constantly innovating in the economic sphere and thus challenging bureaucracy. Thus the kind of managerial capitalism that Schumpeter, Burnham and the paleoconservatives decried might be re-enchanted by entrepreneurial rule. Seen in this way, Donald Trump is the heroic head of a new state, which will make America great again through entrepreneurialism and thus the US being run as if it was a business. In this scenario Trump is literally the CEO of "America Inc" and so technocratic neoliberalism is displaced by an authoritarian neoliberalism, which offers re-enchantment through entrepreneurial role.

We saw in the last chapter some of the tensions among both neoliberals and paleoconservatives concerning rhetorical support for small businesses on the one hand, and corporate monopoly on the other. Similarly, while paleoconservatives talk of continuity between the liberal managerialism of the New Deal era and that of the neoliberal era from the 1980s onwards, they seriously underestimate the changes between the two periods. What this suggests, then, is that the paleoconservative critique of the liberal managerial state is in many respects ahistorical. We have an analysis that borrows heavily from Burnham's critique of liberal managerialism, but also a politics – in Buchanan and Trump – which in many respects draws on nostalgia for the (white, masculinist) 1950s, an era in which the managerial state was fully established. While paleoconservatism is quite right to challenge the view that the state no longer matters, or has somehow withdrawn from public life, it extends this argument to the much more problematic contention that in fact the source of power in society today is control of the means of political organization, rather than ownership of the means of production. For what neoliberalism has entailed is actually an intensification of inequality in part based on the growing financialization of society, and thus the ability of the richest asset owners to increase their wealth. Others – in both Britain and the US – have also become asset owners but they have also seen significant increases in debt, reinforced by stagnant or declining real wages in

low-paid and often insecure service work. This is the source of great resentment and is central to the – limited, uneven – appeal of both Trump and Brexit
among less-privileged groups in society, as we have seen. We have also seen
that much of this is directed at what the paleoconservatives call the new class,
that is, those leading and directing the liberal managerial state. The clear implication is that the cosmopolitan, transnational liberal elite is responsible for the
fact that some have been "left behind" by globalization. But the problem with
this argument is that for most of this so-called new class, they too have faced
significant challenges. This has included stagnant wages, but also the marketization of the public sector through new public management reforms, designed in
part to make universities producers of "fast" knowledge such as that produced
in the competitive marketplace, rather than the "elitist" knowledge associated
with the idea of a public sphere. Some senior managers have benefited from this
process – private companies through outsourcing, senior health consultants,
and heads and vice chancellors in school academies and semi-privatized universities – but this is a highly stratified process, and one that has led to low morale
among many public-sector workers. Seen in this way both paleoconservatives
and conservative Brexiteers are guilty of gross over-simplification and of hom-
ogenizing public-sector workers as a "new class" or a "blob" (Gove 2013) of
privileged producer interests (Buchanan & Tullock 1962). Moreover, this is also
a problem for those libertarians like the late Murray Rothbard and Hans Herman
Hoppe, who support marketization but argue that this can only take place within
specific – white – cultures. They support a populist strategy led by dispossessed
and "native" whites, but then also concede that "it is above all white men that
make up the ruling elite and that have foisted the current mess upon us" (Hoppe
2017). The argument of liberal betrayal by white elites undermines the idea of
separate united cultures based around supposed races or ethnicities, and the
idea that there is a straightforward dispossession of white people.

In terms of the geopolitics of globalization, some of Trump's pronouncements
both before and after he became president – over the Trans-Pacific Partnership
(TPP), NATO, NAFTA, relations with China, the United Nations, environmental agreements and liberal wars of intervention among others – suggested
a significant shift away from the US's international commitments. The practice
has to date been significant but perhaps still more limited than his rhetoric.
The TPP was abandoned but this was likely, or at least a distinct possibility,
in the event of Hillary Clinton becoming president. The US's departure from
the Paris Accord is not irreversible. While relations with the UN and NATO
are undoubtedly different, reflecting in part Trump's ignorance of how these
international institutions function, the US has not left them and does not seem
likely to do so. The administration agreed a largely symbolic and strategically
useless bombing of Syria, much to the delight of American neoconservatives

like Bill Kristol and Max Boot, and liberal internationalists like Hillary Clinton, but events and the president's attention span quickly moved on, not least to the assassination of Qassem Suleimani in January 2020. This did, however, briefly alienate some of his supporters in the "Alt-Right" movement[2] who are committed to a white nationalist isolationism, as did the decision to increase troop deployment in Afghanistan (as well as shady military operations in parts of sub-Saharan Africa such as Niger). Much of this suggests then that Trump has not ripped up the liberal international order and insofar as there has been change, it reflects a mixture of incompetence combined with a belief that the US can make a series of bilateral deals across the world without Trump himself paying much attention to detail. Seen in this way. Trump is not so much isolationist and more someone who believes in the "art of the (bilateral) deal" – but this itself is still a challenge to a rules based multilateral order.

These issues are discussed in depth in the next chapter, but in terms of the Middle American Radicals (MARs) deemed so important to Trump, these issues are probably less important than that of the promise of Making America Great Again through the return of secure jobs that have been lost through globalization. Liberal wars of intervention and their disastrous failure might matter to the MARs, but less in terms of the significance of foreign relations, and somewhat more in terms of high casualty rates in regions already neglected by the liberal managerial state (Weiss 2017). This again feeds into the narrative of resentment discussed in the previous chapter, and brings us back to the question of multiculturalism.

Culture and globalization: cosmopolitanism and multiculturalism

The discussion above does not deal with a further question around globalization, namely that of migration and related debates around multiculturalism, an issue where conservative Brexiteers, paleoconservatives and Trump, and the populist Right share similarly sceptical viewpoints. Much of the argument here relates to debates around culture and globalization, and specifically multiculturalism and the question of migration. We have outlined in some depth throughout

2. The Alt-Right movement includes a variety of patriot, and white supremacist, movements but also one that has a significant online presence, the latter of which has drawn on counter-cultural ideas usually associated with the New Left. Indeed, the Frankfurt School critique of capitalist conformity and the culture industry has in effect been co-opted by a certain strand of Far Right would-be hipsters, critical of the liberal conformity associated with political correctness and a certain strand of identity politics. Paleoconservative intellectuals are themselves not unaware of this cultural Marxism. Above all, see Gottfried (2005). On the Alt-Right movement, see Niewert (2017) and the online culture wars involving the Alt-Right are discussed in Nagle (2017).

the book the problem of low and relatively stagnant wages in the last 30 years. Some conservatives accept that this has indeed been the case but suggest that this is because of the impact of high rates of immigration, which has led to intense competition between workers, especially in low-skilled jobs, which has served to drive real wages down. This, according to Fraser Nelson (2017) is "precisely why a lot of people voted for Brexit", and prominent Brexiteer Iain Duncan Smith even claimed that immigration has led to a 10 per cent fall in wages during the European referendum campaign in Britain (see NIESR 2016). This fits uneasily with post-Brexit scenarios of Britain competing on the basis of low rates of taxation and cheap labour but, leaving that aside, the implication is that with controls on immigration, wages will increase in the context of labour shortages. The basic reason for low wages, then, is, according to this argument, immigration (Miller 2016: 159). Similar arguments have been made that pressure on public services such as health and education have also been caused by immigration. The 2002 European Social Survey found that 57 per cent of the sample UK respondents believed that this was indeed the case, while only 11 per cent believed that migrants were net contributors (Dustmann *et al.* 2010: 2).

The problem with this argument is that it rests on the so-called lump-of-labour fallacy, which assumes that there is a fixed amount of jobs within a national economy, and so a migrant is essentially "taking" a job that would otherwise go to a native-born worker. This argument is problematic both for understanding the quantity of labour and wages within an economy, and indeed the broader relationship between population increase and economic growth. The problem is that while a shortage of labour in one particular sector may push up wages in that sector, that does not mean it will do so in the aggregate. A migrant earning wages does not simply negatively affect wages in the particular sector in which he or she works, but also has wider effects on demand in the economy, which might then serve to stimulate economic activity and indeed wages in other sectors. As Crouch points out:

> Under conditions of tight labour supply, one person's wage increase is another person's price increase. The pursuit of *generally* higher incomes through the enforcement of labour scarcity is a self-defeating project ... If it were really the case that reducing the supply of labour was a positive move, then we should find that towns and regions experiencing sudden population loss should have the most vibrant economies.
>
> (Crouch 2019: 36)

Indeed, at the same time, areas of large influxes of immigrants show no evidence of lower wages or higher unemployment (Wadsworth 2017: 7–8). Iain Duncan Smith's claim that migration led to a 10 per cent decline in wages was based on a misreading of data from a study that actually showed that the impact of migration on low wages was "infinitesimally small" (Portes 2017; and see Nickell & Saleheen 2015). A similar argument is the claim that migrants take all the new jobs in the economy, but this is a fallacy that conflates net and gross increases in employment. Thus, in 2016 net employment growth was around 500,000, and immigrant employment increased by 300,000. This led tabloid newspapers to conclude that immigrants had "taken" the majority of all new jobs for that particular year. But in fact the net employment increase was made up of the difference between 4 million gross new jobs, and 3.5 million gross jobs lost (Wadsworth 2017: 6). The 4 million figure was the appropriate point of comparison with immigrant jobs but this was lost in the hysteria. In terms of the impact on public services, we can also dismiss arguments that in essence scapegoat migrants for the neglect of public services such as health, education and housing. For instance, based on a study of migrants from Central and Eastern Europe from May 2004 to the immediate post-financial crisis period, Dustmann *et al.* (2010) found that in aggregate, they were 59 per cent less likely than hosts to receive state benefits and 57 per cent less likely to live in social housing. Moreover, based on a comparison of those with similar demographic profiles to the host population, migrants were 13 per cent less likely than the host population to receive benefits, and 29 per cent less likely to live in social housing (see also Wadsworth 2017: 10–11).

Much of the debate on immigration in the US replicates these errors. While it is true that the number of migrants – around 41 million in 2014 – is at its highest ever level, migrants as a proportion of the population comprise around 13 per cent, which is comparable to, and sometimes lower than, previous periods in history such as 1900 to 1930 (Casselman 2014). Over 60 per cent have lived in the US for 15 or more years, and most are lawful migrants. Around 47 per cent are naturalized citizens, and many others are lawful permanent residents, on temporary student or work visas, or refugees or asylum seekers. Although it is difficult to be certain about the number of undocumented migrants, the most reliable estimate is that the number was 11.7 million in 2012, down from 12.2 million in 2007 (Casselman 2014). This amounts to less than 4 per cent of the US population. Contrary to popular myth, exploited by Trump and paleoconservative intellectuals (Francis 2004), migrants are less likely to commit crime than the local population, and crime rates are lowest in states with the highest immigration growth rates. In 2015 in the state of Texas, there were 1,794 convictions per 100,000 "natives", compared to 782 for illegal immigrants and just 262 for legal migrants (Nowrasteh 2018a). Migrants cannot claim most benefits, and legal migrants who have to wait a five-year period to receive social security and Medicare are still less likely than native-born Americans to claim welfare benefits (Nowrasteh 2018b). Despite some conservative claims to the contrary, there is no evidence of terrorist camps near the Mexican border (Kaplan 2014). While it is true that Mexico remains the largest source of migrants to the US (not least because NAFTA led to cheap corn imports from the US and impoverished Mexican farmers), and the Mexican border is a major route into the country, net migration from Mexico has fallen significantly. Moreover, the real growth areas in terms of migrations are Asian countries such as India and China, which by 2012 accounted for 12 per cent and 10 per cent of the respective totals (Casselman 2014).

In some respects, however, the debate is less one of arguments about the economic contribution of migrants to a particular economy, and more a cultural one of what kind of society in which one might wish to live. Of course those hostile to migration often draw on spurious arguments such as those discussed above, including the view that migrants are disproportionate welfare recipients. But even when faced with facts, populists like Nigel Farage contend that he would rather be poorer and have fewer migrants rather than the opposite, so that lower economic growth is a price worth paying for less migration (Holehouse 2016). This, then, is less a question of utilitarianism and more one of moral economy, and in particular it is a challenge to the idea of multiculturalism. This can be broadly defined as a belief in the fair and equal treatment of culturally and ethnically diverse populations and in this respect can be linked to cosmopolitan ideas such as universal human rights (Kymlicka 2007). On the other hand, liberal critics of multiculturalism argue that the focus should be on individual rights and universalism, and that attempts to promote the group rights of particular cultures and communities amounts to special treatment, which in turn undermines cultural cohesion. In 2010 and 2011 Angela Merkel, Nicolas Sarkozy and David Cameron all claimed that multiculturalism had failed in Europe (see Bloemraad 2011). While conservative critiques might also argue the case for integration and assimilation rather than multiculturalism, some go further and argue for the existence of separate ethno-cultures (see below). Advocates of multiculturalism respond that while individual rights might be important, so too are group rights, and minority cultures – under certain conditions – should be granted certain rights of existence (Taylor, C. 1992). In this way, social equality and community cohesion can be enhanced through the celebration of cultural difference, provided that the rights of these cultures to exist are not subject to "internal restrictions" that deny the freedom of members of that community, including the right to exit that community (Kymlicka 1995). In more radical forms, critical multiculturalism suggests that culture is intimately connected to power and some cultures have been oppressed through a history of colonialism, racism and imperialism (Hall 2000). This approach, then, emphasizes that "integration failure" is less a product of multicultural policies and more a result of unequal social and economic structures, part of which are racial and ethnic inequalities. There are undoubtedly tensions and questions around the relationship between difference and culture on the one hand, and equality and inclusivity on the other, not least for the political Left committed to the principle of solidarity and thus some degree of similarity. But we will see below that conservative critiques of multiculturalism are largely based on scapegoating.

This brings us back to the ethno-nationalist argument that different cultures can only exist alongside each other, and not within the same cultural space. Sometimes this argument draws on Huntington's clash of civilizations, in that there is an assumption of relatively fixed cultures with insurmountable differences. This does beg the question of why and how such cultures do not exist in a permanent state of conflict and confrontation and, as we have seen in earlier chapters, isolationist policies can quickly give way to aggressively con-frontational ones for this reason. Huntington (1996) himself suggested that, despite cultural differences, peaceful co-existence could take place so long as these different cultures respected cultural difference and did not promote inter-ventionist policies that would lead to conflict. More important, as many have argued, the main problem with Huntington's thesis is his tendency to homogenize cultures and downplay conflicts within and similarities between, dynamic, changing cultures (Halliday 1996). But perhaps more significant – at least for understanding conservatism in the US – is Huntington's later work. In *Who Are We?*, Huntington (2004a) argues (in contrast to the paleoconservatives) that America is a creed and an ideal based on the beliefs of the "original" Protestant settlers, and this is central to American identity. This has been undermined by waves of migration, particularly from Mexico, as well as the supposed threat from Islam. As we saw in Chapter 3, Huntington (2004a) also expressed concern about the denationalization of privileged Americans, in which "Davos Man" had closer ties to fellow "global citizens" rather than other Americans. This argu-ment was closer to the paleoconservative position, which argues that America has been undermined by the rootless cosmopolitan coastal elites or globalists, who have betrayed the dreams of rooted Middle American Radicals. In this way, paleoconservatives celebrate more rooted white Americans who have close ties to their local communities, but who have been undermined by largely Protestant coastal elites (Francis 2016). Indeed, Thomas Fleming (cited in Ashbee 2000: 76) argues that the US is heterogeneous, as it is "rich in local and ethnic diver-sity, but at the same time identifiable in national terms". However, this focus on diversity does not mean that paleoconservatives claim allegiance to some kind of multiculturalism. Instead, like much of the European Far Right, emphasis is placed on rooted cultures and political systems based on ethno-nationalism. This, however, is less one of multiculturalism (though see below), and more an identitarian one based on ethnically similar cultures existing alongside, but sep-arate from, similar ethnically homogeneous cultures. Some European right-wing intellectuals argue for the "return" of grounded political communities based on shared history and culture, or what amounts to an ethno-pluralism (de Benoist 2017). Paleoconservatives have some sympathy with these views, though they do not envisage the break-up of the US, and indeed tend towards more pragmatic alternatives such as the devolution of power back to local states, the weakening of the federal state and coastal elites, and the massive curtailment of immigration (Francis 2016). In both cases emphasis is placed on the importance of local, grounded and culturally similar localities, but ones that exist alongside wider political orders.

While this ethno-pluralism is, by its very nature, bound to take very different forms across nations and localities (much, though not all, of the European Far Right is anti-American as well as anti-EU), what unites them is a rejection of the liberal international order and of what we might call domestic multiculturalism in the name of celebrating essentialist cultures. We have already pointed to the problem of essentialism in Huntington's work – its belief in cultures as unchanging, uncontested and communities of fate – and this can be applied to the paleoconservative and European approaches to ethno-politics. This argument has been developed further by Hazony (2018), who contrasts nations on the one hand, and imperialism and empires on the other, and supports the former on the grounds that nationalism represents an organic, natural order in contrast to artificial empires, which include institutions of global governance such as the European Union. This argument flies in the face of changing conceptions of national identity, which are far from fixed and subject to change in the context of migration, not least in the US. Contrary to Hazony's somewhat archaic claims, European state formation did not reflect the existence of "tribal loyalties" (Carneiro 1970) and indeed in many respects it was the absence of such loyalties that helped to consolidate centralized power (Teschke 2003). Moreover, his argument also rests on the claim that nationalism and imperialism are completely separate ideas and practices, when in fact history shows that the two are intimately linked.[3]

There is a further issue, which is that these views do not so much reject as *displace* multiculturalism (Spektorowski 2003). Alain de Benoist's emphasis on differentialism sounds less like a rejection of multiculturalism *per se*, and more an attempt to shift multiculturalism from the local and national to the global and international spheres. This begs the question of why and how such cultures, which can only conflict with each other in local or national communities, should and could peacefully co-exist at the latter levels but not at the

---

3. In this respect Hazony's arguments rest not only on an essentialist account of culture, but also an account of empire that mirrors that of Enoch Powell (see Chapter 4), in that there is in effect no problem with European empires and expansion to "the Other", but when "the Other" moves to the core, then ethno-nationalism becomes the order of the day.

former. These tensions are clear in the case of geopolitics as well, for example, in Steven Bannon's argument that that the West is at war with Islam, or indeed the appointment of John Bolton, a neoconservative fellow traveller, as US National Security Adviser in 2018 (though he then left the post in 2019). This is but one example of how the question moves quickly from one based on a supposedly objective analysis of irreconcilable cultural difference to one instead based on a political project in which some cultures and polities dominate others. De Benoist himself suggests that "the European race is not the absolute superior race. It is only the most apt to progress" as Indo-European authenticity "implies technological progress" (quoted in Spektorowski 2016: 126; 2000: 299). In this account, a relativist cultural difference on the surface exists alongside a more explicit cultural superiority. Indeed de Benoist has shifted from a position of support for French colonialism in the early 1960s and the Unilateral Declaration of Independence (UDI) in Rhodesia, to one where he now (selectively) uses anti-imperialist arguments associated with the Left (Spektorowski 2000; Bar-On 2013) to reject what he sees as a racist globalism, in which claims to liberal universalism actually involve the imposition of Western values on culturally different societies. This is an argument also made by the paleoconservative Samuel Francis (see Chapter 2), and indeed deployed at times by European Far Right movements (Lanzano 2018); for example, Lega Nord has drawn parallels between the plight of Native Americans in the US and what it chooses to call the cultural genocide of Northern Italy (see Bar-On 2013: 225). Such comparisons are absurd, and echo the argument that the Nazis were not nationalist (Hazony 2018). But the more important point is that this right-wing anti-imperialism and cultural relativism still upholds a cultural and political-economic hierarchy. This involves the stereotyping of other cultures in the name of an ahistorical authenticity, and the promotion of what is in effect a colonial international division of labour in which Europe produces higher-value goods, and the rest of the world produces lower-value agricultural goods (Spektorowski 2000: 299). Moreover, in terms of the practical problems faced in the real world, as opposed to the ideal scenarios envisaged by ethno-nationalists, it often involves a more straightforward hostility to other cultures. Thus, while de Benoist has criticized the National Front for its hostility to immigrants in France and indeed celebrated the right to difference between cultures, his former collaborator Guillaume Faye has taken a far more hostile position on Islam (Bar-On 2013: 187–200), and Francis' ethno-nationalism in the US easily spilled over into an endorsement of white supremacy. In practice, much of the populist Right deploys an identitarian politics that draws on the kind of differentialism endorsed by de Benoist, but equally deploys the more open hostility to "others" espoused by Faye.

Much of this leads to attempts to read off individual acts of crime from supposedly immutable cultural differences, even when immigrant crime rates are lower than the national average (as in the US), and the causes of crime are far more complex than questions of supposed cultural difference. Gun crimes by whites, including right-wing nationalists, are seen as unfortunate random acts of violence while crimes by immigrants are explained away by "culture". This is perhaps most clear in the case of Islam, which in some conservative hands is reduced to a monolithic religion that itself can explain Islamist terrorist actions, even though there is great diversity within the religion of Islam and indeed great diversity and division between Islamist political and terrorist groups (Zubaida 2009). Conservatives of all stripes express varying degrees of hostility to Islam and tend to see it as an existential threat to the Western way of life, a potential "great displacement" (Camus 2018), a new form of the old Red Scare argument for the post-Cold War world (Mudde 2018), and of older Far Right hostility to immigrants in general.

Some take this a step further and argue for a so-called race realism, which revives the long-discredited idea that different outcomes between different "race" groups are rooted in genetic differences (Taylor, J. 1992). Much of this repeats debates over differences in IQ tests and attempts to explain differential outcomes through genetic differences (Jensen 1969; Murray & Herrnstein 1994; Wade 2014), an argument taken up by some movements on the Far Right (see Hawley 2017). Nicholas Wade's (2014) influential book, *A Troublesome Inheritance*, was in fact dismissed by 139 geneticists, many of who he had favourably cited but whose work he had actually caricatured (*New York Times* 2014). Race science essentially argues that there are clear genetic differences, such as the fact that different groups of people have different vulnerabilities to diseases, so it is perfectly possible that this might also apply to intelligence. The problem with this argument is that intelligence, and, even more narrowly, IQ-specific intelligence, is based on thousands of genes and evolution takes place over many millennia, and there is no evidence of cognitive advance rooted in genetics in the last 100,000 years. Moreover, IQ testing has shown considerable variation that cannot be explained by genetics – for instance, in cases where identical twins have been separated in infancy and experienced very different upbringings, and between different ethnic groups measured over a relatively short period of time (Evans 2018). In short, race realism is simply a spurious ideological justification for racism, and nothing more. It is therefore not surprising that much post-1945 racism is rooted in culture and not supposed biological differences. As we have seen this sometimes takes the form of de Benoist's cultural differentialism, but this supposed celebration of differences often gives way to an argument where some cultures are not only different, but better than others. Hazony's (2018) rigid separation of nationalism and imperialism suffers from the same fallacy.

In terms of ethno-nationalism becoming ethno-centrism, there are again some parallels between the radical Right and Brexit, for in some respects the radical

Right is a radicalized version of post-1945 racialized Western liberal democracies, "extremist only by virtue of the strident and shrill tone of radical right wing populist discourse and its uncompromising position" (Betz & Johnson 2017: 79). This argument reflects the limits not of multiculturalism, but of the ways in which racism was not challenged, and the fact of continued discrimination against migrants, not least by those supposed cosmopolitan liberals associated with the third way, particularly in terms of welfare and incarceration policies (see Chapter 3). It is therefore not surprising that centre-right parties have entered coalitions with them, and indeed both centre-left and centre-right have drawn on similar populist rhetoric at times, not least in terms of policies on welfare and law and order (see Chapter 3). Indeed, in 2018, Hillary Clinton suggested that immigration controls were necessary to stop the populist tide (Wintour 2018).[4] This has intensified in the years since as increasing pressure on public services and the welfare state led migrants to become a convenient scapegoat for these social and political problems. Even some further to the left than Clinton have called for controls on immigration to defend the welfare state (Goodhardt 2017; Streeck 2016), or even an essentialized white culture (Miller 2016: 160; Kaufmann 2018),[5] while at least seeming to accept that it has been neoliberal policies and not migrants or refugees that have exacerbated social problems. Like Clinton, this is an argument that allows Far Right populists to set the political agenda, and which naively believes that the Far Right would then somehow halt its exclusionary rhetoric rather than find new targets to scapegoat, not least as the crisis of the welfare state would continue in this context (Crouch 2019: 9).

Important here is the perception that Western societies have been burdened by "floods" of refugees. In fact, in 2017, nine of the top ten countries hosting refugees were from outside Europe or the US, with only Germany making the list. The other countries were Turkey, Pakistan, Uganda, Lebanon, Iran, Bangladesh, Sudan, Ethiopia and Jordan (UNHCR 2018). Factoring in the population of receiving countries changes the list of countries, but does not fundamentally change the fact that the main hosts for refugee countries are countries from the Global South. The top ten recipients based on number of refugees per 1,000 inhabitants in 2017 were Lebanon, Jordan, Turkey, Uganda, Chad, Sweden,

---

4. Indeed, Trump himself suggested more immigration checks in response to the white supremacist terrorist attack in El Paso in August 2019.

5. Kaufmann's (2018) notion of "whiteshift" is based on the idea that white culture should be treated as seriously as anti-racist cultures. This argument is in part made because he rejects the idea of structural racism and so sees white and black culture as equivalents, but he fails to address the many studies that show overwhelming evidence of black disadvantage in liberal democracies (Bonilla-Silva 2014). Moreover, his essentialist account of culture effectively replicates the ethno-nationalism of the Far Right, and does not address the ways in which national culture changes over time.

South Sudan, Sudan, Malta and Djibouti (UNHCR 2017). Similarly, in terms of migrants, EU citizens routinely overestimate the proportion of people in their country born outside the bloc. Estimates vary – for instance, in Britain the estimate is 21 per cent and the actual figure is 8.3 per cent – but on average their estimate is double the actual share (Politico 2018).

But even in narrow electoral terms the argument is problematic. As previous chapters make clear, in both the US and Britain, the argument that the "white working class" simply abandoned the Left for Trump and Brexit is far too simplistic. The rise of the populist Right has coincided with the decline of social democratic parties, but this does not mean that one caused the other. This is a fallacy that unites cosmopolitans like Clinton and Blair with nationalist leftists like Streeck. Moving beyond our two cases, the picture is similarly more complex than the idea of a white working-class flight to right-wing populism. As Mudde (2019) shows, the average vote share for social democratic parties in Western Europe rose to more than 30 per cent in the 1950s and remained stable until the late 1980s. In the late 1990s, the average vote share fell back to just under 30 per cent, only to drop off sharply in the 2000s, so that by 2019 the average share is just above 20 per cent. At the same time, up to the early 1980s, populist radical Right parties were largely irrelevant in Western Europe, polling at about 1 per cent. By the 1990s, this increased to only about 5 per cent. Thus, as the vote share for social democratic parties fell in the 1990s, populist parties did not grow significantly. In the 2000s, Right populist parties did grow but they still average around 10 per cent. The picture is even clearer when we look at individual countries. In Switzerland, the Swiss People's Party almost doubled its support between 1995 and 2015, from 14.9 per cent to 29.4 per cent, but the Social Democratic Party of Switzerland declined by 3 per cent in the same period. In Germany, the Social Democratic Party's decline started after 1998, and especially in 2009, but this was four years before the AfD formed. In the Netherlands, the Dutch Labour Party (PvdA) declined most significantly in the 2017 election, but this was seven years after Geert Wilders' Party for Freedom (PVV) achieved its greatest electoral success. Finally, in 2019, Spain's Social Democratic Party, which had suffered electorally prior to the rise of the populist radical right-wing Vox Party, recovered substantially in this same election, and indeed achieved something of an electoral victory, in the same election that Vox entered parliament with 10.3 per cent of the vote (Mudde 2019).

Specifically applied to the US, there are a number of issues here that require further consideration, which relate to the specific character of populism in the US, the centrality of race and, once again, the question of the so-called white working class. In particular, there is the argument that populism in the Republican Party is not new, and can be dated back to the struggle for Civil Rights. While the US successfully avoided the authoritarianism of much of Europe in the 1930s, the neo-Keynesian New Deal was based in part on a compromise between "progressive" Northern Democrats committed to interventionist policies such as fiscal stimuli, public works programmes and welfare policies, and reactionary Southern Democrats committed to the maintenance of white privilege (Katznelson 2014). By the 1960s, and specifically under President Johnson, Civil Rights legislation undermined the New Deal alliance and the Republicans increasingly won the racist South. As part of a wider realignment in US politics in which the Republicans captured increasing numbers of white working-class voters, the Democrats increasingly moved towards an electoral alliance of the educated white middle class, African Americans and other minorities, which culminated in the "pro-globalization" alliance from the 1990s onwards (see also Chapter 3).

While there is some truth to this argument, we need to treat some of it with caution. The New Deal did indeed promote a racialized "new liberalism" and welfare policies favoured and in some respects reinforced white privilege – and as we have seen the Tea Party is in some respects a response to the extension of welfare beyond the white population. But at the same time – and this is important for understanding not only the dynamics of American electoral politics, but also progressive alternatives to both third way neoliberalism and conservative anti-globalization – it does somewhat over-simplify the story. In particular, it suggests that not very much changed between Roosevelt's election in 1932 and the passage of Civil Rights legislation in the 1960s, and specifically fails to explain significant changes in both the Democrat and Republican Parties. The New Deal in some respects facilitated anti-racist struggles, and indeed its most active opponents were right-wing Republicans and Southern Democrat leaders, both of whom came together to introduce the anti-labour Taft-Hartley Acts in 1947 as well as opposing Civil Rights legislation. Similarly, Civil Rights legislation did not appear from nowhere but reflected social and political realignments that emerged out of the New Deal (Schickler 2016). The South itself benefited from substantial investment in the 1950s under President Eisenhower, and the Republican Party benefited from support in new wealthy suburbs in the "Sunbelt". While 1964 did see the culmination of a racial shift in voting, in which the Democrats captured 85 per cent of the African American vote, by as early as the late 1940s most African Americans had shifted their allegiance to the Democrats (Schickler 2016). It was also in the 1940s, and especially in 1946, when strikes were very common, that the CIO attempted to organize white and African American workers across the race divide. The shift to the Republicans of whites in the South was also a long-term process, one which culminated in support for "state rights" against Civil Rights in 1964, particularly under the candidacy of Barry Goldwater.

Some have argued that since then we have seen another shift, namely that of the movement of white working-class Democrats to the Republican Party. Much of the explanation for this shift is indeed the loss-of-the-South argument associated with Lyndon Johnson, which suggests that once the Democrats took Civil Rights seriously, then they were bound to lose their base among white workers. While there is some validity to this argument, it has been extended in a variety of ways, with some suggesting that white workers are more culturally conservative (and racist) than the rest of the population and this is one reason why they are more likely to vote Republican than Democrat (Haidt 2012). This argument is not dissimilar to an important – and populist – Republican Party strategy document of 1969, authored by Kevin Phillips, called *The Emerging Republican Majority*, which suggested (almost 50 years before Steve Bannon) that the Republicans could win the white working-class vote as the Democrats focused more on culture and rights rather than the economy. Bartels (2005; see also Jacobs 2012) provides data that suggest that in the period from 1952 to 2004, there was a 6 percentage-point decline for Democrats among the so-called white working class, which is (problematically) defined as those white employed Americans without a college degree. This is not, then, a massive swing but even one of this level might be enough to secure electoral victory. However, Bartels also suggests that college-educated voters over this period became more likely to vote Democrat. On the face of it, this sounds like supporting evidence for the third way Democrat position but we might add that college education alone does not guarantee exit from the working class. Indeed, if we factor in income, the evidence suggests that since the 1970s, high-income whites are *less* likely to vote Democrat than lower-income whites. In the 2008 election, Obama narrowly lost to McCain (51 to 47) among low-income whites, but in contrast lost 58 to 40 among all non-college whites (Jacobs 2012: 4–5). Finally, Bartels suggests that the exodus from the Democrat Party is almost completely explained by a shift in voting patterns in the South, so that in the period from 1952 to 2004, Democrat decline among non-college whites was almost 20 percentage points. Indeed, in 2008, Obama won 54 per cent of the vote of whites with incomes under $50,000 outside of the South, compared to 35 per cent in the South (Jacobs 2012: 5). Bartels further argues that in the period from 1984 to 2004, economic issues were twice as likely to determine voting behaviour than cultural issues, the latter of which were actually more important to those that were college-educated. This suggests, then, that the social basis of populism in the US is far more complicated than simply being a response by an angry white working class, an argument we have already made in the context of the Trump vote.

As we saw in Chapter 3, the third way and cosmopolitan liberalism essentially argued that the erosion of manufacturing in the developed world had eroded old class loyalties, and the new service economy presented new opportunities for entrepreneurial individuals. But we also saw that in fact this period experienced an intensification of inequalities. This led to the Left nationalist critique that globalization and its third way advocates had betrayed the "left-behind" white working class (The Full Brexit 2018; Streeck 2019), who were easy prey for right-wing populists (Eatwell & Goodwin 2018). The accusation was also made – with some foundation – that cosmopolitan (neo-)liberals were essentially patronizing in their attitude to the "left-behind". Ironically, the very same third way advocates share a concern with the left-behind, suggesting that there is a need to change their behaviour through state policies such as welfare to work, but also through accepting the need for policies that "win back" the left-behind to (third way) social democracy. This includes policies to "reclaim nationalism" (Mounk 2018), in part through the adoption of a "progressive approach" to immigration (Redgrave 2019). This is an argument ironically shared with Left nationalists and it essentially involves the adoption of nativist policies, the agenda of which is set by populist parties (Mudde 2019). We have already suggested that adapting to populist rhetoric is unlikely to hinder the populist Right, and indeed is more likely to embolden these groups. As we have already argued in Chapter 3, the cosmopolitanism and multiculturalism of third way politicians was always compromised in terms of welfare, incarceration and indeed immigration policies. There was also much rhetoric from British Labour government ministers before 2010 calling for "British jobs for British workers" (Mudde 2019), insisting that Muslim women remove their Niqabs during MPs' surgeries (Younge 2009), that schools had been swamped with the children of asylum-seekers (White and Travis 2002) and indeed that the Empire was a cause for celebration (Brogan 2005). Significant in this respect are the findings of Oesch and Renwald (2017), based on surveys across nine European countries where the populist Right were significant electoral forces from 2000 to 2015. In this period, 31 per cent of production workers and 23 per cent of service workers surveyed voted for radical Right parties. This is not an insignificant figure, but even in the postwar boom a substantial proportion of working-class voters did not vote for social democratic parties and it still does not point to wholesale flight from social democratic to populist Right parties. Moreover, as should be clear from the above, most voters who switch their loyalties away from social democratic parties do not go to the populist Right, but instead to green, radical Left or socially liberal parties, or indeed do not vote. The populist Right tends to win most of its votes from more mainstream right-wing parties (Mudde 2019). This, then, is a more nuanced story than that told by both Left nationalists and cosmopolitan neoliberals, one that overlaps with the British and US case studies discussed in Chapters 4 and 5, in the context of Brexit and Trump.

Conclusion

The focus in this chapter has been mainly on the relationship between globalization and culture, and more specifically the questions of cosmopolitanism, migration and multiculturalism and the nativist challenge to these from the Right. We have seen that this takes a number of forms, but in all cases there is hostility to immigration because it undermines local, national and traditional culture. In this respect the populist Right – including to some extent Trump and US conservatism and Brexit and British conservatism – are committed to some kind of ethno-nationalism even as populists disagree on the extent to which this can be enacted. While the argument takes a quite sophisticated turn in the form of de Benoist's support for cultural difference (an argument mirrored in some respects by Enoch Powell), even this draws on arguments based on an essentialist, unchanging and uncontested understanding of culture. Given that this understanding ultimately rests on stereotypes, it is not surprising that – as in the case of Powell – it also lends itself to a more overt hostility to migrants and an ethno-nationalism in which some cultures are superior to others. This often involves drawing on spurious economic arguments that attempt to represent migrants as a burden on the (welfare) state and a cause of low wages within a country. While previous chapters have suggested that conservative populism in part emerged in response to the problems of neoliberal globalization, this chapter has developed arguments made in earlier chapters that the two are not simply opposing forces. This is partly because, as Muller (2016) has argued, the populist vision and the neoliberal globalization that preceded it are to some extent a mirror image of each other. The global or the national are either partly championed or dismissed through the idea of contrasting a global good with a national bad or vice versa, and the "one people" rhetoric of populism parallels the "one policy" rhetoric of neoliberalism. It is also because in some cases populist parties themselves might support neoliberal economic policies. This is most clear in the case of Brexit and global Britain, but also in the case of the supposedly anti-globalization Trump and his attempt to run America as a business and "make better deals". It is also clear in the case of some populist parties like the AfD, which combine cultural nationalism, including for the welfare state, with more pro-"free market" policies. The next chapter looks more deeply at the so-called free market through a detailed examination of the political economy of globalization, and conservative responses to it.

7

CONSERVATISM AND THE POLITICAL ECONOMY OF (ANTI-)GLOBALIZATION: A CRITIQUE

This chapter expands and extends the critique of conservative responses to globalization outlined in the last chapter. This chapter focuses specifically on the political economy of actually existing globalization. It does so in four sections. First, conservative (and other) arguments both supportive and critical of free trade are considered, through a detailed analysis of the case for comparative advantage and free trade. This opening section problematizes this case, but equally suggests that at least some of the conservative critiques of free trade, including those associated with the Trump administration, are unconvincing and likely to make matters worse. In keeping the focus on the US, the second section then considers the question of US decline and asks whether US (capitalist) hegemony in the international order has declined, or whether in fact it has globalized. The section suggests that it is more a case of the latter than former, and this informs the discussion in the third section. This examines the practice of the Trump administration and questions the viability of protectionism for securing the goal of "making America great again". Equally, however, the section questions the extent to which the Trump administration is not so much isolationist or protectionist, as opposed to using the threat of tariffs to extract concessions from countries on a largely bilateral basis. The section concludes that there are both protectionist and bilateral tendencies in the administration, but neither of these are likely to secure the goal of increasing high-wage manufacturing jobs on a scale envisaged by Trump. The fourth section then returns to the case for free trade through consideration of the argument that Brexit will involve a return to a global Britain, based on spontaneous free trade with countries across the globe, and reinforced by cultural similarities between Anglosphere countries. Here the argument is made that both Trump and Brexit, in different but related ways, underestimate the reality of global value chains and intra-firm trade in the world economy and the ways in which regulation is central to the making of a global economy.

Conservative support for and challenges to free trade

At the heart of both paleoconservative and (possibly) Trumpian views on political economy is the view that globalization has led to US decline, and this is because countries have benefited unfairly at the expense of the US. This argument takes a number of forms. First is the argument that free trade, or the mobility of capital, or both, have led to the deindustrialization of the US. In this case the argument is made for protectionist tariffs to protect US jobs, and/or incentives such as lower rates of corporate taxation, to encourage the return of jobs – above all in manufacturing – to the US. In addition, higher tariffs will discourage companies from overseas outsourcing as the imports from this production will be more expensive. Second is the argument that it is not free trade *per se*, but rather the unfair way in which this has been carried out, that is problematic for the US. While this argument does not preclude the possibility of tariffs, much of the focus here is on extracting better trade deals from other countries. Trade negotiations should therefore discourage practices such as intellectual property theft, currency manipulation to make exports cheaper, the dumping of cheap goods onto foreign markets and the end of restrictions on market access.

To understand what is at stake here we might usefully revisit Ricardo's theory of comparative advantage. Adam Smith had argued for a division of labour in which specialization would increase the total aggregate output in an economy. This principle operated internationally so that countries should not produce goods that they could purchase more cheaply from overseas. Ricardo developed this argument further through his theory of comparative advantage. Based on a two-country, two-product account of international trade, Ricardo argued that even in a situation where one country had an absolute advantage in both products, it still made sense for that country to specialize in production in the good in which it had a relative or comparative advantage. Thus, in his famous example, Portugal produces both cloth and wine with less labour than England. However, Portugal is relatively more efficient at producing wine, and so should specialize in that particular product. If Portugal specialized in wine it would produce 200 barrels a week, and if it specialized in cloth it would produce 600 bolts of cloth. England's equivalent figures are 50 barrels of wine and 500 bolts of cloth. If both countries focus on producing both of these goods, based on half of the labour force concentrating on each good, then the figures would be 125 wine (100 Portugal, 25 England) and 550 cloth (300 Portugal, 250 England). Portugal has an absolute advantage in both; however, it has a lower opportunity cost in wine, in that it sacrifices three bolts of cloth to make one bottle of wine. Through trade, Portuguese winemakers will get more cloth from England for each bottle of wine sold to England, rather than through the purchase of Portuguese cloth for Portuguese wine. Through specialization, total output is increased to 700, with 200 barrels of wine from Portugal and 500 bolts of cloth from England.

This rather neat case for free trade and the exercise of comparative advantage rested on a number of assumptions. In terms of capital, the assumption is that it can move swiftly from producing one product to another, and at the same time this mobility operates within but not between national borders. In other words, capital is nationally mobile but internationally immobile. Equally, in terms of labour, the assumption is made that trade takes place in the context of the full utilization of labour, or what we might today call full employment. This assumes that, like capital, labour will move relatively painlessly, rapidly and without cost, from employment in cloth to employment in wine, or vice versa. From these assumptions we logically arrive at Ricardo's case for specialization. The problem, though, is that these assumptions are highly problematic. Watson (2017), for instance, argues that Ricardo's original formulation of the theory reflected not some hypothetical trading relationship between England and Portugal. It was rather the outcome of specific trading relations between English cloth and Portuguese wine producers, and the powers of the former in brokering a favourable trading agreement both for cloth exports and wealthy imports of Portuguese wine, all of which was sustained from 1703 by British military backing. This in turn condemned Portugal to unequal terms of trade and deficits, but these were financed through gold that was extracted from Brazil, under conditions of African slave labour. In other words, the supposed liberal trading order associated with comparative advantage rested on highly illiberal foundations and unequal power relations. Similarly, the British conversion to free-trade principles in the nineteenth century happened only after it had developed competitive advantage over other countries, and which still involved the use of state power, including military force (see Semmel 1970; Chang 2002; Kiely 2010). Indeed, as we saw in Chapter 5, the US regarded British support for free trade in the nineteenth century as an imperialist conspiracy.

More specifically, while money capital might be as mobile as Ricardo suggests (though this applies internationally as well as nationally), this is not the case for productive capital, or what is in effect technology. Put simply, the Ricardian assumption, or "vice" (Schumpeter 1954), is that capital simply shifts from cloth to wine production, but the machinery necessary to produce one is very different from that needed in the other sector, and so the closure of wine producing technology represents in effect lost capital. Furthermore, if Portugal has an absolute advantage in both products, then there is every incentive for capital to leave England and set up production of both cloth and wine in Portugal. For Ricardo (2004: 290), this makes sense theoretically in terms of efficiency, but also for consumers in both countries that will purchase cheaper goods as a result. The problem with this argument is the failure to consider the effect on incomes in England if production did completely relocate to Portugal. In any case, Ricardo argued that such relocation was unlikely because of the uncertainty of investing in new countries with different laws, including those related to investment (Ricardo 2004: 136–7).

How, then, is this theory relevant for understanding contemporary globalization? In one basic respect it is not, given that capital is far more internationally mobile than Ricardo envisaged. However, in effect the theory has been adapted to take account of this mobility, to explain how specialization works in the international economy, and the fact that there is a clear international division of labour based on specialization. Labour-abundant economies essentially specialize in the production of labour-intensive goods, while capital-abundant economies produce high-margin goods and services. In this way, jobs lost to the developing world tend to be in labour-intensive sectors, but these will be compensated by increased specialization in more skilled and capital-intensive sectors (Krugman 1986; Grossman & Helpman 1991). In this way, NAFTA was seen as a win-win trade deal in which an expanded single market would lead to an increase in specialization across the US, Canada and Mexico. With this specialization, incomes would rise, and so any short-term negatives such as job losses in the US would be compensated for by increased job creation in the US caused through greater specialization and an expanded market, where incomes would rise as a result of its own specialization.

As should by now be clear, however, this assumes a relatively costless shift of both capital and labour from one sector to another, and underestimates the significance of possible reasons why capital might relocate to lower-cost areas and the impact this might have in terms of demand. In terms of both the US and Britain, there has been significant deindustrialization. For today's Ricardians, this is not a problem because both economies have shifted from one based on a comparative advantage in manufacturing goods to one increasingly based on services or high-end manufacturing. This is precisely the argument made by third way theorists who suggest that globalization has given rise to an efficient allocation of goods and services in which labour-abundant developing countries specialize in labour-intensive production, and capital-abundant economies specialize in higher-skilled, capital-intensive production. Insofar as populism involves advocacy of protectionism – and in the case of the US it to some extent has – then this is regarded as yet another example of the irrationality of this backlash against the self-evident advantages of specialization. But this argument rests on precisely the unwarranted assumptions – the Ricardian vice – that are so problematic in the first place. Seen in this way, populist revolts against free trade "are not unthinking reactions against rationality, as mainstream economists like to believe, but reactions to the failure of the real world to conform to the irrational thinking of economists, and the damaging policies that have been imposed by politicians following their advice" (Keen 2017).

Most obviously, as is clear from earlier chapters, the loss of manufacturing jobs in the US has not led to their replacement by higher-wage, skilled work in the service sector, and indeed there have been significant losses in terms of benefits and relative stagnation in terms of wages (see Chapters 3 and 5). The US economy has become more trade-dependent, with trade accounting for around 5 per cent of GDP in the period from 1950 to 1975, but more recently accounting for around 15 per cent of GDP (Guilford 2016). Over more or less the same period, the US share of global GDP has declined from around 40 per cent in 1960 to around 25 per cent by 1980, though interestingly since then it has shifted upwards and downwards between around 22 and 32 per cent. Significantly, though, the latter figure referred to 2002, while the former refers to 2012, a period in which China's rise has been most marked (Patton 2016).

So does this kind of data, alongside that discussed in earlier chapters, mean that Trump and protectionist conservatism are correct? The Trump argument rests in part on a particular understanding of trade as something that is a zero-sum game. Trump the candidate thus argued that China is "stealing our jobs, they're beating us in everything, they're winning, we're losing" and NAFTA is "the worst trade deal maybe ever signed anywhere, but certainly ever signed by this country" (Thiessen 2016; Guilford 2016). Globalization does not work for the US, and trade is a zero-sum game in which one participant wins (has trade surpluses) entirely at the expense of the other (deficit countries). Much was therefore made of the fact that after NAFTA, the US moved from having a trade surplus with Mexico to a trade deficit, which was around $60 billion in 2016 (Erken & Tulen 2017). The figure for China for the same year was a deficit of $350 billion, while for Germany the figure was $80 billion (Erken & Tulen 2017), and these figures reflect that fact that the US has lost out to economic rivals such as Germany, Mexico and China. More specifically, Peter Navarro and Trump have both contended that trade agreements such as NAFTA, as well as wider economic relations, have paved the way for the deindustrialization of the United States. Navarro and Autry (2011) in particular envisage a US labour force where 20 per cent of workers are engaged in manufacturing industry, in contrast to the figure of around 10 per cent in 2016. Trump has made much of the fact that while in 1994 the percentage of the workforce in manufacturing stood at 15 per cent, by 2016 the figure was just 10 per cent (see Benanav 2016).

This argument suggests that in contrast to the win-win, positive-sum game envisaged by the theory of comparative advantage, trade can have negative effects. This is true not only for particular sectors, as some orthodox trade theories recognize (Ohlin 1933; Viner 2018), but also potentially for the wider economy due to the loss of capital that results. Moreover, there appears to be some correlation between relatively recent factory closures and support for Trump in the 2016 election (Davis 2016). This argument might be further reinforced by the fact that after NAFTA was signed, foreign direct investment to Mexico increased, from less than $3 billion in 1994 to $8 billion in 2016, and as much as $11 billion by 2012, before falling back to $6 billion in 2013 (Guilford 2016). In this period, the US trade deficit with Mexico also increased sharply. The assumption of comparative advantage theory, at least when updated to factor in international capital mobility, is that this reflected sound fundamentals, and Mexican specialization in labour-intensive production alongside increased US specialization in higher-value goods and services, some of which could then be exported to the growing Mexican market, was mutually beneficial. However, the problem here is that one of the reasons why capital was invested in Mexico was to take advantage of lower labour costs. Comparative advantage assumes higher income through greater investment, and this higher income is good for both Mexicans (higher living standards) and Americans (a larger market for their products). Indeed, through specialization, there is the possibility of a growing convergence between the US and Mexico, an argument made by twentieth-century versions of comparative advantage theory (Ohlin 1933). However, if one reason for investment is low wages, then the possibility of higher living standards is far from secure. Indeed, in the period from 1993 to 2016, Mexican GDP per capita has risen less (24 per cent) than US GDP per capita (39 per cent) (Guilford 2016).

This is clearly a problem for the assumptions behind orthodox trade theory. Equally, however, these data suggest that there is also a problem for the Navarro-Trump argument that the US is losing at the expense of Mexico. In the period since NAFTA was signed, Mexico has seen no decrease in rates of poverty (around 52 per cent from 1994 to 2012) and only very small wage increases (Weisbrot *et al.* 2017). While it is true that since 1994 US manufacturing jobs as a proportion of all US jobs have fallen, this is also true of Mexico, for over the same period the proportion there fell from 20 to 15 per cent (Benanav 2016). Job losses in US manufacturing are thus hardly being "stolen" by Mexican workers. Furthermore, the decline of manufacturing long pre-dates free-trade agreements like NAFTA. Manufacturing accounted for around 30 per cent of non-farm jobs in 1950, and around 25 per cent by 1970. The figure for 2016 of slightly less than 10 per cent suggests an acceleration since 1970, and indeed the period from 2000 to 2010 saw a sharp decline in manufacturing employment, but long-term manufacturing employment decline has also occurred in manufacturing powerhouses like Germany, even when allowing for the effects of reunification (DeLong 2017). Following NAFTA, there was no sharp increase in unemployment, and indeed in the automobile industry employment actually increased in the period from 1994 to 1997.

Chapter 2 considered the hyper-globalization thesis and we can reconsider it here with specific reference to the idea of a race to the bottom. This suggests a new international division of labour, in which capital takes advantage of cheaper labour and other costs, and therefore manufacturing has left the core countries for the periphery (Frobel *et al.* 1980; Burbach & Robinson 1999). Although this argument is one in which the blame is placed on capital, there is some overlap with the Trump-Navarro view, which suggests that there is a zero-sum game in terms of the location of manufacturing employment.

In stark contrast, Rodrik (2015) has suggested that a process of "premature deindustrialization" is taking place in much of the South, where countries are deindustrializing at low rates of per-capita income compared to the developed world,[1] and moving into low-paid service work and a massive informal sector of urban marginality (Davis 2004; Sumner 2016). Thus, in terms of shares of global manufacturing value added (MVA), and in terms of manufacturing value added's contribution to GDP, we have generally seen a decline in the period from 1970 to 2013 in Western Europe, but also in Latin America and the Caribbean, and sub-Saharan Africa. Meanwhile the shares in both have increased for non-China Asia, and China itself. China's share in global MVA (measured at 1.0) increased from 0 in 1970 to 0.18 in 2013, while the share of MVA to its GDP increased from 0.09 in 1970 to 0.36 in 2013. Latin America's share in global MVA remained the same across the period, at 0.06, while the share of MVA to its GDP declined from 0.20 to 0.16. Sub-Saharan Africa saw a static share in global MVA but a decline in MVA as a share in GDP (from 0.14 to 0.11). While the US's share of global MVA declined from 0.26 to 0.19, the contribution of MVA to its GDP remained the same (Rodrik 2015: table 1). In terms of output, then, we do not see a sharp shift in terms of manufacturing to the South in general, and indeed some decline outside of Asia. This is deemed to be premature deindustrialization because, in contrast to the Global North, much of the South reached peak manufacturing at an earlier point than the Global North. There are a number of possible reasons for this phenomenon. These include competition from China (which may be a bigger problem for the South than it is for the US, as we discuss below), the impact of trade liberalization on industries in the South, the global spread of manufacturing through the deployment of outsourcing and global value chains and higher productivity growth in manufacturing (UNCTAD 2003; Palma 2005). Thus – though we have not yet dealt with the question of China – deindustrialization appears to be a concern for North and South alike, which suggests a more complex scenario than the zero-sum game envisaged by Navarro and Trump.

1. The figure for the developed world is usually cited as around $10,500 based on 1995 purchasing power parity data.

Before we turn to China, we first need to consider why premature deindustrialization might actually matter, and indeed what is meant in this context by the idea of being premature. A longstanding debate in the study of development contends that if you want to develop you must industrialize (Kitching 1982; Kiely 1998). Much of the debate here is over the question of what is meant by development; briefly, the economic argument is that manufacturing is important because it will foster higher rates of growth, which is either the same as, or a precondition for development, in poorer countries. The reasons for this vary, but essentially manufacturing is associated with forward and backward linkages, technological progress, economies of scale and knowledge spill-over. In addition, these factors are associated with a deepening division of labour, specialization at the level of the firm and higher productivity and thus output (Kaldor 1967; Kitching 1982: chapter 1).

The focus on manufacturing brings us back to a consideration of Ricardian trade theory, for output, income and employment is not simply a product of specialization through trade and the exercise of comparative advantage. What is also important is the kinds of goods and services produced within a country. Useful here is *The Atlas of Economic Complexity* (Hausmann *et al.* 2011; see also Keen 2017), which suggests that it is diversity rather than specialization *per se* that is important in determining success in international trade. Particularly important are ubiquity (how many countries export a particular product) and diversity (how many products a specific country exports). As Keen (2017) suggests, in a world of free trade and the exercise of comparative advantage, one would expect flows based on low ubiquity and diversity. However, this is generally only true in the case of developing countries, and not the richer countries of the Global North, which tend to produce and export a wider diversity of goods and those same goods tend to be produced in fewer countries. This diversity is in part a product of earlier processes of manufacturing, which have led to linkages, spill-overs, economies of scale and higher productivity (the last of which has led to the employment of fewer workers and, in this sense, deindustrialization). In contrast, developing countries are often dependent on export revenue from only a small number of products, many of which are produced in a large number of other (usually also developing) countries. It is for reasons such as these that many development economists after 1945 advocated industrialization in the newly independent "third world". This was seen as necessary to overcome what were considered unequal terms of trade between higher-value industrial producers and lower-value primary goods producers, which faced a tendency for prices to fall more rapidly than industrial producers, above all because of intense competition between these "non-ubiquitous", non-diversifying specializers (Prebisch 1959). Seen in this way, specialization through the exercise of comparative advantage in effect recommended a policy of trading into poverty, or "immiserizing growth" (Mackintosh 2004). These countries are overwhelmingly in the Global South and certainly not the US.

This still does not deal with the question of China, where manufacturing employment has expanded over the last 30 years. In the period from 1993 to 2008, Chinese exports grew in real terms by about 500 per cent and by 2010 China had emerged as the world's biggest exporter (Steinfeld 2010: 71). In 1983, direct foreign investment amounted to $1.73 billion spread over 470 projects; by 2006, $193 billion of FDI found its way to 27,514 projects (Steinfeld 2010: 72). Autor *et al.* (2016) suggest that competition from China accounts for as much as 21 per cent of US manufacturing employment decline in the period from 1990 to 2007 (see also Acemoglu *et al.* 2016). This accords with the argument that job losses might be a product of relocation or trade competition in some sectors (Wood 2017), of which China is a major factor. Indeed, Trump has argued that "China is robbing us blind in trade deficits and stealing our jobs" (cited in Lamp 2018: 6), and the 2017 Trade Policy Agenda claimed that the US had lost 5 million manufacturing jobs since China's entry to the WTO in 2001 (Office of the US Trade Representative 2017).

This was the subject of intense debate as early as 2001, when Kletzer (2001) published a paper examining job displacement in low-, medium- and high-competitive importing industries in the US. As Milberg and Winkler (2013: 7–10) suggested, Kletzer's findings were used by both trade pessimists and optimists. But what was clear was that a significant proportion of workers – as much as 63.4 per cent from 1979 to 1999 – were re-employed with an average earnings loss of 13 per cent (Milberg & Winkler 2013: 9). But we should be careful to attribute these losses to trade *per se*, and accept the argument that trade can lead to some job losses, because we have to account for the far greater proportion of job losses *not* accounted for by these factors.[2] Indeed, in the period from 1982 to 2007, when deindustrialization in terms of employment was hugely significant, US manufacturing *output* increased by 131 per cent, which was faster than overall GDP growth (Moody 2017: 10). The sharpest falls in manufacturing employment occurred in periods of recession (1980–2, when 2.5 million manufacturing jobs were lost, 1990–2, when 869,000 manufacturing jobs were lost, and 2007–10, when 2 million manufacturing jobs were lost), which were also periods that saw significant falls in imports (Moody 2017: 12). Now of course these falls in imports did not cause falls in employment, and both reflected recessions, but equally it is mistaken to assume that falls in employment are caused by increases in imports, even if this might hold in specific sectors of the

2. According to Rowthorn and Coutts (2013: 10), the employment share of manufacturing in 23 developed countries fell by 8.7 percentage points, but an estimated 80 per cent of this was due to productivity growth and 20 per cent trade with low-wage economies.

economy. For manufacturing *output* in the US, apart from exceptions such as the period following the 2008 crash, there has been a consistently upward trend. There have been some sectoral declines, such as in furniture, wood products and printing, but these have been more than compensated for by increases in machinery, motor vehicles and parts, other transport equipment, food, beverages and tobacco. Labour productivity from 2006 to 2013 increased in all manufacturing by an estimated 90 per cent, and although a great surge in the computer and electronics sector is a significant part of this story, there were still high rates of productivity increases in sectors like motor vehicles, other transport, electrical equipment and apparel. Hicks and Devaraj (2015) estimate that in the period from 2000 to 2010, 88 per cent of job losses were accounted for by productivity increases rather than trade deals.

So, while we can accept the reality of deindustrialization, and indeed the failure of displaced jobs to be replaced by higher-value ones, it is far less clear that trade *per se* is responsible for these problems. While we might identify job displacement in some sectors, across the whole economy it is far from clear that deindustrialization has occurred because of a wholesale relocation to the developing world. Trump's claim that "We are reclaiming out heritage as a manufacturing nation again … We are going to bring back our jobs" should be seen in this light (cited in Lamp 2018: 7). So, what does this mean in terms of understanding the place of US capital in the global order?

Has US capital declined or globalized?

The wider question of US decline is central to the Trump idea of "making America great again". The symptoms of decline usually include falling US shares of world GDP, US (trade and budget) deficits and growing debt, the fiascos in Afghanistan and Iraq and the 2008 financial crisis and its aftermath, as well as the rise of China. Although this is an argument made by many on the Left (Arrighi 2007; Wallerstein 2003), it is also central to American conservative anti-globalization (Navarro & Autry 2011; Francis 2004; Buchanan 2003). Conversely, it could be argued that actually US hegemony has been central to the making of a global capitalism. US hegemony has not so much declined as globalized, not least because US capital and the US state continue to enjoy significant advantages in the international order. This includes low rates of interest on its debt, higher rates of return on its overseas investment and the related advantages gained from the international role of the dollar (Panitch & Gindin 2012; Starrs 2013; Saull 2012; Gourinchas & Rey 2005; Kiely 2015; Tooze 2018). Thus in 2015, US net investment income, based on measuring overseas liabilities to the US against US liabilities to the rest of the world, was positive, standing at over $200 billion (Mason 2016), which reflects the central role of US companies in the global political economy. Using the Forbes Global 2000 as a benchmark, based on the assets, market value, profit and sales of the top 2,000 corporations, Starrs (2013, 2014) examines the national distribution of profit across 25 broad sectors, both before and after the financial crisis. Comparing 2007 and 2013, US leadership increased in absolute terms in five sectors: business and personal services (from 46 in 2007 to 54 per cent in 2013), casinos, hotels and restaurants (from 52 to 56 per cent), computer hardware and software (from 70 to 72 per cent), financial services (from 47 to 52 per cent) and media (from 60 to 69 per cent). In a further five sectors (aerospace and defence; food, beverages and tobacco; heavy machinery; retail; utilities), US leadership increased relative to its nearest competitor and in a further five (conglomerates; healthcare equipment and services; heavy machinery; oil and gas; transportation) declined after the financial crisis but recovered after 2010. In both 2012 and 2013, the US was the leading country in 18 out of 25 sectors, and had a 40 per cent share in 10 of the 25 (Starrs 2013: 823; 2014: 87). Though China has undoubtedly had some success in "climbing the value chain", it continues to play a subordinate role in global production networks, which are still led by US companies. For example, in 2013, China accounted for 38 per cent of the world telecommunications exports, but Chinese firms account for just 6 per cent of the profit of all firms in that sector. In the same sector, the US accounts for 7.4 per cent of the world's exports, but 59 per cent of the profit share. In clothing, China accounts for 39 per cent of world exports but has no firm in the Forbes Global 2000 in that sector, while the US accounts for 1.3 per cent of exports but 46 per cent of profit share (Starrs 2015: 15–16). According to Credit Suisse's Global Wealth Report of 2015, the US accounts for 46 per cent of the world's millionaires, compared to China's 4 per cent, which reflects the fact that many of these make their money through overseas investment (Starrs 2015: 20). We might therefore argue that US *capitalist hegemony* has been "made great" through globalization.

Trump and the paleoconservatives are correct that Chinese exports have grown significantly in recent years. But we have already seen that these account for at most around one-fifth of job losses in US manufacturing, and it is equally one-sided to assume that China's growth equates to US weakness. One of the most significant factors in terms of Chinese export patterns is that they are highly dependent on the US and European Union markets. Indeed, if these two units are removed from the equation, then China (in both 2005 and 2010) had a trade deficit with the rest of the world. Thus, in 2010 China's trade balance stood at a surplus of $143.3 billion, while its surplus with the US was $201.2 billion and with the EU was $154.9 billion. Thus, its deficit with the rest of the world was over $200 billion, with much of this made up of deficits of around $79 billion each with both South Korea and Japan (Hung 2015: 129). China has a strategy to develop national champions and significant global companies by 2025, but the data we have presented here suggest that China continues to play a significant role in global production networks, and in some respects a subordinate one. Indeed, the continued central role of the dollar as an international reserve currency, combined with cheap goods from China and the payment of low interest to creditors (including China) on US debt, in many ways reflects US strength. Moreover, "Asia's massive investment in low yield US Treasury bonds was tantamount to a tribute payment through which Asian savings were transformed into American's consumption power, prolonging US prosperity but creating a financial bubble in the 1980s and beyond" (Hung 2015: 125).

It is of course true that the 2008 crisis did, in some respects, undermine this scenario, and we return to this question in the concluding chapter. But it should be clear that the 2008 crisis was also not just a problem for the US, but for every country in the international order. We might add in passing that while it is mistaken to view trade as a zero-sum game, as do Trump and Navarro in relation to the US and China, relations between countries attempting to increase their manufacturing production and exports in the world economy are far from a positive-sum game. This is because many countries have attempted to industrialize through the promotion of labour-intensive, low-value manufacturing production where barriers to entry are low (Kaplinsky 2005). It is precisely because barriers to entry are low that many countries enter this competitive race and the effect is to drive down the prices even further because of the intensity of competition. Seen in this way, China's industrialization does undermine the attempts of other countries to follow, through the promotion of low-value manufacturing. However, *this is a problem for other developing countries far more than it is for the US*, as the price of manufacturing exports from developing countries have tended to fall against more complex manufacturing and services from developed countries, including Chinese exports (Maizels *et al.* 1998). This is a very different scenario from Trump's contention that developing countries are stealing American jobs. Indeed, in some respects this is a case of "positive deindustrialization", in which manufacturing employment declines but manufacturing output increases because of higher productivity (Rowthorn & Ramaswamy 1999; Rowthorn & Coutts 2013; Tregenna 2009). This is in contrast to negative deindustrialization, which essentially amounts to a decrease in manufacturing employment and output. It should be obvious from our discussion that positive deindustrialization scenarios could, on the face of it, conform to the expectations of orthodox trade theory, based on the assumption that jobs lost in manufacturing would be replaced by jobs in the service sector. To an extent, as we have seen, this is the case, and in the US from 1973 to 2007, manufacturing employment fell by 25 per cent but manufacturing output rose by 172 per cent (Rowthorn & Coutts 2013: 19). The problem, however, is that most of these jobs have more often than not involved less-well-paid work with fewer benefits[3] – a picture that somewhat muddies the rather stark dichotomies between positive and negative deindustrialization scenarios, as should be clear from the discussion above. In Britain – as the conclusion to Chapter 4 implies – the scenario is one closer to straightforward negative deindustrialization as in the same period manufacturing output rose by 16 per cent while manufacturing employment declined by 58 per cent (Rowthorn & Coutts 2013: 19).

More broadly on trade, we need to highlight a second issue, which relates to the status of so-called trade deals and indeed the WTO itself. In many respects these are less about trade *per se* and more the consolidation and extension of global – and that means above all American – corporate power, particularly as regards intellectual property rights and the extension of the ability to pursue lawsuits against governments in the face of inappropriate regulations. Patents and intellectual property rights in effect give legal backing to such claims as they allow companies to monopolize knowledge for a given period of time, a practice reinforced by the WTO TRIPS (Trade Related Intellectual Property Rights) agreement, first negotiated in 1994 but since subject to considerable debate and controversy. While intellectual property rights should not necessarily be rejected out of hand, the balance is such that the resulting monopoly that arises from the property rights too often exceeds the benefits that is derived from the new knowledge. Since the 1970s, the lifespan of copyrights and patents has been extended in US law, and the WTO TRIPS agreement requires developing countries to adopt increasingly Americanized laws on these issues, and these have been extended by NAFTA and the proposed Trans-Pacific Partnership (see Baker 2016: 80). Over 90 per cent of all patents and most copyrights are held by rich countries,[4] which means that the cost of acquiring new knowledge for developing countries is increasingly expensive. The cost of the increase in technology licence payments alone for developing countries was $45 billion a year in 2004–5 (Chang

3. There is a significant debate on the extent to which jobs lost through imports have been compensated by the growth of jobs in the export sector. Feenstra & Feenstra (2018) thus argue against the pessimism of Autor *et al.* (2016) and suggest that job losses through manufacturing imports have been more or less compensated by job growth in exports. Rowthorn and Coutts (2013) argue that the export sector has not compensated for wider job losses in manufacturing. Importantly, however, they do not place the blame for these losses on trade *per se*, and this is perhaps the most important point. In some respects the arguments around trade *per se* having positive (orthodox trade theory) or negative (Trump, the race to the bottom) effects misses the wider point that we cannot simply focus on trade *per se*, and need to look again at the kinds of goods being traded, and thus the structures of production within countries. See further the discussion of *The Atlas of Economic Complexity* in the text.
4. See more detailed data in Kiely (2015: chapter 8) and Kiely (2016: chapter 3), showing the limits of the rise of the BRICS.

2007: 141). In 2001, the South African government was taken to court by multi-national companies because it had imported cheap generic drugs from India and Thailand to treat HIV/AIDS patients on the grounds that this was contrary to the TRIPS agreement. The MNCs withdrew their case and some even began to send cheap drugs to the African continent, but only under strong pressure from social movements (Chang 2007: 123–4). There has also been great concern that some companies have in effect become monopoly providers to farmers in the developing world, forcing the latter to purchase patented pesticides and herbicides when in the past these farmers used older seeds rather than making such regular purchases, which they can ill afford (Shiva 2001). There have also been cases where firms have claimed a patent over a natural plant, thus claiming a monopoly on something that was previously openly accessible to all. Concern that developing countries are in effect guilty of property theft should be seen in this context, namely that large corporations overwhelmingly located in the developed world, and above all the US, are in effect protecting high rates of profit through intellectual property rights. This is less an issue of developing countries "stealing American jobs" and far more one of corporations maintaining high rates of profit, particularly in sectors like pharmaceuticals. Moreover, the US's commitment to free trade remains selective and indeed, in the period from 2008 to 2016, the US employed far more protectionist measures than any other G20 country (CEPR 2017), reflecting the fact that the US sometimes promotes free trade for others but not for itself.

This final point leads us to the question of the Trump administration in practice, which is considered in the next section.

The Trump administration in practice: isolationist or bilateral?

In practice, the Trump administration's protectionist rhetoric has been real but also inconsistent and has sometimes involved some degree of compromise. The start of the second year saw the introduction of tariffs on certain washing machines and solar panels, followed by more substantial tariffs on imported steel (25 per cent) and aluminium (10 per cent) from selected countries (Milman 2018; Bown 2018). This, however, was still some distance away from a far more blanket 35 per cent tariff that was common in the campaign, and though these could escalate into wider trade disputes, they also need to be kept in perspective. Steel imports were already covered by significant exemptions such as special tariffs, quotes and voluntary export restraints, for around 40 years, and more than 60 per cent of steel was covered by such protection. This special protection particularly affected Chinese imports; China was only the tenth-largest exporter of steel to the US, although China also exports to other countries, such as Turkey, who then export to the US (Greeley 2018). In the case of aluminium, special exemptions have existed since 2009, and again have particularly affected China (Bown 2018). This was followed by (relatively small-scale) retaliation by China, in a number of agricultural sectors dependent on the Chinese market in places where support for Trump in 2016 was significant but also fragile, such as soybeans on the Great Plains, automobiles in the upper Midwest and oil in North and South Dakota and Texas (Green 2018). Considerable stock market volatility followed in 2018, much of which reflected the extent to which the threat of a much bigger trade war was regarded as likely or unlikely. By June and July 2018, trade tensions increased and were extended to a variety of products, and to other countries like Canada as well as the European Union. Trump increased the rhetoric, focusing on specific products and high tariffs, but downplayed the fact that the US itself had tariffs of 350 per cent on some tobacco products, and 55 per cent on some clothing and footwear items (Petroff 2018). But average tariff rates for all products – determined by total tariff revenue divided by the value of imported products – stood at just 2.6 per cent in 2016 (World Bank 2018). According to the World Economic Forum, US exports faced a tariff average of 4.9 per cent, broadly comparable to those faced by China, Japan, Russia and Brazil. While the EU's average was lower this in part was because of the high volume of trade in the tariff-free European single market (Petroff 2018). By the end of 2018, fears over the US budget deficit, the potential effects of tariffs and the end of the stimulus effects of tax cuts meant that stock market volatility was particularly pronounced, including for the share prices of companies like Apple that had global supply chains that were highly integrated with China. This continued into 2019, as tariffs escalated from May onwards (Cassidy 2019) so that by December 2019 it was planned that almost all of China's exports to the US were to be subject to some form of tariff levy (Farrer 2019). This plan was downgraded in October 2019, but it was still clear that tariff escalation had in effect developed into a trade war.

More widely, though, if we are to take the protectionist rhetoric of Trump, Peter Navarro and the paleoconservatives at face value, then we need to consider further the question of what we have already identified as global production networks or value chains, and the feasibility of a pro-capital administration that rhetorically rejects globalization. At a visit to Boeing's North Charleston factory in North Carolina in early 2017, Trump made his usual pronouncements about protecting manufacturing jobs. However, while the new Boeing 787-10 Dreamliner may have been assembled in South Carolina, it relied heavily on components from a number of countries, including Japan, South Korea, India, Italy, France, Sweden, Canada, Mexico and Australia. The planes assembled in the US are delivered to over 60 airlines throughout the world and international suppliers account for about 30 per cent of the plane's components. The Chinese market is particularly important for Boeing; the suppliers are not easily replaceable, as some are full partners that have invested significant capital and are locked in through the whole life of the programme. Shifting suppliers of the wings and batteries would involve granting billions of dollars in compensation to Japanese companies, searching for an American equivalent and massive new start-up costs (Zhang 2017).

The Boeing case is far from exceptional. According to the US Census Bureau, 26.6 per cent of US imports from Mexico in the period from 2007 to 2016 were made up of consumer goods, but as much as 28.1 per cent were of oil, raw materials and industrial inputs, and 35.6 per cent were investment goods. Any attempt to impose a blanket tariff of 40 per cent on Mexican imports would therefore increase the price of US goods, including exports, with likely detrimental effects on employment (Mason 2017). Furthermore, in aerospace in Seattle, the automotive sector in Michigan and electronics in Portland, exports account for at least 15 per cent of local GDP and jobs are thus dependent on such exports (Parilla & Muro 2017). Equally, intermediate goods (as opposed to final goods) account for about 43 per cent of total US imports and as much as 60 per cent of US exports (Erken & Tulen 2017). About 75 per cent of the trade deficit with China in 2016 was accounted for by just three sectors – electronic goods, the wholesale and retail trade, and textiles and footwear. Over 90 per cent of all imports of laptop computers and IT tablets are assembled in China (Erken & Tulen 2017), and trade statistics such as the US deficit with China include value that is effectively imported from elsewhere (Milberg & Winkler 2013: 36). In Mexico, just four sectors account for more than the total US trade deficit with that country – motor vehicles, mining, electronic products and electrical machinery. This reflects the high degree of vertical specialization in international trade, whereby successful exporters are also highly import-intensive (Milberg & Winkler 2013: 36).

These observations reflect the reality of world trade in an increasingly globalized world. Around 60 per cent of world trade is composed of trade between intermediate goods between different parts of the same firm, and 80 per cent is dominated by multinational companies using direct subsidiary or subcontracting and licensing links (UNCTAD 2013). US value added in Mexican motor vehicles is as much as 18.5 per cent and US firms draw heavily on foreign intermediaries – as much as 35.4 per cent in motor vehicles, 33 per cent in fuel and 23.5 per cent in machinery and equipment (Erken *et al.* 2017). According to the OECD, in 2014, 29.4 per cent of Chinese exports have a significant import content and while this is a high figure, other countries also have high import content in their exports. For Germany in the same year, the figure was 25.4 per cent, for the UK it was 21.9 per cent, for Japan 18.4 per cent and for the US it was 15.3 per cent (OECD 2017).

Moreover, even in sectors where there has been a decline in both employment and output – such as steel and aluminium – it is far from clear that protectionism will actually protect manufacturing jobs. For all his free-trade rhetoric, George W. Bush introduced tariffs on steel in 2002. While it is difficult to establish straightforward causality, not least in the context of widespread falls in manufacturing employment, it is true that this did not save jobs in manufacturing. Some estimates suggested that it led to losses in employment in steel-using manufacturing industries, to the tune of 200,000 jobs, including in Rustbelt states like Pennsylvania, Ohio and Michigan. The 2018 tariffs should be seen in the context of a US labour force that employs 60 workers in steel-using industries for every single worker in steel itself (Lowrey 2018; Halzer 2017). Moreover, while employment in steel declined from 205,000 to 125,000 from 1990 to 2015, this is similar to declines in employment in Germany and Japan, and in the same period productivity saw sharp increases, from around 410 tonnes to 800 tonnes per person per year (Crouch 2019: 26–8).

Nonetheless, as we have seen, American millionaires have increasingly made money outside of the United States and some, albeit limited, relocation of jobs does take place in global production networks, some sectors have suffered from heavy trade competition and there is evidence that Trump's support was significant in these counties (Davis 2017). Moreover, in one respect Trump is right to politicize the question of globalization, and we should not reproduce the fallacy of third way technocratic neoliberalism, which suggested that globalization is an irreversible fact of life, and something that exists outside of politics. But Trump and Navarro represent a kind of mirror image of this approach, suggesting that the globalization envisaged by the third way can be replaced by an inevitable but costless "de-globalization" for the United States. It would involve bringing back low-paid manufacturing jobs and not the relatively secure manufacturing jobs of the 1950s. Moreover, *in the aggregate* job losses in manufacturing are more reflective of higher labour productivity and technological change than of relocation.

Much of this project sounds like an attack on globalization and the *movement of capital*, rather more than neoliberalism and *capital per se*. The Trump administration faces the problem that US capital benefits enormously from its global operations, it is locked into deals with foreign suppliers and would carry enormous costs if these were broken, and tariffs on imports could raise consumer prices on finished goods in the US market or export prices in the case of more expensive imported inputs. This would carry risks in terms of inflation and competitiveness, and so hit workers in terms of purchasing power or jobs.

However, this still leaves the question as to whether the Trump administration is really protectionist, or if it is using tariffs to get a better deal with those countries considered to be "ripping off America". As we have seen much of this

concerns issues around intellectual property, technology transfer and investment restrictions, and of course Trump's ongoing concern with trade deficits. In
July 2018, in negotiations with the EU's Jean-Claude Juncker, Trump suggested
a shift towards "total free trade" with the European Union, with zero tariffs
and no non-tariff barriers. This itself may have been a negotiating tool and in
any case this argument rests on the notion that trade can spontaneously take
place without any harmonization of standards, an illusion we consider further
below. Perhaps more significant is the statement by Trump trade representative
Robert Lighthizer to Congress in July 2018, namely that the Trump administration "wants to get to the position where the US is competing with countries
on a bilateral basis and on a no-barrier basis, and then let the United States, let
pure economics make the decision" (cited in Slobodian 2018c). Seen in this way,
the US administration is less isolationist, protectionist or anti-globalization, and
more for an extension of globalization through bilateralism (and in this respect
not so different from Brexiteers on trade). The focus on intellectual property
is not dissimilar to the Reagan administration's use of the 1974 Trade Act to
threaten developing countries if they violated intellectual property provisions
and the use of so-called voluntary export restraints to restrict imports including
of steel, motorcycles, semiconductors and automobiles (Slobodian 2018c). This
point relates to the argument made earlier, namely that for all the isolationist
and paleoconservative rhetoric, Trump is in many respects a neoliberal. Robin
(2018: 260) argues, "(w)here anti-market conservatives historically flew into the
arms ... of the state as an end run around the market, Trump often sees in
matters of the state nothing but the transactions of the market". It is telling that
in 2017 Trump regarded the nuclear threat to Guam as a business opportunity
for its tourist sector, in 2018 justified foreign policy decisions based on arms
sales to Saudi Arabia, and probably feared the Mueller Russian inquiry above all
in terms of exposure of his own business interests (Phillip & Wagner 2017). It is
also not accidental that intelligence services have advised Trump less in terms of
geopolitics and more through the lens of national winners and losers in business
transactions (Schmidt & Barnes 2019).

Similarly, Trump (wrongly) believes that rapid bilateral trade deals can bypass
the bureaucracy of multilateral trade deals and get a "better deal" for the US. Seen
in this way, Trump is less the paleoconservative protectionist and more the pro-
moter of bilateral rather than multilateral trade deals. Much of the claim that the
US faces unfair trade with other countries ignores the history of now developed
countries (including the US) and the ways in which they did not face, or found
ways around, intellectual property laws, and indeed subsidized and protected
their own industries when "climbing up the developmental ladder" (Chang 2002;
Rodrik 2018). The much-lauded "replacement" for NAFTA that was agreed by
executive branches of government in the US, Mexico and Canada in late 2018

was called USMCA by Trump. It was less a complete rejection of the NAFTA agreement and more one where some issues around rules of origin and wages were designed to make the US a more attractive site for investment, but was still a world away from the protectionist rhetoric of Trump the candidate. This reflects the fact that in practice, the Trump administration is less *either* bilateral or protectionist, and more an uneasy combination of the two. In either case, it should be clear that neither protectionism nor the extension of free trade is likely to resolve the issues of deindustrialization, the rise of low-paid service jobs or declining benefits for workers.

Finally, the Trump administration attempted to highlight job growth and the stock market boom as signs that America was indeed great again. While corporate tax cuts no doubt played a part in the stock market boom, this had little impact for most Americans as 80 per cent of stock is owned by 10 per cent of Americans (Reich 2019) and in any case stock market volatility quickly followed. Trump repeatedly claimed that the US has the highest, or one of the highest, rates of corporate taxation in the developed world. But, once exemptions are factored in, the US actually has one of the lowest rates, and indeed in terms of the contribution of corporation tax to government revenue, a rate way below the OECD average. Trump has argued that corporate tax cuts will lead to new investment in the US, but tax cuts for the rich have not led to new high-paid jobs over the last 40 years, and the low contribution of corporation tax to government revenue suggests that corporations do not pay high rates of tax in any case (Ashbee 2017: 20). Much of the argument about tax reform – that cuts will reinvigorate economic activity through heightened investment and therefore (through public–private partnerships) the US federal state can afford to pay private contracts for infrastructure investment – repeats the supply-side economics of the Reagan years, when budget deficits ballooned. In terms of the boom, much of this reflects low interest rates and cheap money, which predates Trump. Moreover, the growth in jobs was no greater than it was under the Obama administration, and most of the new jobs were low-paid services work (such as in health care and food services) and certainly not high-wage, secure jobs in manufacturing (Rushe 2017). In his first year in office, Trump claimed success in any case where jobs appeared to have been saved from relocation, even though the investment decisions predate his presidency – these included investment by Ford, General Motors, Wal-Mart, Intel, Sprint and Lockheed Martin, all of which date back to the Obama era (Greenhouse 2017). Indeed, there are good reasons why productive capital continues to invest in the developed world, including access to final markets, a more developed infrastructure (at least compared to parts of the developing world), the clustering of economic activity and so on. Some companies have indeed sourced back to the US, such as new investment by General Electric in 2012 and the rate of offshoring appeared to slow down in the period 2015 to

2017 (Rothfeder 2016). But none of this is enough to bring back secure jobs to American workers on the scale envisaged by Trump. The tax cuts in 2018 had little impact on investment and instead encouraged share buy-backs designed to stimulate company share prices; indeed, by the third quarter of 2018, investment rose at an annual rate of just 2.5 per cent (Edgecliff-Johnson & Crooks 2018; Reich 2019). Most of the much-trumpeted Carrier jobs "saved" by Trump in late 2016 were actually lost in 2017 (Greenhouse 2017). Much the same point applies to coal mining, where Trump promised to restore jobs in the face of supposedly anti-job environmental regulations, even claiming credit for the opening of the Corsa coal mine in Pennsylvania, even though it had begun digging coal two months before he became president (Greenhouse 2017). Employment in coal mining fell from around 138,000 in 2008 to 98,000 in 2015, and coal's contribution to US electricity provision fell from around 52 per cent in 2009 to 30 per cent in 2017. But coal mining bankruptcies and closures have far more to do with competition from cheap shale gas and technological change than with regulation, a point accepted even by Robert Murray, the US's largest private coal owner (Rushe 2017).

More widely, 2017 saw a 12.1 per cent increase in the trade deficit compared to 2016, including increasing deficits with Mexico and China.[5] In 2018, the deficit rose to $621 billion, its highest annual level since 2008, and a 12.5 per cent increase on the previous year (Politi & Rocco 2019). This is not necessarily a problem for the US economy, but it is a problem for Trump, given his concerns about US trade deficits. In terms of budget deficits, Trump's corporate tax cuts had the effect of increasing the federal deficit, and in the first four months of fiscal year 2019, it increased by 77 per cent compared to the same period in the previous fiscal year (Borak 2019). In this context, interest rates rose, which was a further reason for stock market volatility in 2018. Finally, one might also note Trump's obsession with certain kinds of manufacturing or mining jobs and his great emphasis on coal, automobiles and steel. He pays far less attention to the textiles sector, which is actually more affected by import competition than either coal or steel, but where far more women are employed (Lamp 2018: 9), which again reflects Trump's nostalgia for a 1950s, masculinist, white America. In short, despite Trump's grandstanding, there is little to suggest that the administration made significant headway in terms of its economic promises. For all these reasons, then, the conservative anti-globalization represented by Trump is highly problematic in terms of its analysis and critique of the political economy of "actually existing globalization".

5. *Trading Economics*, "US Balance of trade", available at https://tradingeconomics.com/united-states/balance-of-trade.

Brexit and free trade

What, then, of our other case – that of conservative globalization in Britain associated with Brexit, which in some (though not all) respects is very different from Trump's protectionism? Chapter 4 argued that conservative cases for Brexit are in part based on the belief that Britain can return to its role as a global trading nation, and that this in turn reflected a nostalgia for Britain's former imperial role combined with a belief in hyper-globalization as a political project. We saw that Economists for Brexit (2016) made a case for Brexit on the grounds that the EU constituted a protectionist bloc as against the prospects and opportunities of global free trade. As Finlayson (2016) suggests,

> (f)or these people the EU is a brake on progress: it is too slow and cumbersome, reliant as it is on face-to-face meetings, consultation and consensus, rules and procedures. They see the EU as intervening far too much in the economy (regulating standards, sustaining some employment rights) and far too concerned with shaping our culture and values (all that protecting of local products and brands, forcibly bringing peoples together).

More specifically, Minford (2016) has argued that price differentials are solely the product of EU trade barriers, and so EU harmonization rules are protectionist and designed to keep prices artificially high. In fact, price differentials for specific products reflect a variety of factors and not just trade barriers, such as differences in quality, proximity to the final market, imperfect competition, differential mark-ups, and so on. Moreover, common rules across the EU are not simply trade-restricting as Minford suggests, but instead can be regarded as a precondition for trade to occur at all. It may of course be the case that some rules and standards might raise prices, but without them safety might be compromised. Equally, harmonization has the effect of reducing transaction costs and making trade across national borders easier. Minford assumes an alternative possibility of spontaneous free trade, presumably with competition acting as the effective means of regulation. The problem with this argument is that trade has always relied on institutional preconditions, and this has only increased over time (Barnett 2018). Competition might act as a regulator after the event, but countries rely on preconditions around safety – in food or medicine, for example – before trade can actually take place. There is a whole tradition of thought that rightly points to the ways in which so-called free markets rely on non-market institutional preconditions (Polanyi 2001; Chang 2002). Moreover, as was clear in the discussion of Trump above, these preconditions are of growing importance as international trade is increasingly intra-firm and/

or trade of different components or parts rather than finished goods. In this context, harmonization and the removal of non-tariff barriers facilitate rather than hinder trade and investment. In contrast, the conservative Brexit fantasy of spontaneous free trade essentially ignores the ways in which its proposals would lead to a race to the bottom in standards on the one hand, and an increase in transaction costs on the other.

In practice, most conservative Brexiteers do accept, even if only implicitly, that institutional pre-requisites are important, and it is here that the nostalgia for empire is so important. As we saw in Chapter 4, some conservative Brexiteers call for a turn to the Commonwealth, or a renewed Anglosphere. But this reflects less current economic realities and more a nostalgia for empire, and indeed some of the calls made by the likes of Liam Fox were described in Whitehall as Empire 2.0 – and this was not usually meant as a compliment (Bayliss 2017). Furthermore, there was no period in its imperial history that the British Empire was self-sufficient in trade, and this indeed was one reason why Joseph Chamberlain called for imperial preference (see Chapter 4). In 1913, 28 per cent of British imports came from the Empire, 41 per cent from Europe and 31 per cent from the rest of the world (Edgerton 2019). Exports were similarly global in reach, including coal (Britain was the largest energy exporter up to 1939), cotton goods and railway equipment (Edgerton 2019). The lower value of goods to and from the Empire does not of course mean that it was unimportant, because in part this reflects the unequal and uneven incorporation of the Empire into the world economy (O'Brien 2006). This, however, is hardly an argument that supports the case that the Empire was good for all territories, and instead reflects how it involved subordination. Contrary to some crude versions of dependency, world systems and postcolonial theories (Frank 1969; Blaut 1993; Hobson 2004), this does not mean that British industrialization was a product of colonial plunder alone. Equally, however, in contrast to Eurocentric cases for empire (Ferguson 2003; Lal 2004), the colonial contribution was not an insignificant one and, as well as involving morally repellent practices, the longer-term impact of colonialism was to leave some territories in a subordinate position in the global order (Kiely 2010).

In contrast, Daniel Hannan (2014) argues that the British Empire invented freedom and this was the basis for prosperity across the world as Britain uniquely represented a free-trade empire (though some claim this was true of the Habsburg Empire), in contrast to the protectionist empires of Europe (Slobodian 2018a). This is an argument that in part rests on certain claims about the effects of specialization and comparative advantage in trade, which we have considered above. More specifically, we have argued that the richer economies had more diverse economic structures and this in part reflected levels of industrialization. In the colonial period there was significant deindustrialization in the colonies (Bairoch

1993: 91) – from 1860 to 1914 the developing world's share of manufacturing declined from around 33 to less than 10 per cent (Kozul-Wright 2006: 116). Niall Ferguson (2003: 216), hardly a critic of colonialism, cites evidence that average per-capita income increased in India in the period from 1757 to 1947 by just 14 per cent, compared to 347 per cent in Britain. From 1860 to 1950, per-capita incomes grew from an annual average of $174 to $214, while in the developed world the corresponding figures were $324 and $1,180 (Bairoch 1993: 95). These figures reflected the move to economic diversity in the core countries and specialization in the periphery, as discussed above. Recent cases for liberal empire (Hannan 2018) emphasize the role of Britain in the abolition of slavery, even implying that Britain alone was an agent of abolition (and downplaying slave resistance in the process, not least the Haitian revolution). But they also ignore Britain's central role in both slavery and the slave trade from 1640 to 1807, the use of forced labour and reliance on US slave-produced cotton after abolition, the use of repressive systems of government and governing under some of the worst famines of the nineteenth and twentieth centuries (Nzula *et al.* 1979; Kiely 1996; Davis 2001). Thus, "Britain has, in truth, always been global, and the globe has not always been grateful for it; but now the government preaches internationalism, while erecting trade barriers and curbing migration" (Lis 2017). Liam Fox tweeted in March 2016 that, unlike other countries, Britain "does not need to bury its 20th century history". Much is made here of Britain's isolation in 1940 once Western Europe had fallen to the Nazis, and Britain's role in defeating the Nazis. This is an argument that ignores the fact that 1941 saw the entry into the war of both the United States and the Soviet Union, both of whom were more significant in defeating the Nazis, particularly the latter.

In his resignation letter, the former foreign secretary Boris Johnson (2018b) claimed that the EU had stifled transport regulations designed to improve cycle safety, when in fact the EU had voted for this and it was opposed by the British government – in other words, the very opposite of what Johnson claimed. We return to the question of populism and "post-truth" briefly in Chapter 8, but more relevant for our purposes here is Johnson's claim that the government's July 2018 proposals for what amounted to a "soft Brexit" would reduce Britain to "the status of a colony" (Johnson 2018a). There is the irony that Johnson has actually been an admirer of, indeed an apologist for, colonialism (Sarkar 2018; O'Toole 2019). One might ask then, irrespective of whether or not his statement is true, what precisely is wrong with colonial status? The answer of course is that for Johnson, it is perfectly acceptable for Britain to be a colonizer but not acceptable for it to be a colony, an argument that fully accords with recent cases for empire alongside the rise of Conservative Euroscepticism (Ferguson 2003, 2004; Hannan 2014, 2018; Biggar 2017; see also O'Toole 2019). What should be clear, then, is that Britain was always an awkward partner when it came to the European

Community and European Union, because it hoped to replace its dominant role in the Empire with leadership in Europe (Grob-Fitzgibbon 2016: 290). For many British Conservatives, then, the interdependence of Europe was an unsatisfactory replacement for the dependence of Britain's "partners" in the Empire.

This is also an argument that parallels the ethno-nationalism of paleoconservatism, which as we have seen is usually associated with protectionist and anti-globalization positions and one that in effect supports white nationalism as superior to other cultures. While committed to a global Britain, Johnson shares the ethno-nationalist views that (white) British national culture is superior to other cultures, but puts this to the service of a renewed imperial mission. It is no coincidence that the same week Johnson resigned, he enjoyed the support of President Trump and Steve Bannon, both of whom were in Britain at the time (Reuters 2018). At her Bruges speech in 1988, Thatcher (1988) herself had emphasized Christendom's "recognition of the unique and spiritual nature of the individual".

Advocates of the Anglosphere are somewhat unclear about the form that such a union may take. But this is presented as a strength in contrast to the rigid rules of standardization associated with the European Union. The original Bruges Group Director (and Mont Pelerin Society and leading IEA member) Ralph Harris opposed "the enforcement of unnecessary harmonization from Brussels, followed by spreading European dirigisme" (cited in Slobodian & Plehwe 2019). Here the assumption is that markets promote choice and diversity rather than bureaucratic regulations. But, as should be clear from the discussion in this chapter, this is simply wishful thinking in the context of contemporary globalization, and in fact standardization is a precondition for markets to operate in the first place. The idea that markets are based on a free and equal exchange between consenting individuals is a myth. As Birch (2017: 173) argues, standard – non-consensual, organized and not spontaneous – contracts are necessary for modern capitalism to operate otherwise there would be endless contractual negotiations and therefore massive transaction costs. This is what Durkheim (2013 [1893]) had in mind when he talked of pre-contractual solidarity as the basis for market exchange. It is reflected in the tension of Brexiteers and Trump in their aspiration for a more spontaneous market order while implicitly recognizing the reality of the need for that same market order to be embedded in some kind of pre-market framework (Birch 2017: 173–5). As should be clear by now, in the context of economic globalization, this need for standardization is all the greater as so many economic transactions take place within subsidiaries of the same firm, or subcontractors employed by a parent firm. Seen in this way, even if we accept the (problematic) dichotomy of Trump as anti-globalization and Brexit as hyper-globalization, both positions fail to come to terms with the reality of economic processes being increasingly co-ordinated through global value chains, and that this co-ordination requires more trade rules and regulations, not less. As Bishop (2017) argues, "(t)he more trade we desire, the more these rules proliferate, because the fragmented and infinitely complex nature of modern production, distribution and consumption requires ever more esoteric and finely grained forms of governance". In the name of anti-globalization (Trump and paleoconservatism) or global Britain (Brexit), both positions rhetorically promise that regulations can be rejected. At the same time, this rhetoric is quickly swept under the carpet not least by Brexiteers who, desperate for a trade deal with the US, would have to accept weaker standards on food safety, for example, as US Commerce Secretary Wilbur Ross pointed out in 2017 (Crouch 2019: 10). Moreover, and specifically for the Brexiteers, the argument that leaving the EU opens up the possibilities of all kinds of trade agreements elsewhere ignores some uncomfortable facts, above all that trade agreements with the Commonwealth take place through the EU. At the point of the Brexit referendum in 2016, around 49 per cent of Britain's exports went to the European Union. Germany exports around 33 per cent more to India and as much as 250 per cent more to South Africa than Britain did (Lis 2017). Furthermore, in contrast to the argument, made by hyper-globalization theory and by conservative Brexiteers, that we have shifted to what Liam Fox has called a "post-geography trading world", is unconvincing (cited in Bounds 2016). The gravity theory of trade holds that there is a tendency for trade to diminish through distance (Disdier & Head 2008; Hearne *et al.* 2019), and therefore regionalization is a more dominant tendency than hyper-globalization (Hay 2000). It is indeed the case that trade flows are much greater within, rather than between, regions. Britain is no exception to this rule, in terms of both goods and services (ONS 2017: figure 4). Explanations for why this is the case tend to be speculative, though Minford's argument that this reflects protectionist tendencies is simply an assertion. Instead, we might usefully again point to the fact that so much trade in intermediate goods may both offset reduced transport costs (as supplies may make multiple journeys as part of supply chains), and the fact that proximity is necessary in the context of goods that arrive just in time for further assembly.

More widely, what we have argued in this section, then, is that the case for free trade, as argued by some Brexiteers but also by those who advocated the third way, rests on a number of problematic assumptions around capital and labour mobility and full employment. Equally, however, so does the conservative anti-globalization position, which rests on spurious claims about the causes of deindustrialization, jobs and low wages. Both positions also rest on false assumptions that trade regulations are always and everywhere problematic and can be restricted or even abolished through better trade deals or frictionless open trade. In fact, trade regulations, standards, and so on are often preconditions for trade in the first place. On the other hand, as we saw in earlier chapters, the era of globalization has seen growing inequality, precarity and less secure jobs, reduced pensions, and so on, and these are very real issues. But what should be clear is that these concerns are not reducible either to trade or the growing mobility of capital (or labour). At best we can say that these might be a part of the story, but the restructuring of capitalism has included factors such as the growing importance of finance, significant shifts in taxation specifically against redistributive measures such as income tax, growing wealth and asset inequality, and so on. This is perhaps most stark in the case of Britain, where we saw some evidence for negative deindustrialization after 1980, but the blame for this must surely be placed at the door of successive governments that have effectively allowed the decline of manufacturing on the grounds that this would be compensated by jobs in services and especially financial services. Brexiteers want to *enhance*, rather than roll back, these developments. The Institute of Economic Affairs initially uploaded a document to it website in late 2018, called *Plan A+: Creating a Prosperous Post-Brexit UK* (Singham & Tylecote 2018; see also Ikenson *et al.* 2018), although it had to remove it for breaking Charity Commission guidelines. The case was made that EU regulations were too restrictive and a future trade deal with the US could further extend the market. This involved the removal or reduction of various restrictions such as data protection privacy laws, safety standards in chemicals, transparency requirements placed on pharmaceutical companies and safety standards in food and on the environment. In addition, restrictions on financial services (such as capital requirements and controls on short selling and asset management trading) would be removed, and all services would be open to competition (Lawrence 2018; Farand & Hope 2018). The implementation of Brexit would be necessary for such a trade deal. What was clear by the summer of 2019 was that much of the Conservative Right was prepared to bypass Parliament and in effect carry out a "semi-coup" by the executive in order to carry out the supposed "will of the people", even though a no-deal Brexit was explicitly ruled out in the 2016 referendum campaign. Furthermore, Brexit was supposed to restore the sovereignty of parliament in the face of Brussels, but implementation involved bypassing Parliament in order to compromise "sovereignty" in a proposed bilateral deal with the US. It was more than a coincidence, then, that Prime Minister Boris Johnson appointed a special adviser, Dominic Cummings, who had actually been found to be in contempt of Parliament a few months earlier, and this was followed by an increasingly authoritarian and populist style of leadership in the early autumn of 2019. While there is a great deal of critical literature claiming a lineage from German ordoliberalism to the EU, one might note here how this *anti*-EU project based on authoritarian executive power has more than a passing resemblance to "authoritarian liberalism" (see Chapter 2). It most certainly is not a scenario based on "taking back control". Indeed, Johnson's proposed deal of October 2019 involved a strategy that appeared to rely on the EU to force the British Parliament to in effect support the deal or face the prospect of no deal. This was combined with an election campaign in late 2019 that drew on a classic authoritarian populist distinction between Parliament and the people.

Conclusion

This chapter has focused on the political economy of globalization and particularly theories of trade, both generally and in relation to the contemporary world economy. The chapter has argued that orthodox theories of trade are indeed problematic and that free trade tends to favour those sectors or countries that are relatively strong, competitive and have diverse economies. If free trade is problematic, then it is not surprising that notions of global Britain and the Anglosphere have a history of exclusion based on the promotion of specialized economies in low-value goods, and are tied to Britain's questionable imperial role. On the other hand, the protectionist policies endorsed by Trump are also problematic. First, if this is a bargaining position to change the behaviour of countries on a bilateral basis, then this ignores the ways in which later developers have always deployed protectionist policies in their own process of development, not least the US. Second, if the shift to protectionism is principled rather than tactical, then it is one that simply cannot deal with the reality of American power, and how capital, and US capital, has globalized rather than declined. This has left many in the US marginalized, though of course this was true for African Americans in the supposed Golden Age, and their marginalization persists to this day. What has changed is that this has now affected significant sections of the white population and while the idea of a white working-class surge for the Trump Republican Party is incorrect, it was, as we have seen, significant in certain states in securing electoral victory in 2016. But what this chapter has argued is that there is no prospect of an anti-globalization policy based on a return to an era when manufacturing employed significant sections of the population and paid them relatively high wages with lots of benefits. This is because the erosion of wages, benefits and employment is not simply because of the heightened mobility of capital, though this might exist in some sectors. Rather, it reflects an enhancement of the power of capital, and the erosion of benefits, stagnant wages, growing inequality and increased debt for labour. Ironically, Conservative Brexiteers aim to push this model further through a process of creative destruction and the renewal of a fantasy of global Britain. Moreover, both the American and British cases are based on an illusionary ideal of deregulation in which standards are eroded, and in this respect further undermine any social contract between capital and labour. It is also based on a fiction of spontaneous markets that bears no resemblance to the reality of world markets, which rely on regulation in order to function in the first place. This is not so much the creative destruction of global Britain or Trumpian entrepreneurship, but rather a recipe for fantasy and destruction.

8

CONCLUSIONS

This final chapter provides a concluding summary of the book's main arguments, not through a straightforward outline of the previous chapters, but rather by putting the "crisis of globalization" and the conservative response into a historical context, first alluded to in the second chapter. The first section provides a final summary of conservative anti-globalization, including its strengths and weaknesses. The second section then examines globalization through a focus on current developments in the international order, and how we might think of ("anti-globalization") alternatives within and beyond this order. Finally, we bring these arguments together by focusing on the relationship between conservative populism and the crisis of liberal democracy.

Conservatism and (anti-)globalization

This book has examined conservative responses to globalization and located the rise of conservative populism in the context of the neoliberal turn from the 1980s and the financial crisis of 2008. In this respect it might be argued that this is one of many books that locates the populist turn in the context of the crisis of globalization, focusing in particular on the so-called left-behinds and the conflict between the national and the global. However, the book has more specifically attempted to take these conservative responses seriously, not only in terms of the analysis of political movements, but also in terms of intellectual traditions and conservative political theory. While some attention has been paid to conservative theory in a number of countries, the main two case studies – Britain and the US – were selected because on the face of it they constituted two very different responses to globalization. British Conservatives offer a global Britain as the alternative to the EU, and American conservatism through Trump offers a supposedly isolationist America-first policy. We have seen, however – not only through these two cases, but other conservative populisms discussed briefly in

Chapters 2 and 6 – that the story is more complicated than this. In particular, in drawing on a specific understanding of neoliberalism (Kiely 2018), the argument was made that while the populist revolt is a response to neoliberal globalization, it is not necessarily one that rejects it wholesale, as opposed to the social neo-liberalism of the cosmopolitan, multiculturalist third way. In some respects, and though this varies from country to country, conservative populist responses aim to extend neoliberalism, albeit on socially conservative institutional or cultural foundations. This is also an argument that at least qualifies some accounts of globalization that suggest that the main political conflict in the world today is between a local communitarianism on the one hand, and a "globalist" cosmopol-itanism on the other, a point I return to below.

We have suggested that while deindustrialization, inequality, the fall-out from the crisis of 2008, the fragmentation and marketization of knowledge and the post-political condition cannot, on their own, explain the rise of conservative populism, the latter cannot be properly explained without examining the former. What this book has tried to do, however, is to link this context to a serious examination of the ideas that inform the populist Right, and more significantly conservative globalization and anti-globalization. In particular we have looked at the ways in which conservatives place much of the blame for the recent social and political fall-out on liberal elites and multiculturalism and the promotion of a particular kind of (neo)liberal globalization. We have already rejected both the paleoconservative case for protectionism and the Brexit case for free trade, and argued that economic and cultural critiques of multiculturalism rest on incon-sistencies that hide a much darker project.

But at the same time, conservative critiques that emphasize the technocracy of actually existing neoliberalism, the disasters of liberal military intervention and indeed the emptiness and narcissism of a great deal of contemporary culture are not without merit. As we saw in Chapter 2, there is a Left critique of the cul-ture of modernity, which overlaps with conservative views, based on a critique of liberal individualism, consumer culture and the absence of virtue or shared values in society (Adorno & Horkheimer 2002; Kristol 1970; Gottfried 2001, 2005). Giddens (1994: 15) typifies third way neoliberalism when he suggests that "(g)enerative politics is a politics which seeks to allow individuals and groups to make things happen, rather than have things happen to them, in the context of overall social concerns and goals … it does not situate itself in the old opposition between state and market. It works through providing material conditions, and organisational frameworks, for the life-political decisions taken by individuals and groups in the wider social order." As Kilminster (2008: 134) argues, Giddens "has a blinkered conception of the advantage maximizing, reflective individual who knows no setbacks or disappointments. He has thus reproduced the ideo-logical ideal of omnipotent individuality of the contemporary period." Thus, in the context of (neoliberal) globalization, the force of critique of the liberal individualism is all the greater, as the so-called knowledge economy intensifies divisions between the more and the less educated, and meritocracy provides a convenient ideology to justify both economic and cultural divisions in society. Conservative views around the liberal managerial state (Gottfried 2001), "Davos Man" (Huntington 2004b) and the global elite (Lasch 1996) should therefore not be dismissed out of hand.

We have argued throughout this book that the history of neoliberalism is also the history of a project of de-politicization. The 1930s project was one against the weak Weimar state and the supposed tendency towards totalitarianism in the Western world. The 1970s and 1980s saw a project against neo-Keynesianism, developmentalism and labour movements. One might interpret the current conservative populist turn as a backlash against the politicization of new social movements that rose up in the 1960s, an argument explicitly made by some right-wing thinkers (Willinger 2013). While on the one hand this can be seen as an attempt to re-politicize and re-enchant the world in the face of neoliberal technocracy, on the other it is also an attempt to embed the market in a specific, conservative cultural context, and de-politicize movements of the marginalized. In this respect, it is reactionary, rather than an outright rejection of neoliberalism (Fraser 2017). This is not so much a rejection of, but a different kind of, identity politics. At the same time, we should also note the extent to which the social movements of the 1960s have themselves been de-politicized by their incorporation into the socially liberal neoliberal politics of the third way. To some extent, this has paved the way for the fragmentation of a collectivist political project and its displacement by what amounts to an online and largely university-specific competitive market in different identities. While the Right has certainly exaggerated these tendencies, there is no doubt that they exist.

But the conservative position is itself problematic. Goodwin (2018) has argued that, "(t)oday, looking back, I see that most people never really had an interest in exploring what underpinned Brexit. To many on the liberal Left, Brexit is to be opposed, not understood. There has been no conversation about why people voted for Brexit because conversations require a reply. One side has spoken but, with a few rare exceptions, almost nobody on the other side has thought about what such a reply might be." But as Meek (2019: 7) points out, "Goodwin performs a sleight of hand … he opposes ordinary Leave voters against an arrogant Remainer elite as if those were the two sides of the issue. There is a Remainer elite … but there is also an arrogant Leave elite, the Brexiteers encompassing powerful figures in the media, politics and the traditional landowning class. And just as there are ordinary Leave voters, there are ordinary Remain voters, many of whom, though typically younger and better educated, feel as powerless, angry and betrayed as their counterparts on the other side." Indeed, Goodwin (2018) himself notes:

> Consider what Leavers and Remainers want Britain to prioritise in the coming years. Leavers say Brexit, sharply reducing immigration, curbing the amount spent on overseas aid, and strengthening the armed forces. Remainers say build more affordable homes, raise taxes on high earners, increase the minimum wage, and abolish tuition fees. The only point of consensus is that both want to increase funding for the National Health Service.

Although he makes no comment, the concerns of Remainers – taxing the rich, more homes, higher minimum wages and free higher education – hardly sound like uncritical support for the arrogant liberal elites associated with cosmopolitan neoliberalism. Indeed, Goodwin is at pains to set up a divide between an arrogant Remainer elite and an authentic people supporting Leave. This is an argument that simply *replicates* rather than *explains* the rise of conservative populism – and most certainly does not subject it to anything like a deep critical analysis. Indeed, he argues with his co-author that the Left should tighten borders and prioritize the "national group" over immigrants (Eatwell & Goodwin 2018). As we saw in Chapter 6, this is a policy likely to further galvanize rather than silence the populist Far Right, and the reference to national group begs the question of who actually should be included – and excluded. Given its reliance on crude Huntingtonian cultural essentialism at best, and something far darker at worst, it is no surprise that ethno-nationalists and so-called race realists have welcomed this work (Johnson 2019).

Actually existing globalization and alternatives: a critical assessment

In Chapter 2, I suggested that neoliberalism can in part be seen as a response to the economic crises of the 1930s, when it emerged as an intellectual movement, and the 1970s/1980s, when it emerged as a governing force. In both cases, it was a response to the politicization of mass democracy and neo-Keynesianism in the developed world, and developmentalism and import substitution industrialization in the developing world. However, this begged the question of what then caused the 2008 crisis, which many saw as a product of liberalized financial markets (backed by increasingly marketized states), and which therefore placed the blame for the crisis on the emergence of a predominantly neoliberal global political economy? While this led some to suggest that the era of neoliberalism was over (Fukuyama 2016), as the state played such a central role through bail-outs, the provision (through central banks) of credit and nationalizations, we have already argued that in fact the state has always been central to the promotion of a neoliberal political economy (Panitch & Gindin 2012). Nonetheless, the continued existence of state intervention helped to pave the way for a re-writing of the crisis, so that it became one caused by malign political forces, which varied from country to country, but usually included central banks, interest rate policies, housing policies that distorted the market and government over-spending. Chapter 3 briefly challenged these accounts (see also Kiely 2018: chapter 8), but, whatever their intellectual coherence, this allowed for a reconstruction of the causes of the crisis that blamed certain political forces (see Mirowski 2013; Kiely 2017). Conservative responses to the crisis, then, combined these arguments with the idea that nation states had been corrupted by socially liberal elites, who had more in common with their fellow liberal elites elsewhere (and minorities at home) than their fellow countrymen (and possibly women). In some respects then this was a challenge to globalization and did involve a call for the return of national identity and national sovereignty. At the same time, however, this call for national sovereignty and identity was put to the service of neoliberalism, even if this was and is sometimes qualified, as in the case of Trump and paleoconservatism. Of course, much of the populist Right rail against "globalists" and thus anti-globalization is an important part of the rhetorical appeal of these movements. But much of this is an attack on cosmopolitanism, multiculturalism and multilateralism (and, in the case of the racist Far Right, "globalist" is often a euphemism for Jew) and not a straightforward embrace of anti-globalization or isolationism. There is certainly a more marked tendency towards protectionism in the US case but even here this is combined with a commitment to bilateralism, in which national sovereignty is used to promote "the art of the deal" (Trump & Schwartz 1987).

Furthermore, Feher (2019) argues that the populist turn is not so much a break from neoliberal subjectivity, which emphasized the promotion of human capital, but rather a reconfiguration of a still highly individualist conception of value and human capital, as opposed to a wider notion of a publicly minded citizen. Thus:

> The "globalists" of the 1990s, such as Bill Clinton and Tony Blair, were arguably the first to assume the task of enhancing the human capital of their constituents. Under their stewardship, welfare-to-work programs and easy access to commercial loans purported to improve the employability and solvency of the citizenry. Recently, however, populist firebrands have arguably become the largest suppliers of creditworthiness, by virtue of raising what Steve Bannon calls the "citizenship value" of their base.

Exemplary in this regard, Donald Trump has earned the undying support of his core constituencies by valorizing some key components of their portfolio. While his fellow billionaires enjoy the effects of tax cuts and market deregulations on their estimated net worth, his nativist supporters are grateful that, under the current regime, being or standing by a flag-waving and gun-carrying white male is, once again, a truly valuable asset.

Notwithstanding the "quiet resistance" in the White House, Wall Street greed and rust belt resentment are scarcely on a collision course. In the GOP's big tent, they both receive their fair share of appreciation. Rather than an unfortunate channeling of popular rage against the capitalist corrosion of liberal democracies, the new awakening of nationalist and reactionary values marks yet another step in the speculative *securitization* of human sentiments and attitudes.

Put slightly differently, we can contrast democracy and the "general will" on the one hand, and neoliberalism and populism on the other. Specifically, populism can be regarded as the sum of (majority or large minority) individual wills, rather than the sum of wills that actually consider the different views of fellow citizens. Populism serves to exclude the views of other people as not authentic while neoliberalism individualizes such views and reduces them to self-interest (see further below). While on the face of it populism involves a re-politicization that neoliberals reject, it does so through the individualization, racialization or gendering of grievances. Seen in this way, it is not surprising that politics increasingly takes the form of individualized exit, rather than collective voice (Hirschmann 1970), and Brexit is but one manifestation of this process (Davies 2019). Moreover, the focus on supposedly petty regulations, and the need for these to be overcome, is itself indicative of the process of de-politicization that is central to neoliberalism. Rather than examine major political issues, such as inequality, the environmental crisis and low wages, populist politicians like Boris Johnson prefer to tell stories about petty regulation, which at best distort the truth and at worst involve outright lies. Furthermore, this has involved libertarian rhetoric that challenges the nanny state in Brussels, and its emphasis on food and safety standards, for example (see O'Toole 2018: 112–16). Thus, Boris Johnson and Michael Gove support the right of British families to eat unhealthy food in the name of the freedom of the individual and the fact that, in Gove's words, fatty food gives "comfort, solace and pleasure" (cited in O'Toole 2018: 116). At the same time this attitude can quickly give way to an authoritarianism in which obesity is blamed on individual, lifestyle decisions, and parents need to be policed – and, indeed, according to prominent Brexiteer Julia Hartley Brewer, even possibly arrested. Similarly, in his book about Brexit (Liddle 2019), the well-known right-wing journalist Rod Liddle decries the ways in which blameless people have been held in contempt by a liberal elite. But as O'Toole (2019) points out, the same Liddle wrote in 2014 of "Britain as 'a nation of broken families clamouring about their entitlements siring ill-educated and undisciplined kids unfamiliar with the concept of right and wrong'". O'Toole goes on, "Who described with relish 'the hulking fat tattooed chavmonkey standing in the queue at Burger King'?" In this way, libertarianism and populism are quickly replaced by authoritarianism and elitist contempt (O'Toole 2018: 120).

There are clearly, then, close affinities between neoliberalism and populism and it is far too simplistic to regard them as diametrically opposed to one another. This does not mean of course that all populist conservative movements are simply neoliberal. Many conservative populist movements in Europe have focused more attention on welfare in the context of the aftermath of the 2008 financial crisis and thus qualified some of their "libertarian" economics. But even this is compatible with neoliberalism for two reasons. First, neoliberal welfare policy over the last 30 years has focused more on targeted interventions, rather than unambiguous roll-back of the welfare state. This has taken the form of conditions and less generous individual payments, even as welfare bills have tended to increase at the aggregate level as more people become dependent on welfare (Kiely 2018: chapters 6, 7 and 10). Second, neoliberal governance has tended to be associated with a distinction between the deserving and undeserving poor, an argument made not only by the Anglo-American New Right in the 1980s, but by third way politicians in the 1990s, and one that often took racialized and gendered forms (Cooper 2017). The current populist Right has drawn on this distinction and developed it in more overtly racialized ways, but – as we saw in Chapter 6 – it is not unprecedented, even when compared to the cosmopolitan and multiculturalist third way.

Thus despite the shift away from parts of the liberal international order, and especially the challenge to multilateralism and partial embrace of protectionism, it is far from clear that the rise of conservative populism does represent the unambiguous end of neoliberalism. The shift to neoliberalism in the 1970s and 1980s took place in a variety of national contexts, and was sometimes promoted by parties of the Left (Australia and New Zealand in particular) and in very different contexts in the developing world after 1982. But it was also famously associated with the New Right, particularly in the US and Britain as well as Chile. We might, then, usefully revisit some critical accounts of the rise of the Anglo-American New Right in that era to explore possible parallels with the post-2008 period. Poulantzas (1978: 203–16) argued that in the 1970s, there was a growing authoritarian statism characterized by a crisis of mass politics, the disengagement of social forces from political parties, the increased use of executive power, a focus on security at the expense of rights and an intensification of state attempts to control civil society, in part through the use of populist rhet-oric. Hall (1979) essentially agreed with this prognosis but focused more on the ways in which these developments were mobilized "from the bottom up". In his account, Thatcherism was identified as a hegemonic project in which neoliberal support was mobilized through the identification of fears, enemies and moral panics around issues like the permissive society, trade unions and industrial unrest, economic recession, privileged liberal elites and ethnic minorities (Hall *et al.* 1978). It should be emphasized that this approach to Thatcherism and the Anglo-American New Right does not suggest that hegemony was unproblemat-ically secured by the dominant forces in society (Hall 1979). Rather, hegemony is an ongoing project, which includes more "material" was well as ideological ways to incorporate sections of the population. In our two cases, much of this rested on the provision of financial assets, above all housing, and with that the extension of finance to much of the population (Kiely 2018: chapters 10 and 11). This incorporation was always uneven and highly unequal, but even then, as we have seen, it broke down in 2007–8 and in the period that followed. This cer-tainly undermined neoliberalism, but even with the rise of conservative popu-lism, it has not killed it off. In many respects, the current conservative populism intensifies these processes, this time in response to the social liberalism that can be dated back to the 1960s, but which influenced many governments from the 1990s (Betz 2018).

These developments have had international as well as domestic implications. In many respects, the era of globalization intensified following the neoliberal reforms of the 1980s, and was associated with the boom from 1992 to 2007. This included periodic financial crises, the ongoing destruction of the envir-onment and growing inequality within and in some respects between coun-tries (Kiely 2015). But it also involved the rise of some countries from the South and, perhaps above all, a specific relationship between a rising China and the developed countries, particularly the United States. This was not, contrary to the claims of Trump, an era where manufacturing jobs in the US were "stolen" by China. Deindustrialization did occur, but this was far more because of techno-logical change and the growing intensity of work, and new jobs were largely concentrated in low-paid service work. US workers across the board also saw declining benefits such as pensions and sickness benefits and relatively stag-nant wages. Financialization in some respects partly compensated for these developments. This was facilitated by the creation of new financial instruments, which followed financial liberalization, reinforced by the recycling of credit, including from overseas, including those running trade surpluses with the US, which of course brings us back to China (Schwartz 2009; Tooze 2018). This scen-ario was undermined by rising interest rates before 2007, which in part occurred to deal with inflationary pressures, which included higher commodity prices, also caused in part because of rising demand from China. This in turn undermined the basis for the boom, which turned to bust once it became clear that financial expansion had essentially become a massive Ponzi scheme.

Since then we have not seen the breakdown of this order, but its continuation at a far slower pace in terms of growth, in the absence of any clear alternatives, and the continued dominance of a financial sector that has benefited from policies like quantitative easing (Green 2019). In some respects, the Obama administration attempted to deal with the China question by trying to incorporate it more fully into the liberal international order through the promotion of trade agreements, which would limit its capacity to restrict foreign investment and undermine intellectual property laws (Starrs 2015; Chacko & Jayasuriya 2018). But this is precisely where Trump enters the picture, because his rhetoric had some success in using China anxiety to take a different, America-first, direction. As we have seen, we should not exaggerate Trump's successes in winning the hearts and minds of the American population, let alone the electorate, but like Thatcherism before it, the "project" and "movement" has been one that, in terms of supporters, "pulls them systematically into line with policies and class struggles of the Right" (Hall 1979: 20).

This period has coincided with what we might call an intensification of globalization, and with this what we might describe as two conservative responses to globalization, which draw on both the hyper-globalist and the sceptical positions. However, rather than use these approaches to analyze globalization, conservative responses tend to draw on these as aspirations, and more specifically as political projects to be realized. Thus, while Conservative Brexiteers defend national sovereignty, they do so in order to promote a global Britain that draws on nostalgic appeals to empire, but also attempts to promote and extend hyper-globalization. In the case of contemporary American conservatism, we have a paleoconservative position that defends protectionism and the idea of national sovereignty and a particularist cultural identity, while at the same time there are still some "globalists" in the Trump administration who use the threat of protectionism less to promote isolationism and more to enhance better bilateral deals (Green 2019).

Given these positions, there is a need for some caution in constructing a sharp dichotomy between the national on the one hand, and the global on the other. Nonetheless, much of the globalization debate remains couched in these terms, and those who defend national sovereignty against globalization tend to argue that the decision to participate in institutions of global governance is a political choice, and one that should be avoided. In this way, the national is championed over the global (Streeck 2019). On the other hand, those who argue for the cosmopolitan extension of global governance tend to argue that it is both inevitable and unavoidable on the one hand, and progressive and desirable on the other. In this scenario, the global is championed over the national (Kaldor *et al.* 2003). There are problems with both sides of this argument, not least as both betray what we described as a spatial fetishism in Chapter 2 (see Rosenberg 2000, 2005; Massey 1994: chapter 6), in which analysis of spatial relations takes priority over social relations and politics. Rodrik (2001) has suggested that globalization involves a trilemma in which only two out of three principles – democracy, sovereignty and hyper-globalization – can operate, but not all three of them. This is an argument that, despite Rodrik's (2018) own views, has influenced left-wing cases for Brexit based on the return of national sovereignty and defence of democracy (Streeck 2019), but one does not need to accept the hyper-globalization view to accept the very real constraints faced by states in the world of mobile capital. There is of course a very real democratic deficit in international institutions, but there is also a democratic deficit within nation states, and this would increase in a world based on the supposed recovery of national sovereignty (a world that, for most countries, has never existed as they were colonies). Neoliberalism has not been hegemonic simply because of the existence of international or global forms of governance but rather because national governments have been neoliberal, and in the process have influenced the character and behaviour of international institutions. This is not, then, simply a case of scale, and not one of national good versus global bad, but rather a case of one working through the other. Clearly, then, the national is central but at the same time national governments cannot do without international organizations, and the character of the latter will be strongly influenced by the former. This is most clear in the case of the question of global warming, which simply cannot be dealt with at the national scale, but also even the "neoliberal" EU should be seen in this light. There are neoliberal policies such as limits on state aid, the ways that the euro has disciplined poorer countries (though this could also happen through speculative attacks on national currencies), and rules concerning government deficits. At the same time, state aid and deficit rules have been applied very flexibly (IPPR 2019) and infrastructure projects targeted at poorer regions and (compared to the US, at least) relatively stringent workers' rights and environmental standards are not neoliberal. In other words, these rules have been implemented in different ways, and in part have depended on the wider context of the character of national governments within the EU at a particular point in time. This suggests that any simplistic national/global dichotomy is unconvincing. Indeed, in our cases, the conservative positions we have discussed actually cut across particular spaces and defences of national sovereignty are not simply anti-globalization *per se*.

Nonetheless, the global/national dichotomy is a common one and is based on a spatial fetishism that is also related to questions of nostàlgia, moral economy and support for a pre-globalist past. The paleoconservative Paul Gottfried

(2017: 140) has thus argued that the main political divide today is "between those who wish to preserve inherited communities and their sources of authority and those who wish to 'reform' or abolish these arrangements". In particular, much of the populist Right – though not Conservative Brexiteers – has challenged liberal internationalism, and contended that postwar development has involved the imposition of supposedly universalist principles onto alien cultures (Francis 2016: 471). Chapter 2 noted that this argument has significant overlaps with postcolonial and post-development critiques of Western liberalism (Said 1978; Escobar 1996). The paleoconservative critique of liberal cosmopolitan elites has some parallels with the Marxist theory of a transnational capitalist class (Robinson 2015), at least at the level of analysis, though not in terms of alternatives. But even at the level of alternatives, there is sometimes significant overlap, for instance, in the case of the blue Labour project developed by Maurice Glasman from 2009 (Glasman *et al.* 2011). Like paleoconservatives, and indeed the red Tory tradition (Blond 2010), blue Labour rejects neoliberal globalization and supports the reinvigoration of local communities and social bonds, and is generally hostile to or at least suspicious of immigration and the EU, supporting a communitarian position grounded in local communities. There is also some overlap in terms of wider social movements, and until recently the politics of anti-globalization has mainly been associated with the Left, particularly since the protests at the World Trade Organization in Seattle in 1999 (Kiely 2005). This anti-globalization of the Left has focused on attempting to control the movement of capital through various mechanisms, such as taxes on financial speculation, controls on multinational companies, an increased role for the public sector, closure of the WTO and a reclaiming of the commons. This is a critique that mainly challenges the socio-economic consequences of neoliberal globalization (and not multiculturalism), and so we should not assume that anti-globalization of Left and Right are identical. Nonetheless, some of this is similar to the post-development critique of development, and sometimes this focus on reclamation can lead to a highly questionable nostalgia, which takes it much closer to the conservative critique of globalization. Thus, the late post-development intellectual Majid Rahnema (1997: 318) has argued that "Vernacular societies had a much more realistic view of things. Not blinkered by the myth of equality, they believed that the good of the community was better served by those of its members it considered to be the wisest, the most virtuous, and hence the most 'authoritative' and experienced persons of the groups – those who commanded everyone's respect and deference." In short, postcolonial or de-colonial critiques of Western liberal modernity, development and globalization are not always as novel or radical as their advocates make out, as much of the content of these arguments replicate, or at least overlap with, conservative critiques from within the West. Like the blue Labour position, this tends towards a romanticism that ignores possible hierarchies within local communities, and that tends to assume that such communities are uniformly conservative (Kiely 1999; Finlayson 2011; Berry 2011). Such spatial fetishism also pervades the work of those on the Left who see national sovereignty as the basis for a rejection of the European Union, as if this was sufficient to mount a challenge to the globalizing forces associated with an increasingly global capitalism (see, for instance, The Full Brexit 2018). This is not to say, of course, that the state is simply a prisoner of such forces, but equally neither does the reification of sovereignty guarantee that such forces will be challenged through a simplistic focus on the national. Ironically, one prominent supporter of such a view had previously criticized the left-wing anti-globalization movement on the grounds that "(t)he point of Marx's criticism, then, is to surpass capitalism, not retreat from it" (Heartfield 2003: 288), an argument that could equally be applied to those on the Left that fetishize national sovereignty.

So, do these points mean that we simply accept globalization, and thus return to an endorsement of the socially liberal and cosmopolitan versions of neo-liberalism? It should be clear from the argument in earlier chapters that this is not the case because it leaves aside the question of politics, in terms of principles and strategy. In the case of the US, the rise of the Democrat Leadership Council is central to its adoption of what in effect have been neoliberal principles and policies. While the Republicans advocated supply-side, supposedly anti-regulation and pro-corporate monopoly arguments derived from the Chicago School (Chapter 2), the new Democrats also argued that there was a zero-sum game between the private and public sector, and many government regulations undermined the private sector (Thurow 1980). It was this "neoliberal club" (Rothenberg 1982) that paved the way for the third way of the 1990s, and that explicitly discarded Robert Kennedy's strategy of forging an electoral coalition of marginalized African Americans and organized white workers, in favour of an alliance of African Americans, liberal feminists and university-educated liberals. This conveniently ignores the ways in which news has become just another commodity (including via social media), a product whose "reality" or knowledge is constructed by market exchange, and indeed the ways in which contemporary liberals choose to construct their own knowledge of the world in highly selective ways, often as a simple reflection of identities and experiences. In the context of Trump's victory, the DLC's Al From's (2017) call to "rededicate ourselves to the core new Democrat principles – opportunity, responsibility, community" made little sense either in social or narrowly electoral terms. Similarly, Lee Drutman (2016) of the New America Foundation's call to focus "even more" on "wealthy cosmopolitans" and "global business" betrayed a nostalgia for the boom of the 1990s, and even then failed to see that the new knowledge economy had not worked for all.

What should be clear from the argument made in this book is that while social liberalism is preferable to the conservative reaction that has since occurred, when combined with economic neoliberalism it has led to a number of significant exclusions and an individualism that in effect wishes away and rationalizes such exclusions in the name of meritocracy. As Fraser (2017) argues, the era of globalization has been dominated by a battle between two kinds of neoliberalism. The first, "progressive-neoliberal bloc combined an expropriative, plutocratic economic program with a liberal-meritocratic politics of recognition" (Fraser 2017). In contrast, the New Right's reactionary neoliberalism "combined a similar, neoliberal politics of distribution with a different, reactionary politics of recognition. While claiming to foster small business and manufacturing, reactionary neoliberalism's true economic project centered on bolstering finance, military production, and extractive energy, all to the principal benefit of the global one percent. What was supposed to render that palatable for the base it sought to assemble was an exclusionary vision of a just status order: ethnonational, anti-immigrant, and pro-Christian, if not overtly racist, patriarchal, and homophobic" (Fraser 2017). Conservative (anti-)globalizations have promised a break from both of these neoliberalisms, but in practice have tended to intensify reactionary neoliberalism. Thus, in the case of Trump:

> Far from governing as a reactionary populist, the new president has activated the old bait and switch, abandoning the populist distributive policies his campaign had promised. Granted, he canceled the Trans-Pacific Partnership. But he has temporized on NAFTA and failed to lift a finger to rein in Wall Street. Nor has Trump taken a single serious step to implement large-scale, job-creating public infrastructure projects; his efforts to encourage manufacturing were confined instead to symbolic displays of jawboning and regulatory relief for coal, whose gains have proved largely fictitious. And far from proposing a tax code reform whose principal beneficiaries would be working-class and middle-class families, he signed on to the boilerplate Republican version, designed to funnel more wealth to the one percent (including the Trump family). As this last point attests, the president's actions on the distributive front have included a heavy dose of crony capitalism and self-dealing. But if Trump himself has fallen short of Hayekian ideals of economic reason, the appointment of yet another Goldman Sachs alumnus to the Treasury ensures that neoliberalism will continue where it counts.
>
> (Fraser 2017)

Seen in this way, the turn to conservative populism and anti-globalization is in part based on the failures of the period stretching back to the 1980s and 1990s, and exacerbated by the fallout from 2008, but equally it is not such a radical break as is often assumed. In contrast, much of the discussion of Trump and Brexit and the wider populist turn is based on a particular understanding of the period before 2016 and a sense of bewilderment that the post-Cold War settlement in the West has been undermined. Populism is, thus, dismissed as an irrational response to reason and progress, a replication of a defence of tradition and emotion against the rationality of the Enlightenment (Pinker 2018). The problem with this argument is that it tends to assume that progress is caused by market-friendly policies and that failures are thus the fault of individuals or cultures that fail to be market-friendly (an argument shared by many populists), and that indeed progress has continued in unproblematic ways in recent years (Lent 2018). Seen in this way, any debate between technocratic neoliberalism and the populist turn simply becomes a dialogue of the deaf.

Conservative populism and liberal democracy

In a similar vein, a wide literature has emerged that suggests – in some respects not unreasonably – that democracy is under threat from the rise of irrational forces that seek to undermine Western stability and leadership in the post-Cold War world (Levitsky & Ziblatt 2018; Mounk 2018; Frum 2018). Implicit in much of this work is a particular understanding of both the pre- and post-1989 world. The right-wing version of this argument suggests that the Cold War was a victory for freedom and that this continued and strengthened after 1989, while a more Centre-Left take suggests that freedom was in some respects compromised by the Cold War but it has fully flourished since the collapse of Communism. It is only a slight over-simplification to suggest that that the first position is broadly compatible with neoconservatism and some versions of liberal internationalism, while the latter broadly overlaps with the third way and the turn to cosmopolitan neoliberalism. Each position converges around the view that this End of History has been eroded by the rise of irrational populism. In this account, Trump represents an exceptional threat to what was a previously healthy and functioning democracy (Frum 2018). But it should be clear from the discussion in Chapters 5 and 6 that a racialized populism in the Republican Party predates the Tea Party and Trump era (Skocpol and Williamson 2012: 81–2). Indeed, it can be traced back at least to Goldwater and Nixon, and even before that to what Hofstatdter (2008: 1) called the "paranoid style" of conservative American politics, which embraced fear of the cosmopolitan city and conspiracy theory. Indeed we might go back further to the McCarthyism of the 1950s,[1] and

---

1. Hoftstadter actually traced this back further to the populists of the 1890s, but his attempt to identify a similar social base for 1890s populism and 1950s McCarthyism is problematic and unconvincing.

conservative intellectuals like Willmoore Kendall, William Buckley and Joseph Sobran gave support to white supremacy in both the US and South Africa, and not only in the period before Civil Rights (Heer 2018).

The populism of Brexit can also in part be linked to the fact that the vote was in part a protest against immigration and multiculturalism and a distrust of technocratic elites (Iakhnis *et al.* 2018). But equally, as was alluded to above and discussed in Chapter 6, this involved a construction of a supposedly authentic people. As Freeden (2017: 8; see also the discussion in Chapter 6) points out, this contrasts with the Rousseauian notion of the general will, "which is pains-takingly forged out of a reflective exercise by which each person is individually asked not what is good exclusively for him- or herself (the volonté de tous) but what would be good for everyone else *as well as* the reflecting individual (the volonté générale), who thus participates in the endeavour to identify a common-ality amidst plural differences, a commonality arising 'from the deliberations of a people properly informed'" (Rousseau 1968: 76). In contrast, advocates of the Brexit vote have asserted that their narrow majority represents the will of the (authentic) people and in doing so paper "over normal pluralities and presenting themselves as articulating the true, real or unitary popular voice ... Although the great myth that majoritarianism equals the will of the people has been exploited in many democratic narratives, the implacable insistence that irreversible truths are spelled out in the name of majoritarianism is patently populist. In mature, self-confident democracies winners may willingly make concessions to losers. In the world of populisms – a world inhabited by anxious and unconfident fantasists alongside, and intercutting, the genuinely aggrieved and side-lined – a distaste for tolerance, and distrust of 'others', is a matter of principle, because compromise would be a betrayal of the 'authentic' people" (Freeden 2017: 8).

In one respect, this lack of compromise is a mirror image of the technocratic neoliberalism to which it is a response. For all the talk of compromise, any attempt to challenge the dominance of market-friendly policies was dismissed as irrational, and it was said that there is no alternative and globalization was a force of nature. This technocracy was thus in its own way as uncomprom-ising as the conservative populism that arose in response to it. On the other hand, this sense of resentment towards cosmopolitan neoliberalism is likely to be counter-productive, not least as both the Brexit and Trump project actu-ally propose an extension of precisely the neoliberalism that has led to such anger in the first place. Even when combined with nativism, such as controls on immigration, this only exacerbates the problem as scapegoating and the politics of fear will increase in the context of continued inequality, precarity, and so on. For these reasons, populism is indeed a threat to democracy. But at the same time, we should not see something like the Trump phenomenon as simply an exceptional break from the pre-2016 era. In some respects the rise of populism, conservative anti-globalization, and so on must be explained in part by the failures of the previous era, but also in terms of some continuities with it, not least the erosion of trust brought about by failed wars and dodgy dossiers, expense scandals, corruption, and so on. Above all, those that want to return to a pre-2008 "vital centre",[2] albeit one supportive of neoliberalism rather than the New Deal, underestimate – or simply deny – the ways in which this has failed and why conservative populism has emerged. In terms of democracy, the populist turn represents a reaction to a post-political condition in which the scope for democratic decision-making has been undermined by the dominance of markets and of technocrats running these markets, both real and imagined. In this respect neoliberal technocracy and populism are in effect a mirror image of each other, as "(t)echnocracy holds that there is only policy solution" and "populism claims that there is only one authentic will of the people" (Muller 2016: 97). In both cases, the need for democratic debate is rejected, and populism draws increasingly on executive power that was extended through technocracy as a bulwark against mass democratic rule. Conservative responses to globalization should be seen in a similar light – while in some respects a response to the cosmopolitan version of "progressive neoliberalism", they heighten its reactionary elements, and constitute a dangerous, and self-defeating, development in world politics.

---

2. This was the name of an important book by Schlesinger (1949) that advocated support for the New Deal against totalitarianisms of both Left and Right.

REFERENCES

Acemoglu, D. *et al.* 2016. "Import competition and the great employment sag of the 2000s". *Journal of Labor Economics* 34(S1), 5141–98.

Adorno, T. & M. Horkheimer 2002. *Dialectic of Enlightenment*. Stanford, CA: Stanford University Press.

Alesina, A. & S. Ardagna 1998. "Tales of fiscal adjustment". *Economic Policy* 13(27), 489–585.

Allen, K. & L. Elliot 2016. "UK joins Greece at bottom of wage growth league". *Guardian*, 27 July.

Amsden, A. 1989. *Asia's Next Giant*. Oxford: Oxford University Press.

Anderson, B. 1983. *Imagined Communities*. London: Verso.

Anderson, D. (ed.) 2005. *Decadence*. London: Social Affairs Unit.

Anderson, P. 1964. "The origins of the present crisis". *New Left Review* I/23, 26–53.

Anderson, P. 1992. *English Questions*. London: Verso.

Anderson, P. 2017. "Passing the baton". *New Left Review* II/103, 41–64.

Antonucci, L. *et al.* 2017. "The malaise of the squeezed middle: challenging the narrative of the 'left behind' Brexiter". *Competition & Change* 21(3), 211–29.

Arendt, H. 1966 [1951]. *The Origins of Totalitarianism*. New York: Harcourt.

Arnold, M. 2009 [1869]. *Culture and Anarchy*. Oxford: Oxford University Press.

Aronoff, K. 2016. "Trump and the Tea Party". Available at www.jacobinmag.com/2016/03/tea-party-donald-trump-ted-cruz/ (accessed 13 November 2018).

Arrighi, G. 2007. *Adam Smith in Beijing*. London: Verso.

Ashbee, E. 2000. "Politics of paleoconservatism". *Culture and Society*, March/April, 75–84.

Ashbee, E. 2017. *The Trump Revolt*. Manchester: Manchester University Press.

Ashcroft, M. 2016. "How the United Kingdom voted on Thursday and why". Available at https://lordashcroftpolls.com/2016/06/how-the-united-kingdom-voted-and-why/ (accessed 25 June 2016).

Autor, D. 2019. *Work of the Past, Work of the Future*. AEA Papers and Proceedings, 109, 1–32.

Autor, D., D. Dorn & G. Harrison 2016. "The China shock: learning from labor market adjustment to large changes in trade". NBER Working Paper 21906.

Axford, B. 2013. *Theories of Globalization*. Cambridge: Polity.

Bairoch, P. 1993. *Economics and World History*. Brighton: Harvester-Wheatsheaf.

Baker, D. 2016. *Rigged*. Washington, DC: CEPR.

Baker, D., A. Gamble & S. Ludlum 1993. "Whips or scorpions? The Maastricht vote and the Conservative Party". *Parliamentary Affairs* 46(2), 151–66.

Baker, P. 2019. "We the people: the struggle to define populism". *Guardian*, 10 January. Available at www.theguardian.com/news/2019/jan/10/we-the-people-the-battle-to-define-populism (accessed 11 January 2019).

Bale, T. 2018. "Who leads and who follows?". *Politics* 38(3), 263–77.

Balls, E. 1992. *Euro-monetarism*. London: Fabian Society.

Bannon, S. 2010. *Generation Zero*. Film available at www.youtube.com/watch?v=bsqu9gh6xhk (accessed 13 November 2018).

Barber, B. 2007. *Jihad vs McWorld*. New York: Times Books.

Barnett, A. 2017. *The Lure of Greatness*. London: n.p.

Barnett, A. 2018. "Why Brexit won't work". Available at www.opendemocracy.net/anthony-barnett/why-brexit-won-t-work-eu-is-about-regulation-not-sovereignty (accessed 13 November 2018).

Barnett, T. 2003. "The Pentagon's new map". *Esquire*, March.

Barnett, T. 2005. *The Pentagon's New Map*. New York: Berkley Books.

Bar-On, T. 2013. *Rethinking the French New Right*. London: Routledge.

Bartels, L. 2005. "What's the matter with what's the matter with Kansas?". Available at https://inequality.stanford.edu/sites/default/files/media/_media/pdf/Reference%20Media/Bartels_2006_Social%20Class%20and%20Occupations.pdf (accessed 13 November 2018).

Bartels, L. 2016. "2016 was an ordinary election, not a realignment". *Washington Post*, 10 November.

Bauer, P. 1971. *Dissent on Development*. London: Weidenfeld & Nicholson.

Bauman, Z. 2017. *Retrotopia*. Cambridge: Polity.

Bayliss, C. 2017. "Empire 2.0: UK 'to improve trade links with African Commonwealth nations' after Brexit". *Daily Express*, 6 March.

Beardsworth, R. 2011. *Cosmopolitanism and International Relations Theory*. Cambridge: Polity.

Beck, U. 2000. "The cosmopolitan perspective: sociology of the second age of modernity". *British Journal of Sociology* 51(1), 79–105.

Beck, U. 2006. *Cosmopolitan Vision*. Cambridge: Polity.

Becker, D. & R. Sklar 1987. "Why postimperialism?". In D. Becker *et al.* (eds) *Postimperialism: International Capitalism and Development in the Late Twentieth Century*. Boulder, CO: Lynne Rienner, 1–18.

Becker, G. 1976. *The Economic Approach to Human Behaviour*. Chicago, IL: University of Chicago Press.

Becker, S., T. Fetzer & D. Novy 2017. "Who voted for Brexit? A comprehensive district-level analysis". *Economic Policy* 33(93), 601–50.

Beetham, D. 1977. "Robert Michels – from socialism to fascism part I". *Political Studies* 25(1), 3–24.

Belew, K. 2018. *Bring the War Home*. Cambridge, MA: Harvard University Press.

Bell, D. 1972. "The cultural contradictions of capitalism". *Journal of Aesthetic Education* 6(1/2), 53–65.

Bell, D. 1976. *The Cultural Contradictions of Capitalism*. New York: Basic Books.

Bell, D. 2007. *The Idea of Greater Britain*. Princeton, NJ: Princeton University Press.

Bell, D. 2016. *Reordering the World*. Princeton, NJ: Princeton University Press.

Bellamy, R. 1988. *Modern Italian Social Theory*. Cambridge: Polity.

Benanav, A. 2016. "Precarity rising". Available at www.viewpointmag.com/2015/06/15/precarity-rising/ (accessed 12 October 2016).

Ben-David, D. & B. Loewy 1998. "Free trade, growth and convergence". *Journal of Economic Growth* 3(1), 143–70.

Bennett, J. 2004. *The Anglosphere Challenge*. London: Rowman & Littlefield.

Bennett, J. 2007. *The Anglosphere Century*. Washington, DC: Heritage Foundation.

Bennett, J. 2016. "A time for audacity". Available at www.canzuk.co.uk/single-post/2016/09/05/A-Most-Audacious-Union-How-Britain-Canada-Australia-and-New-Zealand-Can-Work-Together-to-Make-Themselves-a-More-Prosperous-More-Secure-and-More-Independent-Major-Power-in-the-Twenty-First-Century?fb_comment_id=1269784453113546_1540766026015386 (accessed 14 November 2018).

Berry, C. 2011. "Old, new, borrowed or blue? Has blue Labour been duped by conservatism?". Available at www.opendemocracy.net/ourkingdom/craig-berry/old-new-borrowed-or-blue-has-blue-labour-been-duped-by-conservatism (accessed 14 November 2018).

Berry, C. 2013. "Are we there yet? Growth, rebalancing and the pseudo recovery". Sheffield: SPERI Paper no. 7.

Betz, H.-G. 1994. *Radical Right-Wing Populism in Western Europe*. Basingstoke: Palgrave.

Betz, H.-G. 2018. "Everything that is wrong is the fault of 68: regaining cultural hegemony by trashing the left". Available at www.opendemocracy.net/can-europe-make-it/hans-georg-betz/everything-that-is-wrong-is-fault-of-68-regaining-cultural-hegemony-by-trashing-left (accessed 14 November 2018).

Betz, H.-G. & C. Johnson 2017. "Against the current-stemming the tide: the nostalgic ideology of the contemporary populist radical right". In C. Mudde (ed.) *The Populist Radical Right: A Reader*. London: Routledge, 68–82.

Bhagwati, J. & T. Srinivasan 1999. "Outward orientation and development: are revisionists right?". Yale University Economic Growth Center Discussion Paper no. 806, 1–40.

Biggar, N. 2017. "Don't feel guilty about our colonial history". *The Times*, 30 November.

Binkley, S. 2014. *Happiness as Enterprise*. Albany, NY: SUNY Press.

Birch, K. 2015. *We Have Never Been Neoliberal*. London: Zero.

Birch, K. 2016. "Financial economics and business schools: legitimating corporate monopoly". In S. Springer, K. Birch & J. McLeavy (eds) *The Handbook of Neoliberalism*. London: Routledge, 320–30.

Birch, K. 2017. *A Research Agenda for Neoliberalism*. Cheltenham: Elgar.

Bishop, M. 2017. "Brexit and free trade fallacies: part one". Available at http://speri.dept.shef.ac.uk/2017/01/11/brexit-and-free-trade-fallacies-part-one/ (accessed 24 January 2018).

Black, C. 1998. *Britain's Final Choice: Europe or America?* London: Centre for Policy Studies.

Blair, T. 1995. *Let Us Face the Future*. London: Fabian Society.

Blair, T. 1997. Labour Party conference speech. Available at www.britishpoliticalspeech.org/speech-archive.htm?speech=203 (accessed 4 August 2016)

Blair, T. 1998. Labour Party conference speech. Available at www.britishpoliticalspeech.org/speech-archive.htm?speech=204 (accessed 4 August 2016).

Blair, T. 1999a. Labour Party conference speech. Available at www.britishpoliticalspeech.org/speech-archive.htm?speech=205 (accessed 4 August 2016).

Blair, T. 1999b. "Doctrine of the international community". Available at www.number10.gov.uk/Page1297 (accessed 12 June 2009).

Blair, T. 2000. Labour Party conference speech. Available at www.britishpoliticalspeech.org/speech-archive.htm?speech=206 (accessed 4 August 2016).

Blair, T. 2004. *Socialism*. London: Fabian Society.

Blair, T. 2010. *A Journey*. Harmondsworth: Penguin.

Blair, T. & G. Schroeder 1999. *Europe: The Third Way*. London: Labour Party.

Blake, R. 1976. *Conservatism in an Age of Revolution*. London: Churchill.

Blaut, J. 1993. *The Colonizers Model of the World*. New York: Guilford.

Blinder, A. 1997. "Is government too political?". *Foreign Affairs* 76 (November/December), 115–26.

Bloemraad, I. 2011. "'We the people' in an age of migration: Multiculturalism and immigrants: Political integration in comparative perspective". In R. Smith (ed.) *Citizenship, Borders and Human Needs*. Philadelphia, PA: University of Pennsylvania Press, 180–95.

Blond, P. 2010. *Red Tory*. London: Faber.

Blond, P. 2016. "Phillip Blond on post-Brexit Britain". Available at www.respublica.org.uk/press-centre/media-coverage/le-figaro-phillip-blond-post-brexit-britain/ (accessed 14 November 2018).

Bloomberg 2017. "How the populist right is redrawing the map of Europe". Available at www.bloomberg.com/graphics/2017-europe-populist-right/ (accessed 14 November 2018).

Blyth, M. 2013. *Austerity*. Oxford: Oxford University Press.

Blyth, M. 2016. "Global Trumpism". Available at www.foreignaffairs.com/articles/2016-11-15/global-trumpism (accessed 14 November 2018).

Boas, T. & J. Gans-Morse 2009. "Neoliberalism: from new liberal philosophy to anti-liberal slogan". *Studies in Comparative International Development* 44(2), 137–61.

Boettke, P. 2017. "The reconstruction of the liberal project". Available at https://fee.org/articles/the-reconstruction-of-the-liberal-project/ (accessed 14 November 2018).

Boffo, M., B. Fine & A. Saad-Filho 2018. "Neoliberal capitalism: the authoritarian turn". In L. Panitch & G. Albo (eds) *The Socialist Register 2019*. London: Merlin, 247–70.

Bolton, J. 2000. "Should we take global governance seriously?". *Chicago Journal of International Law* 1(2), 205–21.

Bonefeld, W. 2013. "Adam Smith and ordoliberalism: on the political form of market liberty". *Review of International Studies* 39(2), 233–50.

Bonefeld, W. 2016. "Authoritarian liberalism: from Schmitt via ordoliberalism to the euro". *Critical Sociology*, online first, available at http://journals.sagepub.com/doi/abs/10.1177/0896920516662695 (accessed 9 November 2016).

Bonefeld, W. 2017. *The Strong State and the Free Economy*. London: Rowman & Littlefield.

Bonilla-Silva, E. 2014. *Racism without Racists*. London: Rowman & Littefield.

Boot, M. 2003. "The case for American empire". *Weekly Standard*, 15 October.

Borak, D. 2019. "US budget deficit balloons to nearly $1 trillion for fiscal year 2019". CNN Politics. 25 October. Available at https://edition.cnn.com/2019/10/25/politics/trump-us-budget-deficit-2019/index.html (accessed 25 October 2019).

Borch, C. 2012. *The Politics of Crowds*. Cambridge: Cambridge University Press.

Bork, R. 1978. *The Anti-Trust Paradox*. Chicago, IL: University of Chicago Press.

Bounds, A. 2016. "Britain entering a 'post geography trading world' says Liam Fox". *Financial Times*, 29 September.

Bourdieu, P. 1999. *Acts of Resistance*. Cambridge: Polity.

Bourdieu, P. 2003. *Counterfire: Against the Tyranny of the Market*. London: Verso.

Bowman, A. 2015. *What a Waste*. Manchester: Manchester University Press.

Bown, C. 2018. "Trump's steel and aluminium tariffs are counterproductive: here are 5 more things you need to know". Available at https://piie.com/blogs/trade-investment-policy-watch/trumps-steel-and-aluminum-tariffs-are-counterproductive-here-are (accessed 14 November 2018).

Bradford, M. 1999. *The Reactionary Imperative*. Chicago, IL: Open Court.

Brett, E. 1983. *International Money and Capitalist Crisis*. Basingstoke: Macmillan.

Brittan, S. 1975. "The economic contradictions of democracy". *British Journal of Political Science* 5(2), 129–59.

Brockling, U. 2016. *The Entrepreneurial Self*. London: Sage.

Brogan, B. 2005. "It's time to celebrate the empire, says Brown". Available at www.dailymail.co.uk/news/article-334208/Its-time-celebrate-Empire-says-Brown.html (accessed 17 March 2019).

Brooks, D. 2004. *On Paradise Drive*. New York: Simon & Schuster.

Brown, W. 2003. "Neoliberalism and the end of liberal democracy". Available at www.commonhouse.org.uk/wp-content/uploads/2014/02/Brown-2003-Neo-Liberalism-and-the-End.pdf (accessed 26 June 2013).

Brown, W. 2015. *Undoing the Demos*. New York: Zone Books.

Brown, W. 2017. "Apocalyptic populism". *New Humanist*, Winter 2017.

Bruff, I. 2014. "The rise of authoritarian neoliberalism". *Rethinking Marxism* 26(1), 113–29.

Buchanan, J. & G. Tullock 1962. *The Calculus of Consent*. Ann Arbor, MI: University of Michigan Press.

Buchanan, J., J. Burton & R. Wagner 1978. *The Economic Consequences of Mr Keynes*. London: IEA.

Buchanan, P. 1992. "Culture war speech". Available at http://voicesofdemocracy.umd.edu/buchanan-culture-war-speech-speech-text/ (accessed 20 April 2017).

Buchanan, P. 1994. "The isolationist myth". Available at http://buchanan.org/blog/the-isolationist-myth-165.

Buchanan, P. 1998. *The Great Betrayal*. New York: Little, Brown.

Buchanan, P. 1999. *A Republic Not an Empire.* Washington, DC: Regnery.

Buchanan, P. 2002. *The Death of the West.* New York: St Martin's Press.

Buchanan, P. 2003. "Death of manufacturing". *American Conservative,* 11 April.

Buchanan, P. 2004. *Where the Right went Wrong.* New York: Thomas Dunne.

Buchanan, P. 2011. *Suicide of a Superpower.* New York: Thomas Dunne.

Buchanan, P. 2013. "Is Putin one of us?". Available at http://buchanan.org/blog/putin-one-us-6071 (accessed 17 November 2018).

Buchanan, P. 2016. "Trump: middle America's messenger". *American Conservative,* 23 February.

Buckley, W. 1951. *God and Man at Yale.* Chicago, IL: Henry Regnery.

Buckley, W. 1957. "Why the South must prevail". *National Review,* 24 August, 148–9.

Burbach, R. & B. Robinson 1999. "The fin de siecle debate: globalization as epochal shift". *Science and Society* 63(1), 10–39.

Burchill, S. 2013. *Theories of International Relations.* Basingstoke: Palgrave.

Burgin, A. 2012. *The Great Persuasion.* Cambridge, MA: Harvard University Press.

Burke, E. 2003 [1793]. *Reflections on the Revolution in France.* New Haven, CT: Yale University Press.

Burleigh, N. 2017. "Meet the billionaires who run Trump's government". Available at www.newsweek.com/2017/04/14/donald-trump-cabinet-billionaires-washington-579084.html (accessed 24 June 2018).

Burnham, J. 1972. *The Managerial Revolution.* New York: Praeger.

Burnham, J. 2014. *Suicide of the West.* New York: Encounter.

Burnham, P. 1999. "The politics of economic management in the 1990s". *New Political Economy* 14(1), 37–54.

Burnham, P. 2001. "New Labour and the politics of depoliticisation". *British Journal of Politics and International Relations* 3(2), 127–49.

Burnham, W. & T. Ferguson 2014. "Americans are sick to death of both parties: why our political system is in worse shape than we thought", *AlterNet.* Available at www.alternet.org/americans-are-sick-death-both-parties-why-our-politicsworse-shape-we-thought (accessed 14 November 2018).

Burton, M. 2013. *The Politics of Public Sector Reform.* Basingstoke: Palgrave Macmillan.

Bush, S. 2019. "The Conservatives' problem in Peterborough and beyond is that they can never win Brexit", *inews,* 5 June. Available at https://inews.co.uk/opinion/peterborough-by-election-conservatives-brexit/ (accessed 6 June 2019).

Cafruny, A. & M. Ryner 2007. *Europe at Bay.* Boulder, CO: Lynne Rienner.

Cameron, A. & R. Palan 2004. *The Imagined Economies of Globalization.* London: Sage.

Campbell, W. 2009. "Introduction". In W. Röpke (ed.) *The Social Crisis of Our Time.* New Brunswick, NJ: Transaction, xii–xxiv.

Camus, R. 2018. *You Will Not Replace Us!* Open: Chez l'auteur.

Carlson, T. 2018. *Ship of Fools.* New York: Free Press.

Carlyle, T. 2009 [1843]. *Past and Present.* Waikiki: Serenity.

Carneiro, R. 1970. "A theory of the origin of the state". *Science* 169(3947), 733–8.

Carroll, W. 2010. *The Making of a Transnational Capitalist Class.* London: Zed.

Case, A. & A. Deaton 2015. "Rising morbidity and mortality in midlife among white non-Hispanic Americans in the 21st century". *Proceedings of the National Academy of Sciences of the United States of America* 112(49), 15078–83.

Case, A. & A. Deaton 2017. "Mortality and morbidity in the twenty first century". Available at www.brookings.edu/bpea-articles/mortality-and-morbidity-in-the-21st-century/ (accessed 16 April 2017).

Casselman, B. 2014. "Immigration is changing much more than the immigration debate". Available at https://fivethirtyeight.com/features/immigration-is-changing-much-more-than-the-immigration-debate/ (accessed 22 June 2017).

Casselman, B. 2017. "Stop saying Trump's win had nothing to do with economics". Available at https://fivethirtyeight.com/features/stop-saying-trumps-win-had-nothing-to-do-with-economics/ (accessed 16 April 2017).

Cassidy, J. 2019. "The stock market intrudes on the reality of Trump's trade war". *The New Yorker*, 14 May. Available at www.newyorker.com/news/our-columnists/the-stock-market-intrudes-on-the-alternate-reality-of-trumps-trade-war (accessed 14 May 2019).

Castells, M. 1996. *The Rise of the Network Society*. Oxford: Blackwell.

CEPR 2017. "The US pursues selective protectionism not free trade". Available at http://cepr.net/blogs/beat-the-press/u-s-pursues-selective-protectionism-not-free-trade (accessed 24 June 2018).

Cerny, P. 1997. "Paradoxes of the competition state". *Government and Opposition* 32(2), 251–74.

Chacko, P. 2018. "The right turn in India". *Journal of Contemporary Asia* 48(4), 541–65.

Chacko, P. & K. Jayasuriya 2018. "Asia's Conservative moment: understanding the rise of the right". *Journal of Contemporary Asia* 48(4), 529–40.

Chakraborty, A. 2018. "Mis-sold, expensive and overhyped: why our universities are a con". *Guardian*, 20 September.

Chandler, D. 2000. "International justice". *New Left Review* II/6, 55–66.

Chang, H.-J. 2002. *Kicking Away the Ladder*. London: Anthem.

Chang, H.-J. 2006. "Trade and industrial policy during the age of imperialism". In K. Jomo (ed.) *The Long Twentieth Century: Globalization under Hegemony*. Delhi: Oxford University Press, 278–99.

Chang, H.-J. 2007. *Bad Samaritans*. London: Random House.

Chetty, R. *et al.* 2017. "The fading American dream: trends in absolute income mobility since 1940". Available at http://inequality.stanford.edu/sites/default/files/fading-american-dream.pdf (accessed 4 January 2018).

Churchill, W. 2001. *A History of the English-Speaking Peoples* (abridged). London: Orion.

CNN 2016. "Exit polls". Available at https://edition.cnn.com/election/2016/results/exit-polls (accessed 18 April 2017).

Coase, R. 1937. "The nature of the firm". *Economica* 4(16), 386–405.

Coase, R. 1960. "The problem of social cost". *Journal of Law and Economics* 3(1), 1–44.

Coates, D. 2018. *Flawed Capitalism*. Newcastle upon Tyne: Agenda.

Cochrane, J. 2009. "Fiscal stimulus, fiscal inflation or fiscal fallacies". Available at https://faculty.chicagobooth.edu/john.cochrane/research/papers/fiscal2.htm (accessed 9 September 2012).

Cohen, R. 2007. *Global Diasporas*. London: Routledge.

Cole, A. 2012. *American Competitiveness: A Matter of National Security*. Washington, DC: National Security Foundation.

Coleman, J. 1988. "Social capital and the creation of human capital". *American Journal of Sociology* 94, supplement, 95–120.

Coleman, J. 1990. *Foundations of Social Theory*. Cambridge, MA: Harvard University Press.

Coleman, J. 1993. "The rational reconstruction of society". *American Sociological Review* 58(1), 1–15.

Collier, P. 2008. *The Bottom Billion*. Oxford: Oxford University Press.

Comfort, N. 2012. *The Slow Death of British Industry*. London: Biteback.

Congdon, T. 1992. "Home is where our language is". *The Spectator*, 5 September.

Conquest, R. 1999. "Towards an English-speaking union". *The National Interest* 57, 54–60.

Conquest, R. 2001. *Reflections on a Ravaged Century*. New York: Norton.

Conservative Home 2007. "Tories will match Labour's spending plans for next three years". Available at http://conservativehome.blogs.com/torydiary/2007/09/tories-will-mat.html (accessed 16 August 2016).

Constant, B. 1988. *Political Writings*. Cambridge: Cambridge University Press.

Cooper, M. 2017. *Family Values*. Cambridge: Zone.

Cooper, R. 2002. "Why we still need empires". *The Observer*, 7 April.

Cooper, R. 2003. *The Breaking of Nations*. London: Atlantic.

Council of Conservative Citizens 2005. "Statement of principles". Atlanta, GA: Council of Conservative Citizens.

Cramer, K. 2016. *The Politics of Resentment: Rural Consciousness in Wisconsin and the Rise of Scott Walker*. Chicago, IL: University of Chicago Press.

Crouch, C. 2009. "Privatised Keynesianism". *British Journal of Politics and International Relations* 11(3), 382–99.

Crouch, C. 2011. *The Strange Non-Death of Neoliberalism*. Cambridge: Polity.

Crouch, C. 2016. *The Knowledge Corrupters*. Cambridge: Polity.

Crouch, C. 2019. *The Globalization Backlash*. Cambridge: Polity.

Crozier, M., S. Huntington & S. Berger 1975. *The Crisis of Democracy*. New York: New York University Press.

Cushman, T. (ed.) 2005. *A Matter of Principle*. Berkeley, CA: University of California Press.

Dalton, H. 1986. *Second World War Diaries*. London: Cape.

D'Ancona, M. 2016. "Brexit: how a fringe idea took hold of the Tory party". *Guardian*. Available at www.theguardian.com/politics/2016/jun/15/brexit-how-a-fringe-idea-took-hold-tory-party (accessed 15 June 2016).

Dardot, P. & C. Laval 2014. *The New Way of the World*. London: Verso.

Davidson, J. 2012. "Humanitarian intervention as liberal imperialism: a force for good?". *University of Leeds POLIS Journal* 7, 128–64.

Davies, W. 2013. "When is a market not a market?". *Theory, Culture and Society* 30(2), 32–59.

Davies, W. 2014. *The Limits of Neoliberalism*. London: Sage.

Davies, W. 2015a. "The return of social government". *European Journal of Social Theory* 18(4), 431–50.

Davies, W. 2015b. "How friendship became a tool of the powerful". *Guardian*, 7 May.

Davies, W. 2016a. "Brexit will make things worse. Is that why people voted for it?". *Washington Post*, 1 July.

Davies, W. 2016b. "Trump and the charisma of unreason". Goldsmiths PERC. Available at www.perc.org.uk/project_posts/trump-and-the-charisma-of-unreason/ (accessed 28 April 2016).

Davies, W. 2016c. "The difficulty of neoliberalism". Available at www.opendemocracy.net/en/difficulty-of-neoliberalism/ (accessed 22 March 2017).

Davies, W. 2018a. *Nervous States*. London: Cape.

Davies, W. 2018b. "Boris Johnson, Donald Trump and the rise of radical incompetence". *New York Times*, 13 July. Available at www.nytimes.com/2018/07/13/opinion/brexit-conservatives-boris-trump.html (accessed 12 June 2019).

Davies, W. 2019. "England's new rentier alliance". Available at www.perc.org.uk/project_posts/englands-rentier-alliance/ (accessed 1 August 2019).

Davis, A. 2018. *Reckless Opportunists: Elites at the End of the Establishment*. Manchester: Manchester University Press.

Davis, D. 2016. "Britain would be better off out of the EU – and here's why". Available at www.conservativehome.com/platform/2016/02/david-davis-britain-would-be-better-off-out-of-the-eu-and-heres-why.html (accessed 4 February 2017).

Davis, M. 2001. *Late Victorian Holocausts*. London: Verso.

Davis, M. 2004. *Planet of Slums*. London: Verso.

Davis, M. 2017. "The great god Trump and the white working class". Available at www.jacobinmag.com/2017/02/the-great-god-trump-and-the-white-working-class/ (accessed 7 April 2017).

D'Eramo, N. 2013. "Populism and the new oligarchy". *New Left Review* II/82, 5–28.

De Benoist, A. 1996. "Confronting globalization". *Telos* 108, 117–37.

De Benoist, A. 2013. *Carl Schmitt Today*. Budapest: Arktos.

De Benoist, A. 2017. *View from the Right*, Vol. 1. Budapest: Arktos.

De Jong, A. 2016. "The Philippines' new strongman". Available at www.jacobinmag.com/2016/05/philippines-duterte-populism-marcos-neoliberalism (accessed 15 March 2019).

DeLong, J. 2017. "NAFTA and other trade deals have not gutted American manufacturing". Available at www.vox.com/the-big-idea/2017/1/24/14363148/trade-deals-nafta-wto-china-job-loss-trump (accessed 14 March 2018).

De Maistre, J. 1994 [1797]. *Considerations on France*. Cambridge: Cambridge University Press.

Deaton, A. & B. Aten 2014. "Trying to understand the PPPs in ICP 2011: why are the results so different". Available at www.princeton.edu/~deaton/downloads/Deaton_Aten_Trying_to_understand_ICP_2011_V5.pdf (accessed 5 November 2015).

Desai, M. 2000. "Seattle: a tragi-comedy". In B. Gunnell & D. Timms (eds) *After Seattle*. London: Catalyst, 41–5.

Desai, M. 2002. *Marx's Revenge*. London: Verso.

De Smet, B. & K. Bogaert 2017. "Resistance and passive revolution in Egypt and Morocco". In C. Tansel (ed.) *States of Discipline*. London: Rowman & Littlefield, 211–33.

Deudney, D. & J. Ikenberry 1999. "The nature and sources of liberal international order". *Review of International Studies* 25(2), 179–96.

Devine, K. 2019. "Britain's wartime generation are almost as pro-EU as millennials". LSE Brexit blog. Available at https://blogs.lse.ac.uk/brexit/2019/04/05/britains-wartime-generation-are-almost-as-pro-eu-as-millennials/ (accessed 23 May 2019).

Dicken, P. 2015. *Global Shift*. London: Sage.

Diggins, J. 1975. *Up from Communism*. London: Harper and Row.

Dilley, A. 2016. "The Commonwealth is not an alternative to the EU for Britain". Available at http://theconversation.com/the-commonwealth-is-not-an-alternative-to-the-eu-for-britain-57009 (accessed 10 October 2017).

Disch, L. 2010. "The Tea Party: the American 'precariat'". Available at www.opendemocracy.net/en/5050/tea-party-american-precariat/ (accessed 16 June 2018).

Disdier, A. & K. Head 2008. "The puzzling persistance of the distance effect on bilateral trade". *Review of Economics and Statistics* 90(1), 37–48.

Doogan, K. 2009. *New Capitalism?* Cambridge: Polity.

Doran, J. 2008. "$700 billion won't save America from slump". *The Observer*, 28 September.

Dorfman, A. & A. Matellart 2019 [1971]. *How to Read Donald Duck*. London: Pluto.

Dorling, D. 2016. "Brexit: the decision of a divided country". *The BMJ*. Available at www.bmj.com/content/354/bmj.i3697 (accessed 16 June 2017).

Doyle, M. 1984. "Kant, liberal legacies and foreign affairs: part one". *Philosophy and Public Affairs* 12(3), 205–35.

Drolet, J. 2007. "The visible hand of neoconservative capitalism". *Millennium* 35(2), 262–81.

Drolet, J. 2011. *American Neoconservatism*. New York: Columbia University Press.

Drolet, J. & M. Williams 2019a. "Why is there no reactionary international theory?". Manuscript for ISA, Toronto.

Drolet, J. & M. Williams 2019b. "The view from MARS: US paleoconservatism and ideological challenges to the liberal world order". *International Journal* 74(1), 15–31.

Drutman, L. 2016. "Donald Trump will dramatically realign America's political parties". Available at https://foreignpolicy.com/2016/11/11/why-democrats-should-abandon-angry-working-class-whites/ (accessed 4 January 2018).

Dugin, A. 2017. *The Rise of the Fourth Political Theory*. Budapest: Arktos.

Dunkerley, J. 2017. "Chaotic epic: Samuel Huntington's *The Clash of Civilisations and the Remaking of World Order* revisited". In J. Drolet & J. Dunkerley (eds) *American Foreign Policy*. Manchester: Manchester University Press, 137–58.

Dunn, B. 2017. "Against neoliberalism as a concept". *Capital and Class* 41(3), 435–54.

Durkheim, E. 2013 [1893]. *The Division of Labour in Society*. Basingstoke: Palgrave.

Dustmann, C., T. Frattini & C. Halls 2010. "Assessing the fiscal costs and benefits of A8 migration to the UK". *Fiscal Studies* 31(1), 1–41.

Eatwell, R. & M. Goodwin 2017. *National Populism: The Revolt against Liberal Democracy*. London: Pelican.

Economists for Brexit 2016. "The economy after Brexit". Available at https://issuu.com/efbkl/docs/economists_for_brexit_v2 (accessed 3 January 2017).

Economists for Free Trade 2018. "A world trade deal". Available at www.economistsforfreetrade.com/wp-content/uploads/2018/09/A-World-Trade-Deal-The-Complete-Guide-Final-Upload.pdf (accessed 1 May 2019).

Edgar, D. 1986. "The free or the good", in R. Levitas (ed.) *The New Right*. Cambridge: Polity, 55–79.

Edgecliff-Johnson, A. & E. Crooks 2018. "US tax cut said to have little impact on investment". *Financial Times*, 29 October. Available at www.ft.com/content/e9bccd00-db98-11e8-8f50-cbae5495d92b (accessed 29 October 2018).

Edgerton, D. 2019. *The Rise and Fall of the British Nation*. London: Allen Lane.

Edin, K. & H. Schaefer 2015. *$2 a Day*. New York: Houghton Mifflin.

Ehrenfreund, M. 2015. "Bernie Sanders is right: the top 0.1 per cent have as much as the bottom 90 per cent". *Washington Post*, 19 November. Available at www.washingtonpost.com/news/wonk/wp/2015/11/19/bernie-sanders-is-right-the-top-0-1-have-as-much-as-the-bottom-90/?utm_term=.cb622a437373 (accessed 19 November 2015).

El-Elnany, N. 2017. "Brexit is not only an expression of nostalgia for empire, it is also the fruit of empire". Available at https://blogs.lse.ac.uk/brexit/2017/05/11/brexit-is-not-only-an-expression-of-nostalgia-for-empire-it-is-also-the-fruit-of-empire/ (accessed 4 January 2018).

EPI 2016. "Why is recovery taking so long – and who's to blame". Available at www.epi.org/publication/why-is-recovery-taking-so-long-and-who-is-to-blame/ (accessed 10 November 2016).

Erken, H. & M. Tulen 2017. "US global value chain integration: a major impediment for Trump". Available at https://economics.rabobank.com/publications/2017/june/us-global-value-chain-integration-trump-protectionist-trade/ (accessed 20 December 2017).

Erken, H., P. Marey & M. Wijffelaars 2017. "Empty threats: why Trump's protectionist policies would mean disaster". Available at https://voxeu.org/article/why-trump-s-protectionist-trade-agenda-will-fail (accessed 20 December 2018).

Escobar, A. 1996. *Encountering Development*. Princeton, NJ: Princeton University Press.

Evans, R. 2006. *The Third Reich in Power*. Harmondsworth: Penguin.

Evans, G. 2018. "The unwelcome revival of 'race science'". *Guardian*, 2 March.

Farage, N. 2016. "The little people have had enough – not just here but in America too". *The Telegraph*, 9 October.

Farand, C. & M. Hope 2018. "Matthew and Sarah Elliott: how a UK power couple links US libertarians and fossil fuel lobbyists to Brexit". Available at www.desmog.co.uk/2018/11/18/matthew-sarah-elliott-uk-power-couple-linking-us-libertarians-and-fossil-fuel-lobbyists-brexit (accessed 1 August 2019).

Farrer, M. 2019. "US and China begin imposing new tariffs as trade war escalates". *Observer*, 1 September. Available at www.theguardian.com/business/2019/sep/01/us-and-china-begin-imposing-new-tariffs-as-trade-war-escalates (accessed 2 September 2019).

FCIC 2010. *Financial Crisis Inquiry Report*. New York: Public Affairs/Financial Crisis Inquiry Commission.

FCIC 2011. *Financial Crisis Inquiry Report*. New York: Public Affairs/Financial Crisis Inquiry Commission.

Featherstone, L. 2002. *Students Against Sweatshops*. London: Verso.

Febrero, R. & P. Schwartz 1995. "The essence of Becker". In R. Febrero. & P. Schwartz (eds) *The Essence of Becker*. Stanford, CA: Hoover, 95–114.

Feder, L. 2017. "This is how Steve Bannon sees the entire world". Available at www.buzzfeed.com/lesterfeder/this-is-how-steve-bannon-sees-the-entire-world?utm_term=.mp6xZbOzX#.thopJOeyP (accessed 4 January 2018).

Feenstra, R. & A. Sasahara Feenstra 2018. *The "China Shock", Exports and US Employment: A Global Input-Output Analysis*. Working Paper 24022. Available at www.nber.org/papers/w24022.pdf (accessed 12 January 2019).

Feher, M. 2019. "The political ascendancty of creditworthiness". Available at www.publicbooks.org/the-political-ascendancy-of-creditworthiness/ (accessed 17 December 2019).

Felipe, J., A. Mehta & C. Rhee 2015. "Manufacturing matters ... but it's the jobs that count". Asian Development Bank Working Paper no. 40.

Ferguson, N. 2003. *Empire*. London: Penguin.

Ferguson, N. 2004. *Colossus*. London: Allen Lane.

Ferguson, N. 2015. "The UK Labour Party should blame Keynes for their election defeat". *Financial Times*, 11 May.

Ferguson, N. & R. Kagan 2003. The United States is, and should be, an empire: a new Atlantic initiative debate. Washington, DC: American Enterprise Institute for Public Policy Research.

Ferguson, T., P. Jorgensen & J. Chen 2018. "Industrial structure and party competition in an age of hunger games: Donald Trump and the 2016 presidential election". INET Working Paper no. 66.

Fine, B. 2001. *Social Capital or Social Theory*. London: Routledge.

Fine, B. 2012. "Neoliberalism in retrospect? It's financialisation, stupid". In C. Sup, B. Fine & L. Weiss (eds) *Developmnetal Politics in Transition*. Basingstoke: Palgrave, 51–69.

Fine, B. & D. Milonakis 2009. *From Political Economy to Economics*. London: Routledge.

Finlayson, A. 2003. *Making Sense of New Labour*. London: Lawrence & Wishart.

Finlayson, A. 2009. "Financialisation, financial literacy and asset based welfare". *British Journal of Politics and International Relations* 11(3), 400–21.

Finlayson, A. 2011. "Should the left go Blue? Available at www.opendemocracy.net/en/opendemocracyuk/should-left-go-blue-making-sense-of-maurice-glasman/ (accessed 16 April 2017).

Finlayson, A. 2016. "Who won the referendum". Available at www.opendemocracy.net/uk/alan-finlayson/who-won-referendum (accessed 26 June 2016).

Fischer, K. 2009. "The influence of neoliberals in Chile, before, during and after Pinochet". In P. Mirowski & D. Plehwe (eds) *The Road from Mont Pelerin*. Cambridge, MA: Harvard University Press, 305–46.

Fitzhugh, G. 2013 [1854]. *Sociology for the South*. Classics US.

Fleming, T. 2005. "Anarcho-tyranny Rockford style". *Chronicles*, 1 March.

Flinders, M. 2018. "Brexit and anti-politics". In P. Diamond, P. Nedergaard & B. Rosamond (eds) *The Routledge Handbook of the Politics of Brexit*. London: Routledge, 179–91.

Florida, R. 2002. *The Rise of the Creative Class*. New York: Basic Books.

Fonte, J. 2000/1. "Why there is a culture war". Available at www.hoover.org/research/why-there-culture-war (accessed 22 July 2019).

Fonte, J. 2012. *Sovereignty or Submission*. New York: Encounter.

Ford, R. & M. Goodwin 2014. *Revolt on the Right*. London: Routledge.

Foucault, M. 2008 [1978/9]. *The Birth of Biopolitics*. Basingstoke: Palgrave Macmillan.

Francis, S. 1983. "Message from MARs". In G. Schneider (ed.) *Conservatism in America since 1930*. New York: New York University Press, 300–17.

Francis, S. 1992. "Nationalism, old and new". *Chronicles*, June.

Francis, S. 1994. *Beautiful Losers*. Columbia, MO: University of Missouri Press.

Francis, S. 2000. "Capitalism: the enemy". Available at www.chroniclesmagazine.org/2000/August/24/8/magazine/article/10828498/ (accessed 4 January 2018).

Francis, S. 2001. *America Extinguished: Mass Immigration and the Disintegration of American Culture*. Dickville, VA: Americans for Immigration Control Publishers.

Francis, S. 2004. "Why immigrants kill". *VDare*, 29 November. Available at www.vdare.com/francis/041129_kil.htm (accessed 14 November 2017).

Francis, S. 2005. "Refuge of scoundrels: patriotism, true and false, in the Iraq controversy". In D. O'Huallachain & J. Forest Sharpe (eds) *Neo-Conned: Just War Principles: A Condemnation of War in Iraq*. Norfolk, VA: IHS Press, 151–60.

Francis, S. 2014. "Outsourcing: the economic equivalent of ethnic cleansing". Available at www. vdare.com/articles/outsourcing-the-economic-equivalent-of-ethnic-cleansing (accessed 10 June 2017).

Francis, S. 2016. *Leviathan and its Enemies*. New York: Radix.

Frank, A. 1969. *Capitalism and Underdevelopment in Latin America*. New York: Monthly Review Press.

Frank, A. 1981. *Crisis in the Third World*. New York: Monthly Review Press.

Frank, T. 2004. *What's the Matter with America?* London: Secker.

Frank, T. 2016. *Listen Liberal!* New York: Metropolitan.

Fraser, N. 2017. "From progressive neoliberalism to Trump and beyond". *American Affairs* 1(4). Available at https://americanaffairsjournal.org/2017/11/progressive-neoliberalism-trump-beyond/ (accessed 12 December 2018).

Freeden, M. 2017. "After the Brexit referendum: revisiting populism as an ideology". *Journal of Political Ideologies* 22(1), 1–11.

Freedland, J. 2019. "How Brexit is causing the strange death of British conservatism". *Guardian* 7 June. Available at www.theguardian.com/commentisfree/2019/jun/07/brexit-strange-death-british-conservatism (accessed 7 June 2019).

Friedman, J. 2009. "A crisis of politics not economics". *Critical Review* 21(2/3), 127–83.

Friedman, M. 1951. "Neo-liberalism and its prospects". *Farmand*, 17 February, 89–93.

Friedman, M. 1970. "The social responsibility of business is to increase profits". *New York Times Magazine*, 13 September.

Friedman, M. 1976. "Rhodesia". *Newsweek*, 3 May.

Friedman, M. 1978. "Introduction". In W. Simon (ed.) *A Time for Truth*. New York: McGraw Hill, iii–xv.

Friedman, M. 1991. "Where are we headed". Available at http://miltonfriedman.hoover.org/friedman_images/Collections/2016c21/Commonwealth_07_15_1991.pdf (accessed 22 July 2019).

Friedman, M. 1997. "The euro: monetary unity to political disunity". *Project Syndicate*, 28 August.

Friedman, M. 2002 [1962]. *Capitalism and Freedom*. Chicago, IL: University of Chicago Press.

Friedman, T. 2007. *The World is Flat*. New York: Allen Lane.

Friedrich, C. & Z. Brzezinski 1965. *Totalitarian Dictatorship and Autocracy*. Cambridge, MA: Harvard University Press.

Frobel, F., J. Heinrichs & O. Kreye 1980. *The New International Division of Labour*. Cambridge: Cambridge University Press.

From, A. 2017. "Don't be fooled: populism won't help Democrats win again". *Guardian*, 4 January.

Frum, D. 2003. "Unpatriotic conservatives". *National Review*, 25 March. Available at www. nationalreview.com/2003/03/unpatriotic-conservatives-david-frum/ (accessed 2 May 2019).

Frum, D. 2018. *Trumpocracy*. New York: Harper.

Fukuyama, F. 1992. *The End of History and the Last Man*. New York: Free Press.

Fukuyama, F. 2006. *After the Neocons*. London: Profile.

Fukuyama, F. 2016. "US against the world? Trump's America and the new global order". *Financial Times*, 11 November.

Gallagher, J. & R. Robinson 1953. "The imperialism of free trade". *Economic History Review* VI(I), 1–15.

Galston, R. & W. Kristol 2017. "Ideas to recenter America". Available at www.newcenter.org/ideas-to-re-center-america/ (accessed 19 September 2017).

Gamble, A. 1974. *The Conservative Nation*. London: Routledge.

Gamble, A. 1981. *An Introduction to Social and Political Thought*. Basingstoke: Macmillan.

Gamble, A. 1986. "The political economy of freedom". In R. Levitas (ed.) *The Ideology of the New Right*. Cambridge: Polity, 25–54.

Gamble, A. 1988. *The Free Economy and the Strong State*. Basingstoke: Macmillan.

Gamble, A. 1994. *Britain in Decline*. Fourth edition. Basingstoke: Macmillan.

Gamble, A. 1996. *Hayek*. Cambridge: Polity.

Gamble, A. 2001. "Neo-liberalism". *Capital and Class* 75, 127–34.

Gamble, A. 2003. *Between Europe and America*. Basingstoke: Palgrave Macmillan.

Gamble, A. 2005. "Globalization: getting the big picture right". *International Politics* 42(2), 364–71.

Gamble, A. 2009. *The Spectre at the Feast*. Basingstoke: Palgrave Macmillan.

Gamble, A. 2013. "Neoliberalism and fiscal conservatism". In V. Schmidt & M. Thatcher (eds) *Resilient Liberalism in Europe's Political Economy*. Cambridge: Cambridge University Press, 53–76.

Gamble, A. 2014. *Crisis without End?* Basingstoke: Palgrave Macmillan.

Ganz, J. 2018. "The year the clock broke". *The Baffler*, 6 November. Available at https://thebaffler.com/authors/john-ganz (accessed 17 August 2019).

Garcia, A. 2019. "Brazil under Bolsonaro: social base, agenda and perspectives". *SP The Bullet*, 15 April.

Garrett, G. 1998. "Global markets and national politics: collision course or vicious circle?". *International Organization* 52(4), 787–824.

Geiselberger, H. (ed.) 2017. *The Great Regression*. Cambridge: Polity.

Gest, J. 2016. *The New Minority*. Oxford: Oxford University Press.

Giddens, A. 1994. *Beyond Left and Right*. Cambridge: Polity.

Giddens, A. 1998. *The Third Way*. Cambridge: Polity.

Giddens, A. 1999. *Runaway World*. Cambridge: Polity.

Giddens, A. 2000. *The Third Way and its Critics*. Cambridge: Polity.

Giddens, A. 2002. *Which Way for New Labour?* Cambridge: Polity.

Gill, S. 1995. "Globalisation, market civilisation and disciplinary neoliberalism". *Millennium* 24(3), 399–423.

Gilmour, I. 1977. *Inside Right*. London: Hutchinson.

Gladwell, M. 2010. "Small change". *The New Yorker*, 27 September.

Glasman, M. *et al.* (eds) 2011. *The Labour Tradition and the Politics of Paradox*. London: Lawrence & Wishart.

Global Future 2018. *Open Owns the Future*. London: Global Future.

Goldberg, J. 2008. *Liberal Fascism*. New York: Crown.

Goldman, L. 2011. "Conservative political thought from the revolutions of 1848 until the fin-de-siecle". In G. Stedman-Jones (ed.) *The Cambridge History of Nineteenth Century Political Thought*. Cambridge: Cambridge University Press, 691–719.

Goldwater, B. 2007 [1960]. *The Conscience of a Conservative*. Princeton, NJ: Princeton University Press.

Goodhardt, D. 2017. *The Road to Somewhere*. London: Hurst.

Goodwin, M. 2018. "Britain's populist revolt". Available at https://quillette.com/2018/08/03/britains-populist-revolt/ (accessed 26 May 2019).

Gordon, D. 1988. "The global economy: new edifice or crumbling foundations". *New Left Review* I/168, 24–65.

Gottfried, P. 2001. *After Liberalism: Mass Democracy in the Managerial State*. Princeton, NJ: Princeton University Press.

Gottfried, P. 2005. *The Strange Death of Marxism*. Columbia, MO: University of Missouri Press.

Gottfried, P. 2007a. *Conservatism in America: Making Sense of the American Right*. Basingstoke: Palgrave Macmillan.

Gottfried, P. 2007b. "The invincible Wilsonian matrix: 'Universal Human Rights Once Again'". *Orbis* 51(2), 239–50.

Gottfried, P. 2011. "Antecedents of neoconservative foreign policy". *Historically Speaking* 12(1), 33–6.

Gottfried, P. 2016. *Fascism: The Career of a Concept*. DeKalb, IL: Northern Illinois University Press.

Gottfried, P. 2017. *Revisions and Dissents*. DeKalb, IL: Northern Illinois University Press.

Gourinchas, P.-O. & H. Rey 2005. "From world banker to world venture capitalist: US external adjustment and the exorbitant privilege". Available at http://socrates.berkeley.edu/~pog/academic/exorbitant/exorb_privilege_0804.pdfG (accessed 27 May 2014).

Gove, M. 2013. "I refuse to surrender to the Marxist teachers hell-bent on destroying our schools". *Daily Mail*, 23 March.

Gowan, P. 2001 "Neoliberal cosmopolitanism". *New Left Review* II/11, 73–93.

Graeber, D. 2015. *The Utopia of Rules*. London: Melville.

Graff, A., R. Kapur & S. Danuta Walters 2019. "Introduction: gender and the rise of the global right". *Signs* 44(3), 541–60.

Grahl, J. 2004. "The European Union and American power". In L. Panitch & C. Leys (eds) *The Socialist Register 2005*. London: Merlin, 280–96.

Greeley, B. 2018. "China will import more of what it doesn't want to make at home". *Financial Times*, 18 December.

Green, J. 2018. "Trump's trade war hits another red state". Bloomberg Businessweek, 17 April. Available at www.bloomberg.com/news/articles/2018-04-17/chinese-sorghum-tariffs-will-hit-hard-in-trump-friendly-kansas (accessed 18 April 2018).

Green, J. 2019. *Is Globalization Over?* Cambridge: Polity.

Greenleaf, W. 1983. *The British Political Tradition*. London: Methuen.

Greenhouse, S. 2017. "Is Trump really pro-worker". Available at www.nytimes.com/2017/09/02/opinion/sunday/is-trump-really-pro-worker.html (accessed 2 September 2017).

Griffiths, R. 2013. *Fellow Travellers of the Right*. London: Faber.

Grob-Fitzgibbon, B. 2016. *Continental Drift: Britain and Europe from the End of Empire to the Rise of Euroscepticism*. Cambridge: Cambridge University Press.

Grossman, G. & E. Helpman 1991. *Innovation and Growth in the Global Economy*. Cambridge, MA: MIT Press.

Guilford, G. 2016. "Everything we thought we knew about free trade is wrong". Available at https://qz.com/840973/everything-we-thought-we-knew-about-free-trade-is-wrong/ (accessed 16 April 2017).

Haass, R. 2000. "Imperial America". Available at https://monthlyreview.org/wp-content/uploads/2003/05/Imperial_America_Richard_N_Haass.pdf (accessed 11 June 2017).

Haass, R. 2017. *A World in Disarray*. Harmondsworth: Penguin.

Habermas, J. 1999. "Bestiality and humanity: a war on the border between legality and morality". *Constellations* 6(3), 263–72.

Habermas, J. 2001. *The Postnational Constellation*. Boston, MA: MIT Press.

Habermas, J. 2003. *Truth and Justification*. Cambridge, MA: MIT Press.

Habermas, J. 2006. *The Divided West*. Cambridge: Polity.

Haidt, J. 2012. "Why working-class people vote conservative". *Guardian*, 5 June.

Hall, J. & D. Soskice (eds) 2001. *Varieties of Capitalism*. Oxford: Oxford University Press.

Hall, S. 1979. "The great moving right show". *Marxism Today*, January, 54–6.

Hall, S. 1996. "The problem of ideology: Marxism without guarantees". In B. Matthew (ed.) *Marx 100 Years On*. London: Lawrence & Wishart, 57–85.

Hall, S. 2000. "Conclusion: the multicultural question". In B. Hesse (ed.) *Un/settled Multiculturalisms: Diasporas, Entanglements, Transruptions*. London: Zed Books, 209–41.

Hall, S. *et al.* 1978. *Policing the Crisis*. London: Macmillan.

Halliday, F. 1983. *The Making of the Second Cold War*. London: Verso.

Halliday, F. 1996. *Islam and the Myth of Confrontation*. London: I.B.Tauris.

Halper, S. 2010. *The Beijing Consensus*. New York: Basic Books.

Halzer, J. 2017. "Trump's steel tariffs are a surefire way to hurt the rustbelt". *Foreign Policy*, 4 May. Available at http://foreignpolicy.com/2017/05/04/trumps-steel-tariffs-are-a-surefire-way-to-hurt-the-rust-belt/ (accessed 16 December 2017).

Hamilton, A. 2017 [1791]. *Report on the Subject of Manufactures*. Scotts Valley, CA: Create Space.

Hannan, D. 2013. "The anglosphere miracle". Available at www.newcriterion.com/issues/2013/10/the-anglosphere-miracle (accessed 19 December 2013).

Hannan, D. 2014. *Inventing Freedom*. New York: Broadside.

Hannan, D. 2015. "Forget the EU – let's take on the world with our true friends". Available at www.dailymail.co.uk/news/article-2922715/Forget-EU-let-s-world-TRUE-friends-Greek-elections-threaten-shatter-Europe-DANIEL-HANNAN-says-Britain-s-destiny-lies-booming-Commonwealth.html (accessed 20 January 2016).

Hannan, D. 2018. "Capitalist Britain 'literally' overthrew slavery". *Daily Telegraph*, 28 July.

Hanson, P. 1996. "Maiden speech". Available at www.smh.com.au/politics/federal/pauline-hansons-1996-maiden-speech-to-parliament-full-transcript-20160915-grgjv3.html (accessed 4 April 2018).

Harcourt, B. 2011. *The Illusion of Free Markets*. Cambridge, MA: Harvard University Press.

Hardt, M. 2002. "Porto Alegre: today's Bandung". *New Left Review* 2(64), 112–18.

Hardt, M. & T. Negri 2004. *Multitude*. New York: Penguin.

Harris, J. 2018. "Britain's insecure towns aren't left behind: they hold the key to our future". *Guardian*, 17 September. Available at www.theguardian.com/commentisfree/2018/sep/17/britains-insecure-towns-left-behind (accessed 17 September 2018).

Harrison, G. 2004. *The World Bank and Africa*. London: Routledge.

Hartwell, R. 1995. *A History of the Mont Pelerin Society*. Indianapolis, IN: Liberty Fund.

Hartz, L. 1991. *The Liberal Tradition in America*. Boston, MA: Thomson Learning.

Harvey, D. 2005. *A Brief History of Neoliberalism*. Oxford: Oxford University Press.

Haseler, S. 2004. *Super-State: The New Europe and its Challenge to America*. London: I.B.Tauris.

Hausmann, R. *et al.* 2011. *The Atlas of Economic Complexity*. Hollis, NH: Puritan Press.

Havertz, R. 2018. "Right wing populism and neoliberalism in Germany: The AFD's embrace of neoliberalism". *New Political Economy*. Available at www.tandfonline.com/doi/abs/10.1080/13563467.2018.1484715 (accessed 12 March 2019).

Hawley, G. 2016. *Right Wing Critics of American Conservatism*. Kansas City, MO: University of Kansas Press.

Hawley, G. 2017. *Making Sense of the Alt-Right*. New York: Columbia University Press.

Hay, C. 2000. "Contemporary capitalism, globalization, regionalization and the persistence of national variation". *Review of International Studies* 26(4), 509–31.

Hay, C. 2004. "Ideas, interests and institutions in the contemporary political economy of Great Transformations". *Review of International Political Economy* 11(1), 204–26.

Hay, C. 2005. "Globalization's impact on states". In J. Ravenhill (ed.) *Global Political Economy*. Oxford: Oxford University Press, 235–62.

Hay, C. 2007. *Why We Hate Politics*. Cambridge: Polity.

Hay, C. 2011. "Pathology without crisis: the strange demise of the anglo-liberal growth model". *Government and Opposition* 46(1), 1–31.

Hay, C. 2013. *The Failure of the Anglo-Liberal Growth Model*. Basingstoke: Palgrave Macmillan.

Hay, C. & D. Marsh 2001. "Demystifying globalisation". In C. Hay & D. Marsh (eds) *Demystifying Globalisation*. London: Palgrave, 1–14.

Hay, C. & D. Marsh (eds) 2001. *Demystifying Globalization*. Basingstoke: Palgrave Macmillan.

Hay, C. & D. Wincott 2013. *The Political Economy of European Welfare Capitalism*. Basingstoke: Palgrave Macmillan.

Hay, C. & M. Watson 1999. "Globalisation: sceptical notes on the 1999 Reith Lectures". *Political Quarterly* 70(4), 418–25.

Hay, C. & M. Watson 2003. "The discourse of globalisation and the logic of no alternative". *Policy and Politics* 30(4), 289–305.

Hayek, F. 1941. "The Economics of Planning". *The Liberal Review*, Vol. 1, 1–5.

Hayek, F. 1967. *Studies in Philosophy, Politics and Economics*. Chicago, IL: University of Chicago Press.

Hayek, F. 1972 [1948]. *Individualism and Economic Order*. Auburn, AL: Mises Institute.

Hayek, F. 1976. *The Denationalization of Money*. London: IEA.

Hayek, F. 1988. *The Fatal Conceit*. Chicago, IL: University of Chicago Press.

Hayek, F. 2001 [1944]. *The Road to Serfdom*. London: Routledge.

Hayek, F. 2006. *The Constitution of Liberty*. London: Routledge.

Hayek, F. 2010 [1945]. "What price a planned economy?" Available at https://mises.org/library/what-price-planned-economy (accessed 8 May 2016).

Hayek, F. 2013 [1973]. *Law, Legislation and Liberty*. London: Routledge.

Hazeldine, T. 2017. "Revolt of the rustbelt". *New Left Review* II/105, 51–79.

Hazony, Y. 2018. *The Virtue of Nationalism*. New York: Basic.

Head, S. 2016. "The death of British business". *New York Review Daily*. Available at www.nybooks.com/daily/2016/10/18/brexit-death-of-british-business/ (accessed 16 June 2018).

Hearne, D., A. De Ruyter & H. Davis 2019. "The Commonwealth: a panacea for the UK's post-Brexit trade ills?". *Contemporary Social Science* 14(2), 341–60.

Heartfield, J. 2003. "Postmodern desertions: capitalism and anti-capitalism". *Interventions* 5(2), 271–89.

Heer, J. 2018. "Do conservatives know much about conservative history", *The New Republic*, 10 September. Available at https://newrepublic.com/article/151127/conservatives-know-much-conservative-history (accessed 7 January 2019).

Heffer, S. 2008. *Like the Roman: The Life of Enoch Powell*. London: Faber.

Held, D. & A. McGrew 2007. *Globalization/Anti-Globalization*. Cambridge: Polity.

Held, D. *et al.* 1999. *Global Transformations*. Cambridge: Polity.

Heller, H. 2015. "Authoritarian liberalism". *European Law Journal* 21(3), 295–301.

Henderson, A. *et al.* 2016. "England, Englishness and Brexit". *Political Quarterly* 87(2), 187–99.

Henwood, D. 2003. *The New Economy*. New York: Free Press.

Hicks, M. & S. Devaraj 2015. "The myth and the reality of manufacturing in America". Indiana, Ball State University Center for Business and Economic Research.

Hills, J. 2013. "Labour's record on cash transfers, poverty, inequality and the life cycle, 1997–2010". CASE LSE Working Paper no. 5.

Hills, J. 2015. *Good Times, Bad Times*. Bristol: Policy.

Himmelfarb, G. 1995. *The Demoralization of Society*. London: IEA.

Himmelfarb, G. 2008. *The Roads to Modernity*. London: Vintage.

Hindley, B. 1996. *Better Off Out?* London: IEA.

Hindmoor, A. 2018. *What's Left Now*. Oxford: Oxford University Press.

Hirschmann, A. 1970. *Exit, Voice and Loyalty*. Cambridge, MA: Harvard University Press.

Hirst, P., G. Thompson & S. Bromley 2009. *Globalization in Question*. Third edition. Cambridge: Polity.

Hobbes, T. 2014. *Victoria*. Helsinki: Castalia House.

Hobson, J. 2004. *The Eastern Origins of Western Civilisation*. Cambridge: Cambridge University Press.

Hochschild, A. 2016. *Strangers in their Own Land*. New York: New Press.

Hoftstadter, R. 2008 [1964]. *The Paranoid Style in American Politics*. New York: Random House.

Hogg, Q. 1947. *The Case for Conservatism*. Harmondsworth: Penguin.

Hoggart, R. 1957. *The Uses of Literacy*. London: Pelican.

Hohmann, J. 2016. "The daily 202: the Reagan Democrats are no longer Democrats. Will they ever be again?". *Washington Post*, 11 November.

Holehouse, M. 2016. "I'd rather be poorer with fewer migrants, Farage says". *Telegraph*, 7 January.

Holton, R. 2005. *Making Globalization*. Basingstoke: Palgrave Macmillan.

Hood, C. & R. Dixon 2015. *A Government that Worked Better and Cost Less*. Oxford: Oxford University Press.

Hoppe, H. 2017. "Libertarianism and the alt-right". Available at https://misesuk.org/2017/10/20/libertarianism-and-the-alt-right-hoppe-speech-2017/ (accessed 10 August 2019).

Horn, K. 2015. "Controversy over right wing pressure in the Hayek Society". *Cicero*, 20 July. Available at www.cicero.de/kultur/hayek-gesellschaft-liberale-kaempfen-gegen-unterwanderung-von-rechts/59590 (accessed 18 April 2018).

Horwitz, R. 2013. *America's Right*. Cambridge: Polity.

Howe, A. 2007. *Free Trade and Liberal England*. Oxford: Oxford University Press.

Howe, N. 2017. "Where did Stephen Bannon get his worldview? From my book". *Washington Post*, 24 February. Available at www.washingtonpost.com/entertainment/books/where-did-steve-bannon-get-his-worldview-from-my-book/2017/02/24/16937f38-f84a-11e6-9845-576c69081518_story.html?utm_term=.9702ffc33e96 (accessed 24 February 2017).

Hung, H.-F. 2009. "America's head servant?". *New Left Review* II (64), 97–108.

Hung, H.-F. 2015. *The China Boom: Why China will not rule the World*. New York: Columbia University Press.

Huntington, S. 1957. "Conservatism as an ideology". *American Political Science Review* 51(2), 454–73.

Huntington, S. 1996. *The Clash of Civilizations and the Remaking of World Order*. New York: Simon & Schuster.

Huntington, S. 2004a. *Who are We?* New York: Simon & Schuster.

Huntington, S. 2004b. "Dead souls: the denationalization of the American elite". *The National Interest* 75 (spring), 5–18.

Hutt, W. 1964. *The Economics of the Colour Bar*. London: Institute of Economic Affairs.

Iakhnis, E. *et al.* 2018. "Populist referendum: was Brexit an expression of nativist and anti-elitist sentiment?". *University of Strathclyde Research and Politics* 5(2), 1–7.

IFS 2016. *Living Standards, Poverty and Inequality in the UK*. London: IFS.

Ikenberry, J. 2007. *Liberal Order and Imperial Ambition*. Cambridge: Polity.

Ikenson, D., S. Lester & D. Hannan (eds) 2018. *The Ideal US–UK Trade Agreement*. London: IEA. available at https://iea.org.uk/publications/the-ideal-us-uk-free-trade-agreement/ (accessed 11 August 2019).

IMF 1989. *World Economic Outlook*. Washington, DC: IMF.

Independent International Commission on Kosovo 2000. *Kosovo Report*. New York: Oxford University Press.

Inglehart, R. 1977. *The Silent Review*. Princeton, NJ: Princeton University Press.

Inglehart, R. & P. Norris 2009. *Cosmopolitan Communications*. Cambridge: Cambridge University Press.

Inglehart, R. & P. Norris 2017. "Trump, Brexit and the rise of populism: economic have-nots and cultural backlash". Harvard Kennedy School working Paper 16–026.

Inglehart, R. & P. Norris 2019. *Cultural Backlash*. Cambridge: Cambridge University Press.

IPPR 2019. *State Aid Rules and Brexit*. London: Institute for Public Policy Research.

Ipsos Mori 2016. "How Britain voted in the EU referendum". Available at www.ipsos.com/ipsos-mori/en-uk/how-britain-voted-2016-eu-referendum (accessed 5 September 2016).

Ireland, P. 2005. "Shareholder primacy and the distribution of wealth". *Modern Law Review* 68(1), 49–81.

Jabri, V. 2012. *The Postcolonial Subject*. London: Routledge.

Jacobs, E. 2012. "Understanding America's white working class: their politics, voting habits and policy priorities". *Governance Studies at Brookings*, November, 1–17.

Jennings, W. & G. Stoker 2017. "Tilting Towards the Cosmopolitan Axis? Political Change in England and the 2017 General Election". *Political Quarterly* 88(3), 359–69.

Jensen, A. 1969. "How much can we boost IQ and scholastic achievement?". *Harvard Educational Review* 39(1), 1–123.

Johnson, B. 2013. "The Aussies are just like us, so let's stop kicking them out". *Telegraph*, 25 August.

Johnson, B. 2015. *The Churchill Factor*. London: Hodder.

Johnson, B. 2018a. "The rest of the world believes in Britain: it's time we did too". *Telegraph*, 15 July.

Johnson, B. 2018b. "Boris Johnson's letter to the prime minister". Available at www.bbc.co.uk/news/uk-politics-44772804 (accessed 9 July 2018).

Johnson, G. 2019. "National populism is here to stay". Available at www.counter-currents.com/2019/07/national-populism-is-here-to-stay-2/ (accessed 19 July 2019).

Johnson, R. 2016. "Trump: some numbers". Available at www.lrb.co.uk/2016/11/14/rw-johnson/trump-some-numbers (accessed 14 January 2017).

Kagan, R. 2002/3. "One year after: a grand strategy for the west?" *Survival* 44(4), 135–56.

Kagan, R. 2004. *Paradise and Power.* London: Atlantic.

Kagan, R. 2008. *The Return of History and the End of Dreams.* London: Atlantic.

Kagan, R. & W. Kristol (eds) 2000. *Present Dangers: Crisis and Opportunity in American Foreign and Domestic Policy.* San Francisco, CA: Encounter.

Kaldor, M. 2003. *Global Civil Society.* Cambridge: Polity.

Kaldor, M. 2006. *New and Old Wars.* Cambridge: Polity.

Kaldor, M., H. Anheier & M. Glasius 2003. "Global civil society in an era of regressive globalism". In M. Kaldor, H. Anheier & M. Glasius (eds) *Global Civil Society Yearbook 2003.* Oxford: Oxford University Press, 3–33.

Kaldor, N. 1967. *Strategic Factors in Economic Development.* Ithaca, NY: Cornell University Press.

Kane P. 2016. "Leading Brexiteers are pining for us all to embrace a life built on havoc". Available at www.thenational.scot/comment/pat-kane-leading-brexiteers-are-pining-for-all-of-us-to-embrace-a-life-built-on-havoc.18931 (accessed 12 December 2016).

Kant, I. 1957. *Perpetual Peace and Other Essays on Politics, History and Morals.* Indianapolis, IN: Hackett.

Kaplan, R. 2014. "Homeland security says terrorists haven't crossed US Mexico border". Available at www.cbsnews.com/news/homeland-security-says-terrorists-havent-crossed-us-mexico-border/ (accessed 26 April 2016).

Kaplan, L. & W. Kristol 2003. *The War Over Iraq.* New York: Encounter.

Kaplinsky, R. 2005. *Globalization, Poverty and Inequality.* Cambridge: Polity.

Katznelson, I. 2014. *Fear Itself.* New York: Liveright.

Kaufmann, E. 2018. *Whiteshift.* London: Penguin.

Kay, J. 2016. "Jam tomorrow: the meaning of non-tariff trade barriers". Available at www.johnkay.com/2016/10/24/jam-tomorrow-meaning-non-tariff-trade-barriers/ (accessed 12 December 2016).

Keen, S. 2017. "Ricardo's vice and the virtues of industrial diversity". *American Affairs* 1(3). Available at https://americanaffairsjournal.org/2017/08/ricardos-vice-virtues-industrial-diversity/ (accessed 11 June 2018).

Kellner, P. 2019. "Labour will win more votes than it loses by backing another referendum". *Guardian*, 27 February. Available at www.theguardian.com/commentisfree/2019/feb/27/labour-vote-referendum-jeremy-corbyn (accessed 28 February 2019).

Kenny, M. 2017. "Back to the populist future? Understanding nostalgia in contemporary ideological discourse". *Journal of Political Ideologies* 22(3), 256–73.

Kenny, M. & N. Pearce 2018. *Shadows of Empire: The Anglosphere in Contemporary British Politics.* Cambridge: Polity.

Keohane, R. & J. Nye 1977. *Power and Interdependence.* Boston, MA: Little, Brown.

Keynes, J. 1973 [1936]. *The General Theory of Employment, Interest and Money.* London: Macmillan.

Kidd, B. 2009 [1894]. *Social Evolution.* Cambridge: Cambridge University Press.

Kiely, R. 1994. "Development theory and industrialisation: beyond the impasse". *Journal of Contemporary Asia* 24(2), 133–60.

Kiely, R. 1996. *The Politics of Labour and Development in Trinidad.* Mona: University of the West Indies Press.

Kiely, R. 1998. *Industrialization and Development.* London: UCL Press.

Kiely, R. 1999. "The last refuge of the noble savage? A critical account of post-development". *European Journal of Development Research* 11(1), 30–55.

Kiely, R. 2005. *The Clash of Globalisations.* Leiden: Brill.

Kiely, R. 2008. "Poverty through 'insufficient exploitation and/or globalization?': globalized production and new dualist fallacies". *Globalizations* 5(3), 419–32.

Kiely, R. 2010. *Rethinking Imperialism.* Basingstoke: Palgrave Macmillan.

Kiely, R. 2014. "Imperialism or globalization? … or imperialism *and* globalization: theorizing the international after Rosenberg's 'post-mortem'". *Journal of International Relations and Development* 17(2), 274–300.

Kiely, R. 2015. *The BRICs, US Decline and Global Transformations.* Basingstoke: Palgrave Macmillan.

Kiely, R. 2016. *The Rise and Fall of Emerging Powers.* Basingstoke: Palgrave Macmillan.

Kiely, R. 2017. "From authoritarian liberalism to economic technocracy". *Critical Sociology*, online first available at http://journals.sagepub.com/doi/abs/10.1177/0896920516668386 (accessed 4 April 2017).

Kiely, R. 2018. *The Neoliberal Paradox.* Cheltenham: Elgar.

Kilibarda K. & D. Roithmayr 2016. "The myth of the rustbelt revolt". Available at www.slate.com/articles/news_and_politics/politics/2016/12/the_myth_of_the_rust_belt_revolt.html (accessed 14 December 2016).

Kilminster, R. 2008. "Narcissism or informalization? Christopher Lasch, Norbert Elias and social diagnosis". *Theory, Culture and Society* 25(3), 110–38.

Kimmel, M. 2013. *Angry White Men.* New York: Nation Books.

Kimmel, M. 2018. *Healing from Hate.* Berkeley, CA: University of California Press.

Kirk, R. 2008. *The Conservative Mind.* BN Publisher.

Kitching, G. 1982. *Development and Underdevelopment in Historical Perspective.* London: Methuen.

Kletzer, L. 2001. *Job Losses from Imports.* Washington, DC: Peterson Institute for International Economics.

Klein, N. 2000. *No Logo.* London: Picador.

Klos, F. 2017. *Churchill's Last Stand.* London: Bloomsbury.

Knafo, S. 2013. *The Making of Modern Finance.* London: Routledge.

Kolozi, P. 2017. *Conservatives Against Capitalism.* New York: Columbia University Press.

Konings, M. 2017. "From Hayek to Trump: the logic of neoliberal democracy". In L. Panitch & G. Albo (eds) *The Socialist Register 2018.* London: Merlin, 48–73.

Kornacki, S. 2018. "When Trump ran against Trumpism". Available at www.nbcnews.com/think/opinion/when-trump-ran-against-trump-ism-story-2000-election-ncna915651 (accessed 30 June 2019).

Kozul-Wright, R. 2006. "Globalization, now and again". In K. Jomo (ed.) *Globalization Under Hegemony.* New Delhi: Oxford University Press, 100–32.

Kozul-Wright, R. & P. Rayment 2004. "Globalization reloaded: an UNCTAD perspective". UNCTAD Discussion Papers no. 167, 1–50.

Krippner, G. 2012. *Capitalizing on Crisis.* Cambridge, MA: Harvard University Press.

Kristol, I. 1970. "'When virtue loses her loveliness' – some reflections on capitalism and the 'free society'". *The National Interest* 31, 3–15.

Kristol, I. 1995. *Neoconservatism.* New York: Ivan Dee.

Kristol, I. 2000 "The two welfare states". *Wall Street Journal*, 19 October.

Kristol, W. & R. Kagan 1996. "Toward a neo-Reaganite foreign policy". *Foreign Affairs* 75(4), 18–32.

Krueger, A. 1974. "The political economy of the rent-seeking society". *American Economic Review* 64(3), 291–303.

Krueger, A. 1998. "Why trade liberalisation is good for growth". *Economic Journal* 109, 1513–22.

Krugman, P. 1986. *Strategic Trade Policy and the New International Economics.* Cambridge, MA: MIT Press.

Kuhn, M., M. Schularick & U. Steins 2018. "Income and wealth inequality in America 1949–2016". Available at www.wiwi.uni-bonn.de/kuhn/paper/Wealthinequality_7June2018_edt.pdf (accessed 22 February 2019).

Kwarteng, K. *et al.* 2012. *Britannia Unchained.* Basingstoke: Palgrave Macmillan.

Kymlicka, W. 1995. *Multicultural Citizenship.* Oxford: Oxford University Press.

Kymlicka, W. 2007. *Multicultural Odysseys.* Oxford: Oxford University Press.

Kynaston, D. 2001. *The City of London*, Vol. 4. London: Chatto and Windus.

Lal, D. 1984. *The Poverty of "Development Economics".* London: IEA.

Lal, D. 2004. *In Praise of Empires.* Basingstoke: Palgrave Macmillan.

Lal, D. 2008. *Reviving the Invisible Hand.* Princeton, NJ: Princeton University Press.

Lamp, N. 2018. *How Should We Think about the Winners and Losers from Globalization?* Queens University Legal Research Paper No. 2018/102.

Landa, I. 2010. *The Apprentice's Sorcerer.* Chicago, IL: Haymarket.

Langley, P. 2008. *The Everyday Life of Global Finance.* Oxford: Oxford Universty Press.

Lanier, L. 1977. "A critique of the philosophy of progress". In J. Ransom (ed.) *I'll Take My Stand.* Baton Rouge, LA: Louisiana State University, 122–54.

Lanktree, G. 2017. "Donald Trump may be losing the rust belt and the 'deplorables' – but he has one big way to win them back". Available at www.newsweek.com/trump-losing-rust-belt-and-deplorables-694835 (accessed 4 January 2018).

Lanzano, C. 2018. "Why are Italian fascists approvingly quoting Samora Machel and Sankara". Available at https://africasacountry.com/2018/09/twisting-pan-africanism-to-promote-anti-africanism (accessed 16 December 2018).

Larner, W. 2000. "Neoliberalism: policy, ideology, governmentality". *Studies in Political Economy* 63, 5–25.

Lasch, C. 1996. *The Revolt of the Elites and the Betrayal of Democracy.* New York: Norton.

Lassiter, M. 2006. *The Silent Majority.* Princeton, NJ: Princeton University Press.

Lauryssens, S. 1999. *The Man Who Invented the Third Reich.* London: The History Press.

Lavoie, D. 1985. *National Economic Planning.* Cambridge, MA: Ballinger.

Lawrence, F. 2018. "Who is behind the push for a post-Brexit trade deal with the US". *Guardian*, 4 December. Available at www.theguardian.com/commentisfree/2018/dec/04/post-brexit-free-trade-deal-us-rightwing-thinktanks (accessed 11 August 2019).

Lawson, N. 2016. "Brexit will complete Margaret Thatcher's economic revolution". *Telegraph*, 26 September.

Lazear, E. 2000. "Economic imperialism". *Quarterly Journal of Economics* 115(1), 99–146.

Lazzarato, M. 2012. *The Making of Indebted Man.* Boston, MA: MIT Press.

Le Baron, G. 2016. "The coming crisis: the dangers of indecent work". Available at http://speri.dept.shef.ac.uk/2016/06/22/the-coming-crisis-the-dangers-of-indecent-work/ (accessed 7 February 2017).

Le Bon, G. 1960. *The Crowd.* New York: Viking.

Leggett, W. 2014. "The politics of behaviour change". *Politics and Policy* 42(1), 3–19.

Lenin, V. 1977 [1916]. "Imperialism: the highest stage of capitalism". In *Selected Works.* Moscow: Progress Publishers.

Lent, J. 2018. "Steven Pinker's ideas are fatally flawed: these eight graphs show why". Available at www.opendemocracy.net/en/transformation/steven-pinker-s-ideas-are-fatally-flawed-these-eight-graphs-show-why/ (accessed 3 January 2019).

Letts, Q. 2017. *Patronising Bastards.* London: Constable.

Levitas, R. 2005. *The Inclusive Society?* Basingstoke: Palgrave Macmillan.

Levitsky, S. & D. Ziblatt 2018. *How Democracies Die.* Cambridge, MA: Harvard University Press.

Lewis, P. *et al.* 2018. "Revealed: the rise and rise of populist rhetoric". *Guardian*, 6 March, available at www.theguardian.com/world/ng-interactive/2019/mar/06/revealed-the-rise-and-rise-of-populist-rhetoric (accessed 7 March 2019).

Liddle, R. 2019. *The Great Betrayal.* London: Constable.

Lis, J. 2017. "To the Commonwealth, 'Global Britain' sounds like nostalgia for something else". Available at www.newstatesman.com/politics/staggers/2017/02/commonwealth-global-britain-sounds-nostalgia-something-else (accessed 30 April 2018).

List, F. 1966 [1841]. *The National System of Political Economy.* New York: Augustus Kelley.

Littler, J. 2018. *Against Meritocracy.* London: Routledge.

Lloyd, J. 2000. "The anglosphere project". *New Statesman*, 13 March.

Lloyd, J. 2001. *The Protest Ethic.* London: Demos.

Lowrey, A. 2018. "Trump's 'smart tariffs' don't make economic sense". *The Atlantic*, 1 March.

Lucas, C. 2019. "A letter to my country – we must united to prevent a Trumpian Brexit". Available at www.newstatesman.com/politics/uk/2019/07/caroline-lucas-letter-my-country-we-must-unite-prevent-trumpian-brexit (accessed 1 August 2019).

Mackintosh, M. 2004. "Gaining from trade". In S. Bromley, M. Mackintosh & W. Brown (eds) *Making the International.* London: Pluto, 33–72.

Maizels, A., T. Palaskas & T. Crowe 1998. "The Prebisch Singer hypothesis revisited". In D. Sapford & J. Chen (eds) *Development Economics and Policy.* Basingstoke: Palgrave Macmillan, 95–110.

Mance, H. 2016. "Britain has had enough of experts, says Gove". *Financial Times*, 3 June.

Mandelson, P. & R. Liddle 1996. *The Blair Revolution.* London: Faber.

Mannheim, K. 1993 [1927]. "Conservative thought". In K. Wolff (ed.) *From Karl Mannheim.* New York: Transaction, 260–350.

Marcuse, H. 2002 [1964]. *One Dimensional Man.* London: Routledge.

Martell, L. 2017. *The Sociology of Globalization.* Cambridge: Polity.

Mason, J. 2016. "Dealing with the trade deficit". Available at http://jwmason.org/wp-content/uploads/2015/05/Mason-2016-Dealing-with-the-Trade-Deficit.pdf.

Mason, J. 2017. "What we get wrong when we talk trade". Available at www.jacobinmag.com/2017/01/trump-mexico-trade-tariff-import-pena-nieto (accessed 18 November 2017).

Mason, P. 2009. *Meltdown.* London: Verso.

Mason, P. 2019. *Clear Bright Future.* London: Allen Lane.

Massey, D. 1994. *Space, Place and Gender.* Cambridge: Polity.

Massey, D. 2005. *For Space.* London: Sage.

May, T. 2016. "Conservative speech on Brexit". Available at www.politicshome.com/news/uk/political-parties/conservative-party/news/79517/read-full-theresa-mays-conservative (accessed 7 February 2017).

May, T. 2017. "Brexit speech". Available at www.independent.co.uk/news/uk/home-news/fulltexttheresamaybrexitspeechglobalbritaineueuropeanunionlatest-a7531361.html (accessed 7 February 2017).

Mayer, A. 1981. *The Persistence of the Old Regime, Europe to the Great War.* New York: Pantheon.

Mazarr, M. 2003. "George W. Bush, idealist". *International Affairs* 79(3), 503–22.

Mazower, M. 2001. *Dark Continent.* Harmondsworth: Penguin.

McGirr, L. 2001. *Suburban Warriors.* Princeton, NJ: Princeton University Press.

McGoey, L. 2015. "The philanthropy hustle". Available at www.jacobinmag.com/2015/11/philanthropy-charity-banga-carnegie-gates-foundation-development/ (accessed 4 January 2017).

McQuarrie, M. 2016. "Trump and the revolt of the rustbelt". Available at http://blogs.lse.ac.uk/usappblog/2016/11/11/23174/ (accessed 11 November 2016).

McQuarrie, M. 2017. "Revolt of the Rustbelt". *British Journal of Sociology* 68(1), 120–52.

Mearsheimer, J. 2001. *The Tragedy of Great Power Politics.* New York: Norton.

Mearsheimer, J. 2006. "China's unpeaceful rise". *Current History* (April), 160–2.

Meek, J. 2019. *Dreams of Leaving and Remaining.* London: Verso.

Meyer, F. 1969. *The Conservative Mainstream.* New York: Arlington.

Mieville, C. 2005. *Between Equal Rights.* Leiden: Brill.

Milberg, W. & D. Winkler 2013. *Outsourcing Economics.* Cambridge: Cambridge University Press.

Mill, J. 2010 [1861]. *Considerations on Representative Government.* Cambridge: Cambridge University Press.

Miller, D. 2016. *Strangers in our Midst.* Cambridge, MA: Harvard University Press.

Milman, O. 2018. "Donald Trump tariffs on panels will cost US solar industry thousands of jobs". *Guardian*, 24 January.

Min, D. 2011. *Why Wallison is Wrong about the Genesis of the US Housing Crisis.* Washington, DC: Center for American Progress.

Minford, P. 2016. "Understanding UK trade agreements with the EU and other countries". Cardiff Economics Working Paper No. E2016/1.

Minford, P. 2017. *From Project Fear to Project Prosperity.* London: Economists for Free Trade.

Mirowski, P. & D. Plehwe (eds) 2009. *The Road from Mont Pelerin.* Cambridge, MA: Harvard University Press.

Mirowski, P. 2009. "Post-face: defining neoliberalism". In P. Mirowski & D. Plehwe (eds) *The Road from Mont Pelerin.* Cambridge, MA: Harvard University Press, 417–55.

Mirowski, P. 2013. *Never Let a Serious Crisis Go to Waste.* London: Verso.

Mirowski, P. 2014. "The political movement that dare not speak its name". INET Working Paper no. 23.

Mirowski, P. 2017. "Hell is truth seen too late". Available at www.ineteconomics.org/uploads/papers/Mirowski-Hell-is-Truth-Seen-Too-Late.pdf (accessed 6 June 2018).

Mises, L. 1944. *Bureaucracy.* New Haven, CT: Yale University Press.

Mondon, A. 2017. "Limiting democratic horizons to a nationalist reaction: populism, the radical right and the working class". *Javnost* 24(4), 355–74.

Moody, K. 2017. *On New Terrain.* Chicago, IL: Haymarket.

Moore, M. 2017. "Trump's approval ratings plummets in three key states, polls find". Available at www.marketwatch.com/story/trumps-job-approval-rating-plummets-in-three-key-states-polls-find-2017-08-21 (accessed 16 April 2018).

Morphet, J. 2017. *Beyond Brexit.* Bristol: Policy.

Mosca, G. 2012 [1939]. *The Ruling Class.* Ulan Press.

Mouffe, C. 2006. *The Return of the Political.* London: Verso.

Mound, J. 2017. "What Democrats must do". Available at www.jacobinmag.com/2017/09/democratic-party-2016-election-working-class (accessed 16 April 2018).

Mount, F. 2012. *The New Few, or, A Very British Oligarchy.* London: Simon and Schuster.

Mounk, Y. 2018. *The People versus Democracy.* Cambridge, MA: Harvard University Press.

Moynihan, D. 1965. *The Negro Family.* Washington, DC: Department of Labor.

Mudde, C. 2004. "The populist zeitgeist". *Government and Opposition* 39(4), 541–63.

Mudde, C. 2007. *Populist Radical Right Parties in Europe.* Cambridge: Cambridge University Press.

Mudde, C. 2010. "The populist radical right: a pathological normalcy". *West European Politics* 33(6), 1167–86.

Mudde, C. 2016. "Introduction to the populist radical right". In C. Mudde (ed.) *The Populist Radical Right: A Reader.* London: Routledge, 1–10.

Mudde, C. 2018. *The Far Right in America.* London: Routledge.

Mudde, C. 2019. "Why copying the populist right isn't going to save the left". Availble at www.theguardian.com/news/2019/may/14/why-copying-the-populist-right-isnt-going-to-save-the-left (accessed 14 May 2019).

Mulholland, M. 2011. *Bourgeois Liberty and the Politics of Fear.* Oxford: Oxford University Press.

Muller, J.-W. 2016. *What is Populism?* Philadelphia, PA: University of Pennsylvania Press.

Muro, M. & S. Liu 2016. "Another Clinton Trump divide: High output American versus low output America". Available at www.brookings.edu/blog/the-avenue/2016/11/29/another-clinton-trump-divide-high-output-america-vs-low-output-america/ (accessed 16 June 2018).

Murray, C. 1984. *Losing Ground.* New York: Basic Books.

Murray, C. & R. Herrnstein 1994. *The Bell Curve*. New York: Free Press.

Nagle, A. 2017. *Kill All Normies*. London: Zero.

Nairn, T. 1977. *The Break Up of Britain*. London: New Left Books.

Nairn, T. 1988. *The Enchanted Glass*. London: Radius.

Nalapat, M. 2011. "India and the anglosphere". *The New Criterion* 37(9).

Nash, G. 2008. *The Conservative Intellectual Movement in America since 1945*. Wilmington: ISI.

National Review 2016. "Against Trump". 15 February, 14–16.

Navarro, P. & G. Autry 2011. *Death by China*. New York: Prentice Hall.

Needham, C. 2007. *The Reform of Public Services under New Labour*. Basingstoke: Palgrave Macmillan.

Nelson, F. 2016. "Of course Britain is open for business: that was the point of Brexit". Available at https://blogs.spectator.co.uk/2016/07/course-britain-open-business-point-brexit/ (accessed 18 July 2016).

Nelson, F. 2017. "This is precisely why a lot of people voted for Brexit". Available at https://twitter.com/frasernelson/status/885759150625624064?lang=en (accessed 14 July 2017).

New York Times 2014. "Letter: a troublesome inheritance". Available at www.nytimes.com/2014/08/10/books/review/letters-a-troublesome-inheritance.html (accessed 8 August 2014).

Nickell, S. & J. Saleheen 2015. "The impact of immigration on occupational wages: the evidence from Britain". Bank of England Staff Working Paper, no. 574.

NIESR 2016. "Immigration and wages: getting the numbers right". Available at www.niesr.ac.uk/blog/immigration-and-wages-getting-numbers-right (accessed 16 October 2017).

Niewert, D. 2017. *Alt-America*. London: Verso.

Nisbet, R. 2010 [1953]. *The Quest for Community*. Wilmington, DE: ISI.

Nowrasteh, A. 2018a. "Criminal immigrants in Texas: illegal immigrant conviction and arrest rates for homicide, sex crimes, larceny, and other crimes". Available at www.cato.org/publications/immigration-research-policy-brief/criminal-immigrants-texas-illegal-immigrant (accessed 6 January 2019).

Nowrasteh, A. 2018b. "The 14 most common arguments against immigration and why they are wrong". Available at www.cato.org/blog/14-most-common-arguments-against-immigration-why-theyre-wrong (accessed 6 January 2019).

NSS 2002. "The National Security Strategy of the United States of America". Available at www.whitehouse.gov/nsc/nss.html (accessed 4 March 2003).

Nzula, A., I. Potekhin & A. Zusmanovich 1979. *Forced Labour in Colonial Africa*. London: Zed.

Oakeshott, M. 1962. *Rationalism in Politics*. London: Methuen.

O'Brien, P. 1991. "The foundations of European industrialization: from the perspective of the world". *Journal of Historical Sociology* 4(3), 288–317.

O'Brien, P. 2006. "Colonies in a globalizing economy, 1815–1948". In B. Gills & W. Thompson (eds) *Globalization and Global History*. London: Routledge, 248–91.

OECD 2010. *Perspectives on Global Development, 2010: Shifting Wealth*. Paris: OECD Development Centre.

OECD 2017. "International trade, foreign direct investment and global value chains". Available at www.oecd.org/investment/UNITED-KINGDOM-trade-investment-statistical-country-note.pdf (accessed 24 June 2018).

Oesch, D. & L. Renwald 2017. *Electoral Competition in Europe's Tripolar Political Space*. European University Institute Max Weber Programme, Working Paper 2017/02.

Office of the US Trade Representative 2017. "2017 Trade Policy Agenda and 2016 Annual Report". Available at https://ustr.gov/sites/default/files/files/reports/2017/AnnualReport/AnnualReport2017.pdf (accessed 9 August 2018).

Ohlin, B. 1933. *Inter-Regional and International Trade*. Cambridge, MA: Harvard University Press.

Ohmae, K. 1990. *Borderless World*. Cambridge, MA: Harvard University Press.

Ohmae, K. 2008. *The End of the Nation State*. New York: Harper Collins.

Olusoga, D. 2017. "Empire 2.0 is dangerous nostalgia for something that never existed". *Guardian*, 19 March. Available at www.theguardian.com/commentisfree/2017/mar/19/empire-20-is-dangerous-nostalgia-for-something-that-never-existed (accessed 20 March 2017).

O'Meara, M. 2013. *New Culture, New Right*. Budapest: Arktos.

O'Neill, J. 2013. *The Growth Map*. London: Portfolio Penguin.

ONS 2017. "UK trade: December 2017". Available at www.ons.gov.uk/economy/nationalaccounts/balanceofpayments/bulletins/uktrade/december2017 (accessed 4 June 2018).

Ortega y Gasset, J. 1960 [1929]. *The Revolt of the Masses*. New York: Norton.

Otjes, S. *et al.* 2018. "It's not economic interventionism, stupid: reassessing the political economy of right wing populist parties". *Swiss Political Science Review* 24(3), 270–90.

O'Toole, F. 2018. *Heroic Failure*. London: Apollo.

O'Toole, F. 2019. "The Great Betrayal by Rod Liddle review – a disingenuous, dishonest Brexit polemic". *Guardian*, 17 July. Available at www.theguardian.com/books/2019/jul/17/great-betrayal-rod-liddle-brexit-review (accessed 17 July 2019).

Owsley, F. 2001. "The pillars of agrarianism". In J. Ransom (ed.) *I'll Take My Stand*. Charlottesville, VA: University of Virginia Press, 190–210.

Ozden, B., I. Akca & A. Bekman 2017. "Antinomies of authoritarian neoliberalism in Turkey". In C. Tansel (ed.) *States of Discipline*. London: Rowman & Littlefield, 189–209.

Palen, M.-W. 2016. *The Conspiracy of Free Trade*. Cambridge: Cambridge University Press.

Palley, T. 2012. *From Financial Crisis to Stagnation*. Oxford: Oxford University Press.

Palma, G. 2005. "Four sources of deindustrialization and a new concept of the Dutch disease". In J. Ocampo (ed.) *Beyond Reforms: Structural Dynamics and Macroeconomic Vulnerability*. Stanford, CA: Stanford University Press, 71–116.

Palma, G. 2009. "The revenge of the market on the rentiers: why neo-liberal reports of the end of history turned out to be premature". *Cambridge Journal of Economics* 33(4), 829–69.

Panitch, L. & S. Gindin 2012. *The Making of Global Capitalism*. London: Verso.

Pareto, V. 1966. *Sociological Writings*. London: Pall Mall.

Parilla, J. & M. Muro 2017. "US metros most exposed to a Trump trade shock". Available at www.brookings.edu/blog/the-avenue/2017/01/27/u-s-metros-most-dependent-on-trade/ (accessed 30 January 2017).

Parmar, I. 2009. "Foreign policy fusion: liberal interventionists, conservative nationalists and neoconservatives – the new alliance dominating the US foreign policy establishment". *International Politics* 46(2/3), 177–209.

Patton, M. 2016. "China will surpass the US in 2018". Available at www.forbes.com/sites/mikepatton/2016/04/29/global-economic-news-china-will-surpass-the-u-s-in-2018/#234219c224af (accessed 16 June 2017).

Payne, C. 2012. *The Consumer, Credit and Neoliberalism*. London: Routledge.

Pearce, N. 2013. "Is there any austerity in the UK". Available at www.opendemocracy.net (accessed 7 June 2015).

Perraton, J. 2003. "The scope and implications of globalisation". In J. Michie (ed.) *A Handbook of Globalisation*. Cheltenham: Elgar, 37–60.

Petroff, A. 2018. "Tariffs aren't the biggest problem for American exporters". Available at https://money.cnn.com/2018/06/07/news/economy/trump-tariffs-trade-us-eu/index.html (accessed 4 January 2019).

Pew Research Center 2015. "The hollowing of the American middle class". Available at www.pewsocialtrends.org/2015/12/09/1-the-hollowing-of-the-american-middle-class/ (accessed 20 October 2018).

Phillip, A. & J. Wagner 2017. "Trump as a conventional Republican?" *Washington Post*, 13 April.

Phillips, K. 1969. *The Emerging Republican Majority*. New York: Arlington House.

Phillips-Fein, K. 2009. *Invisible Hands*. New York: Norton.

Pieterse, J. 2004. *Globalization and Culture*. London: Rowman & Littlefield.

Piketty, T. 2014. *Capital in the Twenty First Century*. Cambridge, MA: Harvard University Press.

Pinker, S. 2018. *Enlightenment Now*. Harmondsworth: Penguin.

Pinto, E. 2009. "Acorn and the housing bubble". *Wall Street Journal*, 12 November.

PNAC 1997. "Project for the New American Century: Statement of Principles". Available at newamericancentury.org (accessed 15 June 2007).

Pocock, J. 1992. *The Discovery of Islands*. Cambridge: Cambridge University Press.

Podhoretz, N. 1983. "Appeasement by any other name". *Commentary*, July 1983.

Polanyi, K. 2001 [1944]. *The Great Transformation*. New York: Beacon Press.

Politi, J. & M. Rocco 2019. "Blow to Trump as US trade deficit hits ten year high". *Financial Times*, 6 March. Available at www.ft.com/content/93faa9b2-4012-11e9-b896-fe36ec32aece (accessed 6 March 2019).

Politico 2018. "Where Europe's migrants are". Available at www.politico.eu/article/europe-migration-refugees-where-migrants-are/ (accessed 6 January 2019).

Pollitt, C. 1990. *Managerialism and the Public Services*. Oxford: Blackwell.

Portes, J. 2017. "Why you're wrong if you think that clamping down on immigration from Europe will help low paid British workers". *Independent*, 18 July. Available at www.independent.co.uk/news/business/comment/uk-europe-immigration-brexit-freedom-movement-eu-citizens-low-paid-british-workers-theresa-may-a7846686.html (accessed 18 July 2017).

Portes, J. 2018. "Austerity really has hit poor people the hardest". *Guardian*, 14 March.

Posner, R. 1981. *The Economics of Justice*. Cambridge, MA: Harvard University Press.

Posner, R. 1987. "The regulation of the market in adoptions". *Boston University Law Review* 67, 59–72.

Posner, R. 1990. *The Problem of Jurisprudence*. Cambridge, MA: Harvard University Press.

Posner, R. 2001. *Anti-Trust Law*. Chicago, IL: University of Chicago Press.

Post, C. 2017. "How the Donald came to rule". Available at www.jacobinmag.com/2017/02/how-the-donald-came-to-rule (accessed 16 February 2017).

Poulantzas, N. 1978. *State, Power, Socialism*. London: Verso.

Powell, E. 1965. *A Nation not Afraid*. London: Hodder & Stoughton.

Powell, E. 1971. *Common Market: The Case Against*. Tadworth: Elliot Right Way Books.

Powell, E. 1977. *Joseph Chamberlain*. London: Thames & Hudson.

Prebisch, R. 1959. "Commercial policy in the underdeveloped countries", *American Economic Review* 44, 251–73.

Progress 2015. "Editorial: 'The new Spanish Inquisition'". *Progress*, 18 December.

Rahnema, M. 1997. "Towards post-development: searching for signposts, a new language, a new paradigm". In M. Rahnema & V. Bawtree (eds) *The Post-Development Reader*. London: Zed, 304–29.

Raimondo, J. 2000. *An Enemy of the State: The Life of Murray Rothbard*. Amherst, NY: Prometheus.

Ransom, J. 1977. *I'll Take My Stand*. Baton Rouge, LA: Louisiana State University Press.

Rattansi, A. 2011. *Multiculturalism: A Very Short Introduction*. Oxford: Oxford University Press.

Redgrave, H. 2019. "Balanced migration: a progressive approach". Available at https://institute.global/insight/renewing-centre/balanced-migration-progressive-approach (accessed 7 March 2019).

Reich, R. 2019. "Trump offers socialism for the rich and capitalism for everyone else". *Guardian*, 11 February. Available at www.theguardian.com/commentisfree/2019/feb/11/trump-offers-socialism-for-the-rich-capitalism-for-everyone-else (accessed 12 February 2019).

Reinert, E. 2007. *How Rich Countries got Rich and Why Poor Countries Stay Poor*. London: Constable.

Reuters 2018. "Ex-Trump strategists targets Britain in anti-EU campaign". Available at https://uk.reuters.com/article/uk-europe-politics-bannon/ex-trump-strategist-bannon-targets-britain-in-anti-eu-campaign-idUKKBN1KH260 (accessed 27 July 2018).

Ricardo, D. 2004 [1817]. *On the Principles of Political Economy and Taxation.* Indianapolis, IN: Liberty Fund.

Ritzer, G. 1993. *The McDonaldization of Society.* Newbury Park, CA: Pine Forge.

Ritzer, G. 1997. *The McDonaldization Thesis.* London: Sage.

Roberts, A. 2006. *A History of the English-Speaking People since 1900.* London: Orion.

Roberts, A. 2016. "CANZUK: after Brexit, Canada, Australia, New Zealand and Britain can unite as a pillar of western civilisation". *Telegraph,* 13 September. Available at www.telegraph.co.uk/news/2016/09/13/canzuk-after-brexit-canada-australia-new-zealand-and-britain-can/ (accessed 13 September 2016).

Roberts, S., A. Secor & M. Sparke 2003. "Neoliberal geopolitics". *Antipode* 35(5), 886–97.

Robin, C. 2018. *The Reactionary Mind.* Oxford: Oxford University Press.

Robinson, B. 2004. *A Theory of Global Capitalism.* Baltimore, MD: Johns Hopkins University Press.

Robinson, B. 2015. "The transnational state and the BRICs". *Third World Quarterly* 36(1), 1–21.

Rodrik, D. 2001. *The Global Governance of Trade as if Development Really Mattered.* Geneva: United Nations Development Programme.

Rodrik, D. 2002. "Comments on 'Trade, Growth and Poverty' by D. Dollar & A. Kraay". Available at www.ksghome.harvard.edu (accessed 3 March 2007).

Rodrik, D. 2015. "Premature deindustrialization". Harvard University, unpublished paper.

Rodrik, D. 2018. *Straight Talk on Trade.* Princeton, NJ: Princeton University Press.

Roediger D. 2017. "Who's afraid of the white working class? On Joan Williams' 'White Working Class: Overcoming Class Cluelessness in America'". *Los Angeles Review of Books,* 17 May.

Röpke, W. 1957. *Welfare, Freedom and Inflation.* London: Pall Mall.

Röpke, W. 1969. *Against the Tide.* Vienna: Ludwig von Mises Institute.

Röpke, W. 1998 [1958]. *A Humane Economy.* Wilmington, DE: ISI Books.

Röpke, W. 2009 [1950]. *The Social Crisis of Our Time.* New Brunswick, NJ: Transaction.

Rosenberg, J. 2000. *The Follies of Globalisation Theory.* London: Verso.

Rosenberg, J. 2005. "Globalization theory: a postmortem". *International Politics* 42(1), 2–74.

Rosenberg, J. 2007. "And the definition of globalization is? A reply to *In at the Death* by Barrie Axford". *Globalizations* 4(3), 417–21.

Rostow, W. 1960. *The Stage of Economic Growth.* Cambridge: Cambridge University Press.

Rothbard, M. 1974. *Egalitarianism as a Revolt against Nature and other Essays.* Washington, DC: Libertarian Review Press.

Rothenberg, R. 1982. "The neoliberal club". *Esquire,* 1 February.

Rothfeder, J. 2016. "Why Donald Trump is wrong about manufacturing jobs and China". *The New Yorker,* 14 March.

Rousseau, J. 1968 [1762]. *The Social Contract.* Harmondsworth: Penguin.

Rowthorn, R. & K. Coutts 2013. "Deindustrialisation and the balance of payments in advanced countries". University of Cambridge Centre for Business Research working Paper no.453. Available at www.cbr.cam.ac.uk/fileadmin/user_upload/centre-for-business-research/downloads/working-papers/wp453.pdf (accessed 11 November 2017).

Rowthorn, R. & R. Ramaswamy 1999. "Growth, trade and deindustrialization", *IMF Staff Papers,* 46(1), 18–41.

Runciman, D. 2005. *The Politics of Good Intentions.* Princeton, NJ: Princeton University Press.

Russett, B. 1993. *Controlling the Sword.* Cambridge, MA: Harvard University Press.

Rushe, D. 2017. "Trump's growth problem: jobs boost masks trouble ahead for US economy". Available at www.theguardian.com/business/2017/jul/09/us-economy-trump-growth-wages (accessed 9 July 2017).

Sachs, W. (ed.) 1992. *The Development Dictionary.* London: Zed.

Said, E. 1978. *Orientalism.* Harmondsworth: Penguin.

Salam, R. 2018. *Melting Pot or Civil War.* New York: Sentinel.

Sampson, A. 1962. *Anatomy of Britain.* London: Hodder and Stoughton.

Sandel, M. 2012. *What Money Can't Buy*. London: Allen Lane.

Sarkar, A. 2018. "The colonial past is another country. Let's leave Boris Johnson there". *Guardian*, 10 July. Available at www.theguardian.com/commentisfree/2018/jul/10/past-boris-johnson-colonial-brexit-colony (accessed 10 July 2018).

Sasse, B. 2018. *Them*. New York: St Martin's Press.

Saull, R. 2012. "Rethinking hegemony". *International Studies Quarterly* 56(2), 323–38.

Saunders, R. 2019. "The closing of the conservative mind". *New Statesman*, 12 June.

Savage, M. 2015. *Social Class in the 21st Century*. London: Pelican.

Schickler, E. 2016. *Racial Re-alignment: The Transformation of American Liberalism, 1932–1965*. Princeton, NJ: Princeton University Press.

Schiller, H. 1969. *Mass Communications and American Empire*. New York: Kelley.

Schlesinger, A. 1949. *The Vital Centre*. New York: International.

Schmidt, M. & J. Barnes 2019. "Trump's targeting of intelligence agencies gains a harder edge". *New York Times*, 25 May.

Schmitt, C. 1962. "L'Ordre du monde après la deuxième guerre mondiale". In C. Jouin (ed.) *Carl Schmitt. La Guerre Civile Mondiale, Essais 1943–1978*. Paris: Ère.

Schmitt, C. 1976 [1932]. *The Concept of the Political*. New Brunswick, NJ: Rutgers University Press.

Schmitt, C. 1985 [1922]. *Political Theology*. Cambridge, MA: MIT Press.

Schmitt, C. 1988 [1923]. *The Crisis of Parliamentary Democracy*. Cambridge, MA: MIT Press.

Schmitt, C. 1998 [1932]. "Sound economy – strong state". In R. Cristi (ed.) *Carl Schmitt and Authoritarian Liberalism*. Cardiff: University of Wales Press, 212–32.

Schofield, C. 2013. *Enoch Powell and the Making of Postcolonial Britain*. Cambridge: Cambridge University Press.

Scholte, J. 2000. *Globalization: A Critical Introduction*. First edition. Basingstoke: Palgrave Macmillan.

Scholte, J. 2005. *Globalization: A Critical Introduction*. Second edition. Basingstoke: Palgrave Macmillan.

Schumpeter, J. 1951. *Imperialism and Social Classes*. Oxford: Blackwell.

Schumpeter, J. 1954. *The History of Economic Analysis*. New York: Oxford University Press.

Schumpeter, J. 1976 [1942]. *Capitalism, Socialism and Democracy*. London: Routledge.

Scotchie, J. 1999. *The Paleoconservatives: New Voices from the Old Right*. New York: Transaction.

Scott, A. 1996. "Bureaucratic revolutions and free market utopias". *Economy and Society* 25(1), 89–110.

Scott, A. 1997. "Introduction – globalization: social process or political rhetoric". In A. Scott (ed.) *The Limits of Globalization*. London: Routledge, 1–22.

Schwartz, B. 2011. *The White Man's World*. Oxford: Oxford University Press.

Schwartz, H. 2009. *Sub-Prime Nation*. Ithaca, NY: Cornell University Press.

Seeley, J. 2001 [1883]. *The Expansion of England*. Boston, MA: Adamant.

Semmel, B. 1960. *Imperialism and Social Reform*. London: Allen & Unwin.

Semmel, B. 1970. *The Rise of Free Trade Imperialism*. Cambridge: Cambridge University Press.

Shaikh, A. (ed.) 2005. *Globalization and the Myths of Free Trade*. London: Routledge.

Shariatmadari, D. 2017. "How the war on Islam became central to the Trump doctrine". *Guardian*, 30 January. Available at www.theguardian.com/us-news/2017/jan/30/war-on-islam-central-trump-doctrine-terrorism-immigration (accessed 30 January 2017).

Shiva, V. 2001. *Protect or Plunder*. London: Zed.

Singham, S. & R. Tylecote 2018. *Plan A+: Creating a Prosperous Post-Brexit UK*. London: IEA. Available at https://f.hypotheses.org/wp-content/blogs.dir/3671/files/2018/09/PLAN-A-final-document.pdf (accessed 11 August 2019).

Sklair, L. 2001. *The Transnational Capitalist Class*. Oxford: Wiley Blackwell.

Skocpol, T. & V. Williamson 2012. *The Tea Party and the Remaking of Republican Conservatism.* Oxford: Oxford University Press.

Slobodian, Q. 2018a. *Globalists.* Cambridge, MA: Harvard University Press.

Slobodian, Q. 2018b. "Hayek's populist bastards". Available at www.publicseminar.org/2018/02/neoliberalisms-populist-bastards/ (accessed 12 January 2019).

Slobodian, Q. 2018c. "You live in Robert Lighthizer's world now". Available at https://foreignpolicy.com/2018/08/06/you-live-in-robert-lighthizers-world-now-trump-trade/ (accessed 6 August 2018).

Slobodian, Q. & D. Plehwe 2019. "Neoliberals against Europe". In W. Callinson & Z. Manfredi (eds) *Mutant Neoliberalism.* New York: Fordham University Press, 89–111.

Snyder, T. 2017. *On Tyranny.* Harmondsworth: Penguin.

Spektorowski, A. 2000. "The French new right: differentialism and the idea of ethnophilian exclusionism". *Polity* 33(2), 283–303.

Spektorowski, A. 2003. "The new right: ethno-regionalism, ethno-pluralism and the emergence of a neo-fascist 'third way'". *Journal of Political Ideologies* 8(1), 111–30.

Spektorowski, A. 2016. "Fascism and post-national Europe: Drieu La Rochelle and Alain de Benoist". *Theory, Culture and Society* 33(1), 115–38.

Spengler, O. 1991 [1926]. *Decline of the West.* Oxford: Oxford University Press.

Spengler, O. 2015 [1931]. *Man and Technics.* London: Arktos.

Srnicek, N. 2017. *Platform Capitalism.* Cambridge: Polity.

Stager, U., C. Pagel & C. Cooper 2019. "A no deal Brexit is not the wish of the country but is now the preferred outcome of Leave voters". Available at https://blogs.ucl.ac.uk/grand-challenges/2019/04/10/a-no-deal-brexit-is-not-the-wish-of-the-country-but-is-now-the-preferred-outcome-for-leave-voters/ (accessed 10 October 2019).

Standing, G. 2011. *The Precariat.* London: Bloomsbury.

Starr, H. 1997. "Democracy and integration: why democracies don't fight each other". *Journal of Peace Research* 32(2), 153–62.

Starrs, S. 2013. "American economic power hasn't declined – it globalized! Summoning the data and taking globalization seriously". *International Studies Quarterly* 57(4), 817–30.

Starrs, S. 2014. "The chimera of global convergence". *New Left Review* II (87), 81–96.

Starrs, S. 2015. "China's rise is designed in America, assembled in China". *China's World* 2(2), 9–20.

Steinfeld, E. 2010. *Playing Our Game.* Cambridge: Cambridge University Press.

Stigler, G. 1971. "The theory of economic regulation". *Bell Journal of Economics and Management Science* 3, 3–18.

Stoddard, L. 2019. *The Rising Tide of Color.* New York: Blurb.

Stokes, D. 2018. "Trump, American hegemony and the future of the liberal international order". *International Affairs* 94(1), 133–50.

Strauss, W. & N. Howe 1997. *The Fourth Turning.* New York: Bantam.

Streeck, W. 2014. *Buying Time.* London: Verso.

Streeck, W. 2016. *Exploding Europe: Germany, the Refugees and the British Vote to Leave.* University of Sheffield: SPERI Paper no. 31.

Streeck, W. 2019. "Reflections on political scale". *Jurisprudence*, February. DOI: 10.1080/20403313.2018.1554939.

Sumner, A. 2016. *Global Poverty.* Oxford: Oxford University Press.

Sylvest, C. 2009. *British Liberal Internationalism.* Manchester: Manchester University Press.

Talbot, C. 2016. "The myth of neoliberalism". Available at https://colinrtalbot.wordpress.com/2016/08/31/the-myth-of-neoliberalism/ (accessed 7 February 2017).

Talmon, J. 1970. *The Origins of Totalitrian Democracy.* New York: Secker and Warburg.

Tansel, C. (ed.) 2017. *States of Discipline.* London: Rowman & Litttlefield.

Taylor, A. 2016. "Barry Goldwater: insurgent conservatism as constitutive rhetoric". *Journal of Political Ideologies* 21(3), 242–60.

Taylor, C. 1992. *Multiculturalism and the Politics of Recognition*. Princeton, NJ: Princeton University Press.

Taylor, J. 1992. *Paved with Good Intentions*. New York: Carroll & Graf.

Teschcke, B. 2003. *The Myth of 1648*. London: Verso.

Thackeray, D. & R. Toye 2019. "Debating Empire 2.0". In S. Ward & A. Rasch (eds) *Embers of Empire in Brexit Britain*. London: Bloomsbury, 15–24.

Thatcher, M. 1988. "Speech to the College of Europe". Available at www.margaretthatcher.org/document/107332 (accessed 10 January 2018).

The Economist 2016. "The new political divide". 30 July. Available at www.economist.com/leaders/2016/07/30/the-new-political-divide (accessed 30 July 2016).

The Full Brexit 2018. "Founding Statement". Available at www.thefullbrexit.com/about (accessed 30 November 2018).

Thiessen, M. 2016. "Why, despite his insults, the Chinese love Trump". Available at www.newsweek.com/why-despite-his-insults-chinese-love-trump-465807 (accessed 13 March 2017).

Thompson, E. 1965. "The peculiarities of the English". In R. Miliband & J. Savile (eds) *The Socialist Register 1965*. London: Merlin, 311–62.

Thurow, L. 1980. *The Zero Sum Society*. New York: Basic Books.

Timothy, N. 2016. "Port Talbot, globalisation – and the governing class that gains from mass immigration while the poorer classes lose out". Conservative Home, 5 April. Available at www.conservativehome.com/thecolumnists/2016/04/nick-timothy-port-talbot-should-make-us-question-the-unthinking-liberalism-of-our-governing-classes.html (accessed 28 October 2018).

Tocqueville, A. 1997 [1893]. *Recollections: The French Revolution of 1848*. New Brunswick, NJ: Transaction.

Tocqueville, A. 2004 [1835]. *Democracy in America*. New York: Bantam.

Tomlinson, J. 1991. *Cultural Imperialism*. Baltimore, MD: Johns Hopkins University Press.

Tomlinson, J. 1999. *Globalisation and Culture*. Cambridge: Polity.

Tomlinson, J. 2007. *The Culture of Speed*. London: Sage.

Tooze, A. 2018. *Crashed*. London: Allen Lane.

Toye, J. 1987. *Dilemmas of Development*. Oxford: Blackwell.

Trading Economics 2018. "US balance of trade". Available at https://tradingeconomics.com/united-states/balance-of-trade (accessed 14 April 2019).

Tregenna, F. 2009. "A new theoretical analysis of deindustrialisation". *Cambridge Journal of Economics* 38(6), 1373–90.

Triantafillou, P. 2017. *Neoliberal Power and Public Management Reforms*. Manchester: Manchester University Press.

Trump, D. & T. Schwartz 1987. *The Art of the Deal*. New York: Random House.

Trump, D. 2017. "The inaugural address". 20 January. Available at www.whitehouse.gov/briefings-statements/the-inaugural-address/ (accessed 21 January 2018).

Turner, R. 2008. *Neoliberal Ideology: History, Concepts, Policies*. Edinburgh: Edinburgh University Press.

UNCTAD 1998. *World Investment Report 1998*. Geneva: UNCTAD.

UNCTAD 2002a. *The Least Developed Countries Report 2002*. Geneva: UNCTAD.

UNCTAD 2002b. *Trade and Development Report 2002*. Geneva: UNCTAD.

UNCTAD 2002c. *World Investment Report 2002*. Geneva: UNCTAD.

UNCTAD 2003. *World Investment Report 2003*. Geneva: UNCTAD.

UNCTAD 2004. *The Least Developed Countries Report 2004*. Geneva: UNCTAD.

UNCTAD 2004. *Trade and Development Report 2004*. Geneva: UNCTAD.

UNCTAD 2006. *Trade and Development Report 2006*. Geneva: UNCTAD.

UNCTAD 2007. *World Investment Report 2007*. Geneva: UNCTAD.

UNCTAD 2008. *Trade and Development Report 2008*. Geneva: UNCTAD.

UNCTAD 2010. *World Investment Report 2010.* Geneva: UNCTAD.

UNCTAD 2012. *Trade and Development Report 2012.* Geneva: UNCTAD.

UNCTAD 2013. *World Investment Report 2013.* Geneva: UNCTAD.

UNCTAD 2014. *World Investment Report 2014.* Geneva: UNCTAD.

UNCTAD 2016. *World Investment Report 2016.* Geneva: UNCTAD.

UNHCR 2017. *Global Trends 2017.* Available at www.unhcr.org/globaltrends2017/ (accessed 12 December 2018).

UNHCR 2018. "Figures at a glance". Available at www.unhcr.org/uk/figures-at-a-glance.html (accessed 12 December 2018).

Urry, J. 2014. *Offshore.* Cambridge: Polity.

Venugopal, R. 2015. "Neoliberalism as concept". *Economy and Society* 44(2), 165–87.

Viereck, P. 2005 [1949]. *Conservatism Revisited.* New York: Transaction.

Viner, J. 2018. *Studies in the Theory of International Trade.* London: Routledge.

Vogel, S. 1998. *Freer Markets, More Rules.* Ithaca, NY: Cornell University Press.

Volcoviel, V., N. Groom & S. Di Savino 2017. "Trump declares end to 'war on coal' but utilities aren't listening". Available at www.reuters.com/article/us-usa-trump-climate-power/trump-declares-end-to-war-on-coal-but-utilities-arent-listening-idUSKBN1770D8 (accessed 2 January 2018).

Wacquant, L. 2009. *Punishing the Poor.* Durham, NC: Duke University Press.

Wacquant, L. 2010. "Crafting the neoliberal state: workfare, prison fare and social insecurity". *Sociological Forum* 25(2), 197–220.

Wade, N. 2014. *A Troublesome Inheritance.* Harmondsworth: Penguin.

Wade, R. 1990. *Governing the Market.* Princeton, NJ: Princeton University Press.

Wade, R. 2017. "Is Trump wrong on trade? A partial defense based on production and employment". *Real World Economics Review* 79, 43–63.

Wadsworth, J. 2017. "Immigration and the UK economy". LSE Centre for Economic Performance. Available at http://cep.lse.ac.uk/pubs/download/ea039.pdf (accessed 12 December 2018).

Wallerstein, I. 2003. *The Decline of American Power.* New York: New Press.

Wallison, P. 2009. "Cause and effect: government policy and the housing crisis". *Critical Review* 21(2/3), 365–76.

Walt, S. 2011. "The myth of American exceptionalism". Available at https://foreignpolicy.com/2011/10/11/the-myth-of-american-exceptionalism/ (accessed 14 September 2017).

Watson, M. 2013. "New Labour's 'paradox of responsibility' and the unravelling of its macroeconomic policy". *British Journal of Politics and International Relations* 15(1), 6–22.

Watson, M. 2017. "Historicising Ricardo's comparative advantage theory, challenging the normative foundations of liberal international political economy". *New Political Economy* 22(3), 257–72.

Watson, M. 2018. *The Market.* Newcastle upon Tyne: Agenda Publishing.

Watson, M. & C. Hay 2003. "The discourse of globalisation and the logic of no alternative: rendering the contingent necessary in the political economy of New Labour". *Policy and Politics*, 31(3), 289–305.

Weaver, R. 1948. *Ideas Have Consequences.* Chicago, IL: University of California Press.

Weber, M. 1994. *From Max Weber: Essays in Sociology.* London: Routledge.

Weeks, J. 2012. "Understanding the crisis". Available at www.res.org.uk/view/article3Apr12Correspondence.html (accessed 14 June 2015).

Weisbrot, M. *et al.* 2017. "Did NAFTA help Mexico". Available at http://cepr.net/publications/reports/did-nafta-help-mexico-an-update-after-23-years (accessed 16 June 2018).

Weiss, L. 2012. "The myth of the neoliberal state". In K. Chang, B. Fine & L. Weiss (eds) *Developmental Politics in Transition.* London: Routledge, 15–35.

Weiss, P. 2017. "Clinton lost because PA, WI, and MI have high casualty rates and saw her as pro-war, study says". Available at http://mondoweiss.net/2017/07/clinton-because-communities/ (accessed 17 March 2018).

Wellings, B. & H. Baxendale 2015. "Euroscepticism and the anglosphere: traditions and dilemmas in contemporary English nationalism". *Journal of Common Market Studies* 53(1), 123–39.

Weyrich, P. & W. Lind 2007. "The next conservatism". Available at www.theamericanconservative.com/articles/the-next-conservativism/ (accessed 23 November 2018).

Weyrich, P. & W. Lind 2009. *The Next Conservatism*. South Bend, IN: St Augustine's Press.

White, M. & A. Travis 2002. "Blunkett defends 'swamping' remark". *Guardian*, 25 April. Available at www.theguardian.com/politics/2002/apr/25/immigrationandpublicservices.immigration (accessed 17 May 2019).

Will, G. 1981. "A shrill assault on Mr Lincoln". *Washington Post*, 29 November. Available at www.washingtonpost.com/archive/opinions/1981/11/29/a-shrill-assault-on-mr-lincoln/453b1986-761e-4a86-9b71-759ce0729f87/?utm_term=.491f047540a9 (accessed 26 October 2018).

Willetts, D. (ed.) 1996. *The Conscience of the World*. London: Hurst.

Williams, J. 2017. *White Working Class*. Cambridge, MA: Harvard Business Review Press.

Williams, M. 2004. "What is the national interest? The neoconservative challenge to IR theory". *European Journal of International Relations* 11(3), 307–37.

Williams, M. 2007. *Culture and Security*. London: Routledge.

Willinger, M. 2013. *Generation Identity*. Budapest: Arktos.

Winlow, S. & S. Hall 2013. *Rethinking Social Exclusion*. London: Sage.

Wintour, P. 2018. "Hillary Clinton: Europe must curb immigration to stop right-wing populists". *Guardian*, 22 November. Available at www.theguardian.com/world/2018/nov/22/hillary-clinton-europe-must-curb-immigration-stop-populists-trump-brexit (accessed 23 November 2018).

Wood, A. 2017. "How globalisation affected manufacturing around the world". Available at https://voxeu.org/article/how-globalisation-affected-manufacturing-around-world (accessed 12 January 2018).

Wood, E. 1991. *The Pristine Culture of Capitalism*. London: Verso.

Wooldridge, A. 1995. *Meritocracy and the Classless Society*. London: Social Market Foundation.

World Bank 1981. *Accelerated Development in Sub-Saharan Africa*. Washington, DC: World Bank.

World Bank 1987. *World Development Report 1987*. Oxford: Oxford University Press.

World Bank 1989. *World Development Report 1989*. Oxford: Oxford University Press.

World Bank 1992. *Governance and Development*. Washington, DC: World Bank.

World Bank 1993. *The East Asian Miracle*. Oxford: Oxford University Press.

World Bank 1994. *Adjustment in Africa*. Oxford: Oxford University Press.

World Bank 1997. *World Development Report 1997*. Oxford: Oxford University Press.

World Bank 1999. *World Development Report 1999*. Oxford: Oxford University Press.

World Bank 2002. *Globalization, Growth and Poverty*. Oxford: Oxford University Press.

World Bank 2015. *World Development Report 2015*. Oxford: Oxford University Press.

World Bank 2018. "Tariff rate, applied, simple mean, all products (%)". Available at https://data.worldbank.org/indicator/tm.tax.mrch.sm.ar.zs (accessed 18 February 2019).

Wren-Lewis, S. 2015. "The austerity con". *London Review of Books* 37(4), 9–11.

Wren-Lewis, S. 2016. "New Labour and neoliberalism". Available at https://mainlymacro.blogspot.co.uk/2016/08/new-labour-and-neoliberalism.html (accessed 1 September 2016).

Yglesias, M. 2017. "Trump won by running as a moderate Republican". Available at www.vox.com/policy-and-politics/2017/7/11/15941846/trump-moderate-republican (accessed 3 February 2018).

Younge, G. 2009. "When you watch the BNP on TV, remember Jack Straw started all this". *Guardian*, 21 October. Available at www.theguardian.com/commentisfree/2009/oct/21/jack-straw-bnp-griffin-hain (accessed 17 May 2019).

Zhang, B. 2017. "Trump's 'America First' policies are catapulting Boeing into dangerous territory". Available at http://uk.businessinsider.com/boeing-trump-administration-policies-effects-2017-2 (accessed 3 February 2018).

Ziai, A. 2007. *Exploring Post-Development*. London: Routledge.

Zolo, D. 1997. *Cosmopolis*. London: Wiley.

Zubaida, S. 2009. *Islam, the People and the State*. London: I.B.Tauris.

INDEX